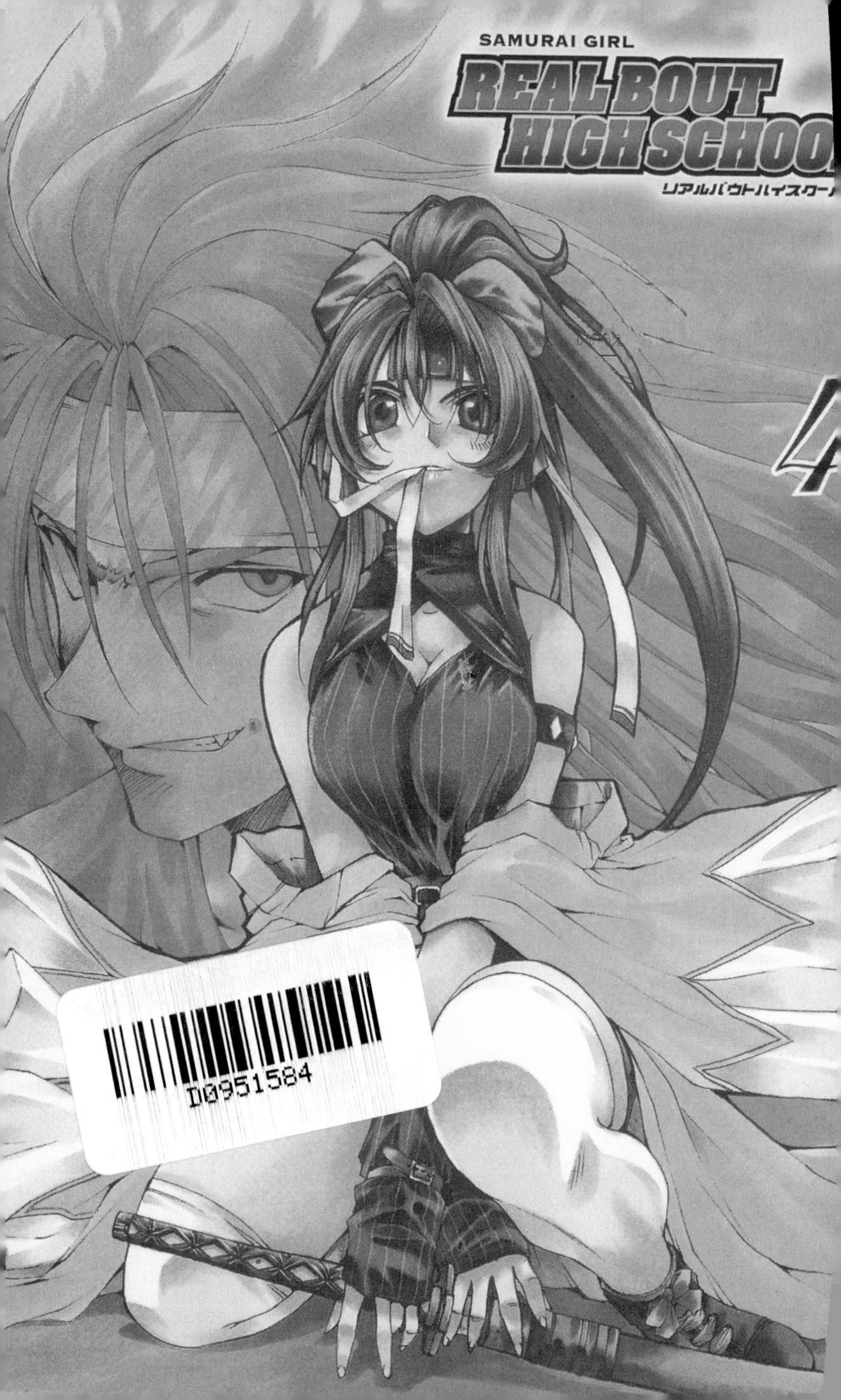
SAMURAI GIRL
REAL BOUT
HIGH SCHOO
リアルバウトハイスクー
4

SAMURAI GIRL
REAL BOUT HIGH SCHOOL
リアルバウトハイスクール

Volume 4

Art by Sora Inoue
Story by Reiji Saiga

TOKYOPOP®

Los Angeles • Tokyo

Translator – Dan Kanemitsu
Graphic Designer – Justin Renard
English Adaptation – Luis Reyes
Cover Designer – Rod Sampson

Senior Editor – Luis Reyes
Production Manager – Mario M. Rodriguez
Art Director – Matt Alford
VP of Production – Ron Klamert
Publisher – Stuart Levy

Email: editor@TOKYOPOP.com
Come visit us at www.TOKYOPOP.com

A  manga
TOKYOPOP® Presents
Real Bout High School Vol. 4 by Sora Inoue and Reiji Saiga
TOKYOPOP® is a registered trademark of Mixx Entertainment, Inc.

ISBN: 1-59182-021-9
First TOKYOPOP® Printing: September 2002

10 9 8 7 6 5 4 3 2

Printed in the USA

THE STORY THUS FAR . . .

More than anything else, Ryoko wants to be a great woman, and she has set on achieving this goal in life by taking up the code of the warrior and becoming one of the best Kendo combatants at Daimon High School. However, she buries her insecurities and emotions well beneath her gruff exterior, harboring a romantic longing for her Kendo sparring partner, Tatsuya. Unfortunately, he has transferred to another school, leaving our little samurai girl to find her own emotional strength.

Of course, life at Daimon High Shool isn't exactly the easiest stretch in a student's academic career. Too many martial arts groups vie for too few training studios, a situation that prompts spontaneous and large scale battles on campus. Luckily, Principal Todo - a man defined as much by his bloodlust as by his committment to educa- tion - has set up the K-Fight system in which students and teachers can settle disputes, differences of opinion and personal vendettas through sanctioned combat. When do students find time to study? When they're laid up in the hospital licking their wounds.

In the more pacifist wings of Daimon High, the student body presi- dent has designs on using the K-Fight system for a more noble pur- pose, a purpose that may inherently open up the doors for Ryoko to find her higher purpose.

SAMURAI GIRL

REAL BOUT HIGH SCHOOL

リアルバウトハイスクール

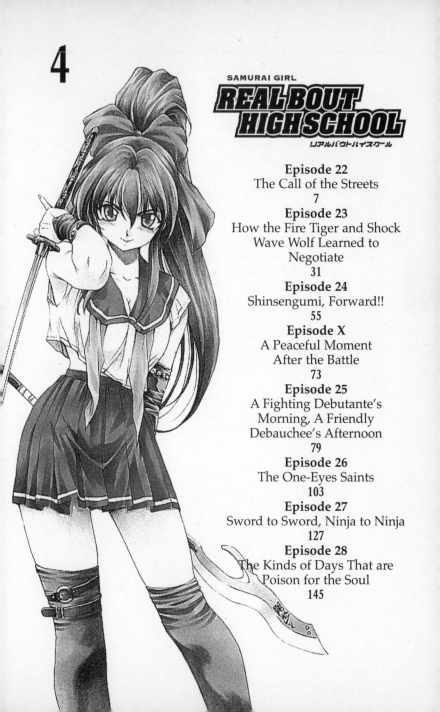

4

SAMURAI GIRL

REAL BOUT HIGH SCHOOL

リアルバウトハイスクール

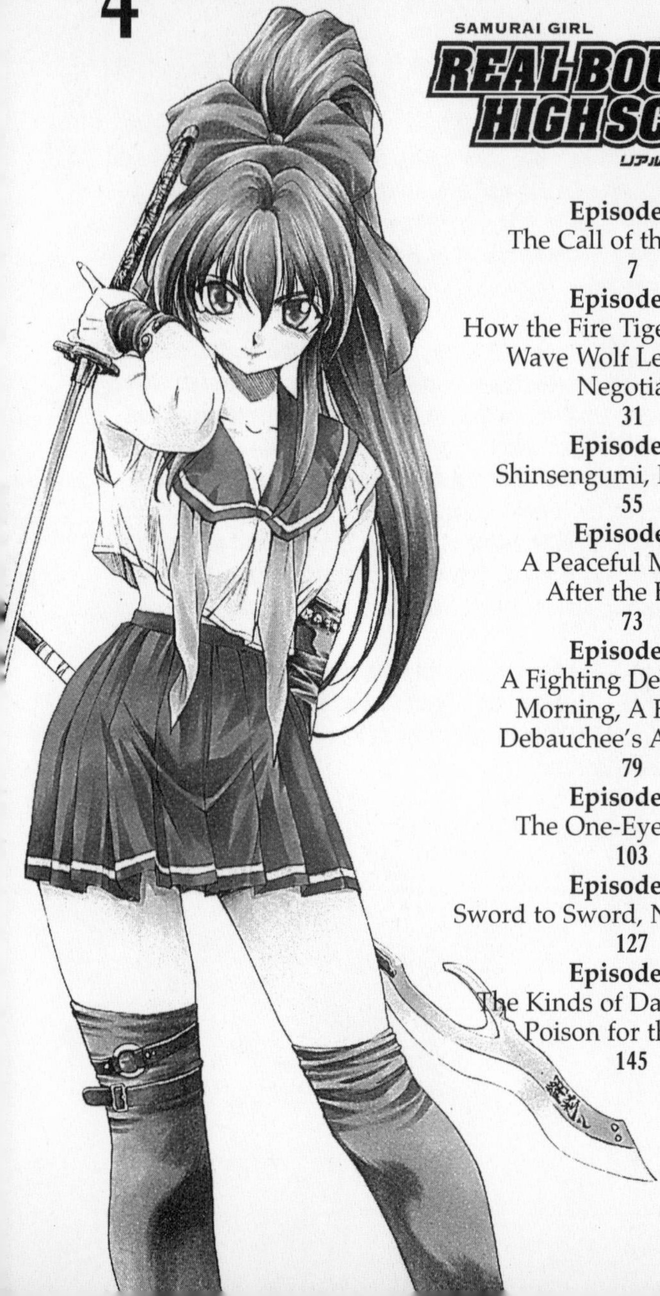

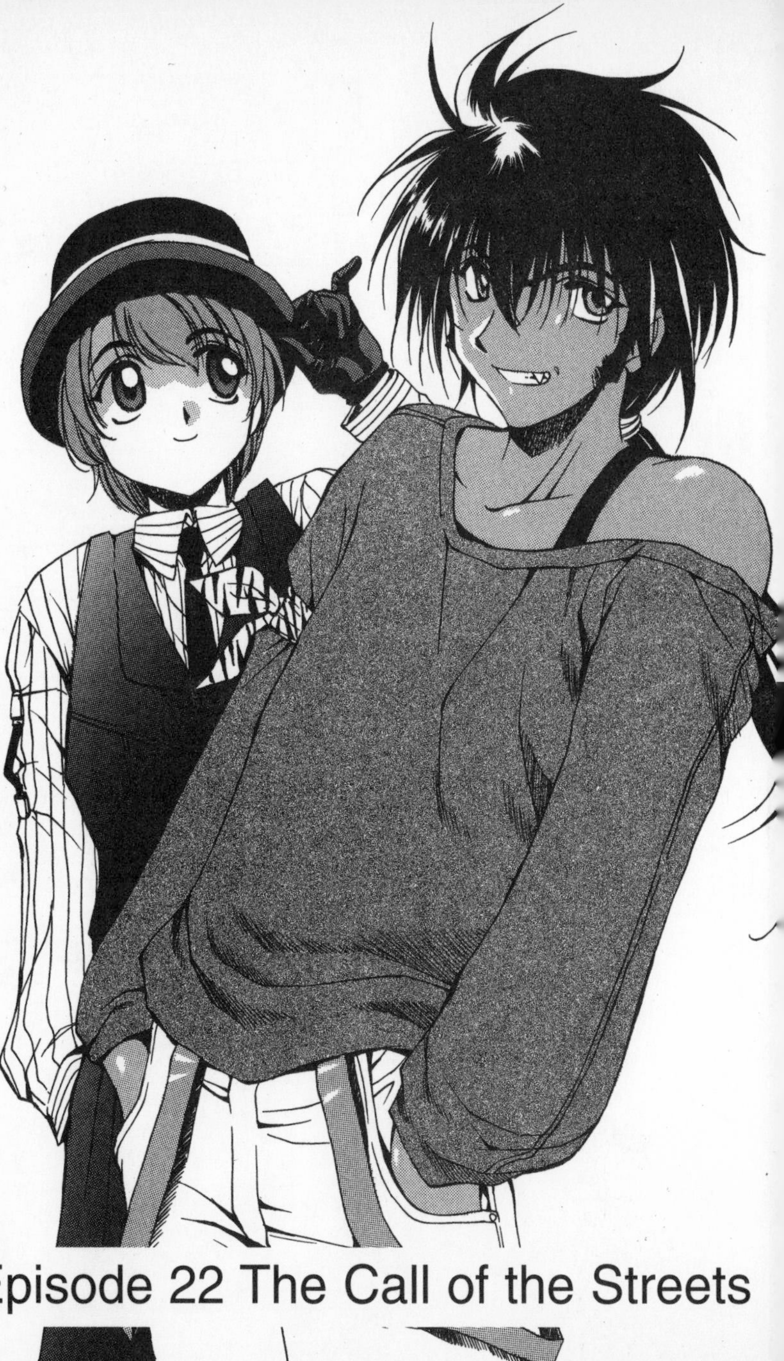

Episode 22 The Call of the Streets

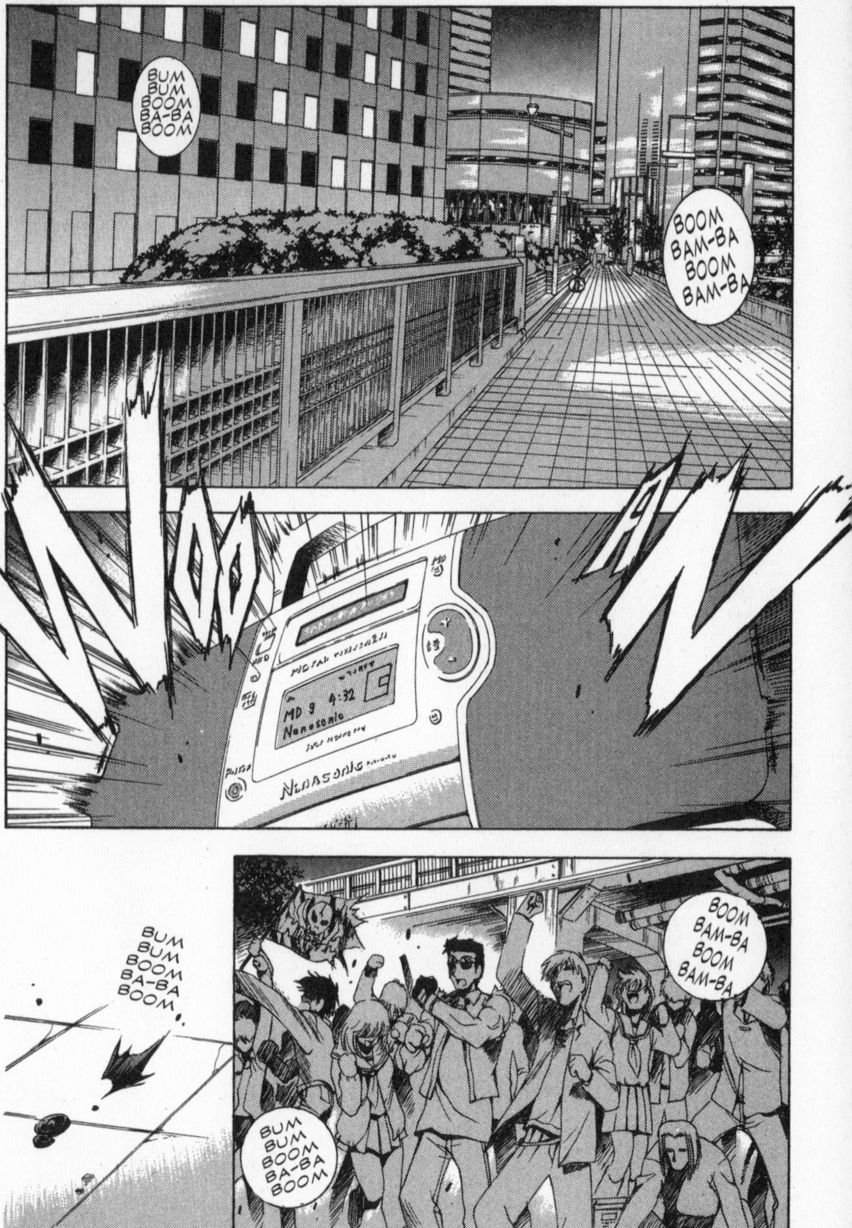
BOOM BAM-BA BOOM BAM-BA
BUM BUM BOOM BA-BA BOOM
MD 9 4:32
Nanasonic
BOOM BAM-BA BOOM BAM-BA
BUM BUM BOOM BA-BA BOOM..
BUM BUM BOOM BA-BA BOOM

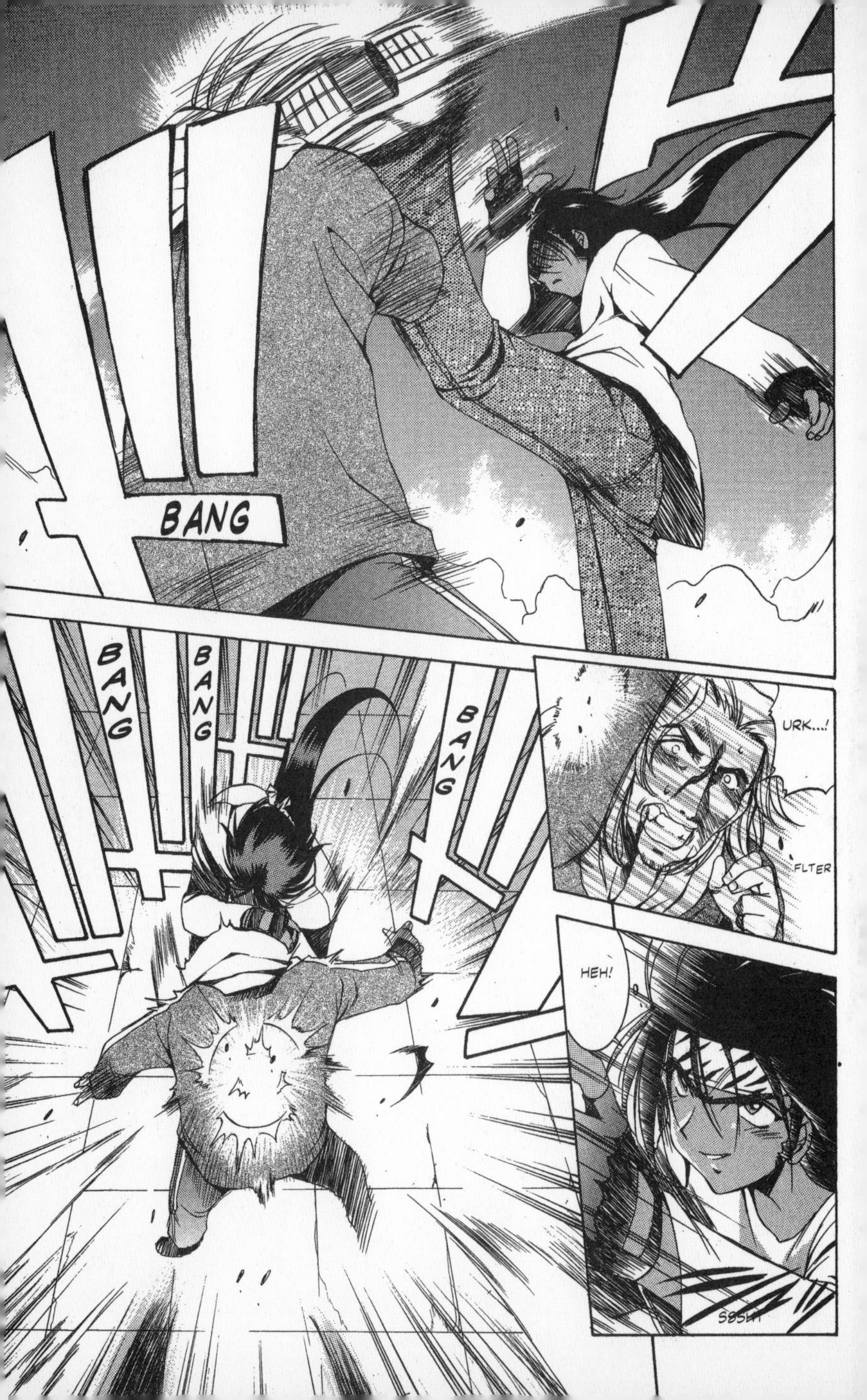
BANG
URK...!
FLTER
HEH!
SSSHT
BANG
BANG
BANG

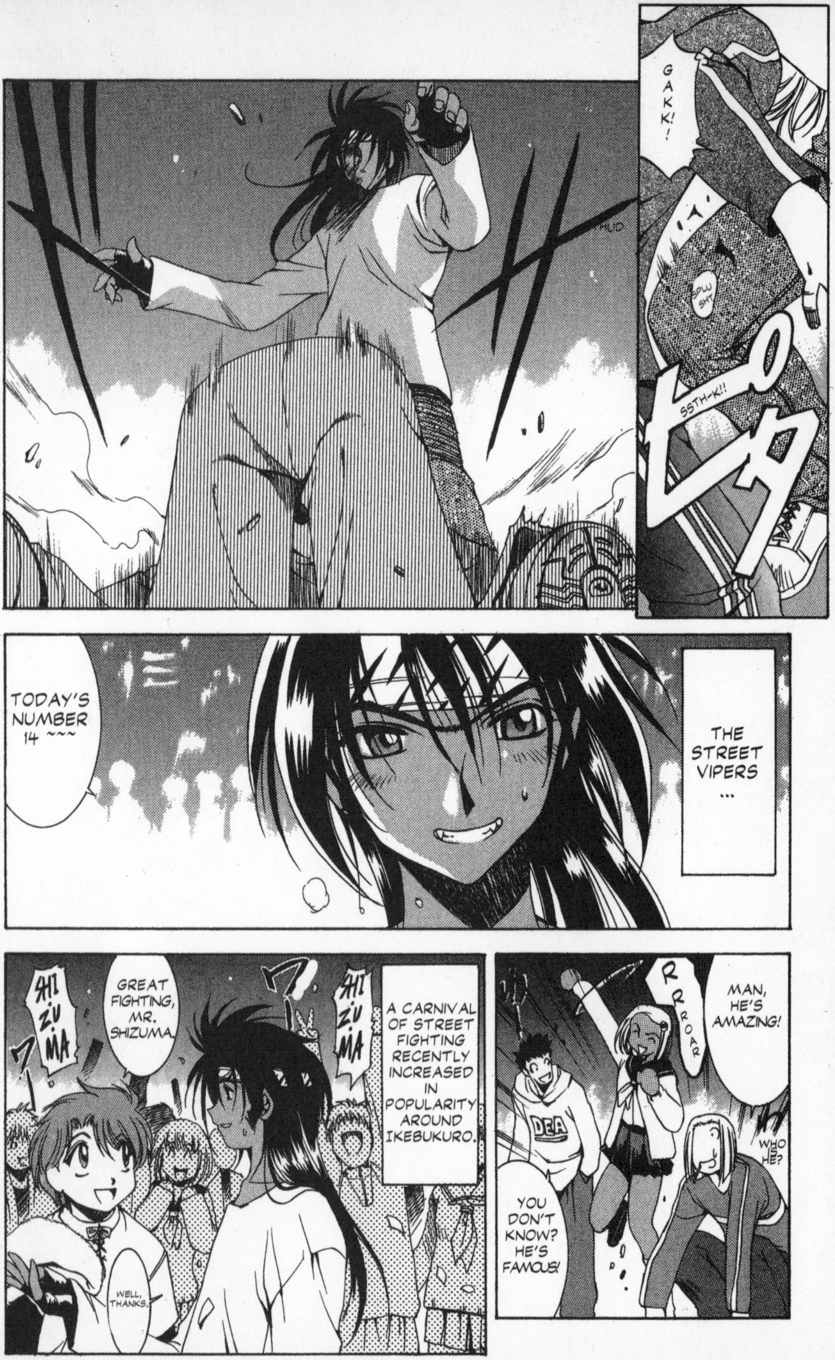
GAKK!
SPLU SHT
SSTH-K!!
HUD
THE STREET VIPERS ...
TODAY'S NUMBER 14 ~~~
MAN, HE'S AMAZING!
RRROAR
WHO IS HE?
YOU DON'T KNOW? HE'S FAMOUS!
A CARNIVAL OF STREET FIGHTING RECENTLY INCREASED IN POPULARITY AROUND IKEBUKURO.
SHI-ZU-MA
GREAT FIGHTING, MR. SHIZUMA.
SHI-ZU-MA
WELL, THANKS.

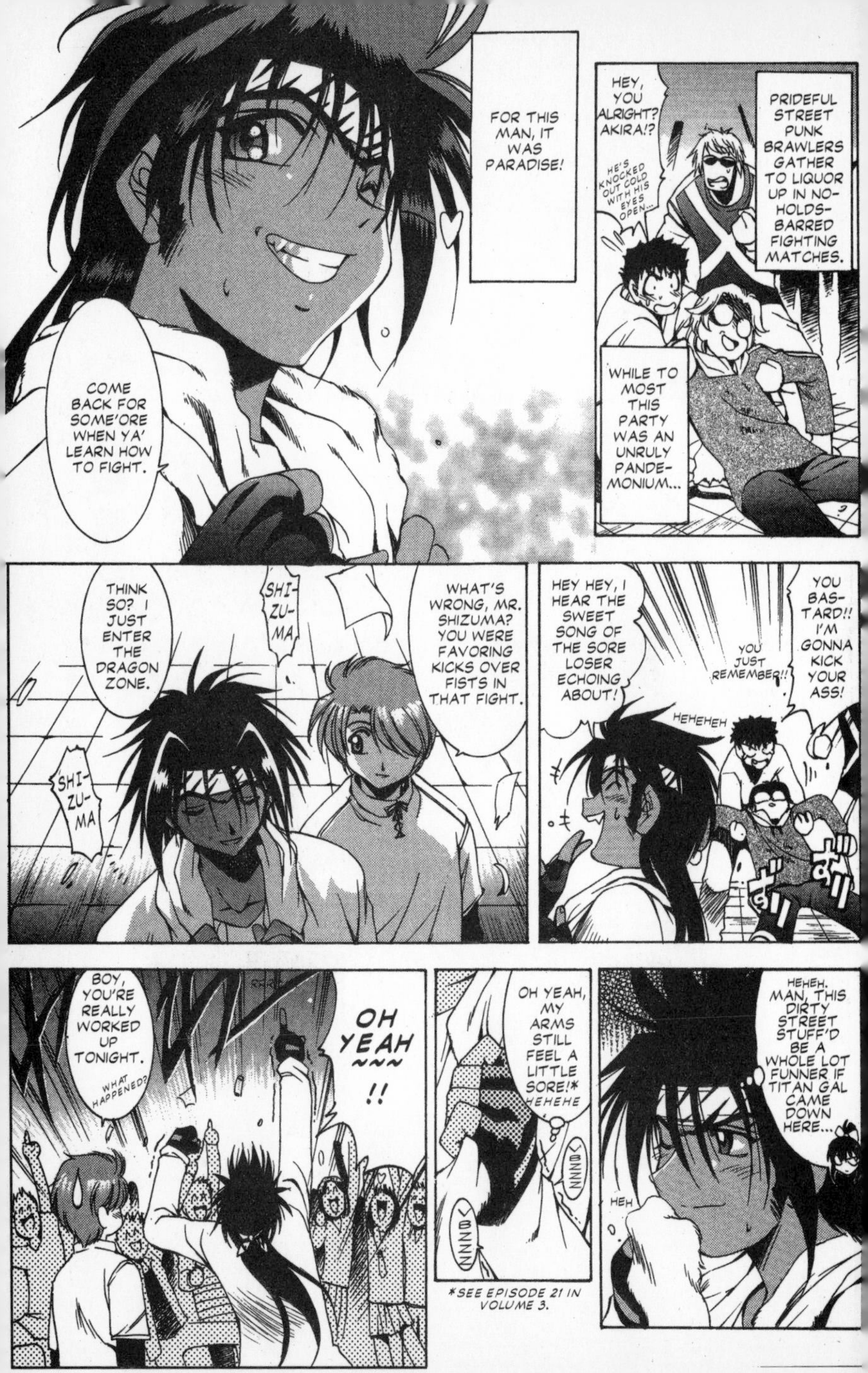
PRIDEFUL STREET PUNK BRAWLERS GATHER TO LIQUOR UP IN NO-HOLDS-BARRED FIGHTING MATCHES.
HEY, YOU ALRIGHT? AKIRA!?
HE'S KNOCKED OUT COLD WITH HIS EYES OPEN...
WHILE TO MOST THIS PARTY WAS AN UNRULY PANDEMONIUM...
FOR THIS MAN, IT WAS PARADISE!
COME BACK FOR SOME'ORE WHEN YA' LEARN HOW TO FIGHT.
YOU BASTARD!! I'M GONNA KICK YOUR ASS!
YOU JUST REMEMBER!!
HEY HEY, I HEAR THE SWEET SONG OF THE SORE LOSER ECHOING ABOUT!
HEHEHEH
WHAT'S WRONG, MR. SHIZUMA? YOU WERE FAVORING KICKS OVER FISTS IN THAT FIGHT.
SHI-ZU-MA
THINK SO? I JUST ENTER THE DRAGON ZONE.
SHI-ZU-MA
HEHEH. MAN, THIS DIRTY STREET STUFF'D BE A WHOLE LOT FUNNER IF TITAN GAL CAME DOWN HERE...
HEH
OH YEAH, MY ARMS STILL FEEL A LITTLE SORE!* HEHEHE
OH YEAH ~~~ !!
BOY, YOU'RE REALLY WORKED UP TONIGHT.
WHAT HAPPENED?

*SEE EPISODE 21 IN VOLUME 3.

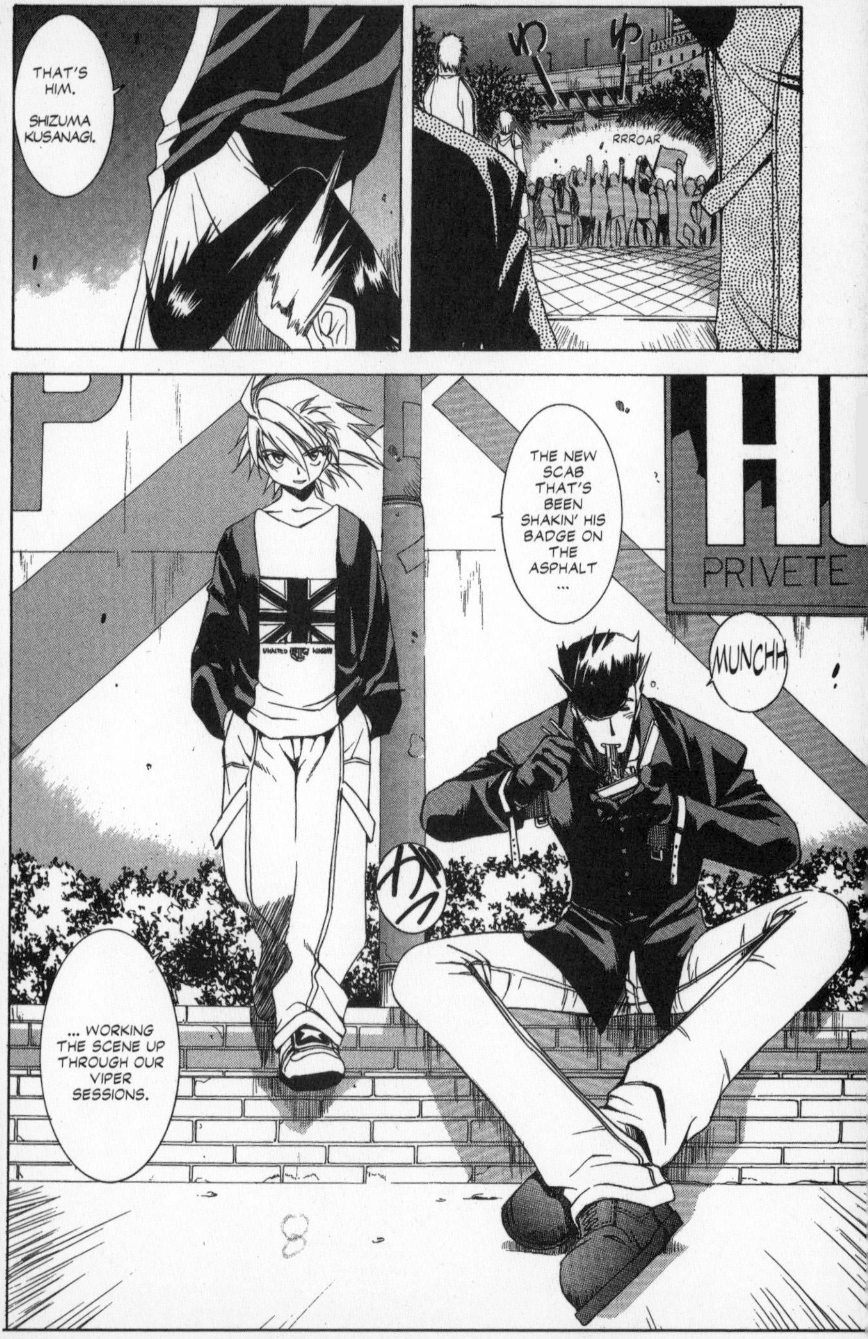
RRROAR
THAT'S HIM.
SHIZUMA KUSANAGI.
HI
PRIVETE
THE NEW SCAB THAT'S BEEN SHAKIN' HIS BADGE ON THE ASPHALT ...
MUNCHH
... WORKING THE SCENE UP THROUGH OUR VIPER SESSIONS.

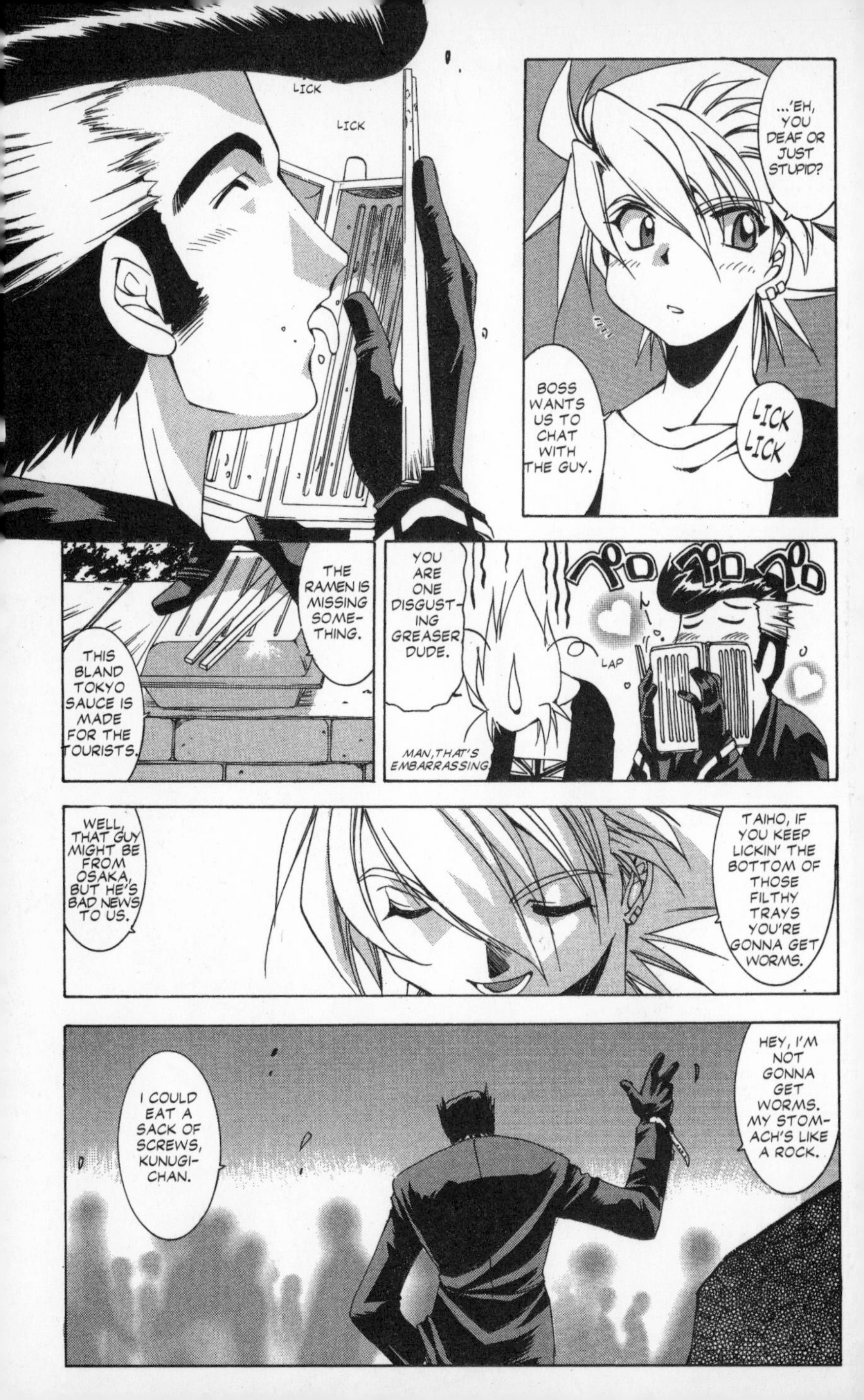
...'EH, YOU DEAF OR JUST STUPID?
BOSS WANTS US TO CHAT WITH THE GUY.
LICK LICK
LICK
LICK
ペロ ペロ ペロ
YOU ARE ONE DISGUSTING GREASER DUDE.
LAP
MAN, THAT'S EMBARRASSING
THE RAMEN IS MISSING SOMETHING.
THIS BLAND TOKYO SAUCE IS MADE FOR THE TOURISTS.
TAIHO, IF YOU KEEP LICKIN' THE BOTTOM OF THOSE FILTHY TRAYS YOU'RE GONNA GET WORMS.
WELL, THAT GUY MIGHT BE FROM OSAKA, BUT HE'S BAD NEWS TO US.
HEY, I'M NOT GONNA GET WORMS. MY STOMACH'S LIKE A ROCK.
I COULD EAT A SACK OF SCREWS, KUNUGI-CHAN.

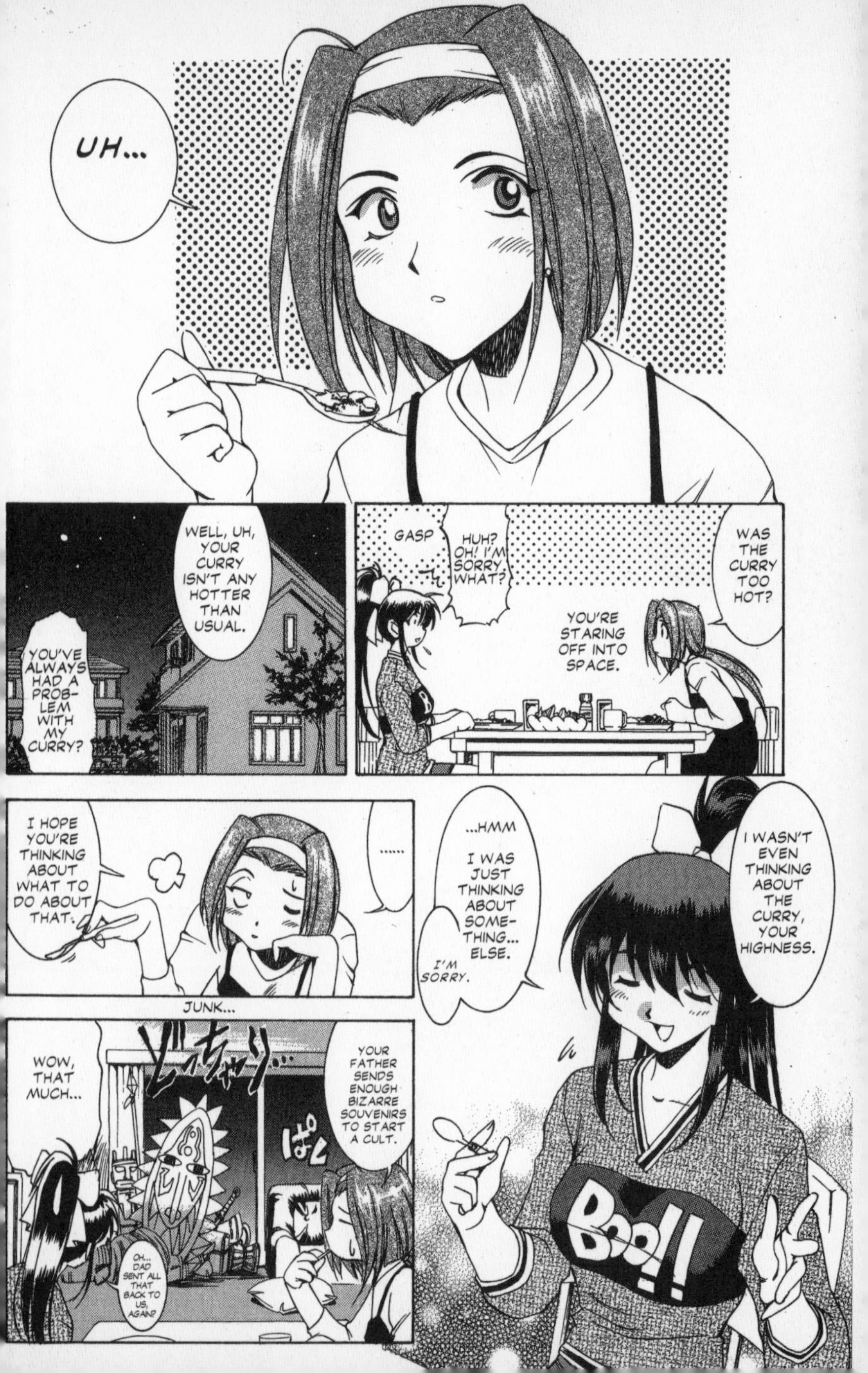
UH...
WAS THE CURRY TOO HOT?
YOU'RE STARING OFF INTO SPACE.
HUH? OH! I'M SORRY WHAT?
GASP
WELL, UH, YOUR CURRY ISN'T ANY HOTTER THAN USUAL.
YOU'VE ALWAYS HAD A PROB-LEM WITH MY CURRY?
I WASN'T EVEN THINKING ABOUT THE CURRY, YOUR HIGHNESS.
...HMM
I WAS JUST THINKING ABOUT SOME-THING... ELSE.
I'M SORRY.
......
I HOPE YOU'RE THINKING ABOUT WHAT TO DO ABOUT THAT.
JUNK...
YOUR FATHER SENDS ENOUGH BIZARRE SOUVENIRS TO START A CULT.
WOW, THAT MUCH...
OH... DAD SENT ALL THAT BACK TO US, AGAIN?

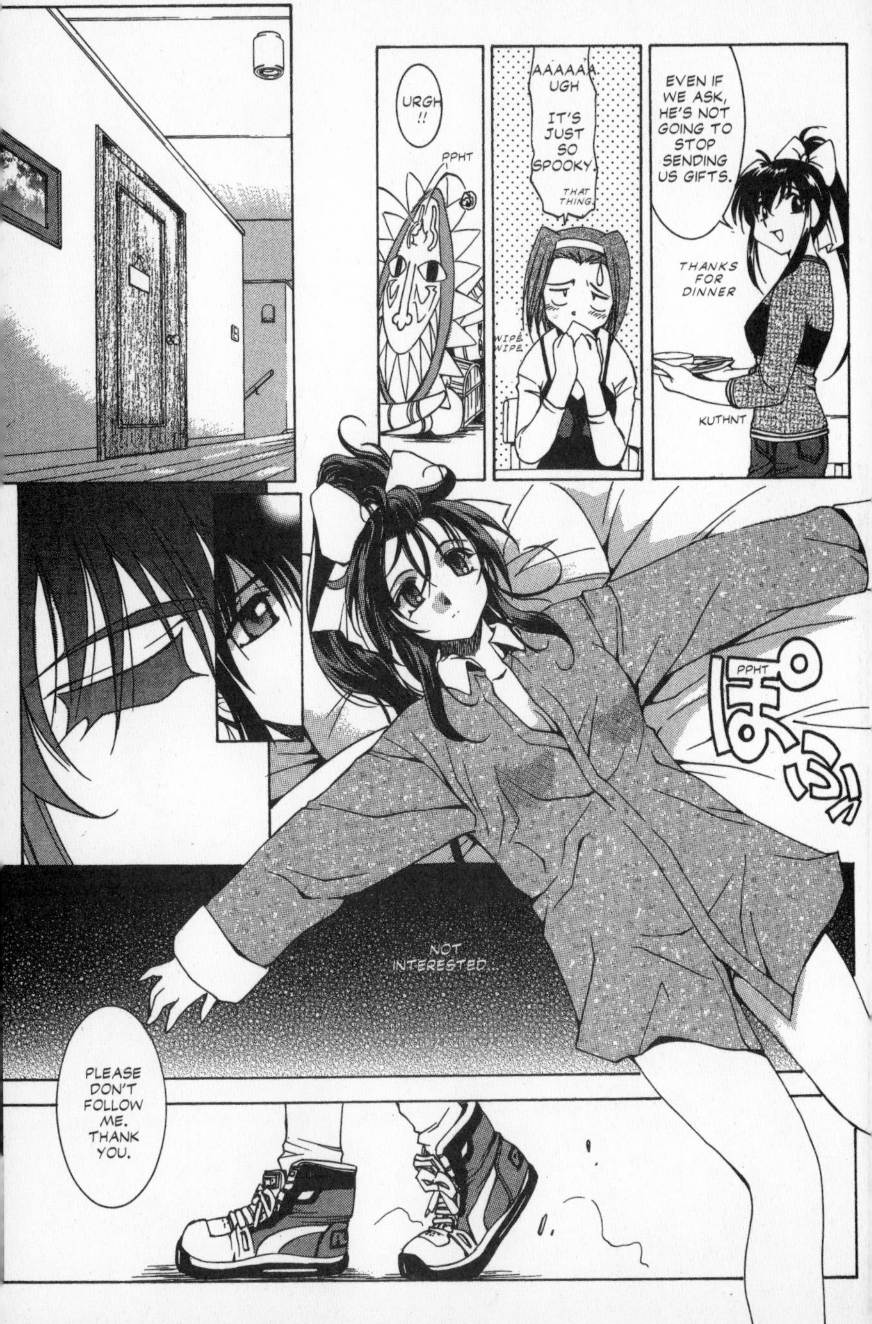
EVEN IF WE ASK, HE'S NOT GOING TO STOP SENDING US GIFTS.
THANKS FOR DINNER
KUTHNT
AAAAAAUGH
IT'S JUST SO SPOOKY.
THAT THING.
WIPE WIPE
URGH!!
PPHT
PPHT
NOT INTERESTED...
PLEASE DON'T FOLLOW ME. THANK YOU.

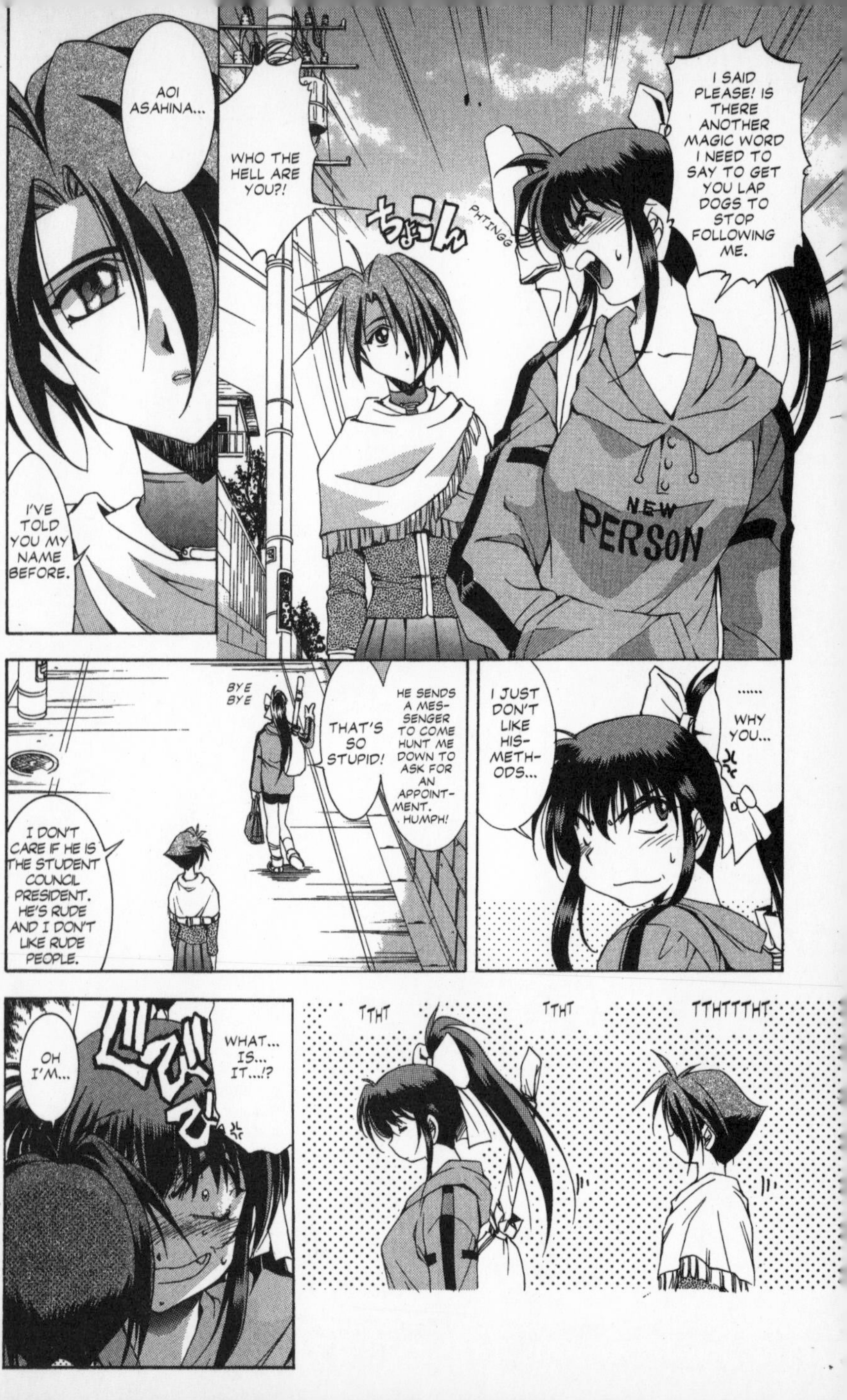
I SAID PLEASE! IS THERE ANOTHER MAGIC WORD I NEED TO SAY TO GET YOU LAP DOGS TO STOP FOLLOWING ME.
PHTINGG
ちょこん
WHO THE HELL ARE YOU?!
AOI ASAHINA...
I'VE TOLD YOU MY NAME BEFORE.
......
WHY YOU...
I JUST DON'T LIKE HIS-METH-ODS...
HE SENDS A MES-SENGER TO COME HUNT ME DOWN TO ASK FOR AN APPOINT-MENT. HUMPH!
THAT'S SO STUPID!
BYE BYE
I DON'T CARE IF HE IS THE STUDENT COUNCIL PRESIDENT. HE'S RUDE AND I DON'T LIKE RUDE PEOPLE.
TTHTTTHT
TTHT
TTHT
WHAT... IS... IT...!?
OH I'M...

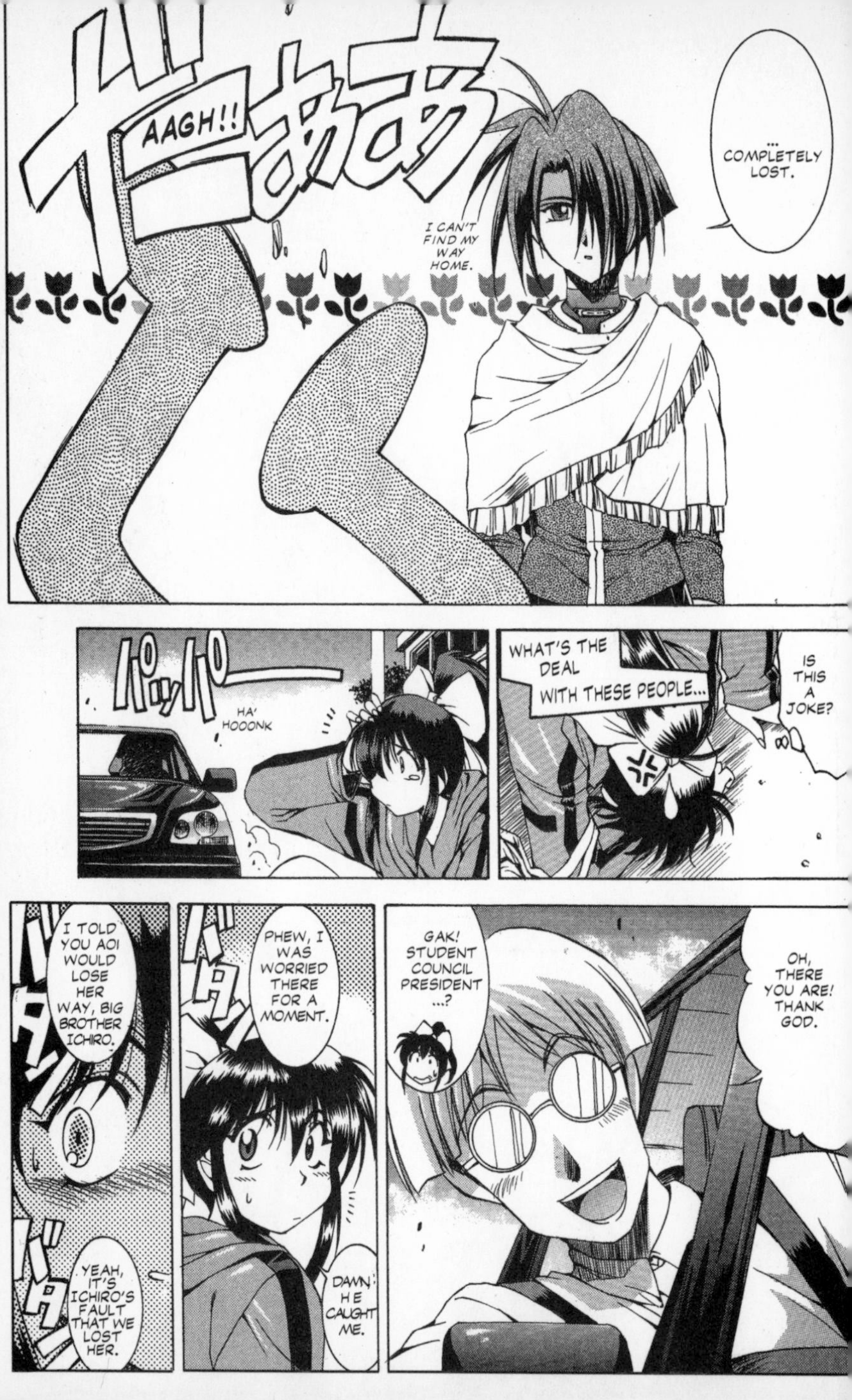

...COMPLETELY LOST.
I CAN'T FIND MY WAY HOME.
AAGH!!
IS THIS A JOKE?
WHAT'S THE DEAL WITH THESE PEOPLE...
HA' HOOONK
OH, THERE YOU ARE! THANK GOD.
GAK! STUDENT COUNCIL PRESIDENT ...?
PHEW, I WAS WORRIED THERE FOR A MOMENT.
DAMN! HE CAUGHT ME.
I TOLD YOU AOI WOULD LOSE HER WAY, BIG BROTHER ICHIRO.
YEAH, IT'S ICHIRO'S FAULT THAT WE LOST HER.

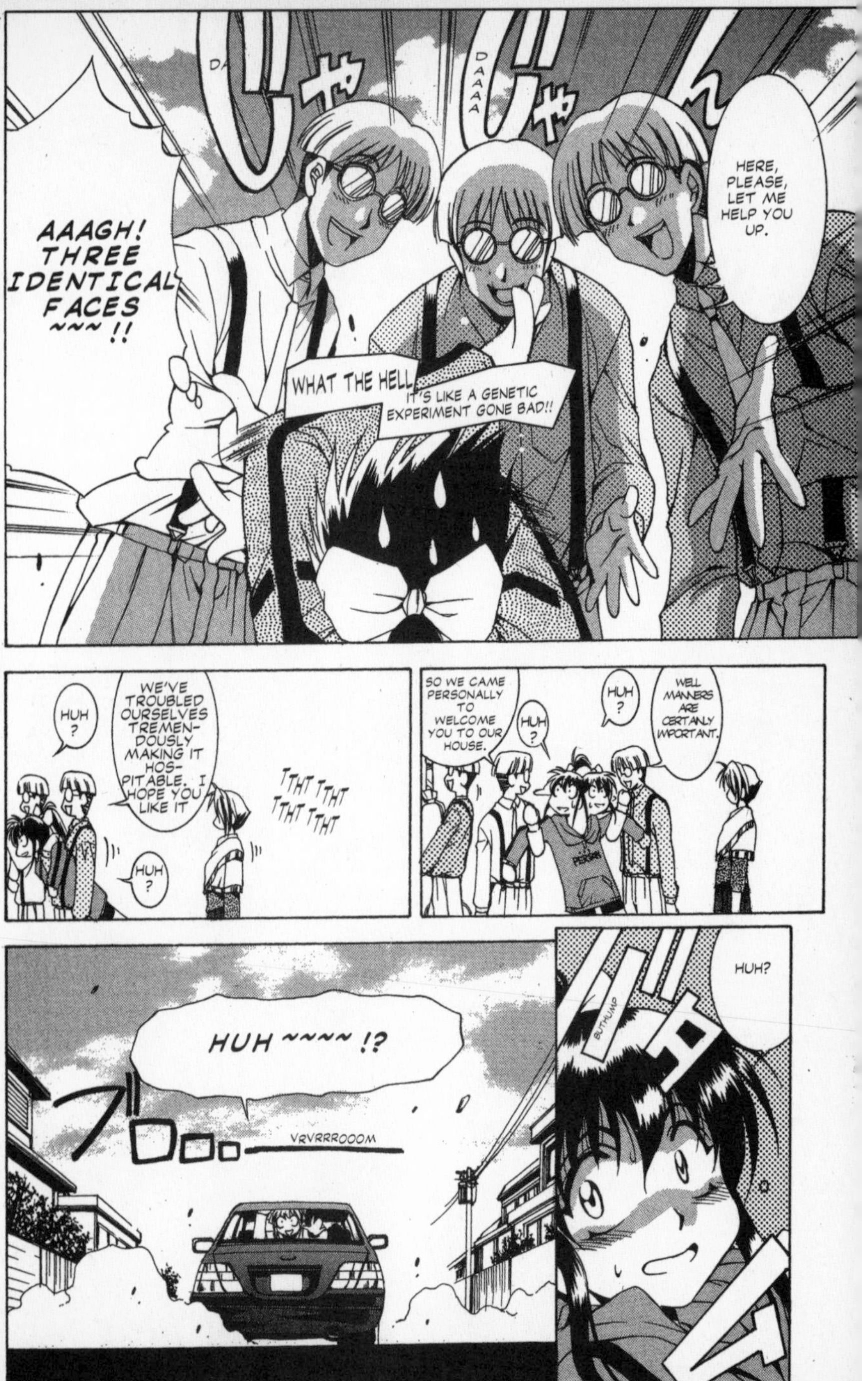
HERE, PLEASE, LET ME HELP YOU UP.
DAAAA
DA
WHAT THE HELL
IT'S LIKE A GENETIC EXPERIMENT GONE BAD!!
AAAGH! THREE IDENTICAL FACES ~~~ !!
WELL MANNERS ARE CERTANLY IMPORTANT.
HUH ?
SO WE CAME PERSONALLY TO WELCOME YOU TO OUR HOUSE.
HUH ?
TTHT TTHT TTHT TTHT
WE'VE TROUBLED OURSELVES TREMENDOUSLY MAKING IT HOSPITABLE. I HOPE YOU LIKE IT
HUH ?
HUH ?
HUH?
BUTHUMP
HUH ~~~~ !?
VRVRRROOOM

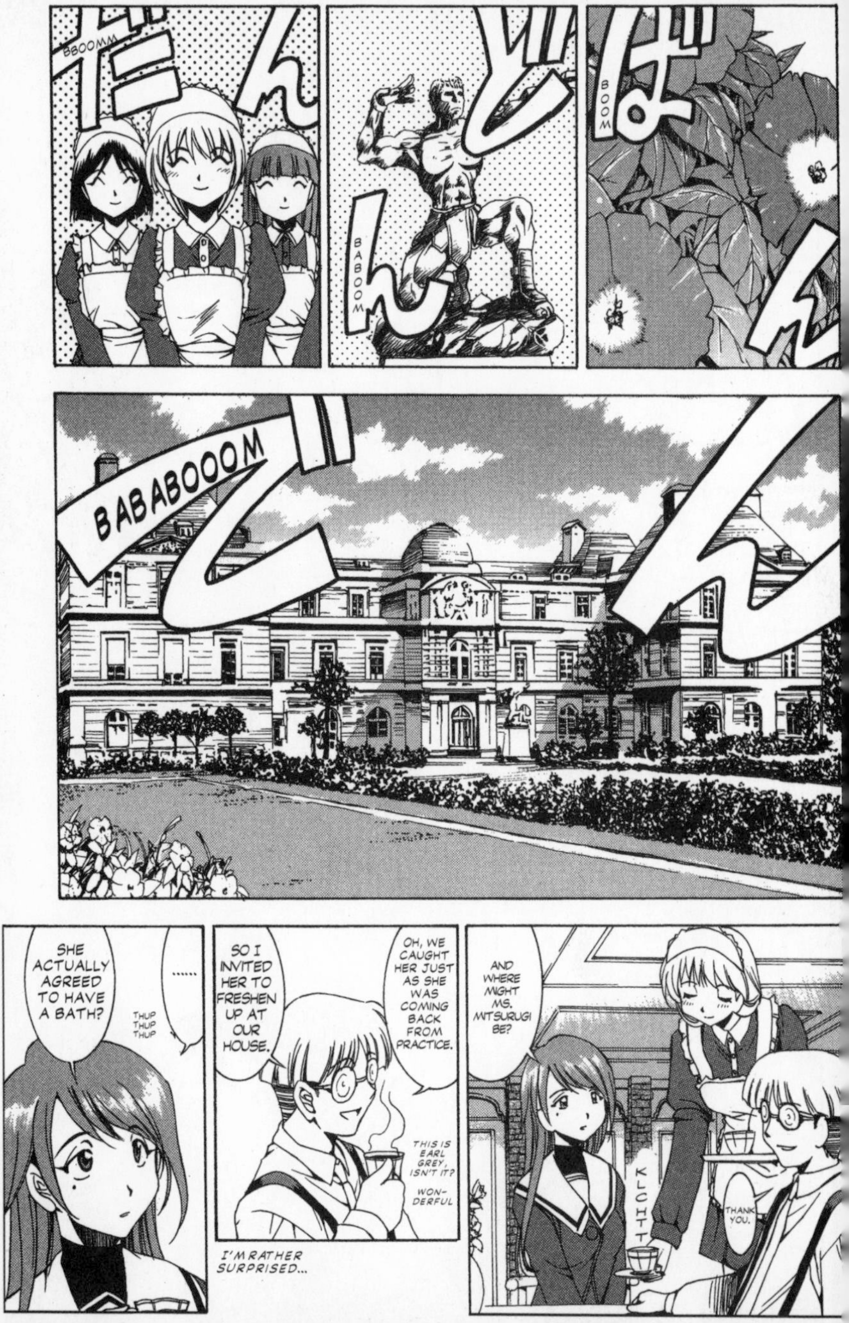
ばん
BOOM
どん
BABOOM
だん
BBOOMM
でん
BABABOOOM
AND WHERE MIGHT MS. MITSURUGI BE?
KLCHTT
THANK YOU.
OH, WE CAUGHT HER JUST AS SHE WAS COMING BACK FROM PRACTICE.
SO I INVITED HER TO FRESHEN UP AT OUR HOUSE.
THIS IS EARL GREY, ISN'T IT? WONDERFUL
......
THUP THUP THUP
SHE ACTUALLY AGREED TO HAVE A BATH?
I'M RATHER SURPRISED...

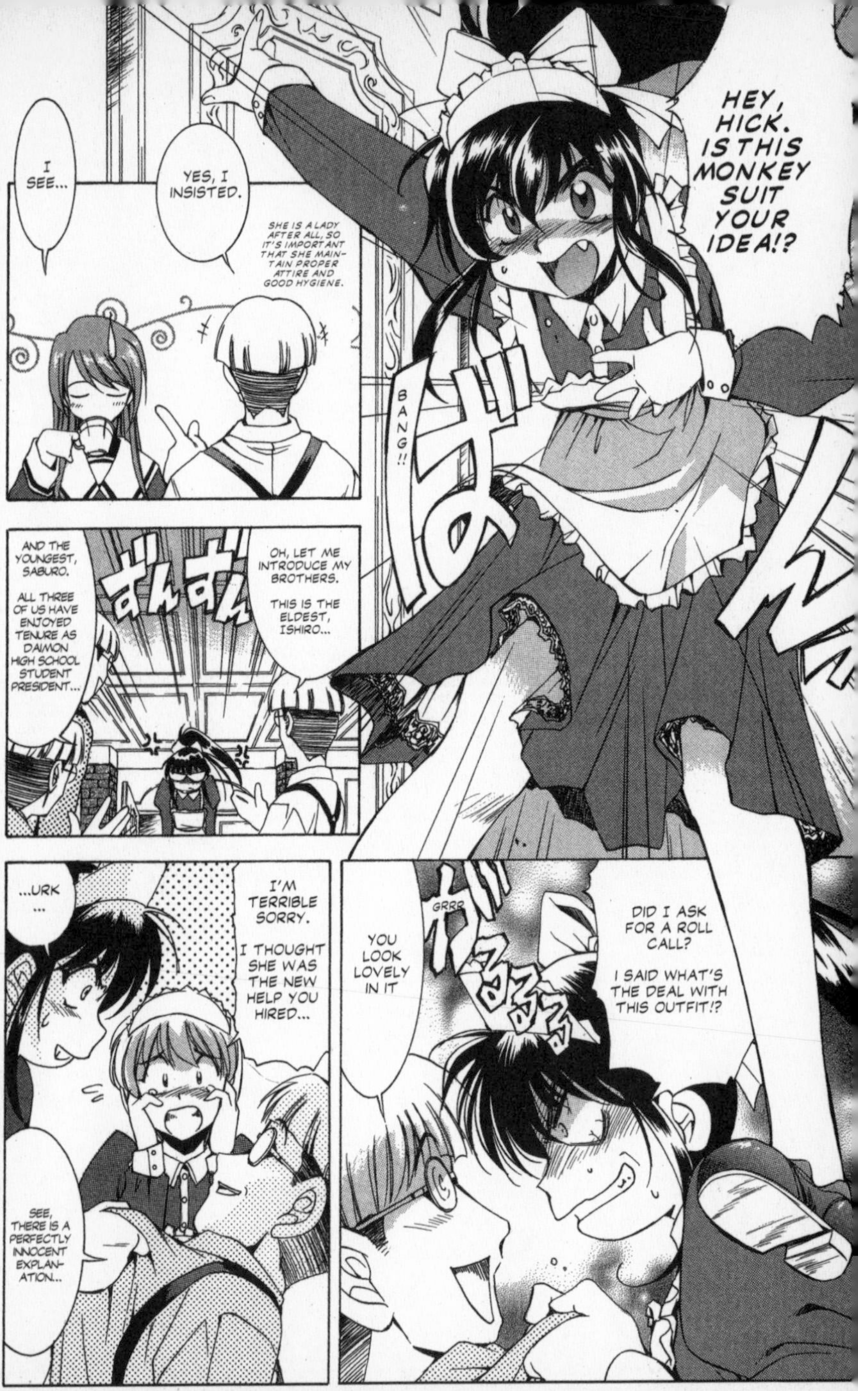
HEY, HICK. IS THIS MONKEY SUIT YOUR IDEA!?
BANG!!
YES, I INSISTED.
SHE IS A LADY AFTER ALL, SO IT'S IMPORTANT THAT SHE MAIN-TAIN PROPER ATTIRE AND GOOD HYGIENE.
I SEE...
OH, LET ME INTRODUCE MY BROTHERS.
THIS IS THE ELDEST, ISHIRO...
ずんずん
AND THE YOUNGEST, SABURO.
ALL THREE OF US HAVE ENJOYED TENURE AS DAIMON HIGH SCHOOL STUDENT PRESIDENT...
DID I ASK FOR A ROLL CALL?
I SAID WHAT'S THE DEAL WITH THIS OUTFIT!?
GRRR
がるるる
YOU LOOK LOVELY IN IT
I'M TERRIBLE SORRY.
I THOUGHT SHE WAS THE NEW HELP YOU HIRED...
...URK ...
SEE, THERE IS A PERFECTLY INNOCENT EXPLAN-ATION...

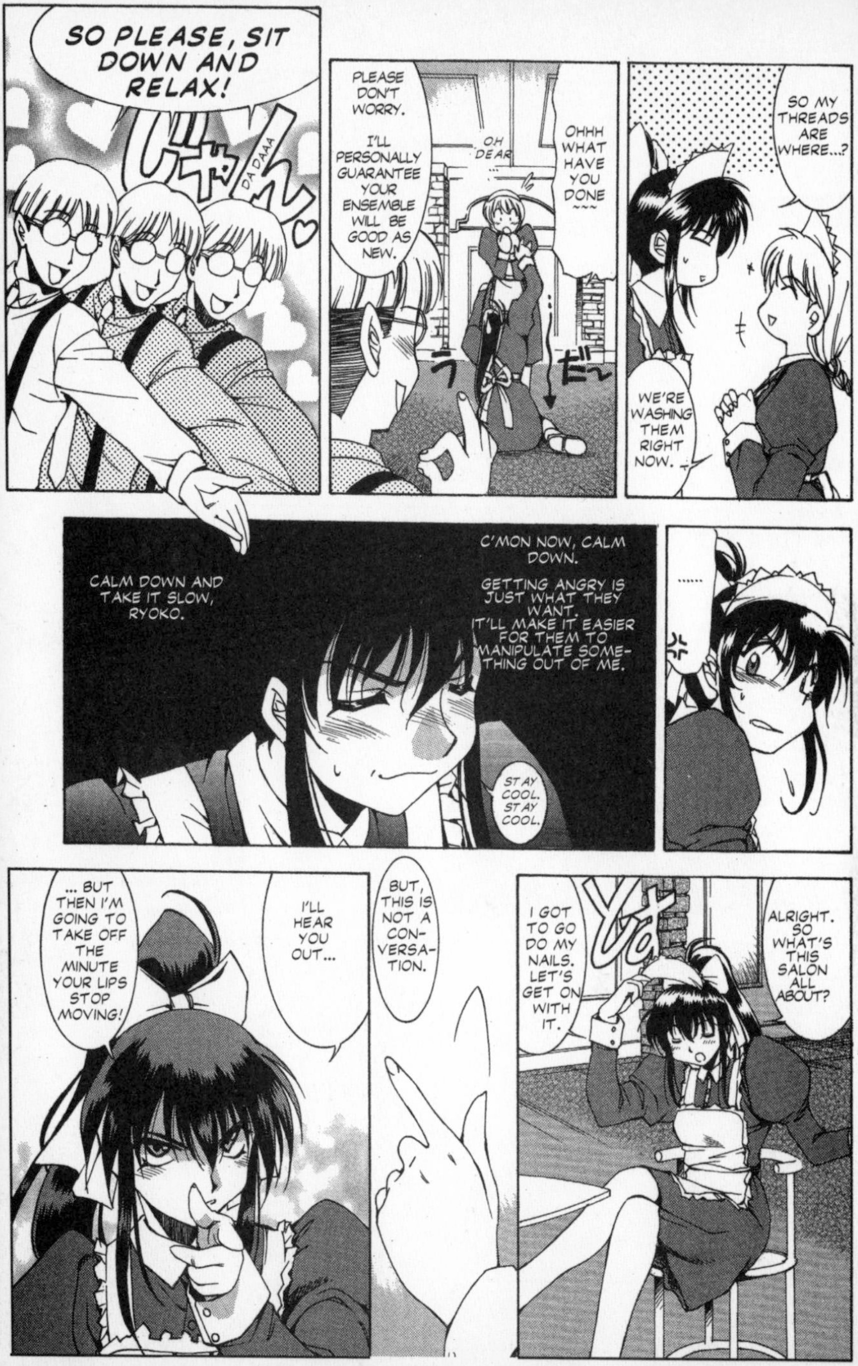
SO MY THREADS ARE WHERE...?
WE'RE WASHING THEM RIGHT NOW.
OHHH WHAT HAVE YOU DONE ~~~
OH DEAR ...
PLEASE DON'T WORRY.
I'LL PERSONALLY GUARANTEE YOUR ENSEMBLE WILL BE GOOD AS NEW.
SO PLEASE, SIT DOWN AND RELAX!
DA DAAA
......
C'MON NOW, CALM DOWN.
GETTING ANGRY IS JUST WHAT THEY WANT. IT'LL MAKE IT EASIER FOR THEM TO MANIPULATE SOMETHING OUT OF ME.
CALM DOWN AND TAKE IT SLOW, RYOKO.
STAY COOL. STAY COOL.
ALRIGHT. SO WHAT'S THIS SALON ALL ABOUT?
I GOT TO GO DO MY NAILS. LET'S GET ON WITH IT.
BUT, THIS IS NOT A CONVERSATION.
I'LL HEAR YOU OUT...
... BUT THEN I'M GOING TO TAKE OFF THE MINUTE YOUR LIPS STOP MOVING!

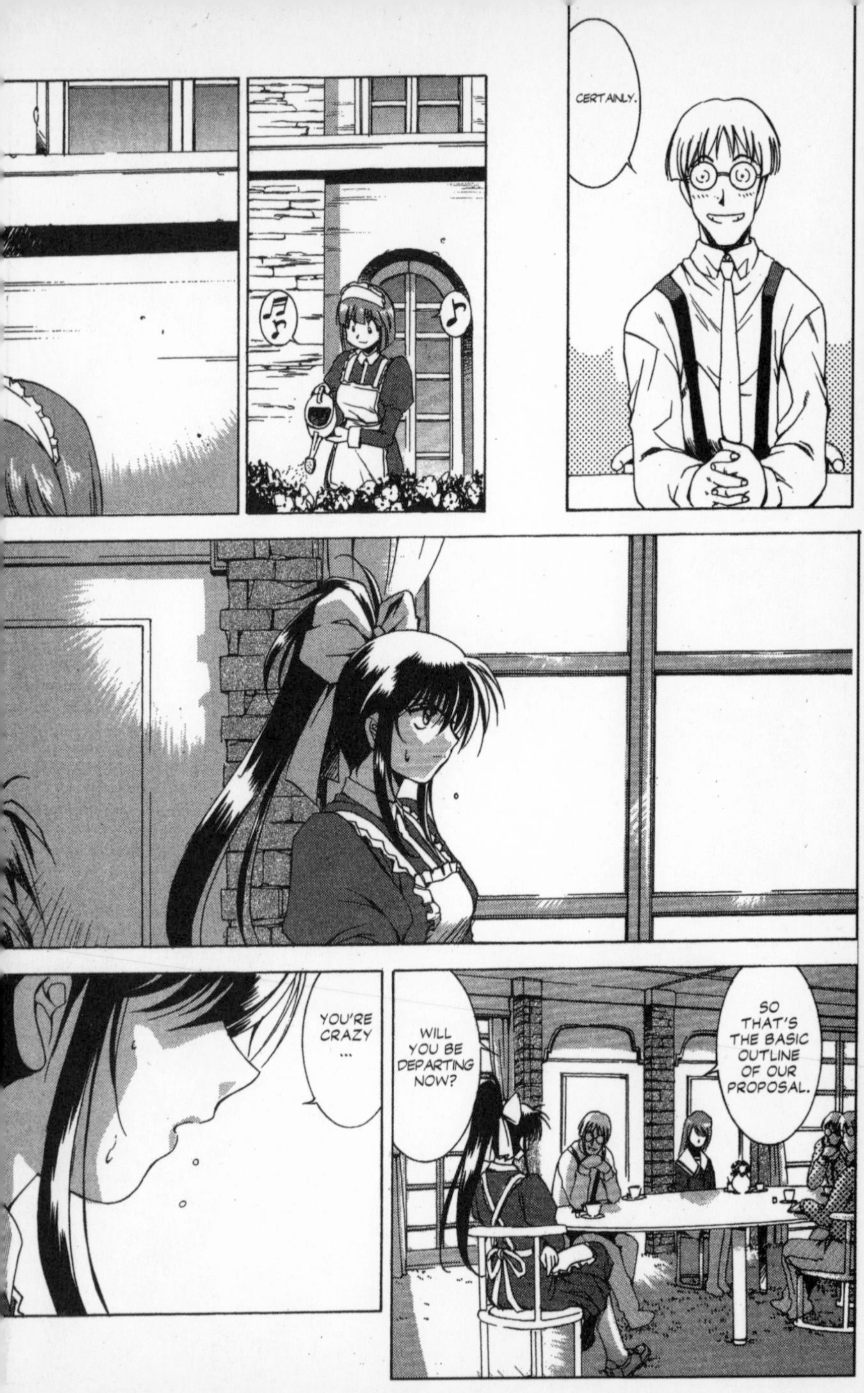
CERTAINLY.
SO THAT'S THE BASIC OUTLINE OF OUR PROPOSAL.
WILL YOU BE DEPARTING NOW?
YOU'RE CRAZY ...

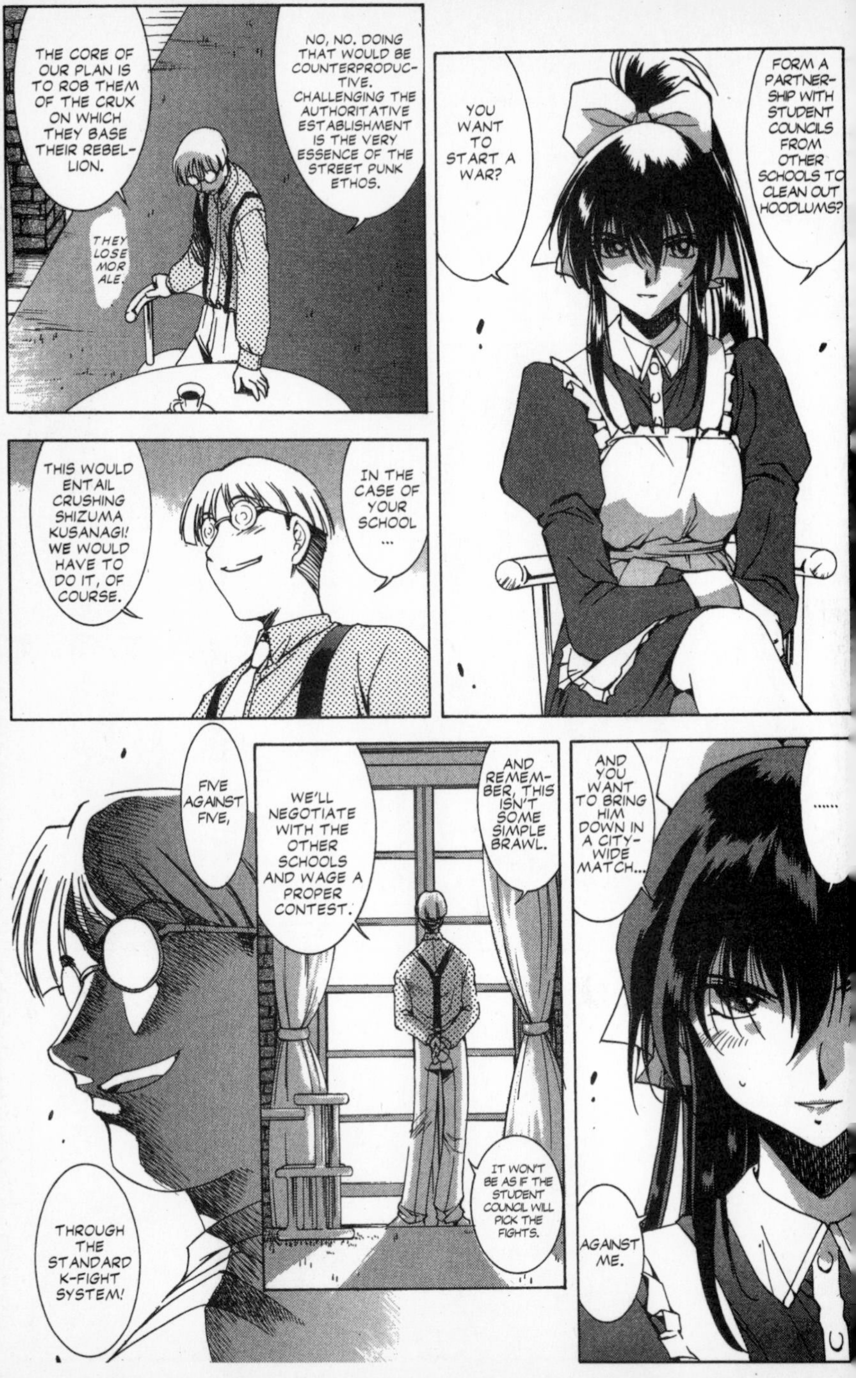
FORM A PARTNERSHIP WITH STUDENT COUNCILS FROM OTHER SCHOOLS TO CLEAN OUT HOODLUMS?
YOU WANT TO START A WAR?
NO, NO. DOING THAT WOULD BE COUNTERPRODUCTIVE. CHALLENGING THE AUTHORITATIVE ESTABLISHMENT IS THE VERY ESSENCE OF THE STREET PUNK ETHOS.
THE CORE OF OUR PLAN IS TO ROB THEM OF THE CRUX ON WHICH THEY BASE THEIR REBELLION.
THEY LOSE MORALE.
IN THE CASE OF YOUR SCHOOL...
THIS WOULD ENTAIL CRUSHING SHIZUMA KUSANAGI! WE WOULD HAVE TO DO IT, OF COURSE.
......
AND YOU WANT TO BRING HIM DOWN IN A CITY-WIDE MATCH...
AGAINST ME.
AND REMEMBER, THIS ISN'T SOME SIMPLE BRAWL.
WE'LL NEGOTIATE WITH THE OTHER SCHOOLS AND WAGE A PROPER CONTEST.
IT WON'T BE AS IF THE STUDENT COUNCIL WILL PICK THE FIGHTS.
FIVE AGAINST FIVE,
THROUGH THE STANDARD K-FIGHT SYSTEM!

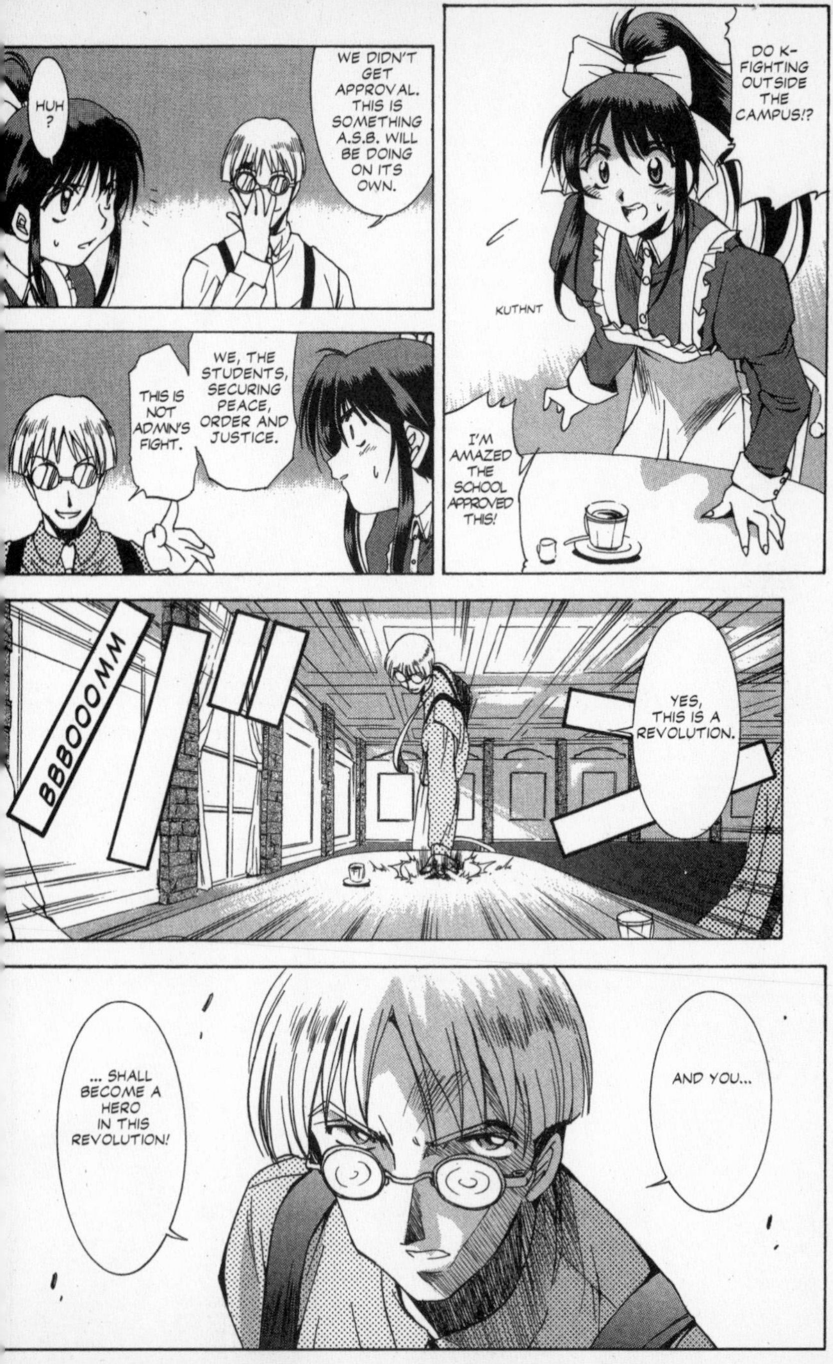
DO K-FIGHTING OUTSIDE THE CAMPUS!?
KUTHNT
I'M AMAZED THE SCHOOL APPROVED THIS!
WE DIDN'T GET APPROVAL. THIS IS SOMETHING A.S.B. WILL BE DOING ON ITS OWN.
HUH?
WE, THE STUDENTS, SECURING PEACE, ORDER AND JUSTICE.
THIS IS NOT ADMIN'S FIGHT.
YES, THIS IS A REVOLUTION.
BBBOOOMM
AND YOU...
... SHALL BECOME A HERO IN THIS REVOLUTION!

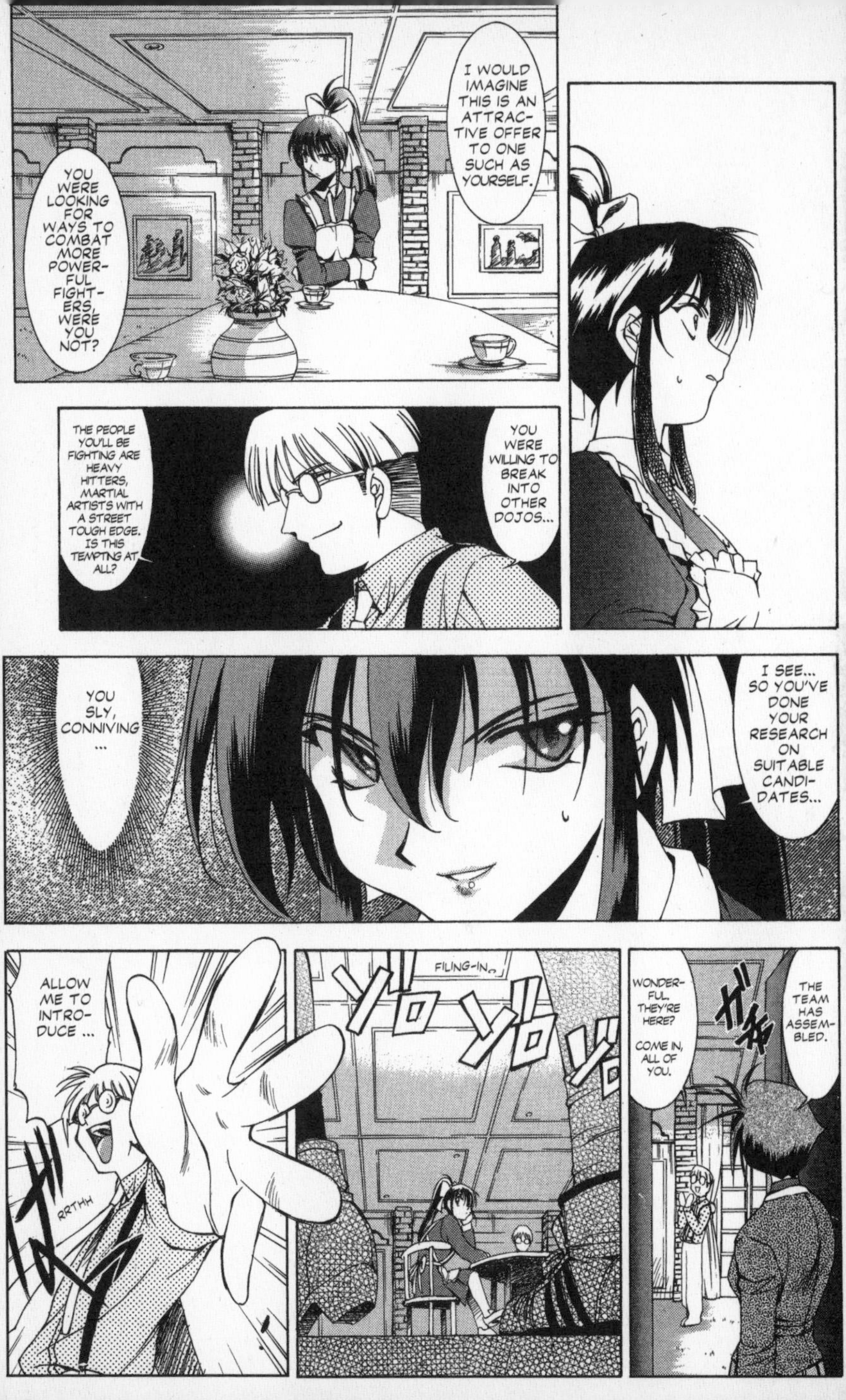
I WOULD IMAGINE THIS IS AN ATTRACTIVE OFFER TO ONE SUCH AS YOURSELF.
YOU WERE LOOKING FOR WAYS TO COMBAT MORE POWERFUL FIGHTERS, WERE YOU NOT?
YOU WERE WILLING TO BREAK INTO OTHER DOJOS...
THE PEOPLE YOU'LL BE FIGHTING ARE HEAVY HITTERS, MARTIAL ARTISTS WITH A STREET TOUGH EDGE. IS THIS TEMPTING AT ALL?
I SEE... SO YOU'VE DONE YOUR RESEARCH ON SUITABLE CANDIDATES...
YOU SLY, CONNIVING ...
THE TEAM HAS ASSEMBLED.
WONDERFUL. THEY'RE HERE?
COME IN, ALL OF YOU.
FILING-IN
ゾロ ゾロ
ALLOW ME TO INTRODUCE ...
RRTHH

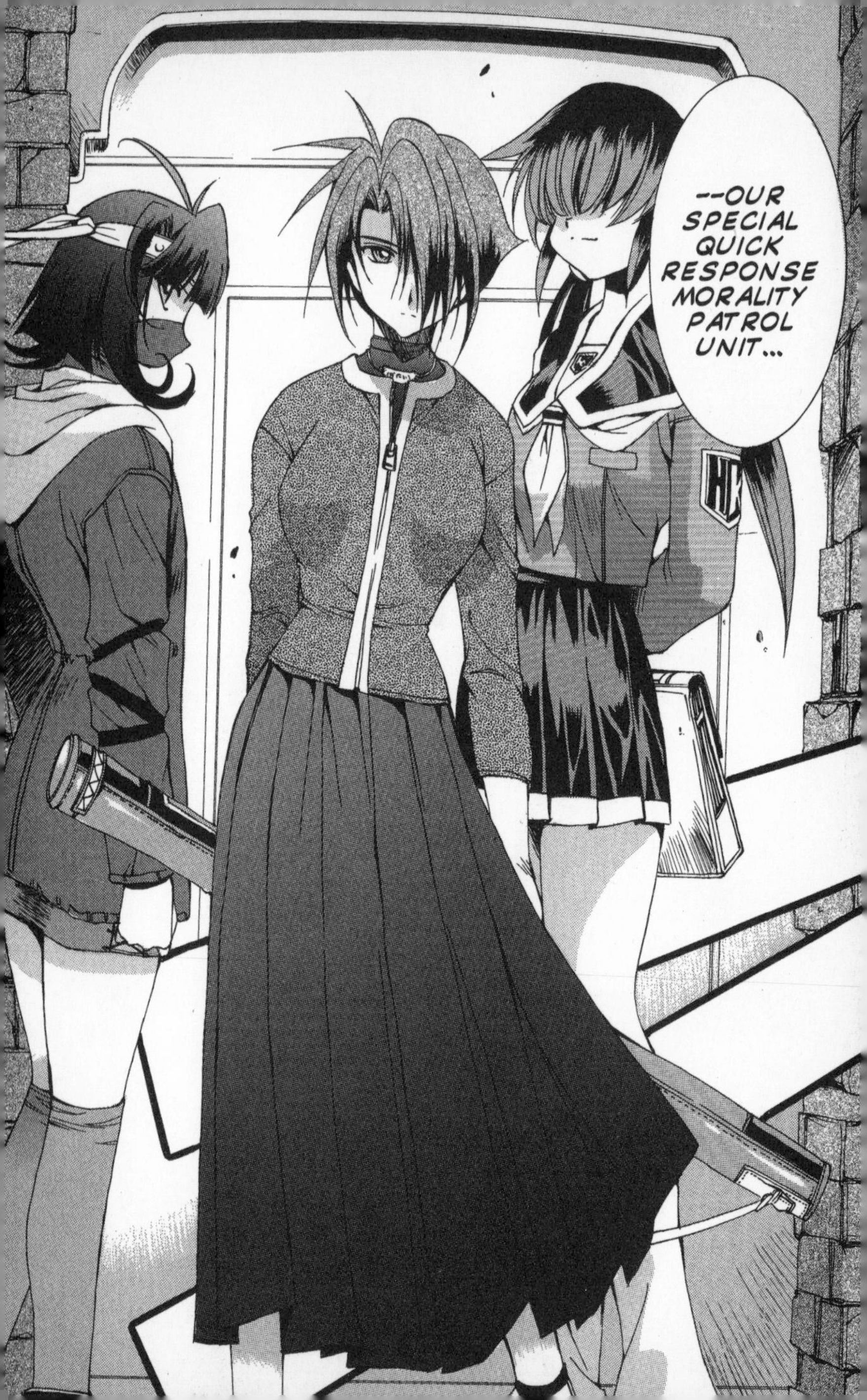
--OUR SPECIAL QUICK RESPONSE MORALITY PATROL UNIT...

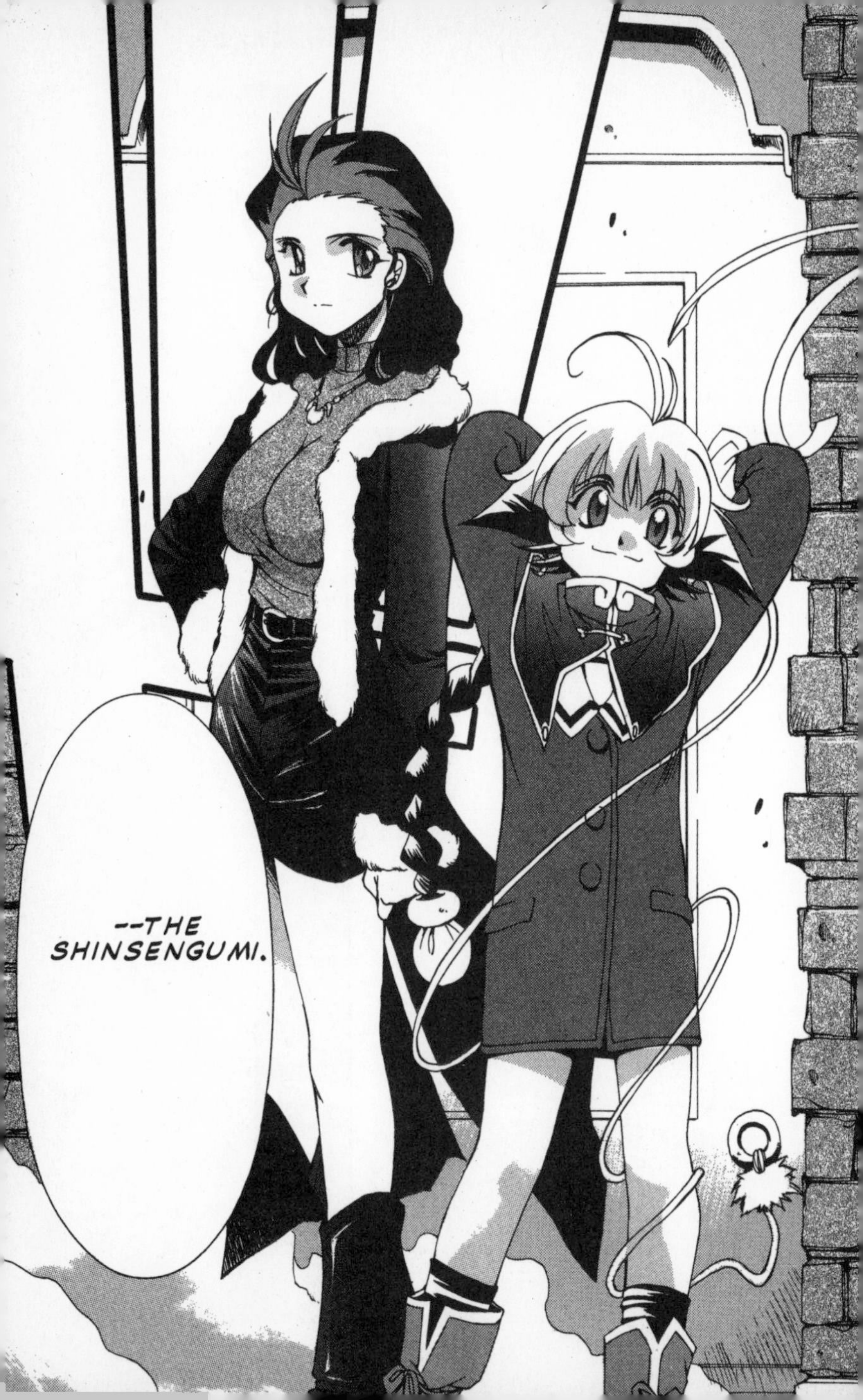
--THE SHINSENGUMI.

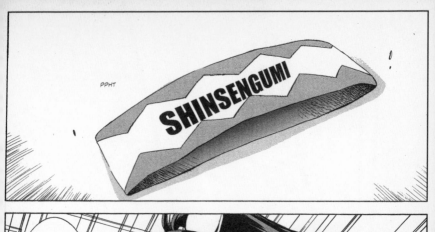

PPHT

SHINSENGUMI

AND YOU WILL BE ITS CAPTAIN.

I'LL AWAIT YOUR ANSWER WITH TINGLING ANTICIPATION.

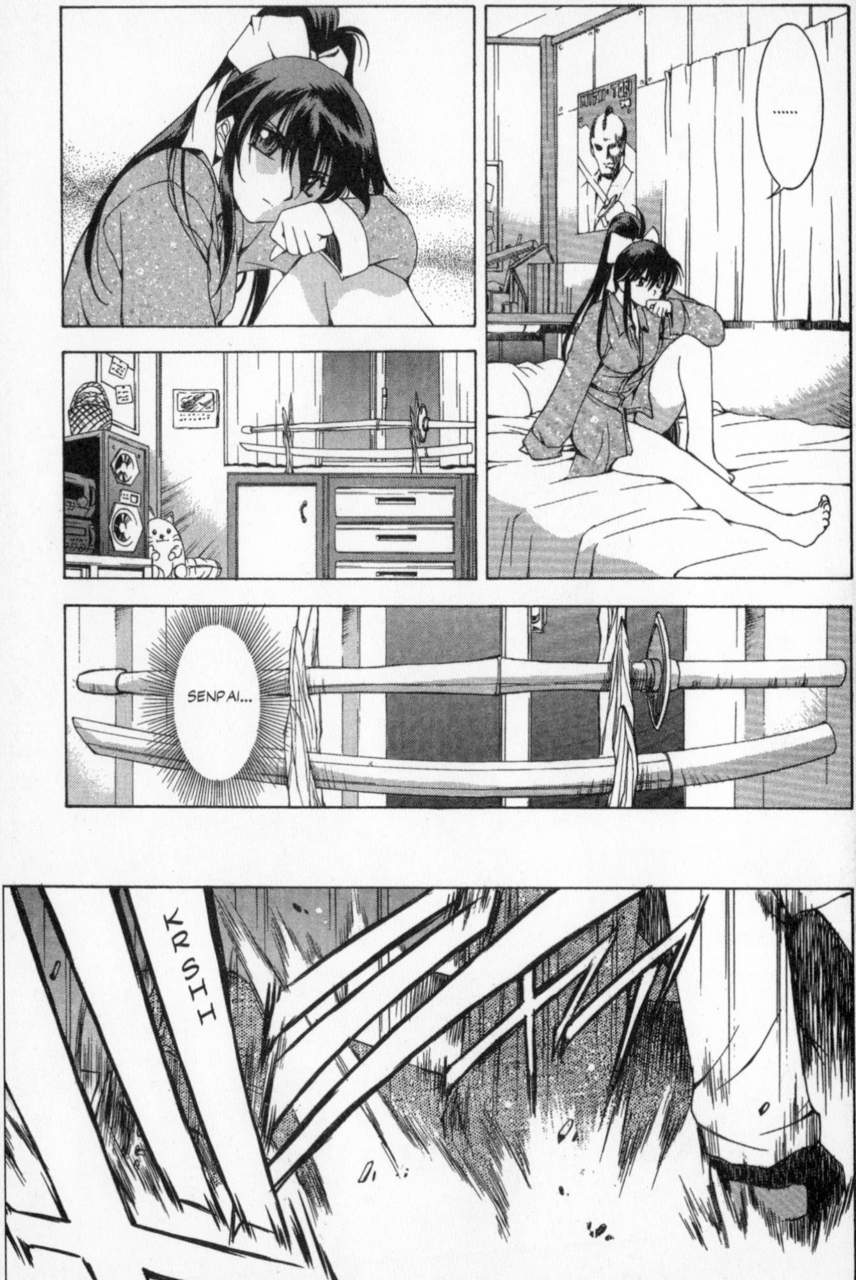

......
SENPAI...
KRSII

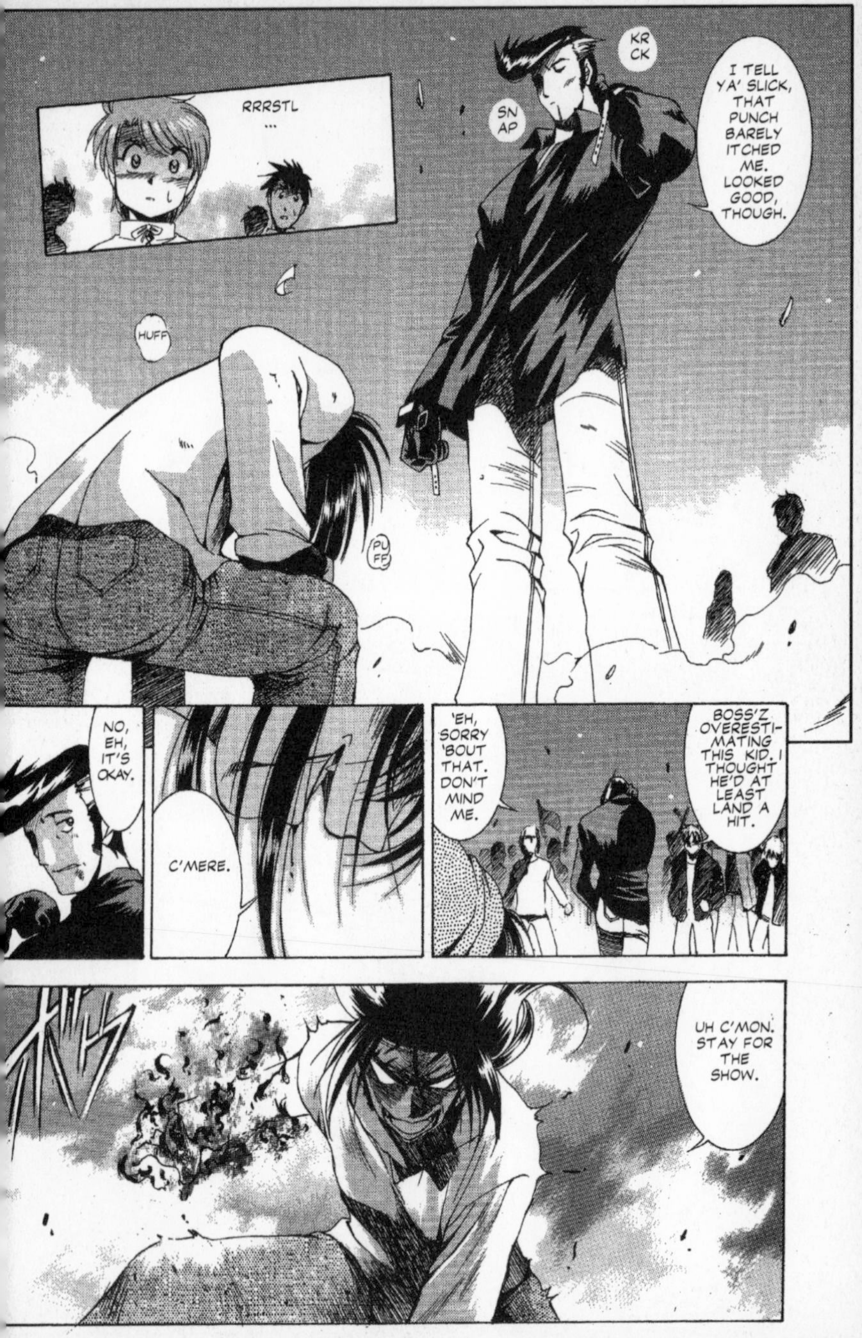
KR CK
I TELL YA' SLICK, THAT PUNCH BARELY ITCHED ME. LOOKED GOOD, THOUGH.
SN AP
RRRSTL ...
HUFF
PU FF
BOSS'Z OVERESTI-MATING THIS KID. I THOUGHT HE'D AT LEAST LAND A HIT.
'EH, SORRY 'BOUT THAT. DON'T MIND ME.
C'MERE.
NO, EH, IT'S OKAY.
UH C'MON. STAY FOR THE SHOW.

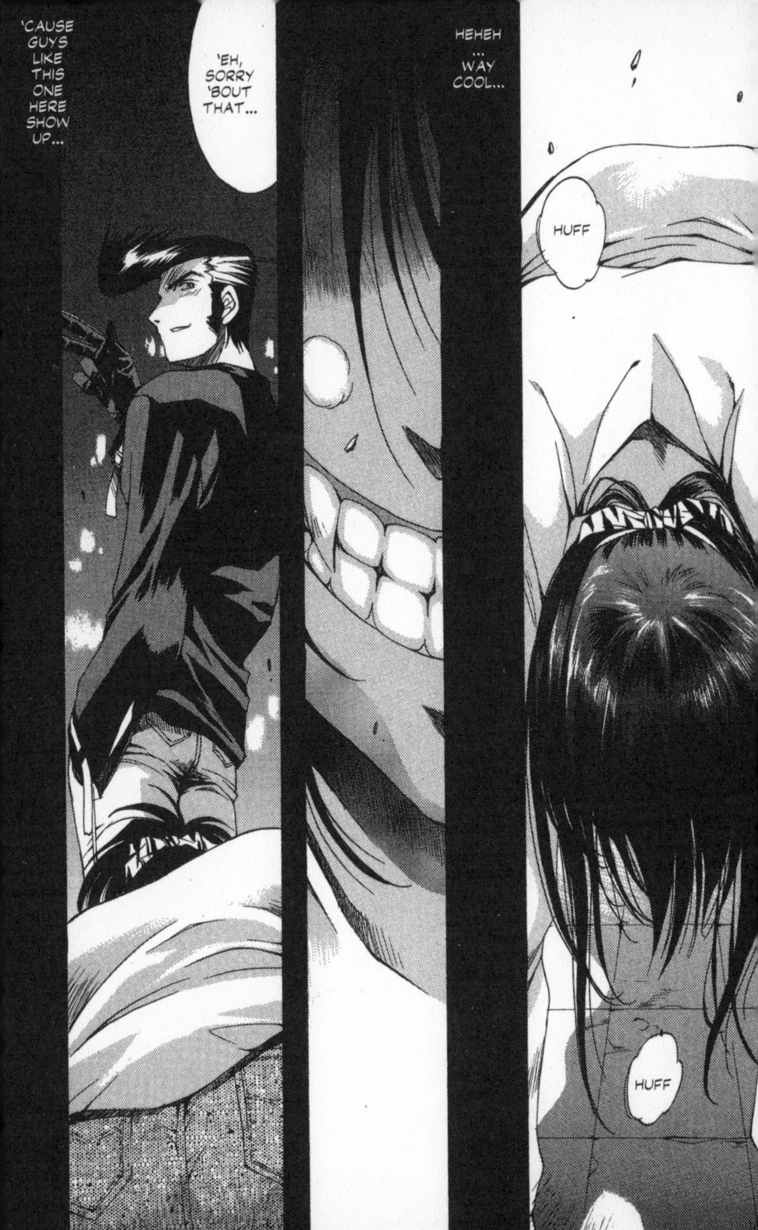
HUFF
HUFF
HEHEH ... WAY COOL...
'EH, SORRY 'BOUT THAT...
'CAUSE GUYS LIKE THIS ONE HERE SHOW UP...

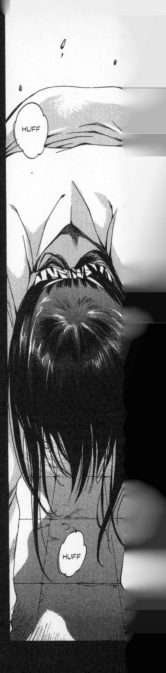

Episode 23 How the Fire Tiger and Shock Wave Wolf Learned to Negotiate

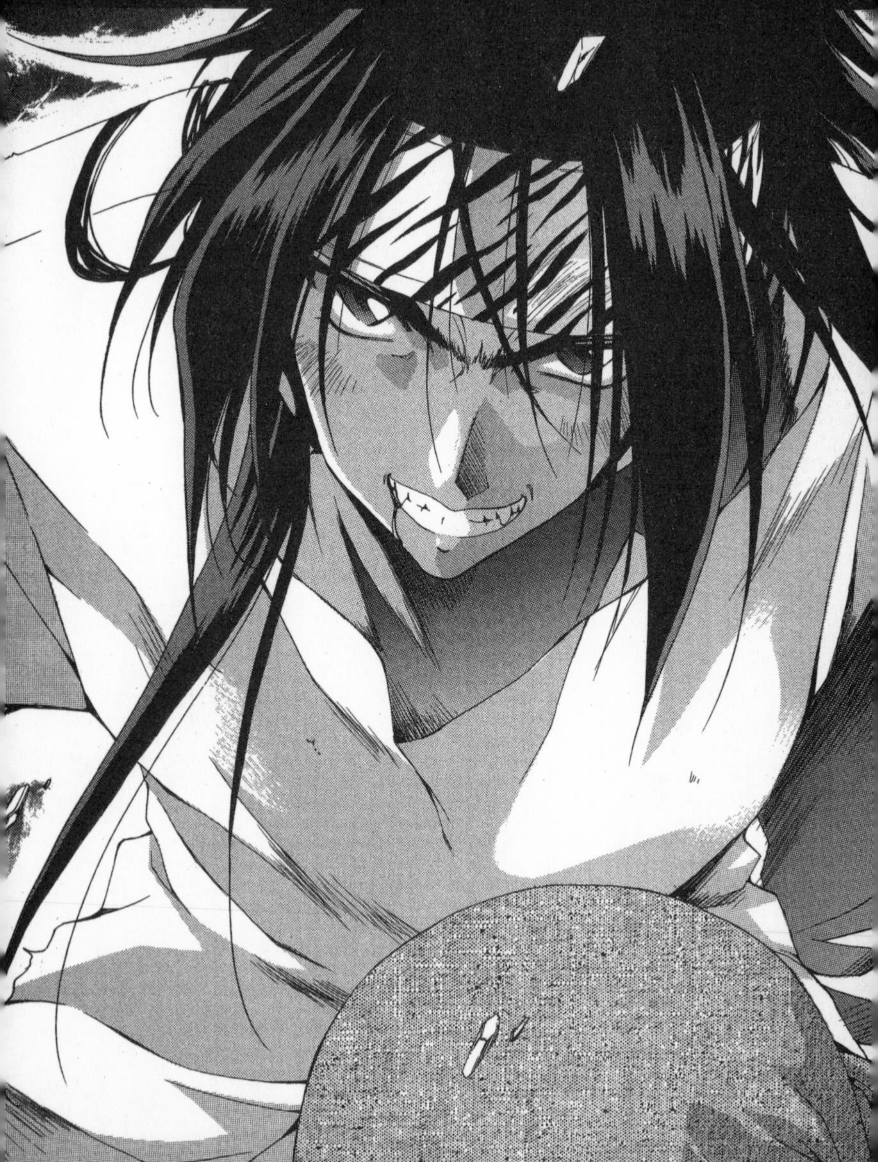

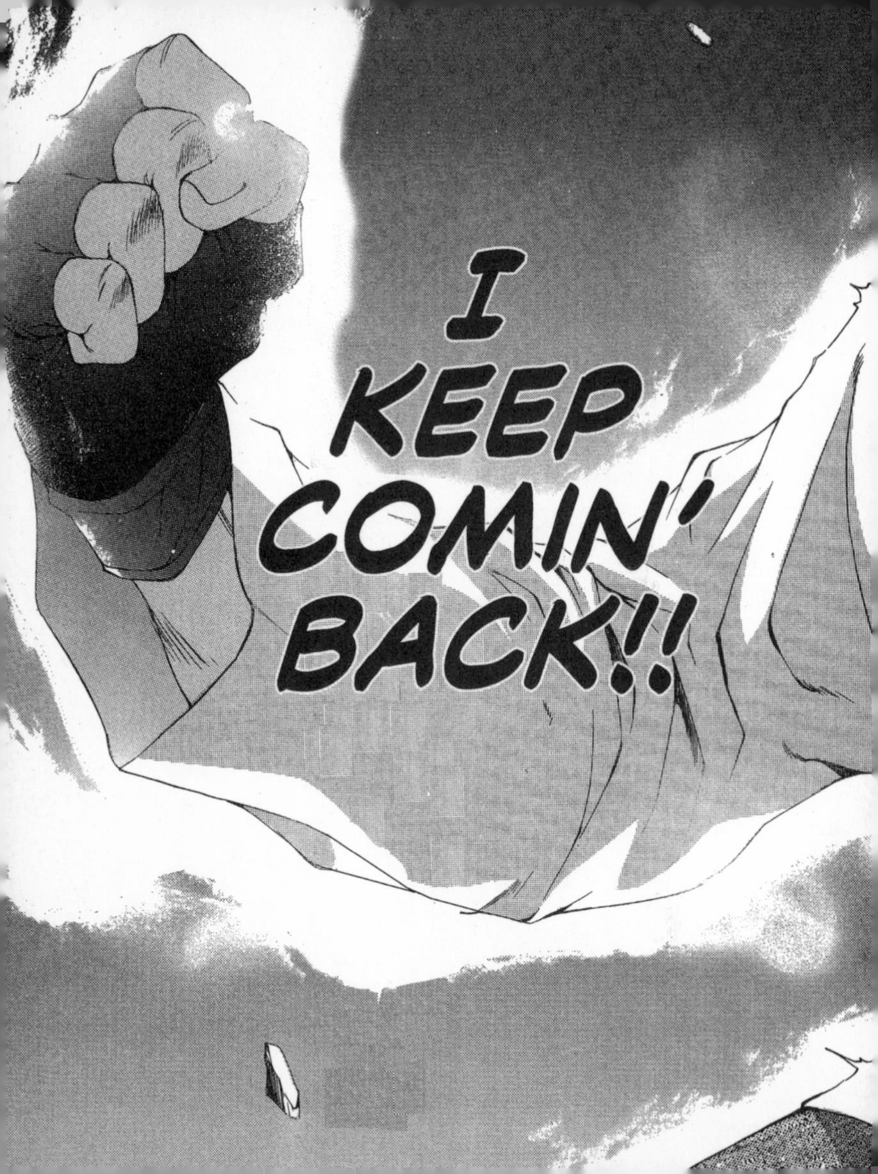
I KEEP COMIN' BACK!!

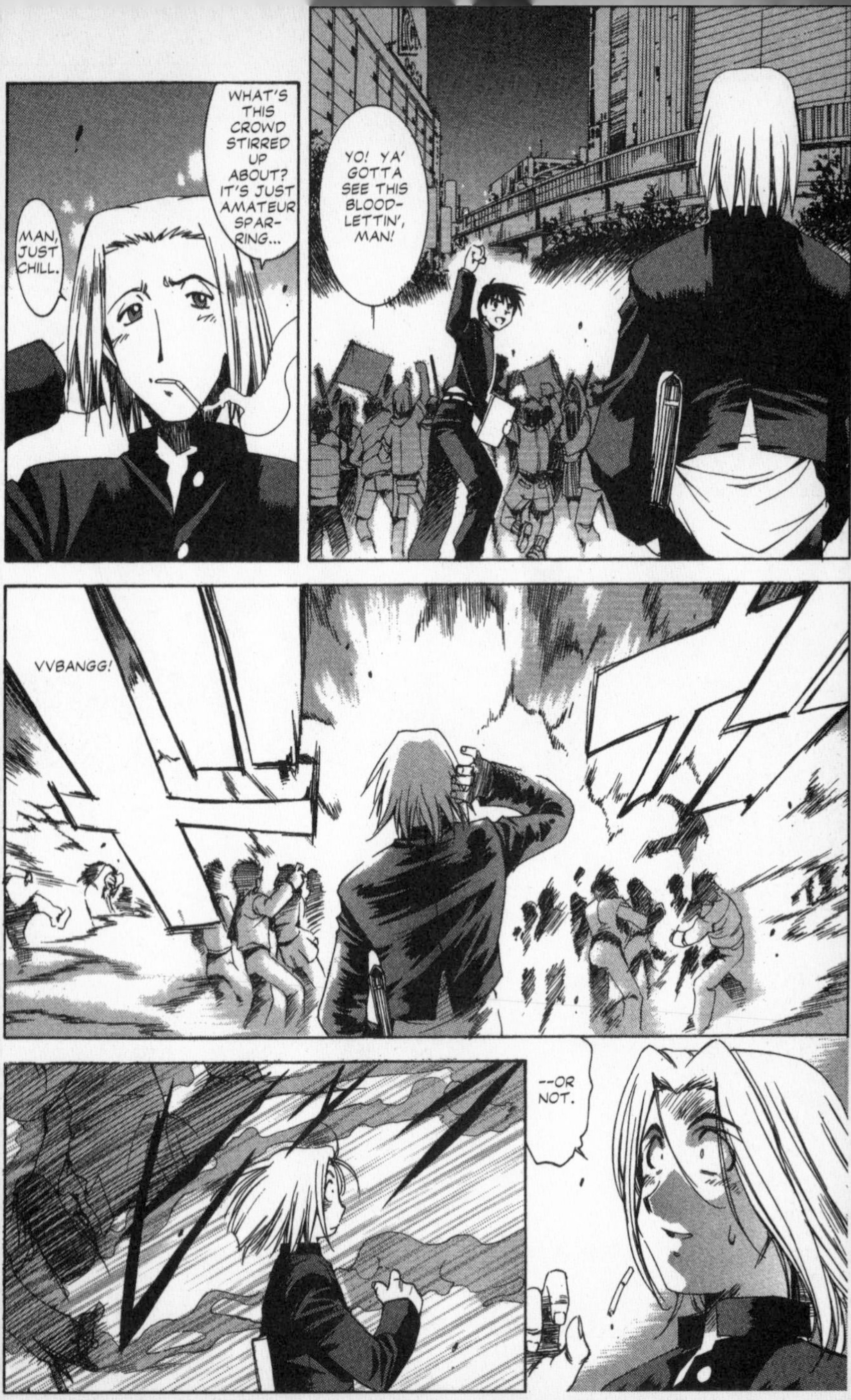
YO! YA' GOTTA SEE THIS BLOOD-LETTIN', MAN!
WHAT'S THIS CROWD STIRRED UP ABOUT? IT'S JUST AMATEUR SPAR-RING...
MAN, JUST CHILL.
VVBANGG!
--OR NOT.

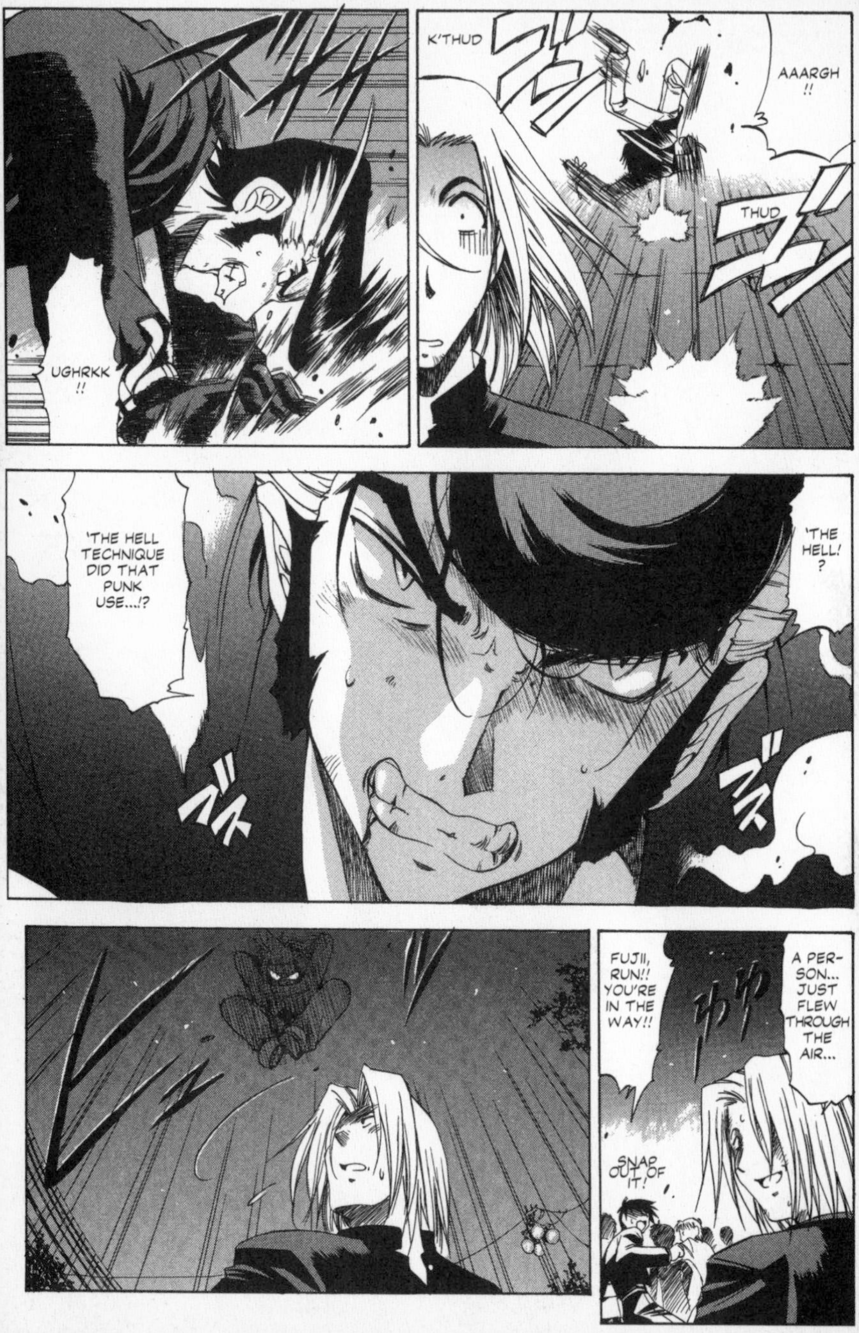

AAARGH !!
K'THUD
THUD
UGHRKK !!
'THE HELL! ?
'THE HELL TECHNIQUE DID THAT PUNK USE...!?
A PER-SON... JUST FLEW THROUGH THE AIR...
FUJII, RUN!! YOU'RE IN THE WAY!!
SNAP OUT OF IT!

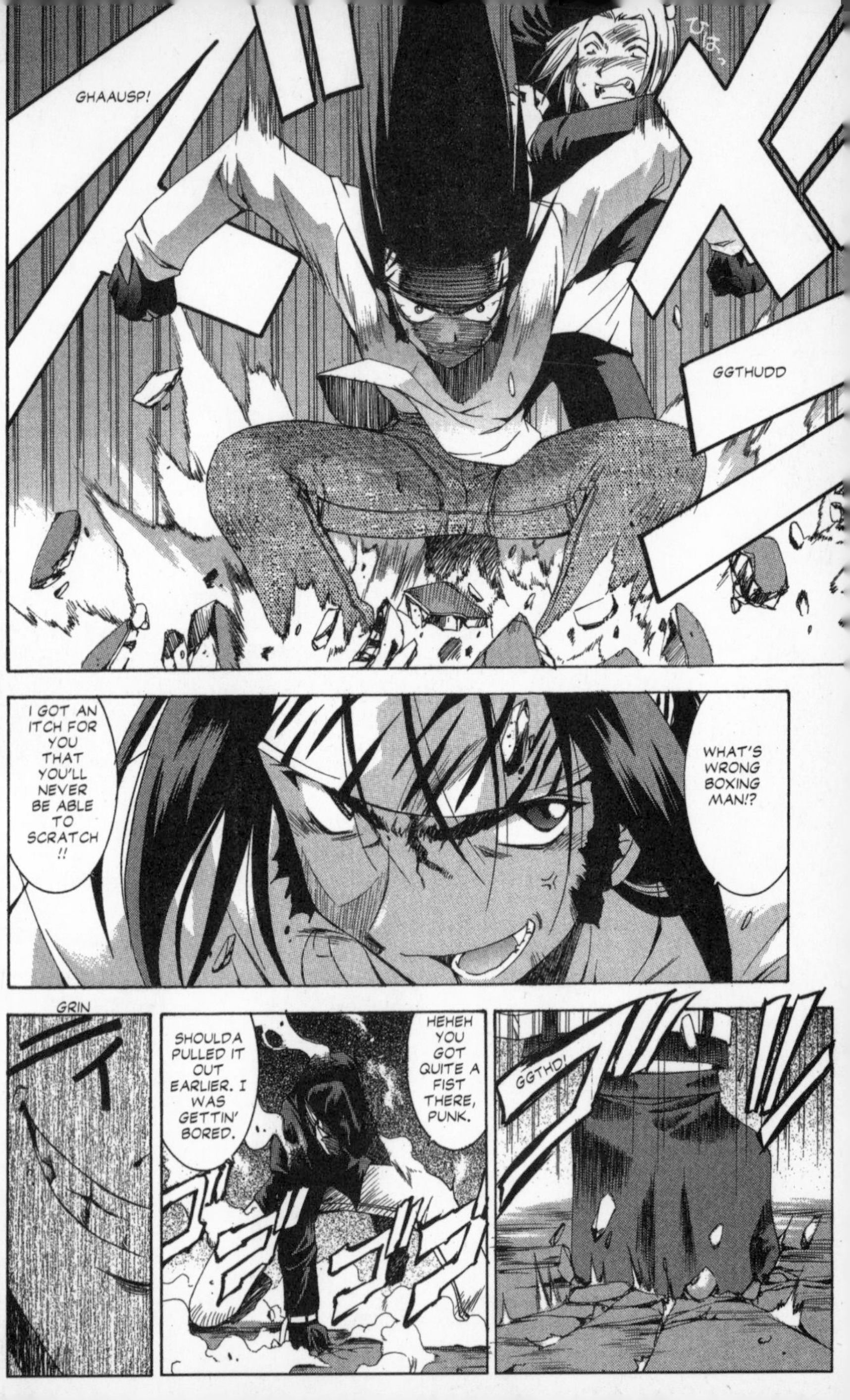
GHAAUSP!
GGTHUDD
WHAT'S WRONG BOXING MAN!?
I GOT AN ITCH FOR YOU THAT YOU'LL NEVER BE ABLE TO SCRATCH !!
GGTHD!
HEHEH YOU GOT QUITE A FIST THERE, PUNK.
SHOULDA PULLED IT OUT EARLIER. I WAS GETTIN' BORED.
GRIN

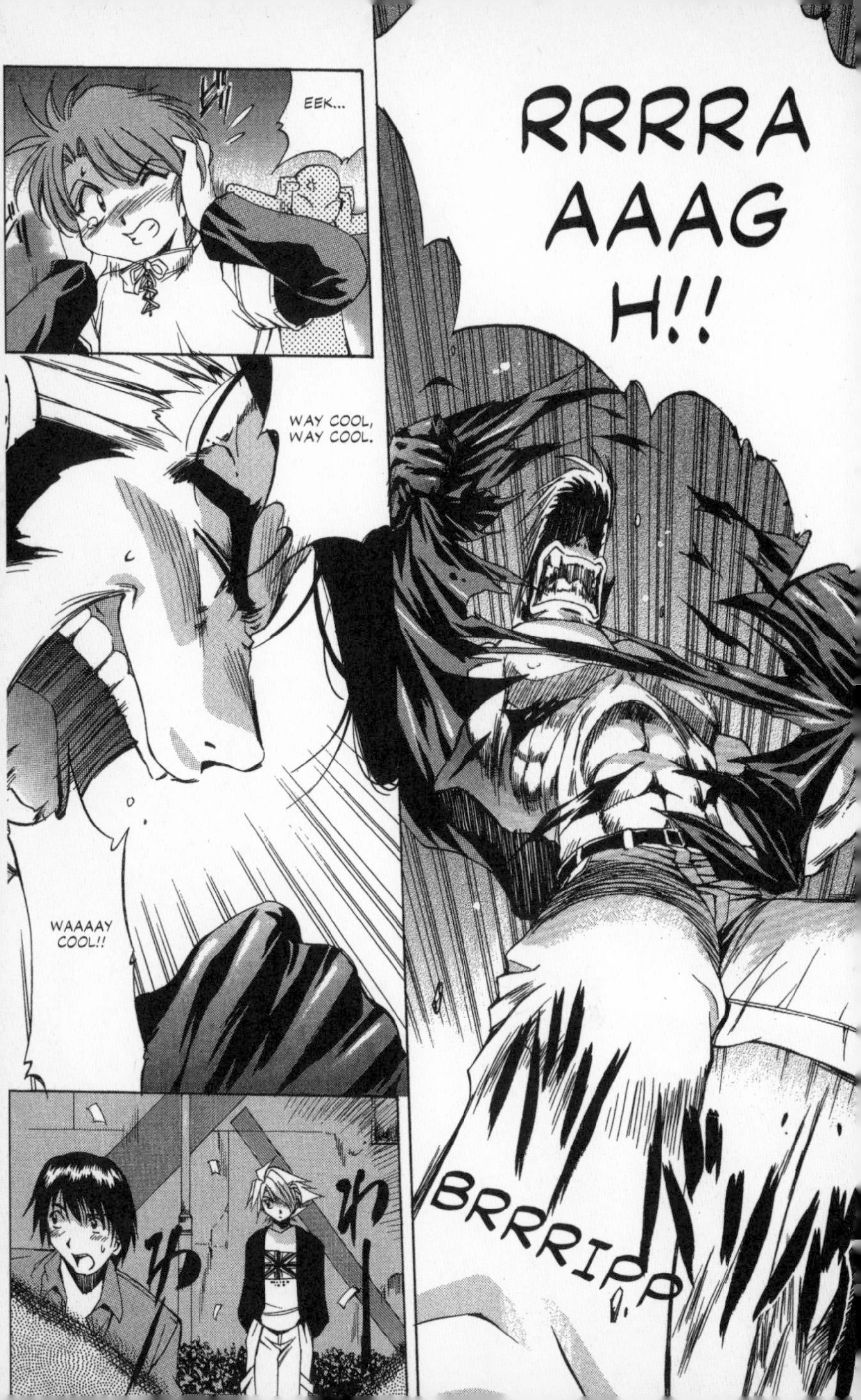
RRRRA AAAG H!!
BRRRRIPP
EEK...
WAY COOL, WAY COOL.
WAAAAY COOL!!

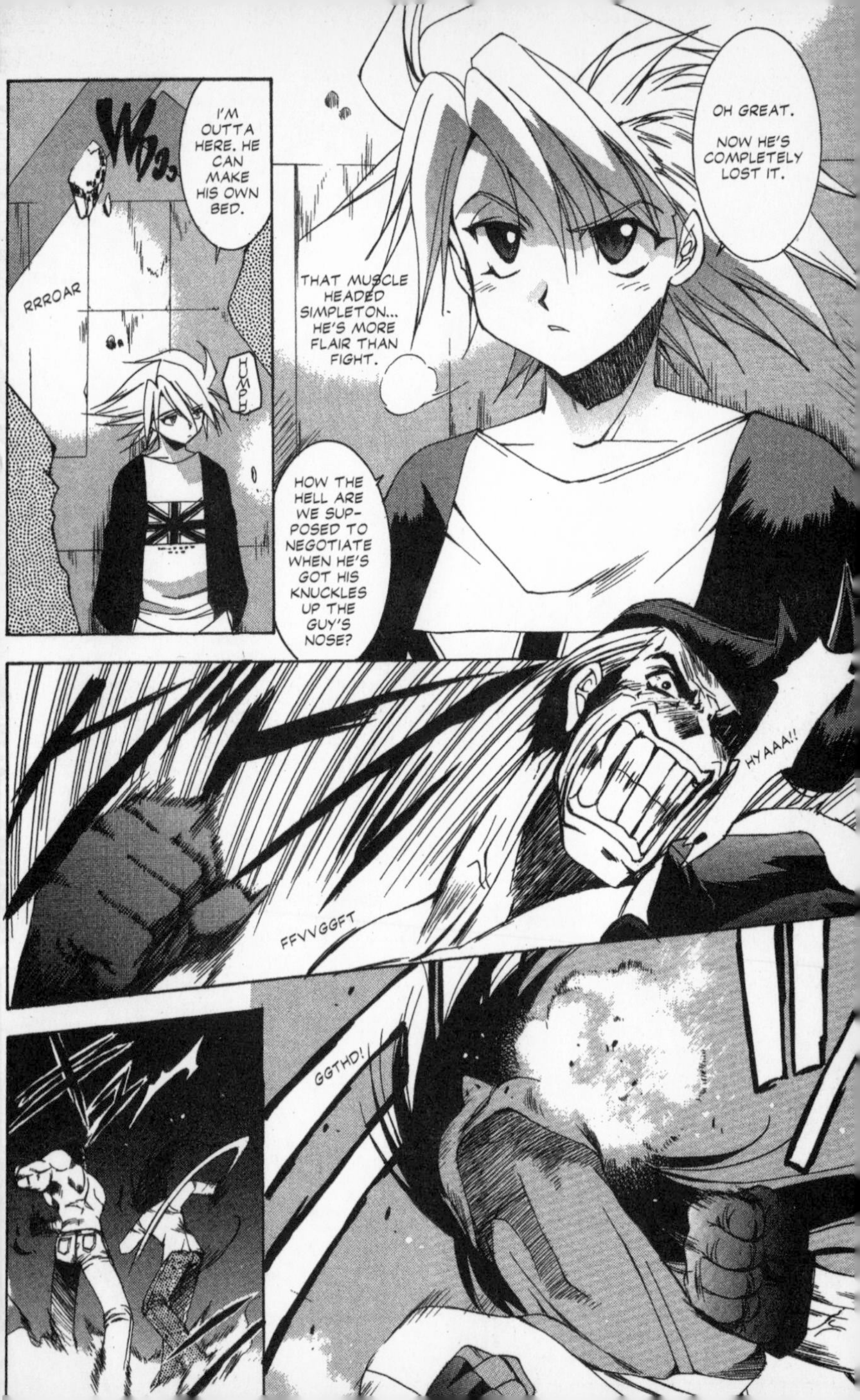
OH GREAT.
NOW HE'S COMPLETELY LOST IT.
THAT MUSCLE HEADED SIMPLETON... HE'S MORE FLAIR THAN FIGHT.
HOW THE HELL ARE WE SUPPOSED TO NEGOTIATE WHEN HE'S GOT HIS KNUCKLES UP THE GUY'S NOSE?
I'M OUTTA HERE. HE CAN MAKE HIS OWN BED.
RRROAR
HUMPH
HYAAA!!
FFVVGGFT
GGTHD!

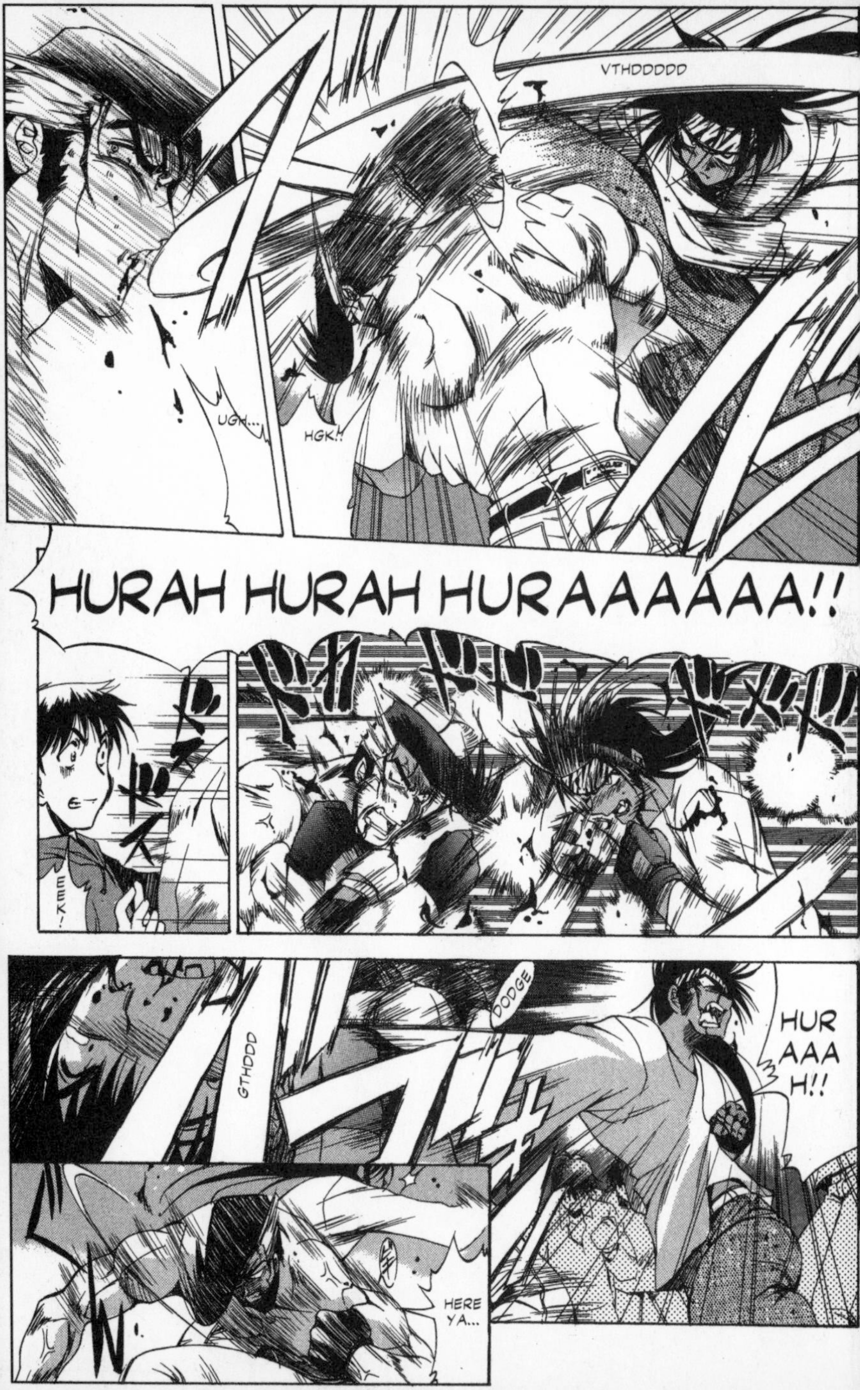
VTHDDDDD
HGK!!
UGH...
HURAH HURAH HURAAAAAAA!!
EEK!
HUR AAA H!!
DODGE
GTHDDD
HERE YA...

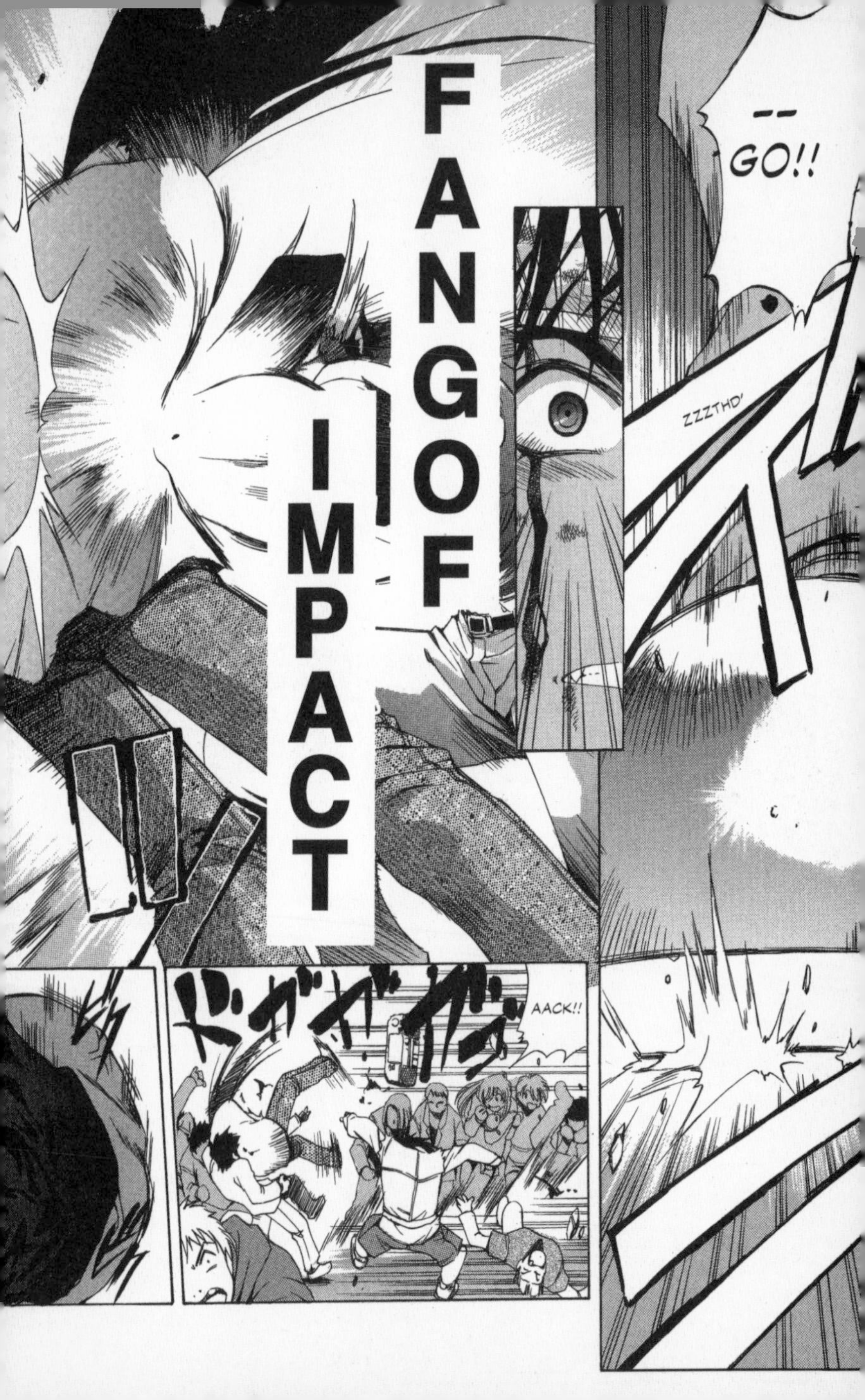
-- GO!!
ZZZTHD'
FANG OF IMPACT
AACK!!

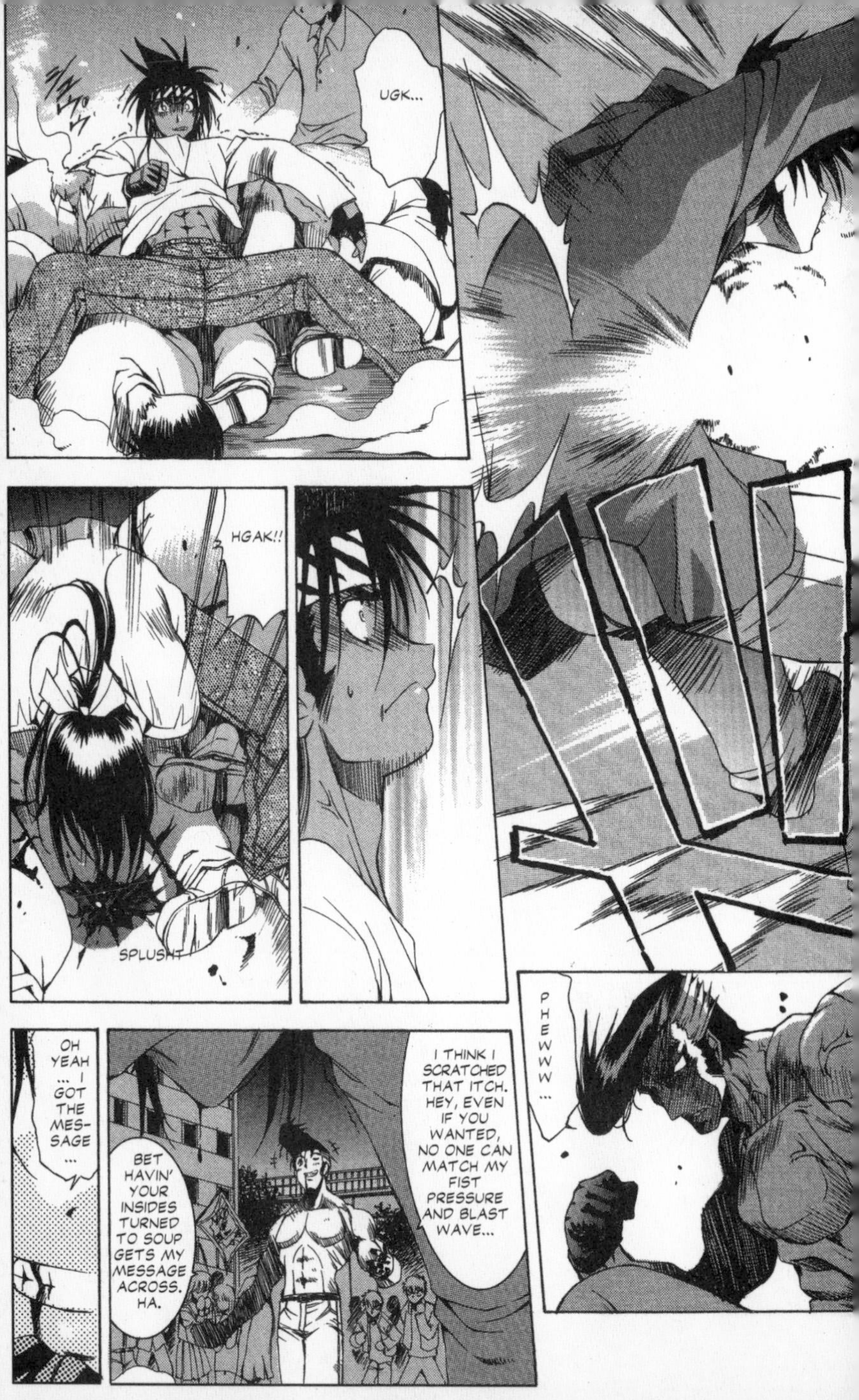
UGK...
HGAK!!
SPLUSH
PHEWWW...
I THINK I SCRATCHED THAT ITCH. HEY, EVEN IF YOU WANTED, NO ONE CAN MATCH MY FIST PRESSURE AND BLAST WAVE...
BET HAVIN' YOUR INSIDES TURNED TO SOUP GETS MY MESSAGE ACROSS. HA.
OH YEAH... I GOT THE MES-SAGE...

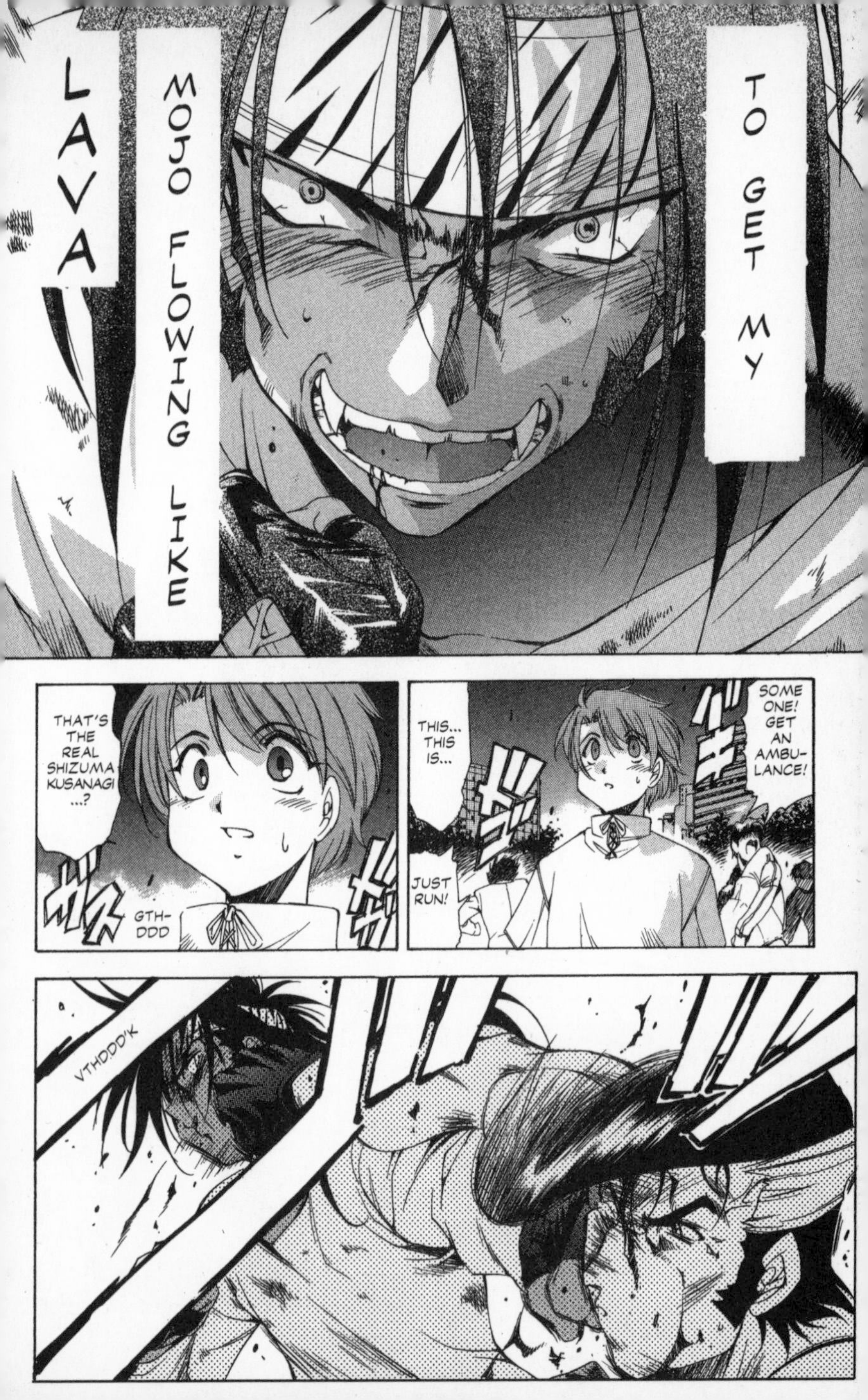
TO GET MY
MOJO FLOWING LIKE
LAVA
SOME ONE! GET AN AMBULANCE!
THIS... THIS IS...
JUST RUN!
THAT'S THE REAL SHIZUMA KUSANAGI ...?
GTH-DDD
VTHDDD'K

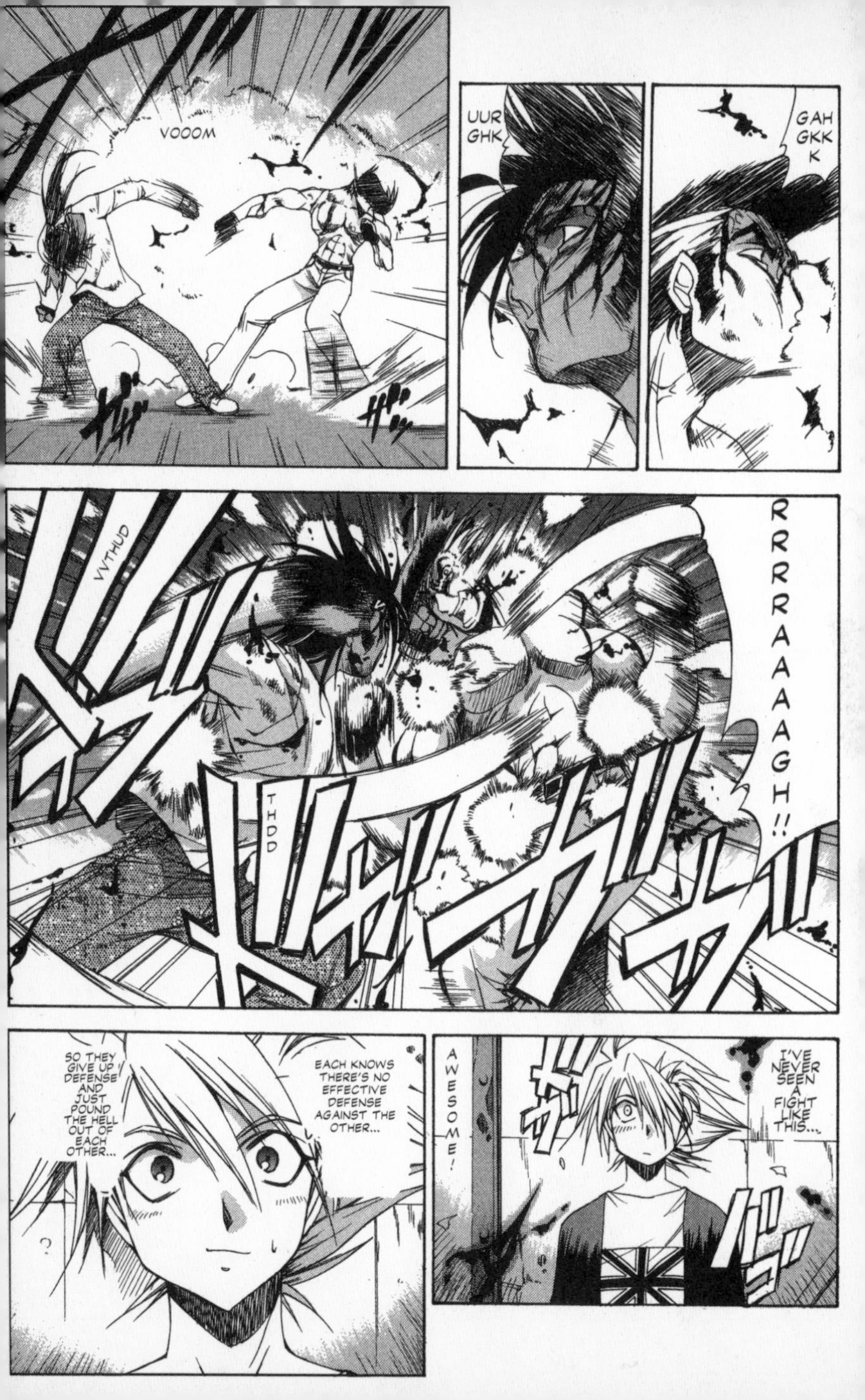
GAH GKKK K
UUR GHK
VOOOM
RRRRAAAAAGH!!
VVTHUD
THDD
I'VE NEVER SEEN A FIGHT LIKE THIS...
AWESOME!
EACH KNOWS THERE'S NO EFFECTIVE DEFENSE AGAINST THE OTHER...
SO THEY GIVE UP DEFENSE AND JUST POUND THE HELL OUT OF EACH OTHER...

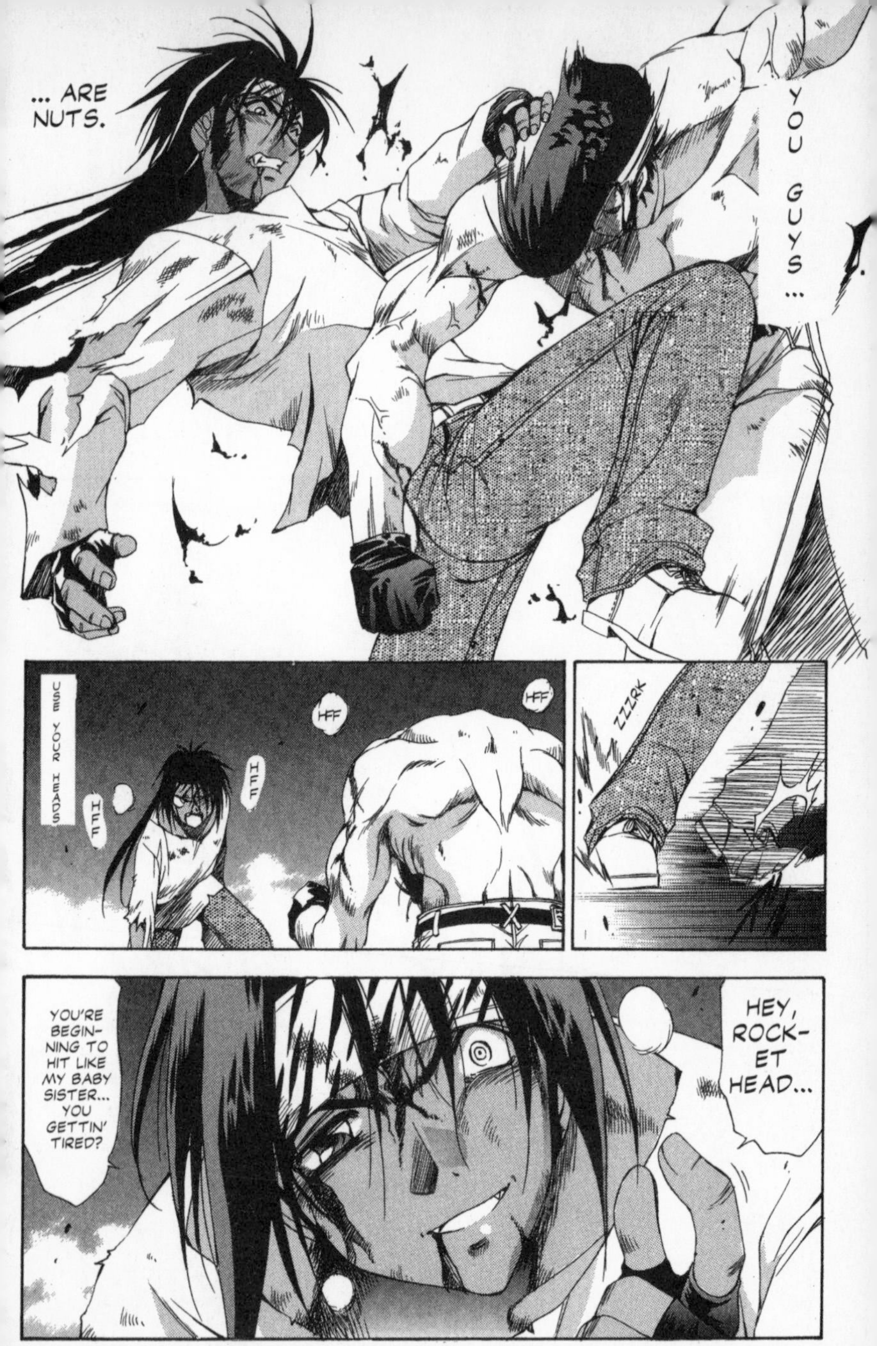
YOU GUYS ...
... ARE NUTS.
ZZZRK
HFF
HFF
HFF
HFF
USE YOUR HEADS
HEY, ROCK-ET HEAD...
YOU'RE BEGIN-NING TO HIT LIKE MY BABY SISTER... YOU GETTIN' TIRED?

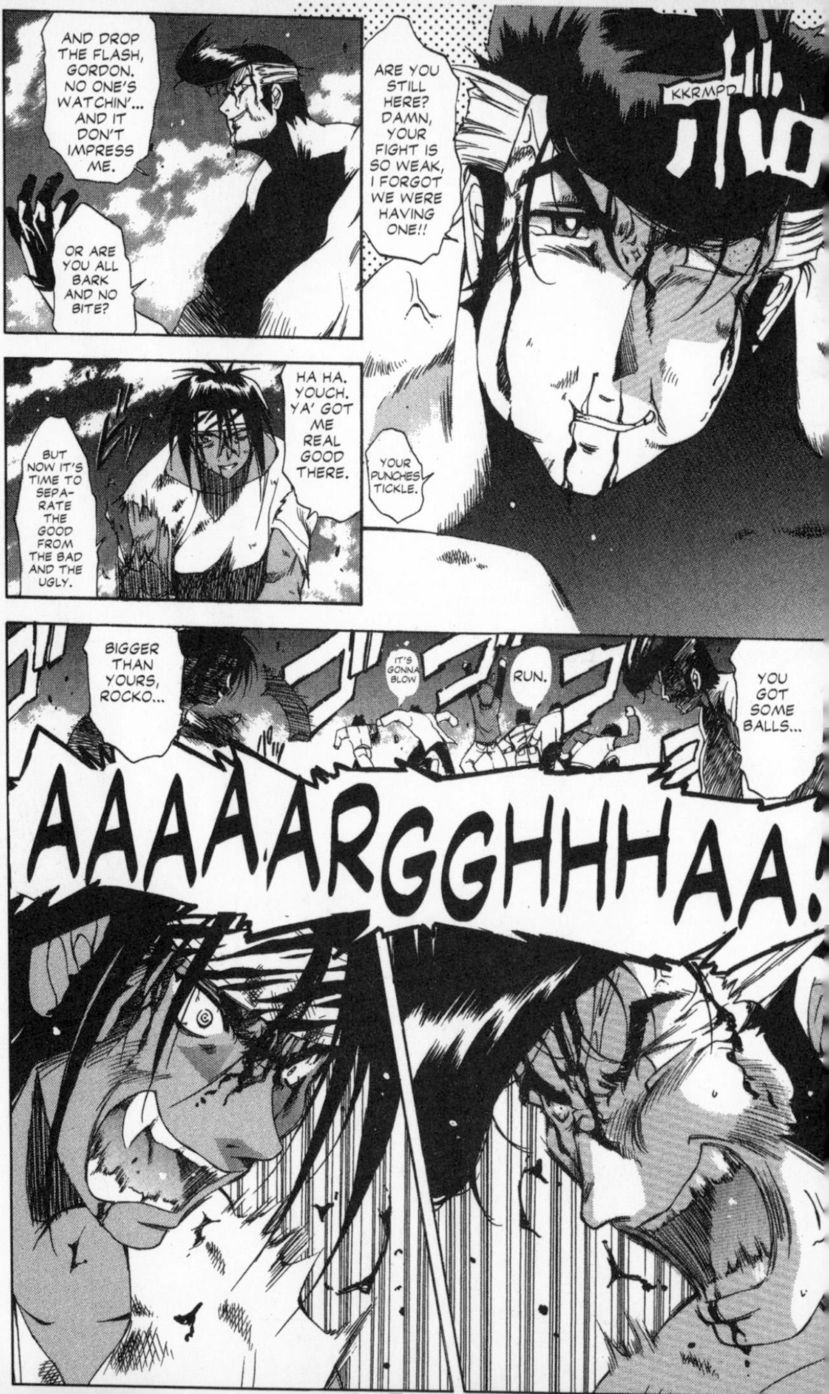
KKRMPD
ARE YOU STILL HERE? DAMN, YOUR FIGHT IS SO WEAK, I FORGOT WE WERE HAVING ONE!!
YOUR PUNCHES TICKLE.
AND DROP THE FLASH, GORDON. NO ONE'S WATCHIN'... AND IT DON'T IMPRESS ME.
OR ARE YOU ALL BARK AND NO BITE?
HA HA. YOUCH. YA' GOT ME REAL GOOD THERE.
BUT NOW IT'S TIME TO SEPA-RATE THE GOOD FROM THE BAD AND THE UGLY.
YOU GOT SOME BALLS...
RUN.
IT'S GONNA BLOW
BIGGER THAN YOURS, ROCKO...
AAAAARGGHHAA!

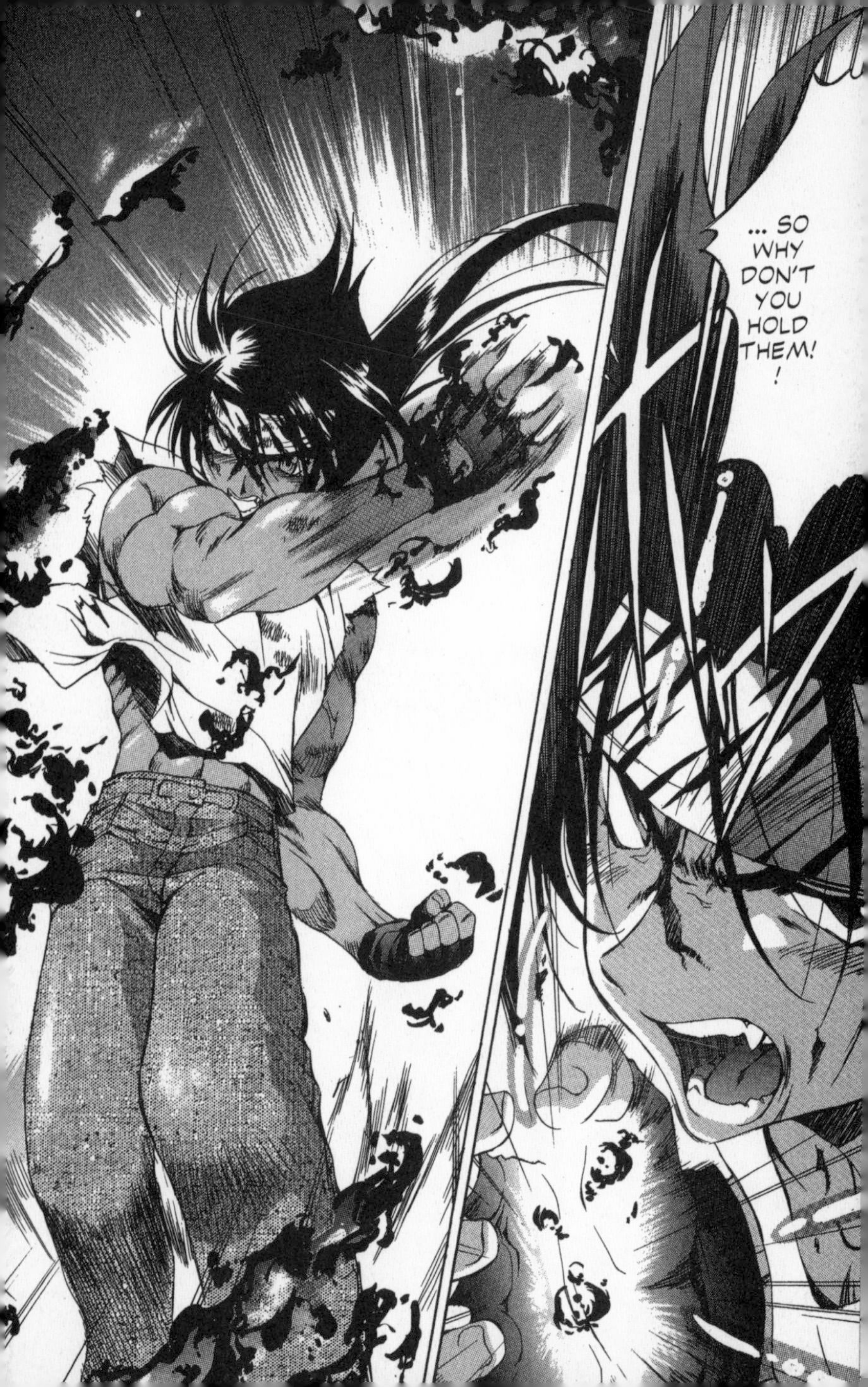
... SO WHY DON'T YOU HOLD THEM!!

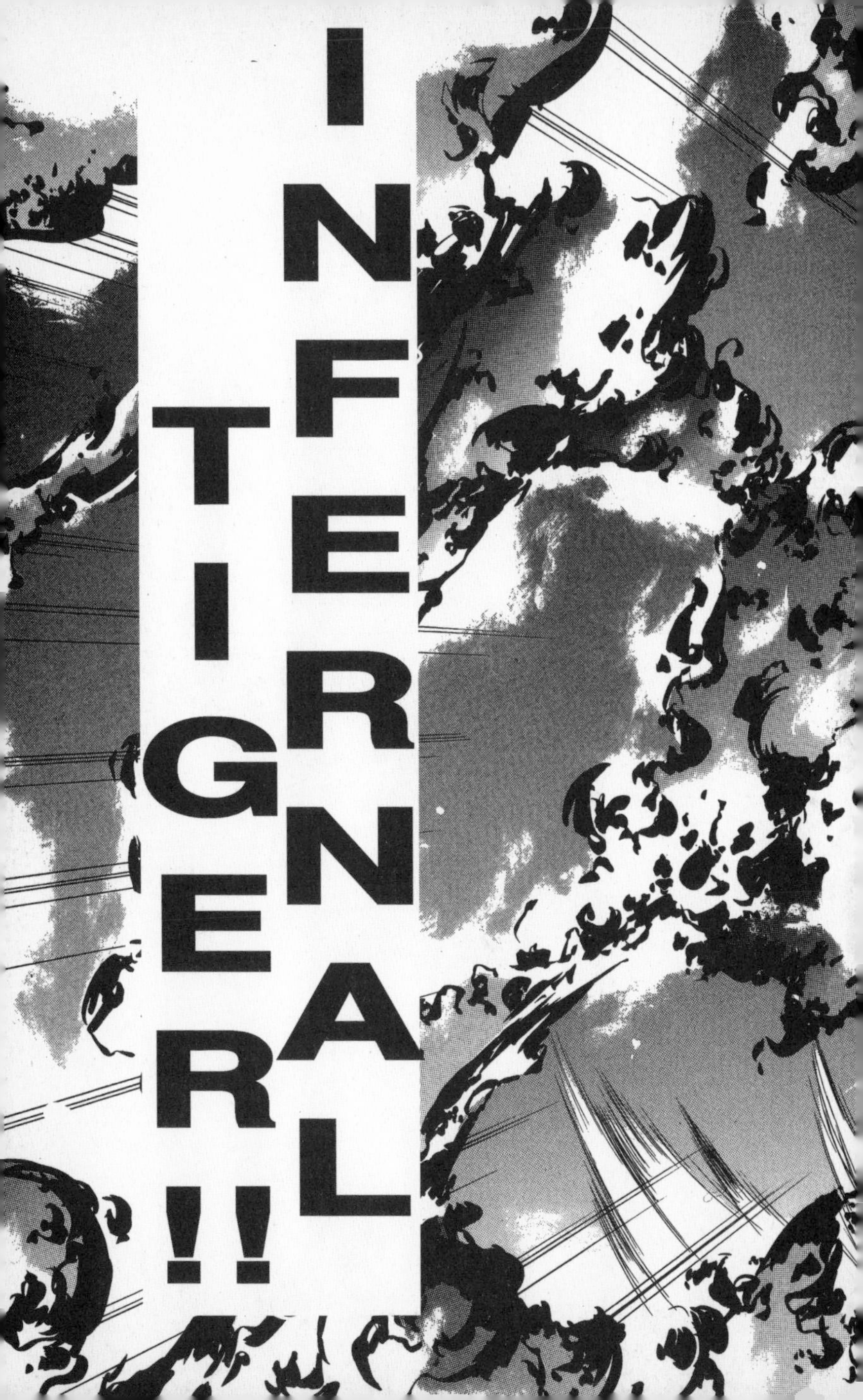
INFERNAL
TIGER!!

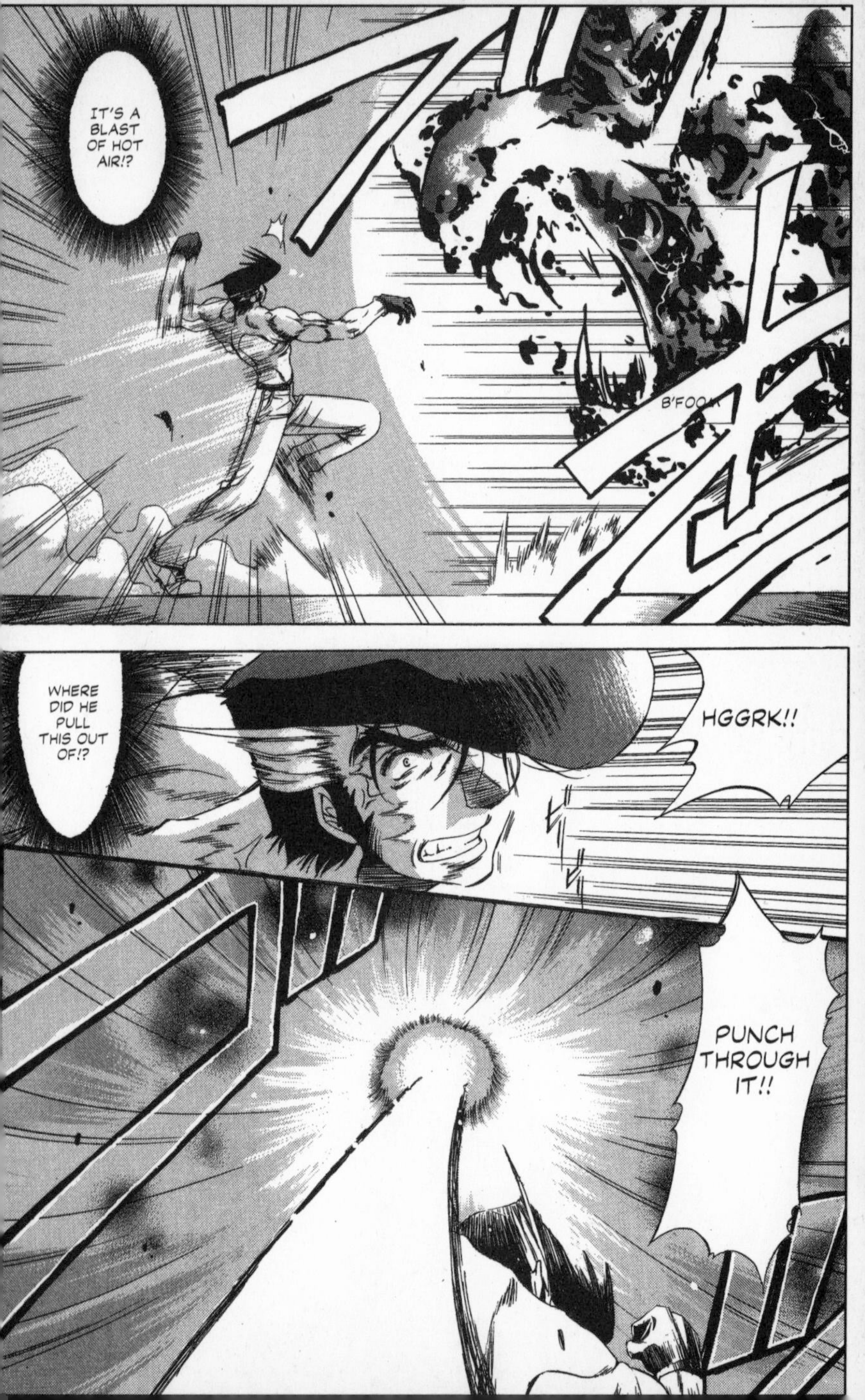
IT'S A BLAST OF HOT AIR!?
B'FOOK
HGGRK!!
WHERE DID HE PULL THIS OUT OF!?
PUNCH THROUGH IT!!

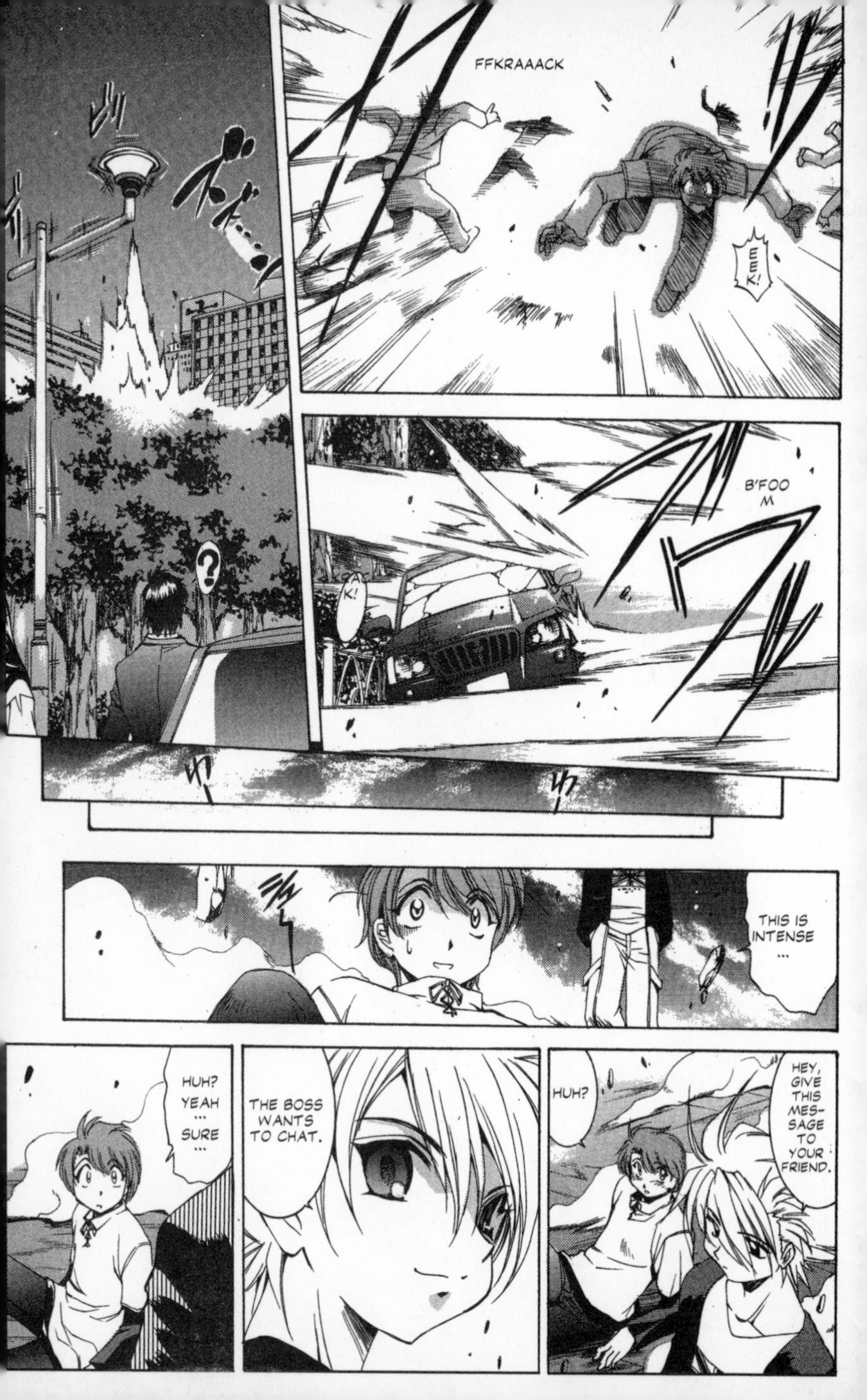
FFKRAAACK
EEK!
B'FOOM
AK!
THIS IS INTENSE ...
HEY, GIVE THIS MESSAGE TO YOUR FRIEND.
HUH?
THE BOSS WANTS TO CHAT.
HUH? YEAH ... SURE ...

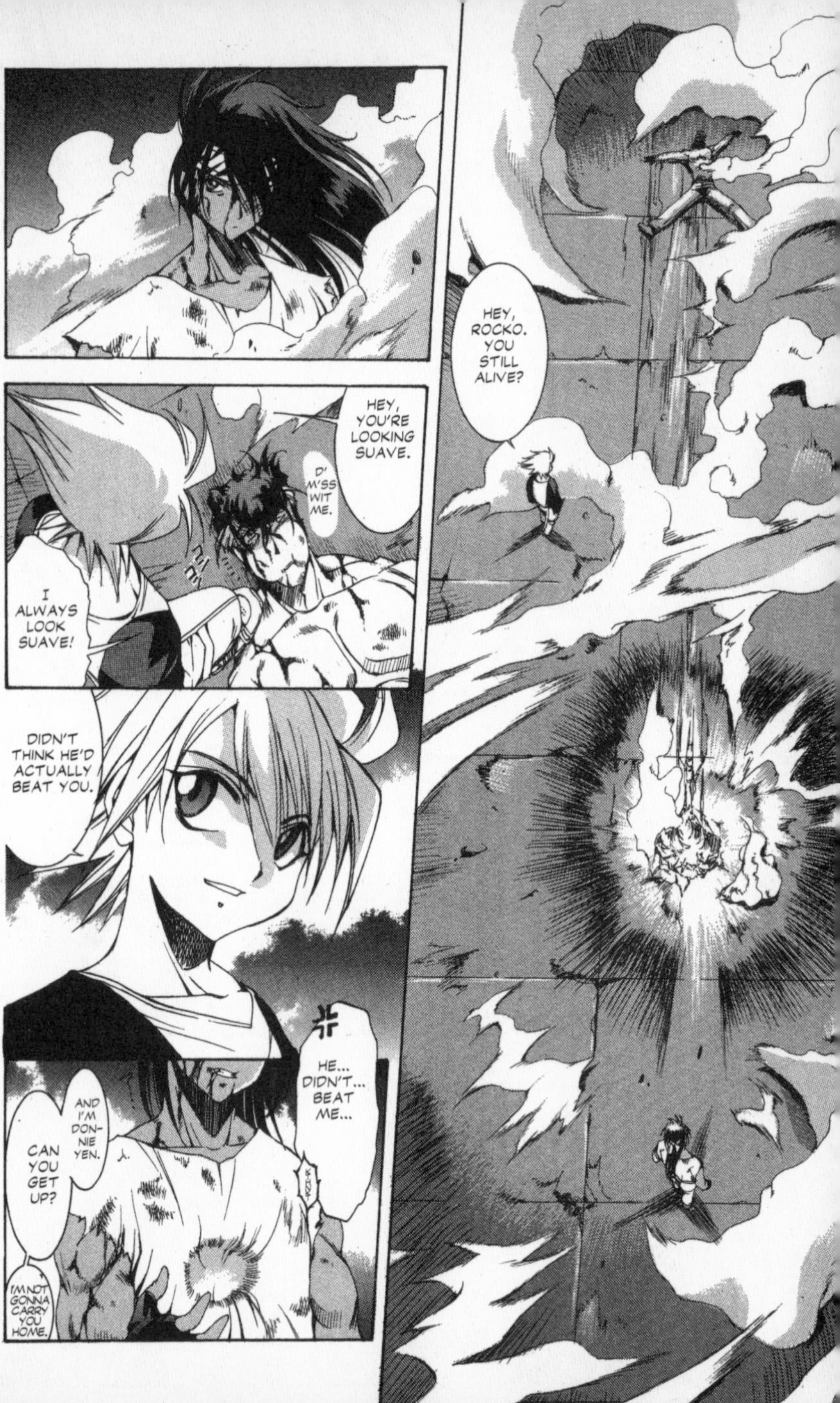
HEY, ROCKO. YOU STILL ALIVE?
HEY, YOU'RE LOOKING SUAVE.
D' M'SS WIT ME.
I ALWAYS LOOK SUAVE!
DIDN'T THINK HE'D ACTUALLY BEAT YOU.
HE... DIDN'T... BEAT ME...
AND I'M DON-NIE YEN.
CAN YOU GET UP?
I'M NOT GONNA CARRY YOU HOME.

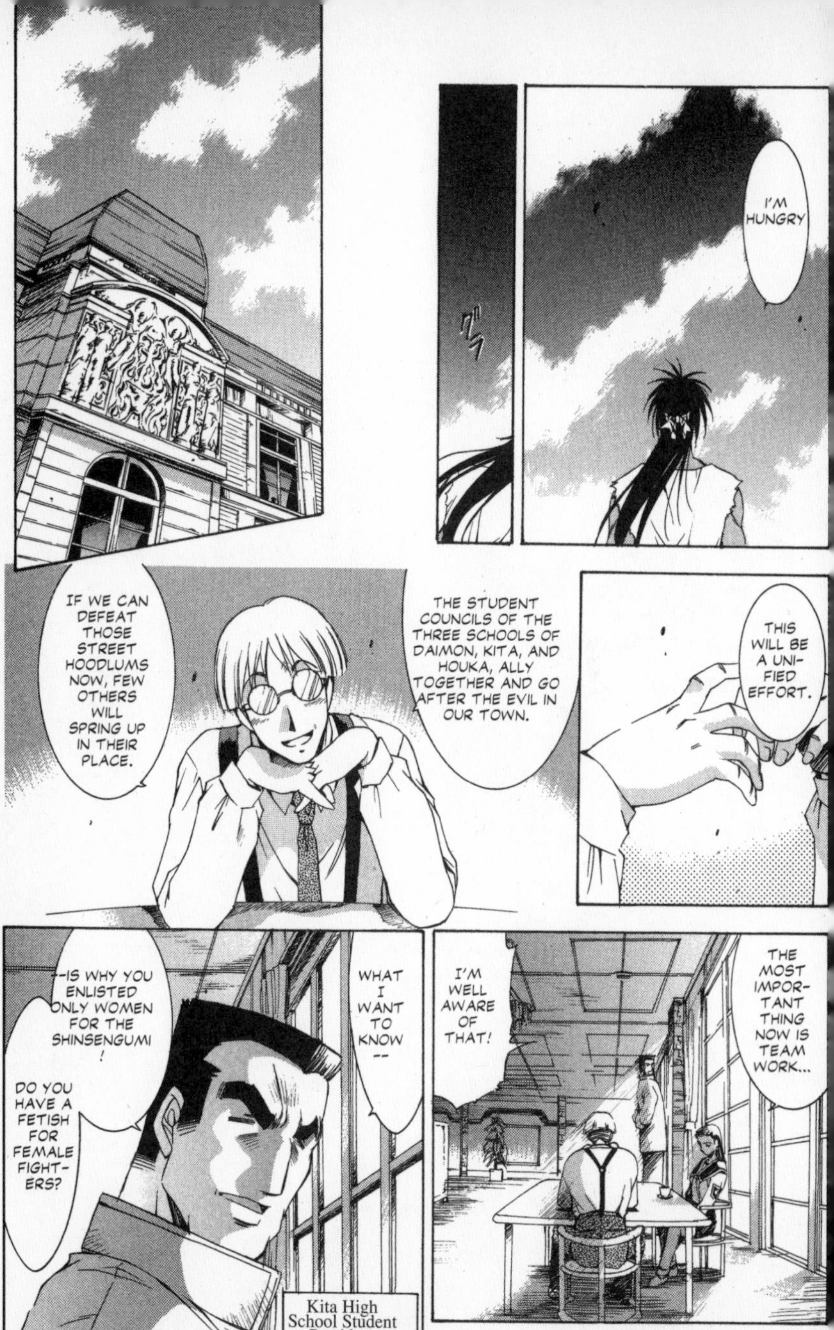
I'M HUNGRY
THIS WILL BE A UNIFIED EFFORT.
THE STUDENT COUNCILS OF THE THREE SCHOOLS OF DAIMON, KITA, AND HOUKA, ALLY TOGETHER AND GO AFTER THE EVIL IN OUR TOWN.
IF WE CAN DEFEAT THOSE STREET HOODLUMS NOW, FEW OTHERS WILL SPRING UP IN THEIR PLACE.
THE MOST IMPORTANT THING NOW IS TEAM WORK...
I'M WELL AWARE OF THAT!
WHAT I WANT TO KNOW--
--IS WHY YOU ENLISTED ONLY WOMEN FOR THE SHINSENGUMI!
DO YOU HAVE A FETISH FOR FEMALE FIGHTERS?
Kita High School Student President Tomoya Nagase

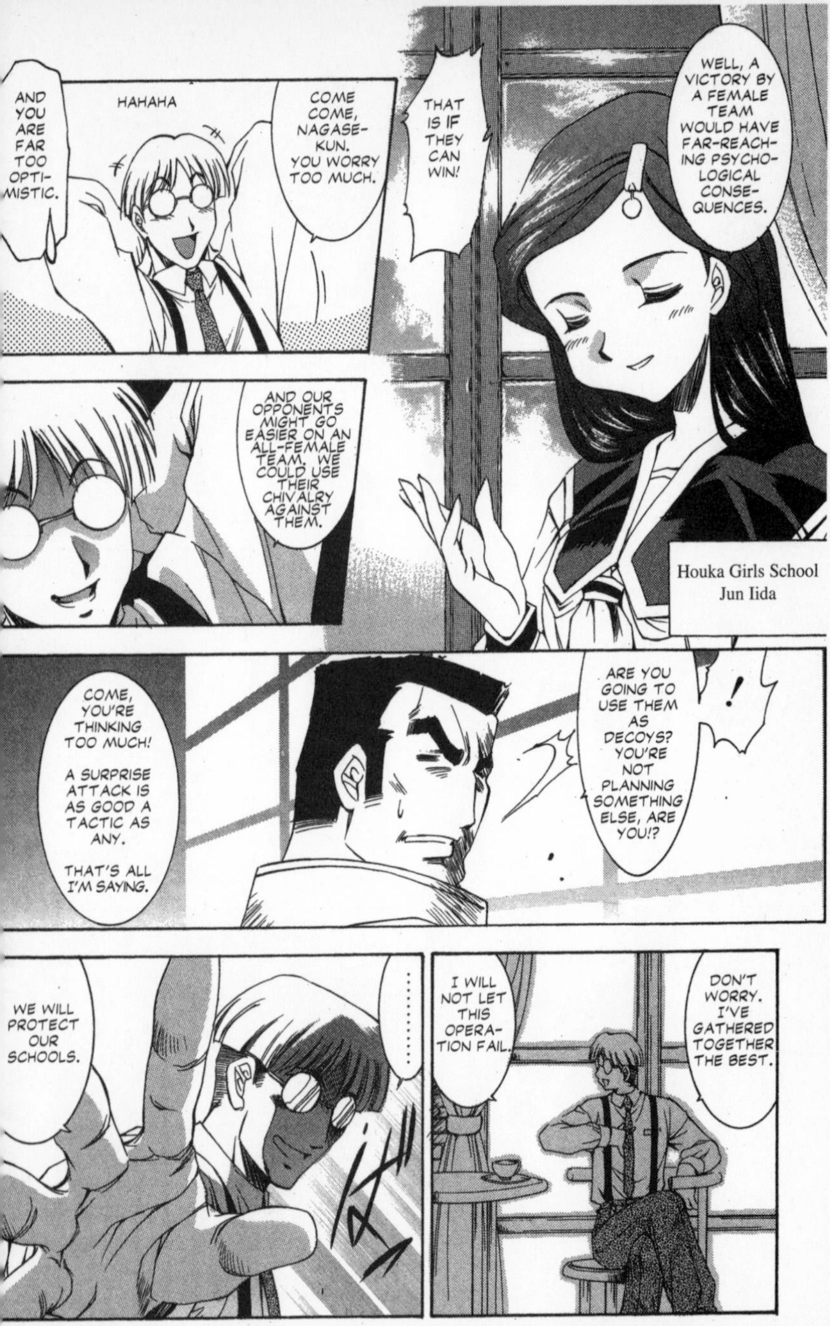
WELL, A VICTORY BY A FEMALE TEAM WOULD HAVE FAR-REACHING PSYCHOLOGICAL CONSEQUENCES.
THAT IS IF THEY CAN WIN!
Houka Girls School
Jun Iida
COME COME, NAGASE-KUN. YOU WORRY TOO MUCH.
HAHAHA
AND YOU ARE FAR TOO OPTIMISTIC.
AND OUR OPPONENTS MIGHT GO EASIER ON AN ALL-FEMALE TEAM. WE COULD USE THEIR CHIVALRY AGAINST THEM.
!
ARE YOU GOING TO USE THEM AS DECOYS? YOU'RE NOT PLANNING SOMETHING ELSE, ARE YOU!?
COME, YOU'RE THINKING TOO MUCH!
A SURPRISE ATTACK IS AS GOOD A TACTIC AS ANY.
THAT'S ALL I'M SAYING.
DON'T WORRY. I'VE GATHERED TOGETHER THE BEST.
I WILL NOT LET THIS OPERATION FAIL.
......
WE WILL PROTECT OUR SCHOOLS.

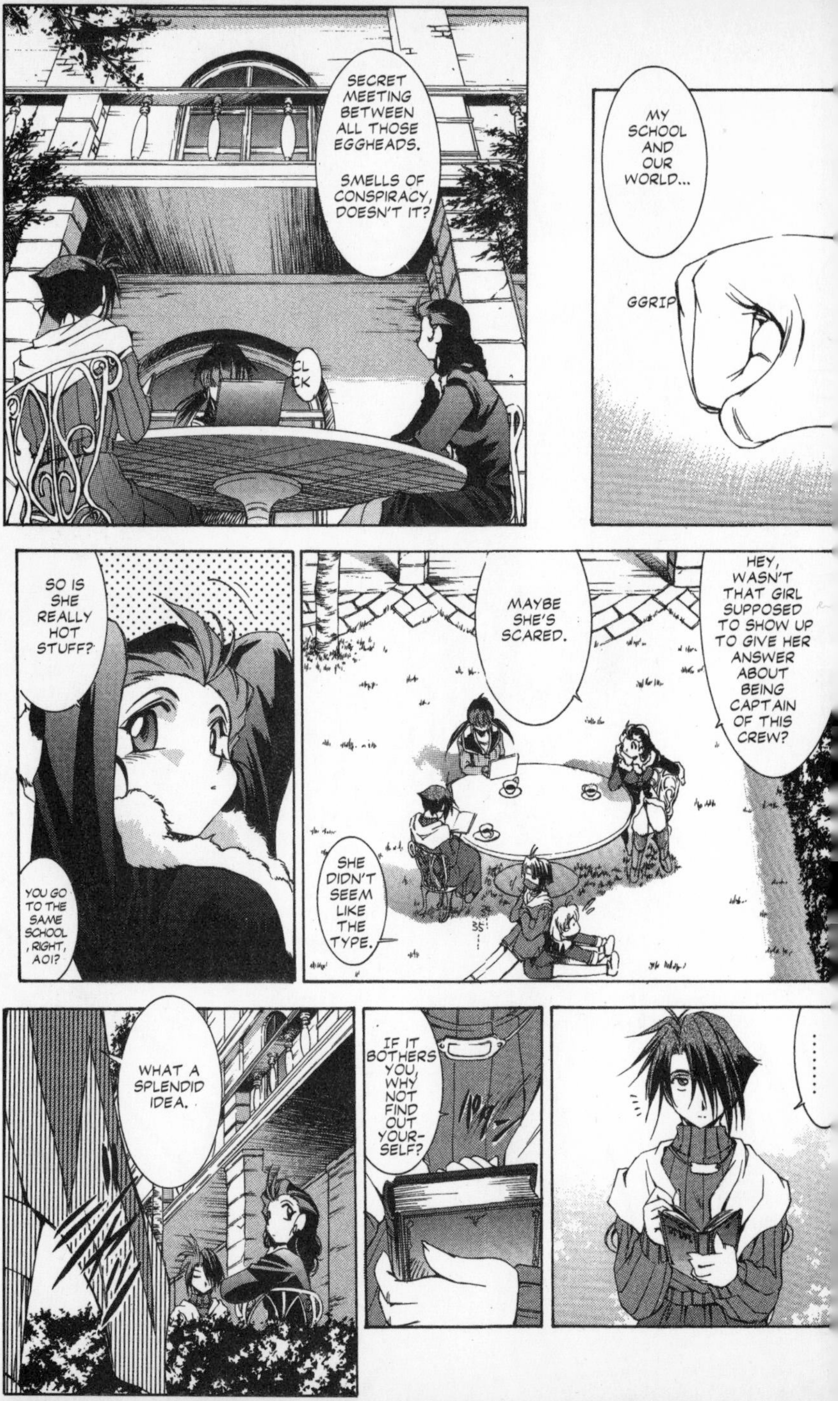
MY SCHOOL AND OUR WORLD...
GGRIP
SECRET MEETING BETWEEN ALL THOSE EGGHEADS.
SMELLS OF CONSPIRACY, DOESN'T IT?
CLICK
HEY, WASN'T THAT GIRL SUPPOSED TO SHOW UP TO GIVE HER ANSWER ABOUT BEING CAPTAIN OF THIS CREW?
MAYBE SHE'S SCARED.
SHE DIDN'T SEEM LIKE THE TYPE.
SO IS SHE REALLY HOT STUFF?
YOU GO TO THE SAME SCHOOL, RIGHT, AOI?
....
IF IT BOTHERS YOU, WHY NOT FIND OUT YOUR-SELF?
WHAT A SPLENDID IDEA.

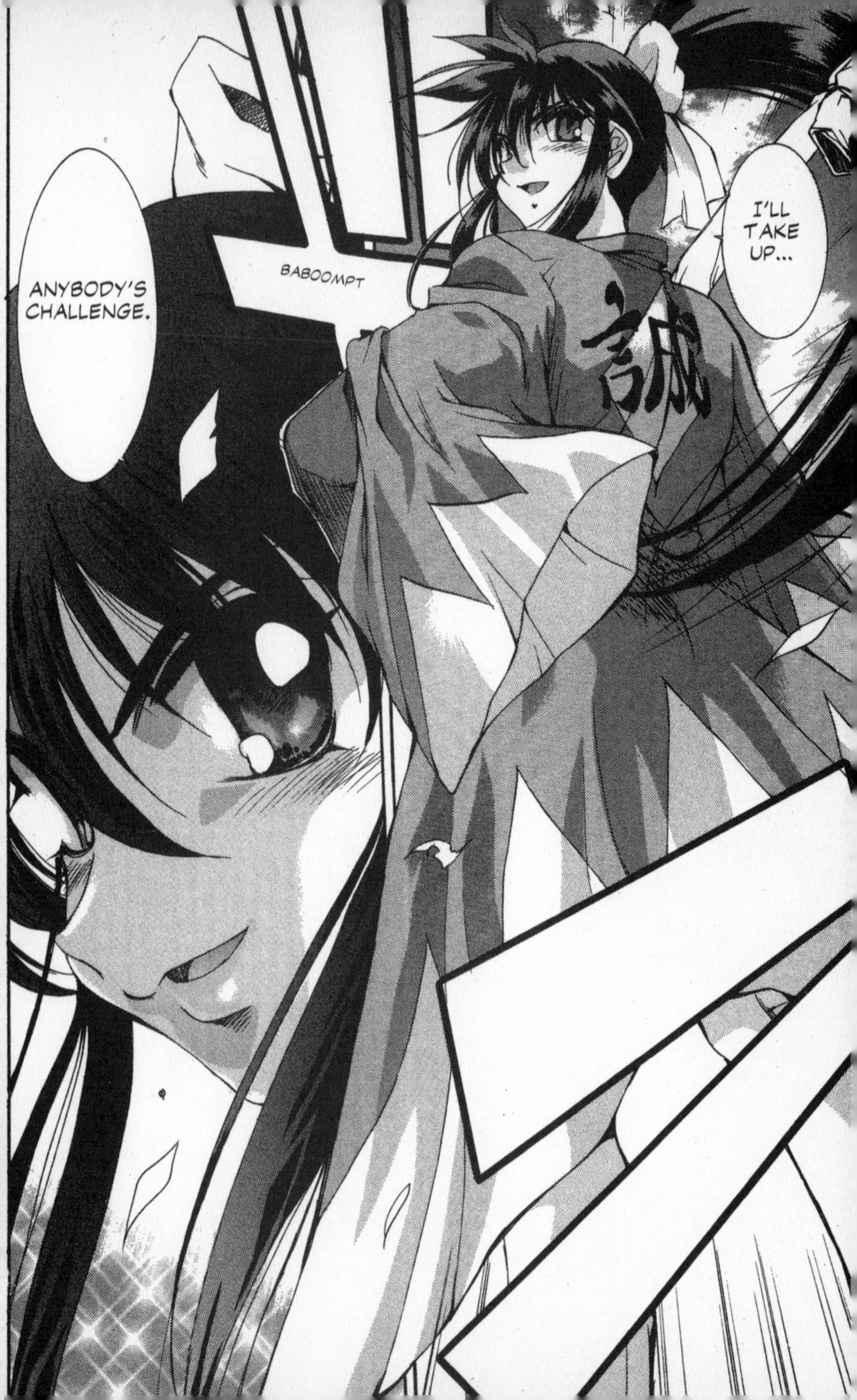
I'LL TAKE UP...
BABOOMPT
ANYBODY'S CHALLENGE.

Episode 24
Shinsengumi, Forward!!

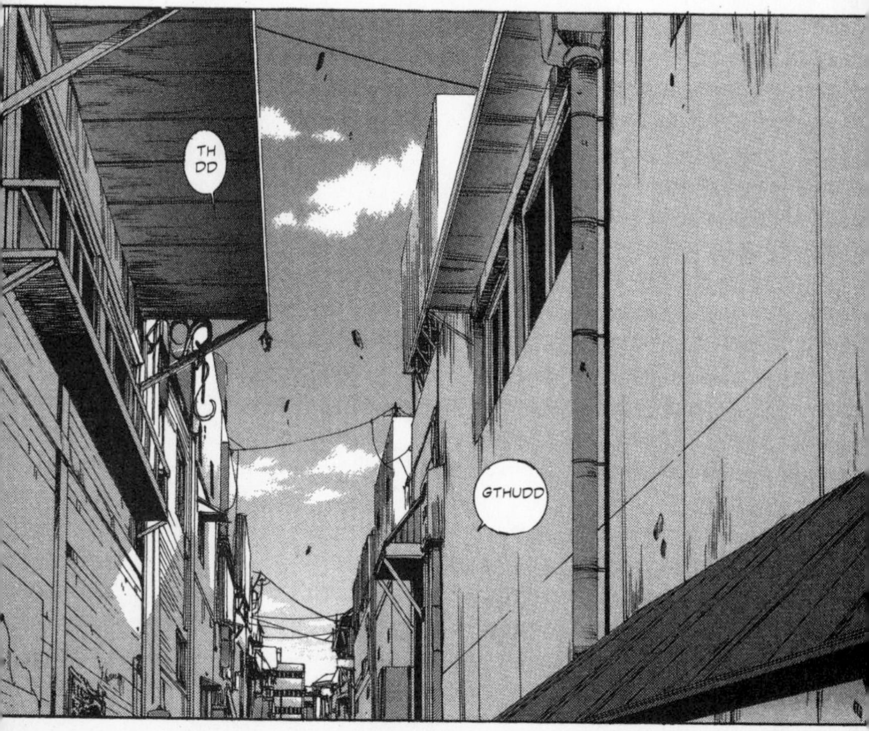
GTHUDD
TH DD

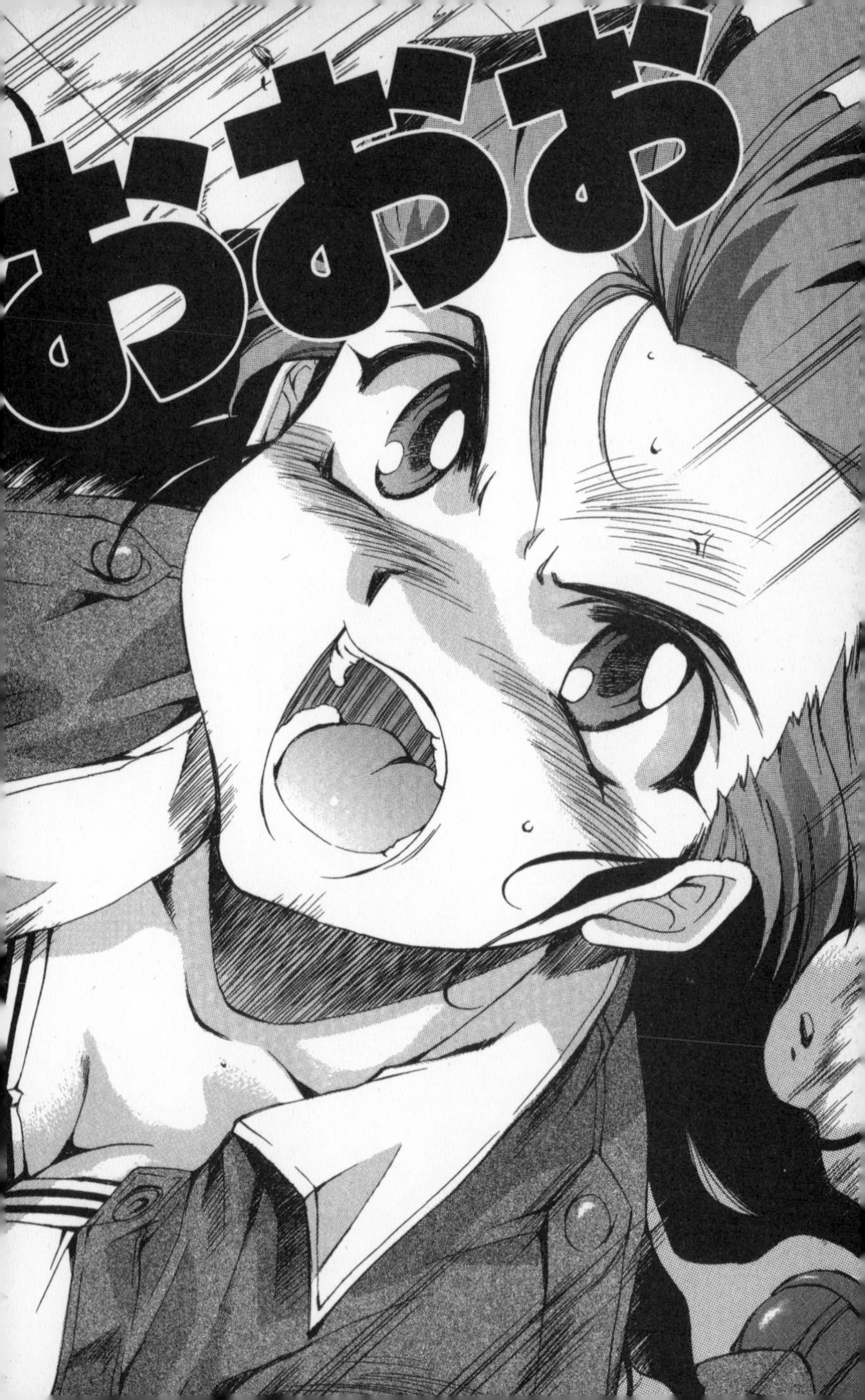
お゛お゛お゛

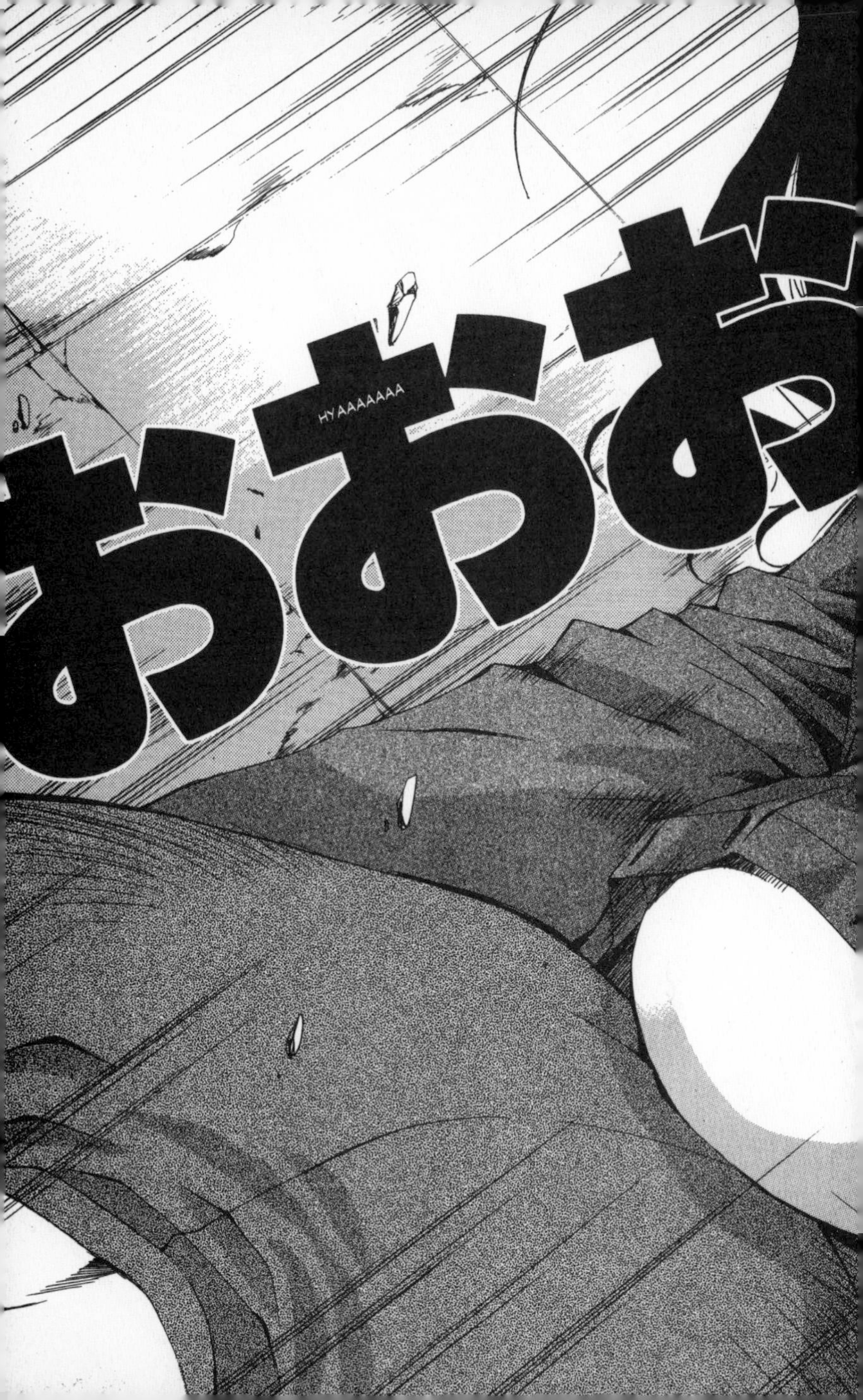
おおお
HYAAAAAAA

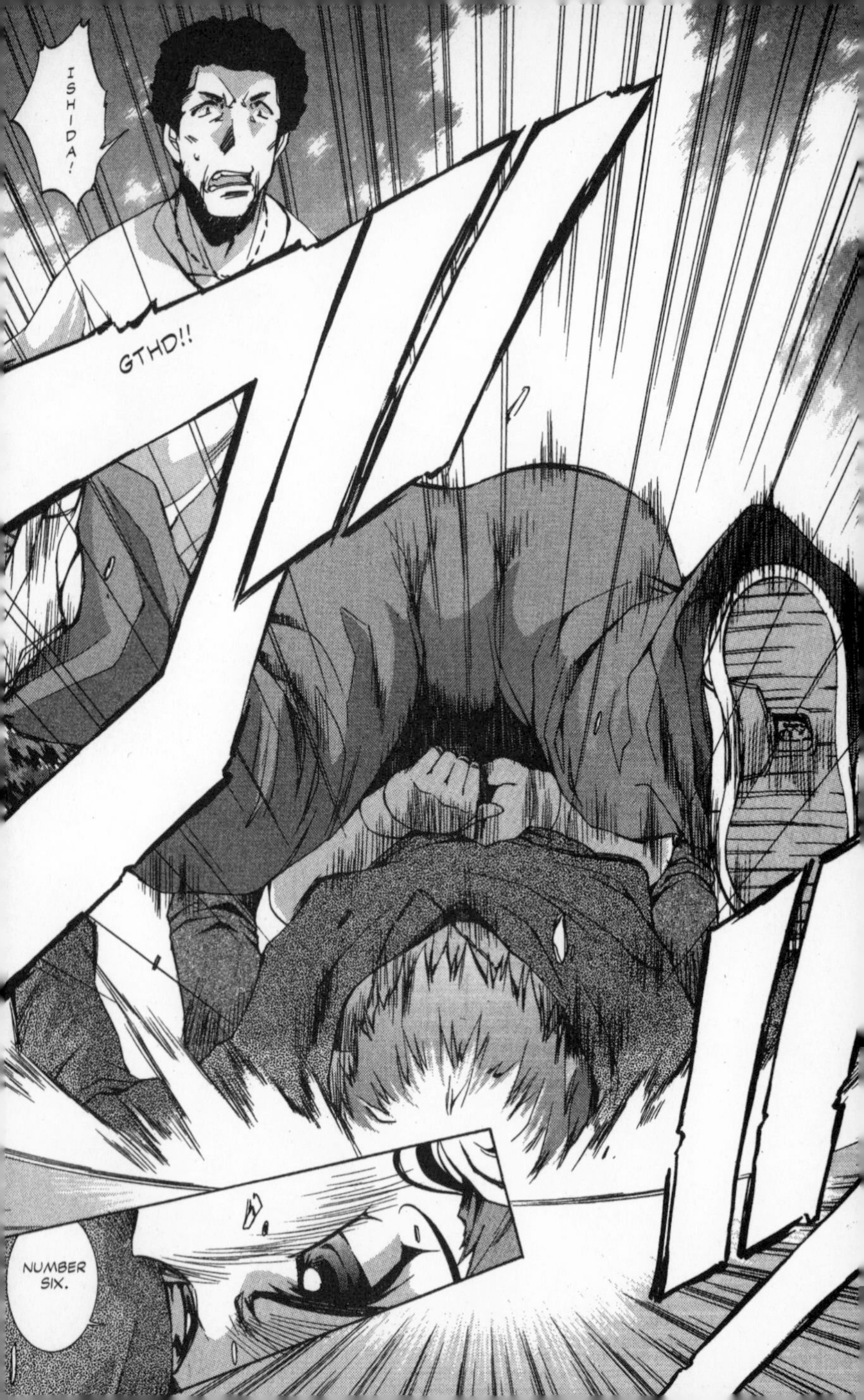
ISHIDA!
GTHD!!
NUMBER SIX.

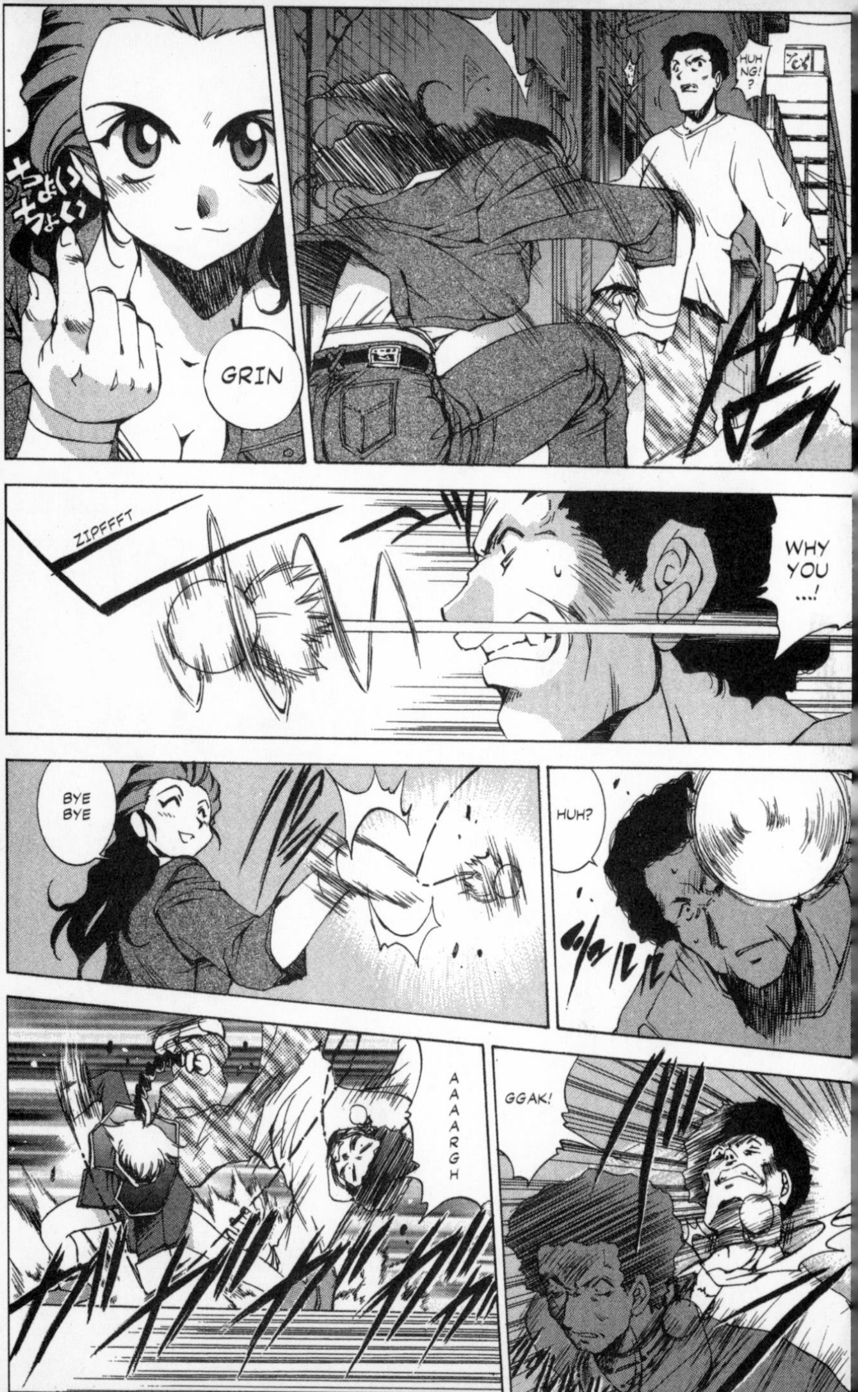

HUH NG! ?
ちょいちょい
GRIN
WHY YOU ...!
ZIPFFFT
HUH?
BYE BYE
GGAK!
AAAARGH

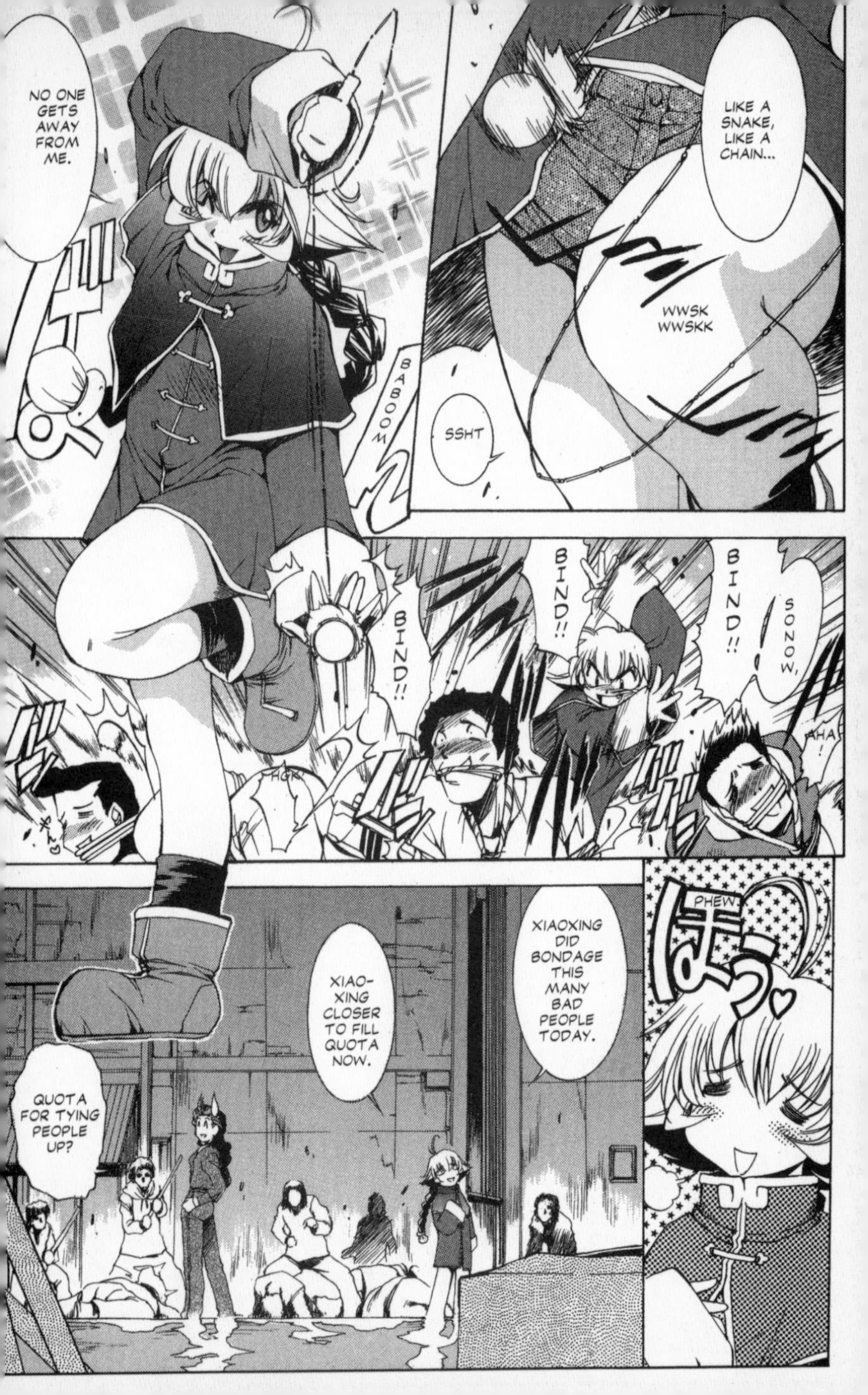
LIKE A SNAKE, LIKE A CHAIN...
WWSK WWSKK
SSHT
BABOOM
SO NOW,
BIND!!
BIND!!
BIND!!
AHA!
HGK
NO ONE GETS AWAY FROM ME.
PHEW
XIAOXING DID BONDAGE THIS MANY BAD PEOPLE TODAY.
XIAO-XING CLOSER TO FILL QUOTA NOW.
QUOTA FOR TYING PEOPLE UP?

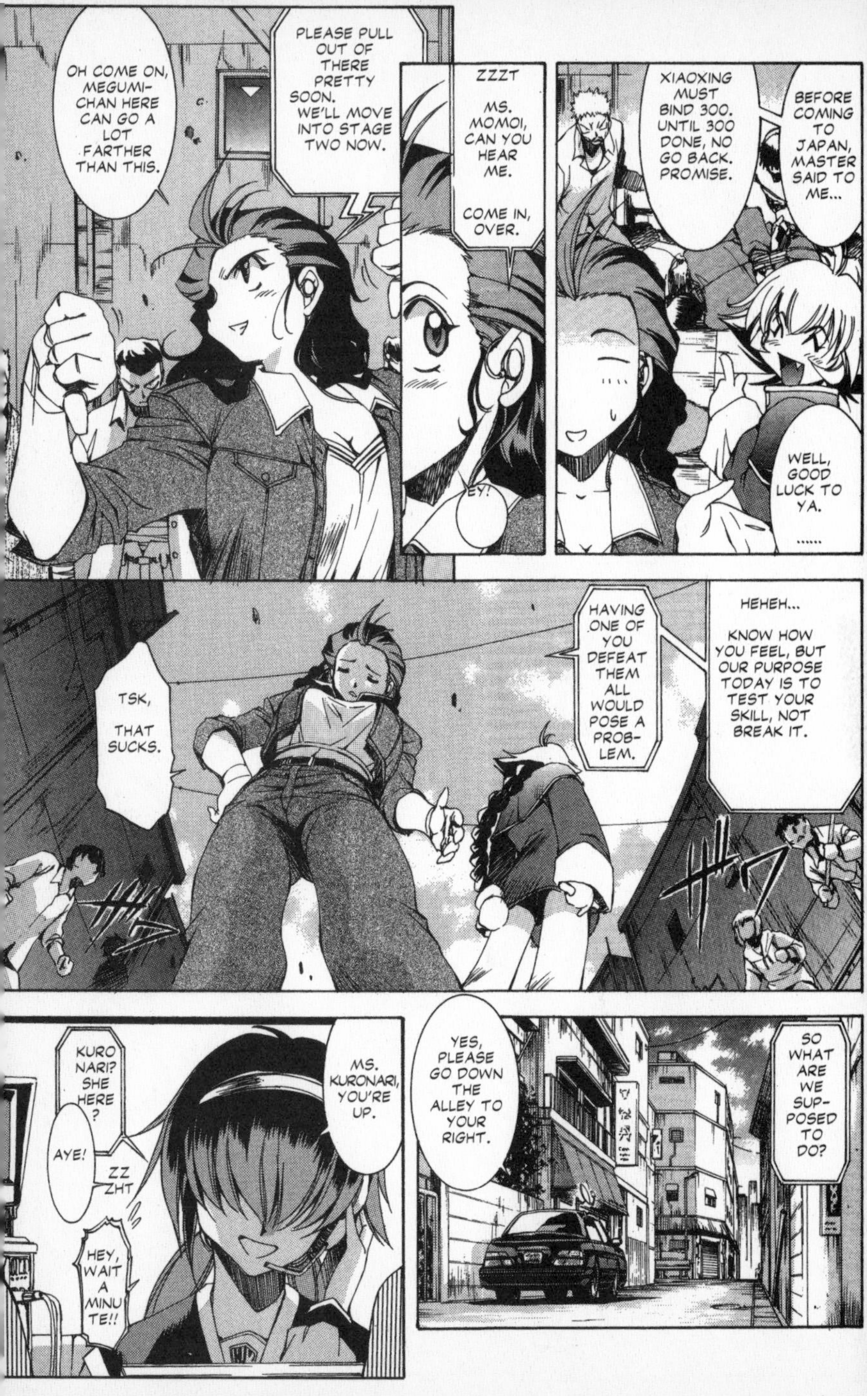
BEFORE COMING TO JAPAN, MASTER SAID TO ME...
XIAOXING MUST BIND 300. UNTIL 300 DONE, NO GO BACK. PROMISE.
WELL, GOOD LUCK TO YA.
......
ZZZT
MS. MOMOI, CAN YOU HEAR ME.
COME IN, OVER.
EY!
PLEASE PULL OUT OF THERE PRETTY SOON. WE'LL MOVE INTO STAGE TWO NOW.
OH COME ON, MEGUMI-CHAN HERE CAN GO A LOT FARTHER THAN THIS.
HEHEH...
KNOW HOW YOU FEEL, BUT OUR PURPOSE TODAY IS TO TEST YOUR SKILL, NOT BREAK IT.
HAVING ONE OF YOU DEFEAT THEM ALL WOULD POSE A PROB-LEM.
TSK,
THAT SUCKS.
SO WHAT ARE WE SUP-POSED TO DO?
YES, PLEASE GO DOWN THE ALLEY TO YOUR RIGHT.
MS. KURONARI, YOU'RE UP.
KURO NARI? SHE HERE?
AYE!
ZZ ZHT
HEY, WAIT A MINU TE!!

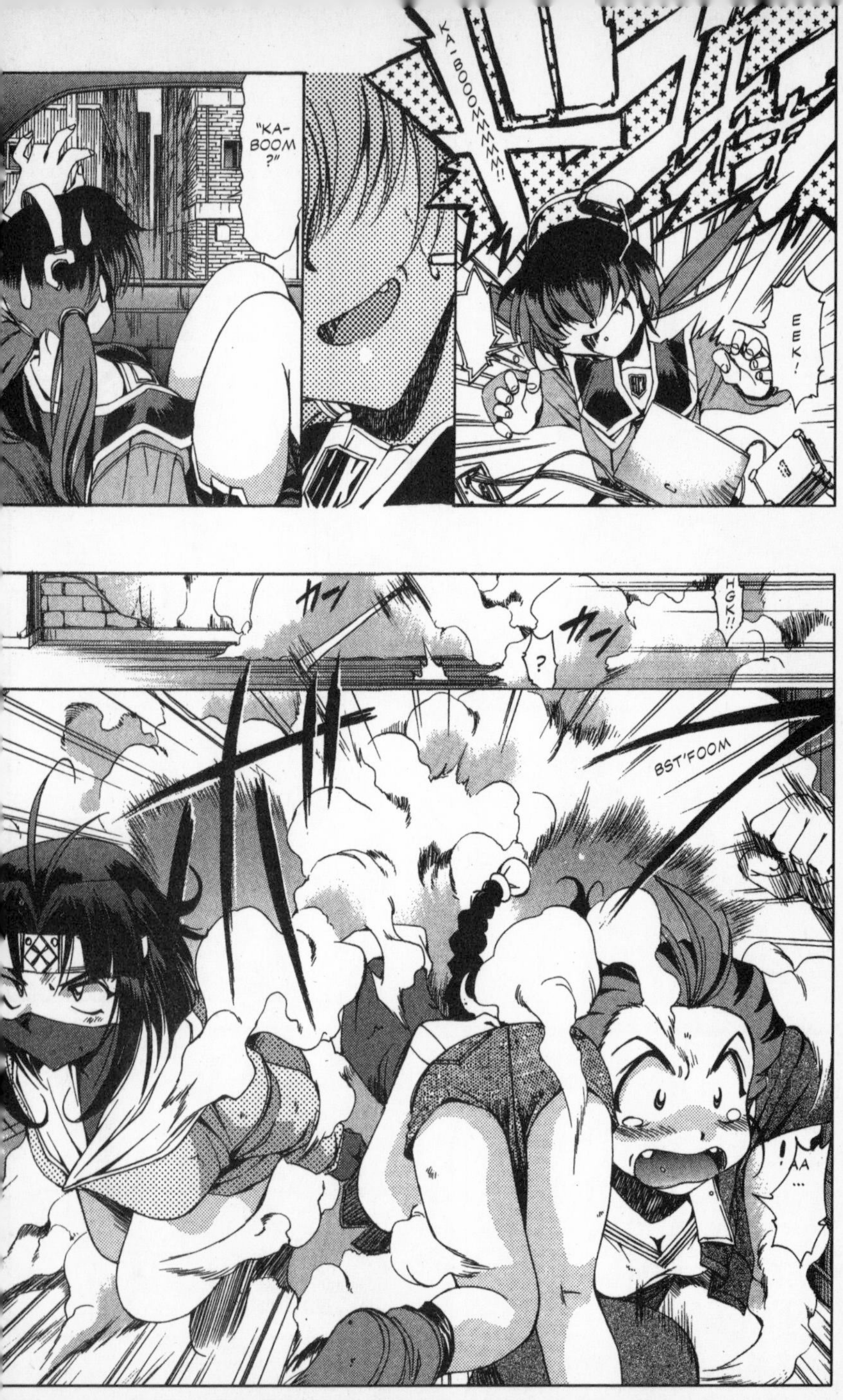
KA-BOOOMMMMM!!
EEK!
"KA-BOOM?"
HGK!!
?
BST'FOOM
! AA ...

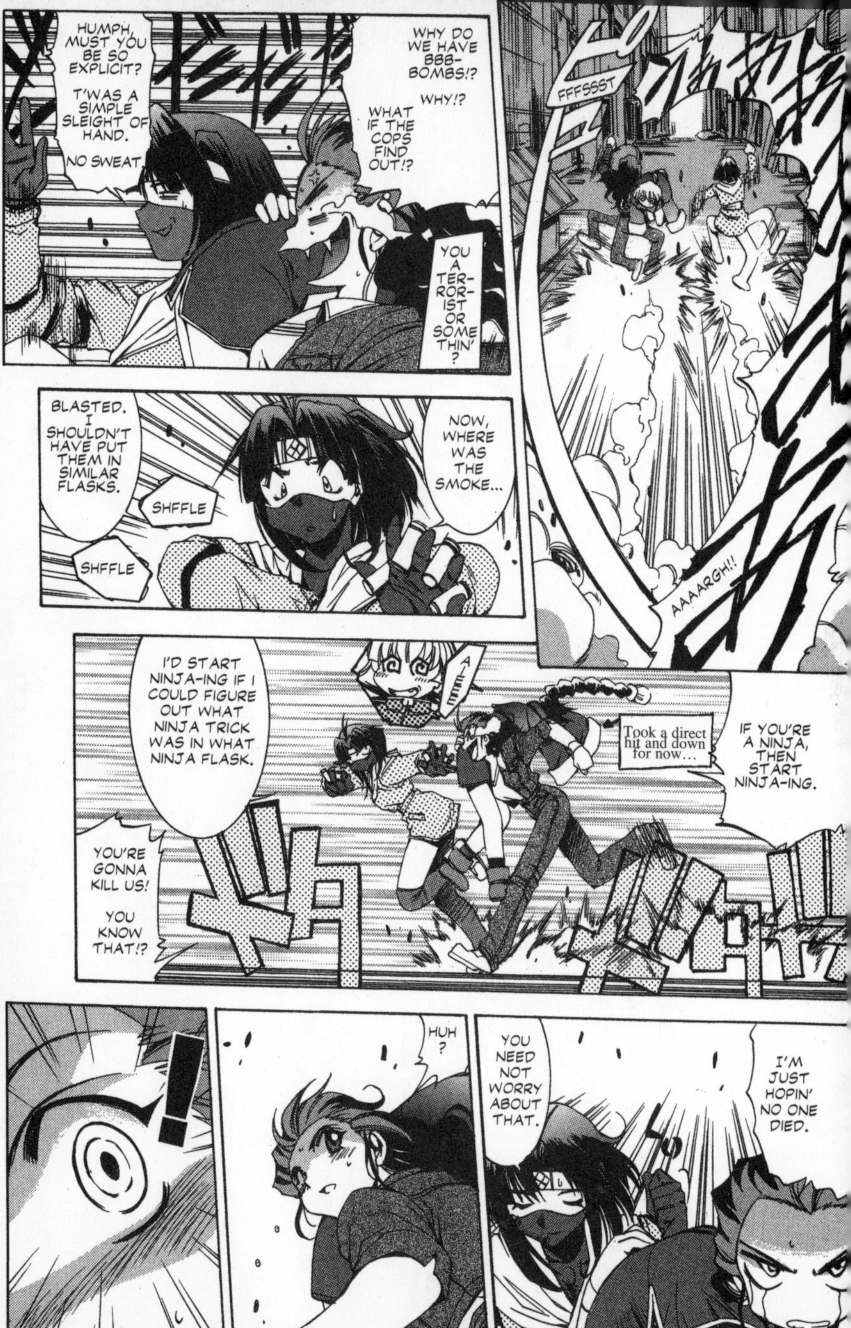
FFFSSST
AAAARGH!!
WHY DO WE HAVE BBB-BOMBS!?
WHY!?
WHAT IF THE COPS FIND OUT!?
YOU A TER-ROR-IST OR SOME THIN'?
HUMPH, MUST YOU BE SO EXPLICIT?
T'WAS A SIMPLE SLEIGHT OF HAND.
NO SWEAT.
NOW, WHERE WAS THE SMOKE...
BLASTED. I SHOULDN'T HAVE PUT THEM IN SIMILAR FLASKS.
SHFFLE
SHFFLE
IF YOU'RE A NINJA, THEN START NINJA-ING.
Took a direct hit and down for now...
AIEEE
I'D START NINJA-ING IF I COULD FIGURE OUT WHAT NINJA TRICK WAS IN WHAT NINJA FLASK.
YOU'RE GONNA KILL US!
YOU KNOW THAT!?
I'M JUST HOPIN' NO ONE DIED.
YOU NEED NOT WORRY ABOUT THAT.
HUH?
!

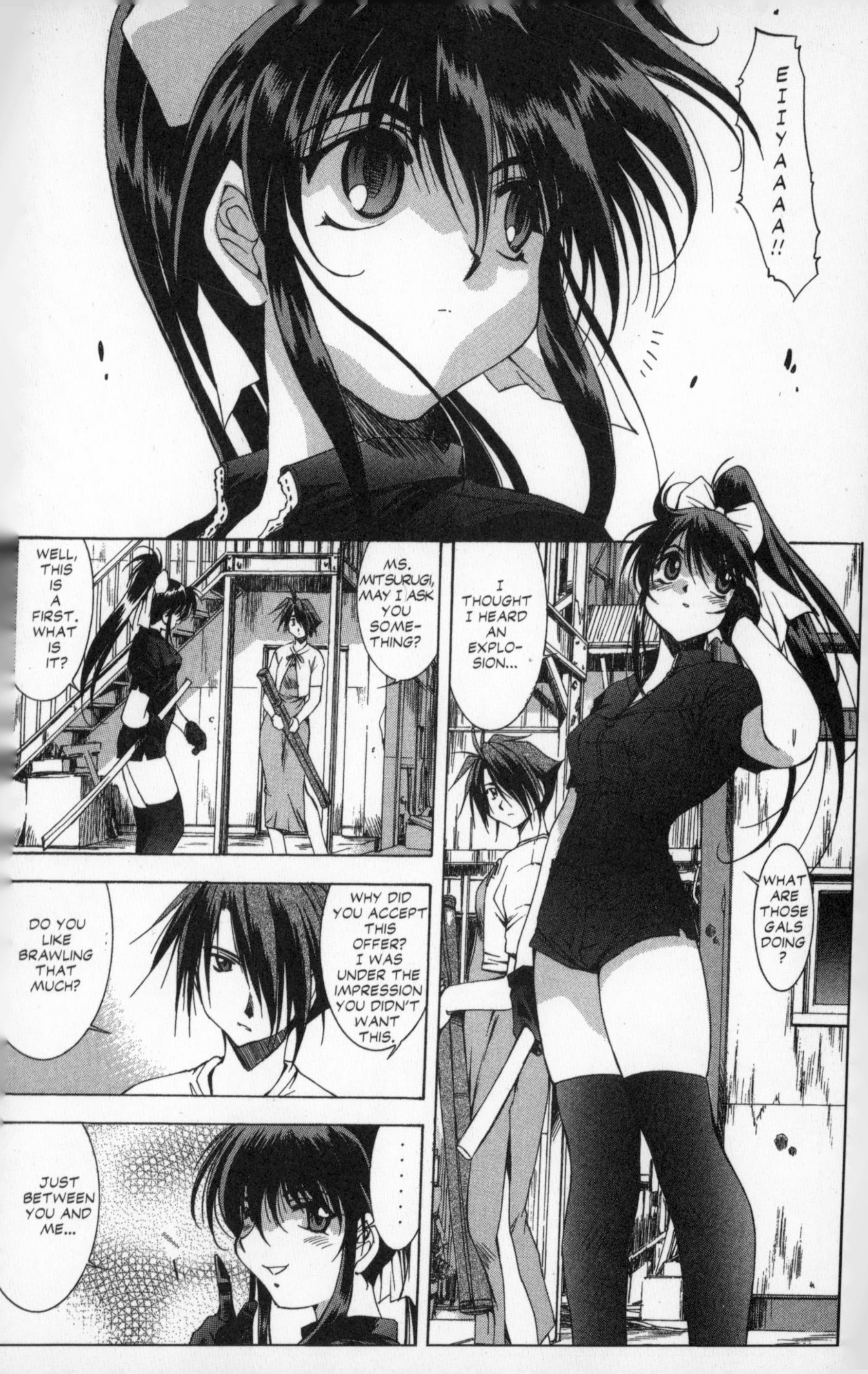
EIIYAAAAA!!
I THOUGHT I HEARD AN EXPLOSION...
WHAT ARE THOSE GALS DOING?
MS. MITSURUGI, MAY I ASK YOU SOMETHING?
WELL, THIS IS A FIRST. WHAT IS IT?
WHY DID YOU ACCEPT THIS OFFER? I WAS UNDER THE IMPRESSION YOU DIDN'T WANT THIS.
DO YOU LIKE BRAWLING THAT MUCH?
......
JUST BETWEEN YOU AND ME...

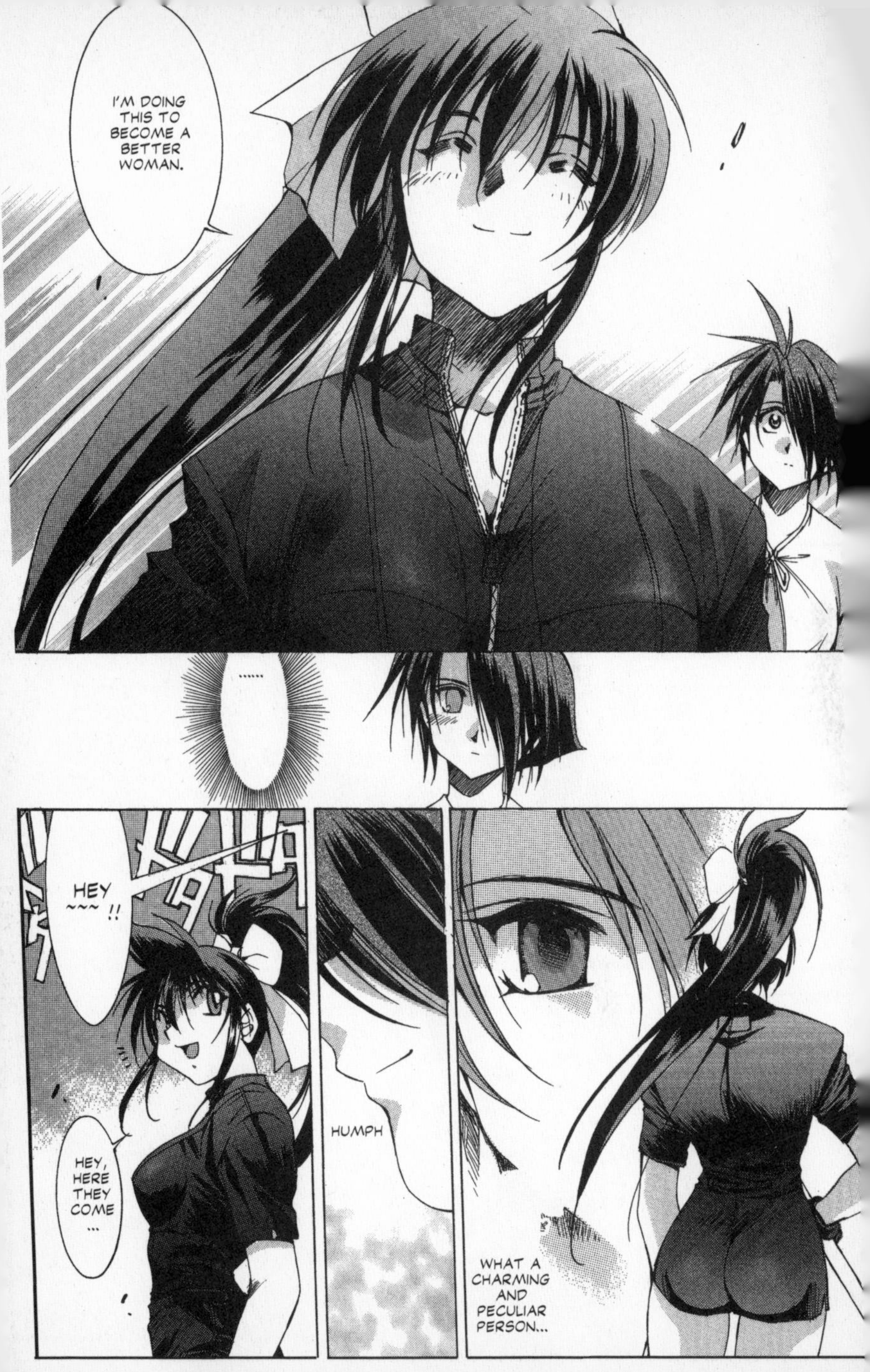
I'M DOING THIS TO BECOME A BETTER WOMAN.
!
......
WHAT A CHARMING AND PECULIAR PERSON...
HUMPH
HEY ~~~ !!
HEY, HERE THEY COME ...

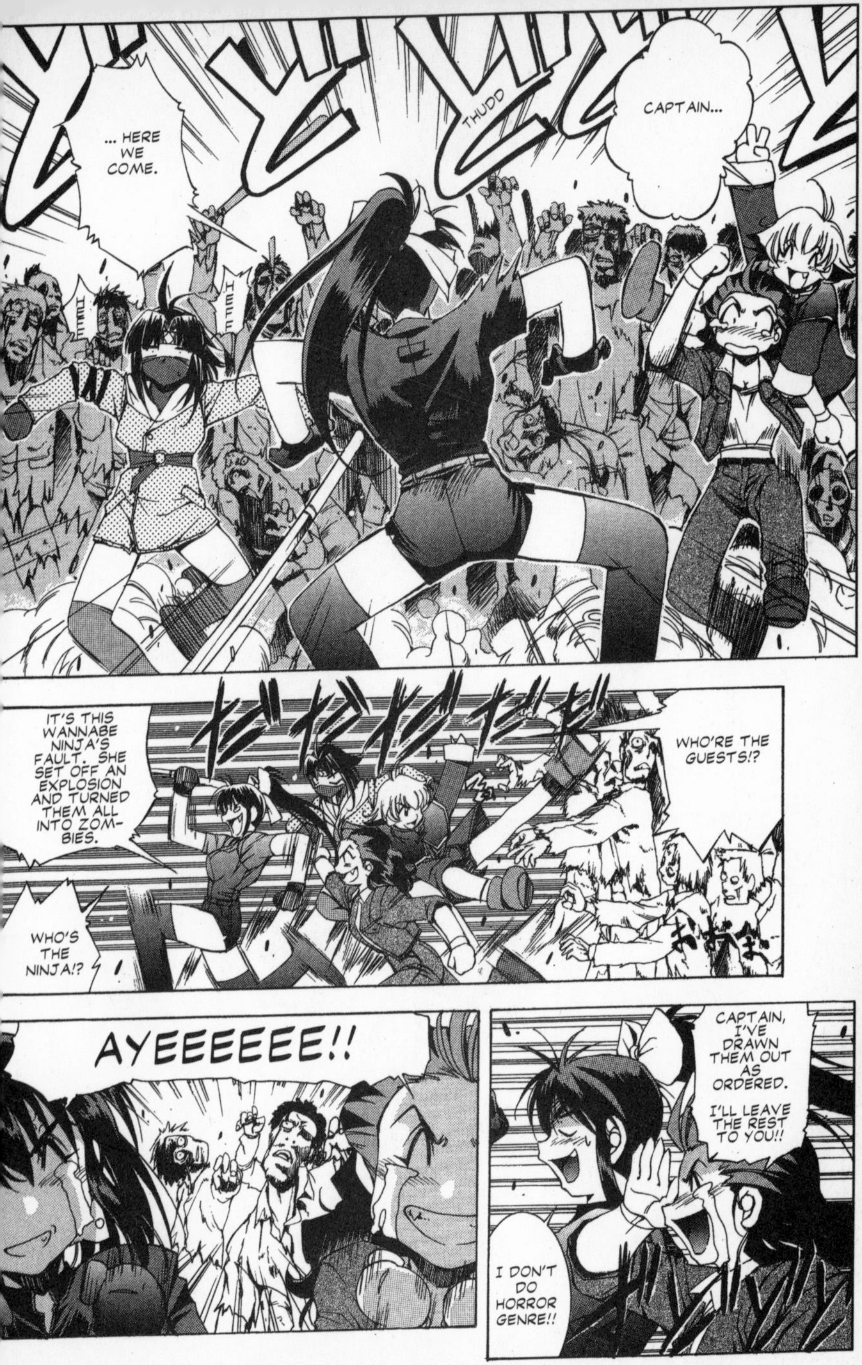
CAPTAIN...
THUDD
HEFF
HEFF
... HERE WE COME.
WHO'RE THE GUESTS!?
IT'S THIS WANNABE NINJA'S FAULT. SHE SET OFF AN EXPLOSION AND TURNED THEM ALL INTO ZOM-BIES.
WHO'S THE NINJA!?
CAPTAIN, I'VE DRAWN THEM OUT AS ORDERED.
I'LL LEAVE THE REST TO YOU!!
I DON'T DO HORROR GENRE!!
AYEEEEEEE!!

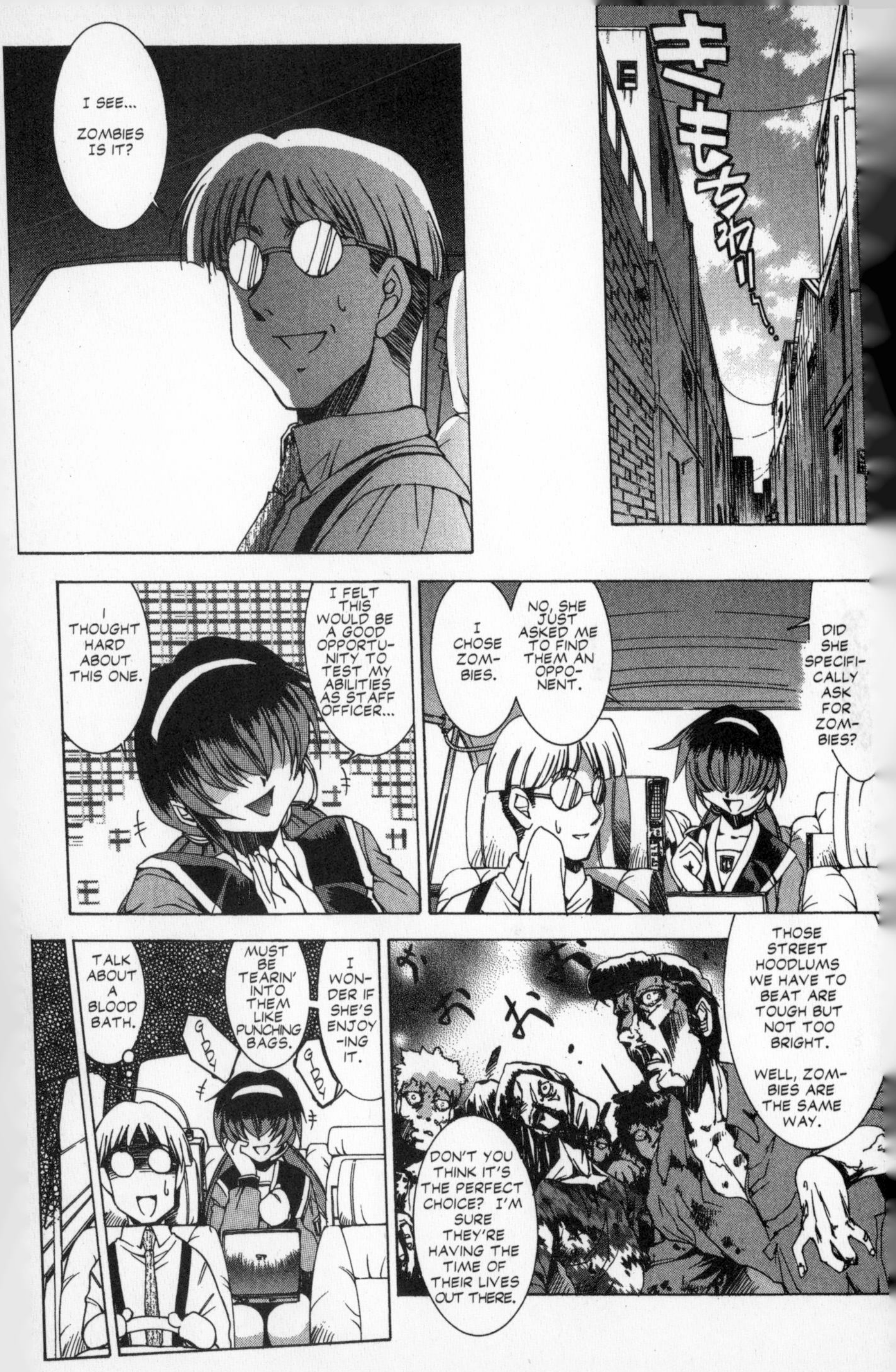
きもちわり
I SEE...
ZOMBIES IS IT?
DID SHE SPECIFICALLY ASK FOR ZOMBIES?
NO, SHE JUST ASKED ME TO FIND THEM AN OPPONENT.
I CHOSE ZOMBIES.
I FELT THIS WOULD BE A GOOD OPPORTUNITY TO TEST MY ABILITIES AS STAFF OFFICER...
I THOUGHT HARD ABOUT THIS ONE.
THOSE STREET HOODLUMS WE HAVE TO BEAT ARE TOUGH BUT NOT TOO BRIGHT.
WELL, ZOMBIES ARE THE SAME WAY.
DON'T YOU THINK IT'S THE PERFECT CHOICE? I'M SURE THEY'RE HAVING THE TIME OF THEIR LIVES OUT THERE.
I WONDER IF SHE'S ENJOYING IT.
MUST BE TEARIN' INTO THEM LIKE PUNCHING BAGS.
TALK ABOUT A BLOOD BATH.

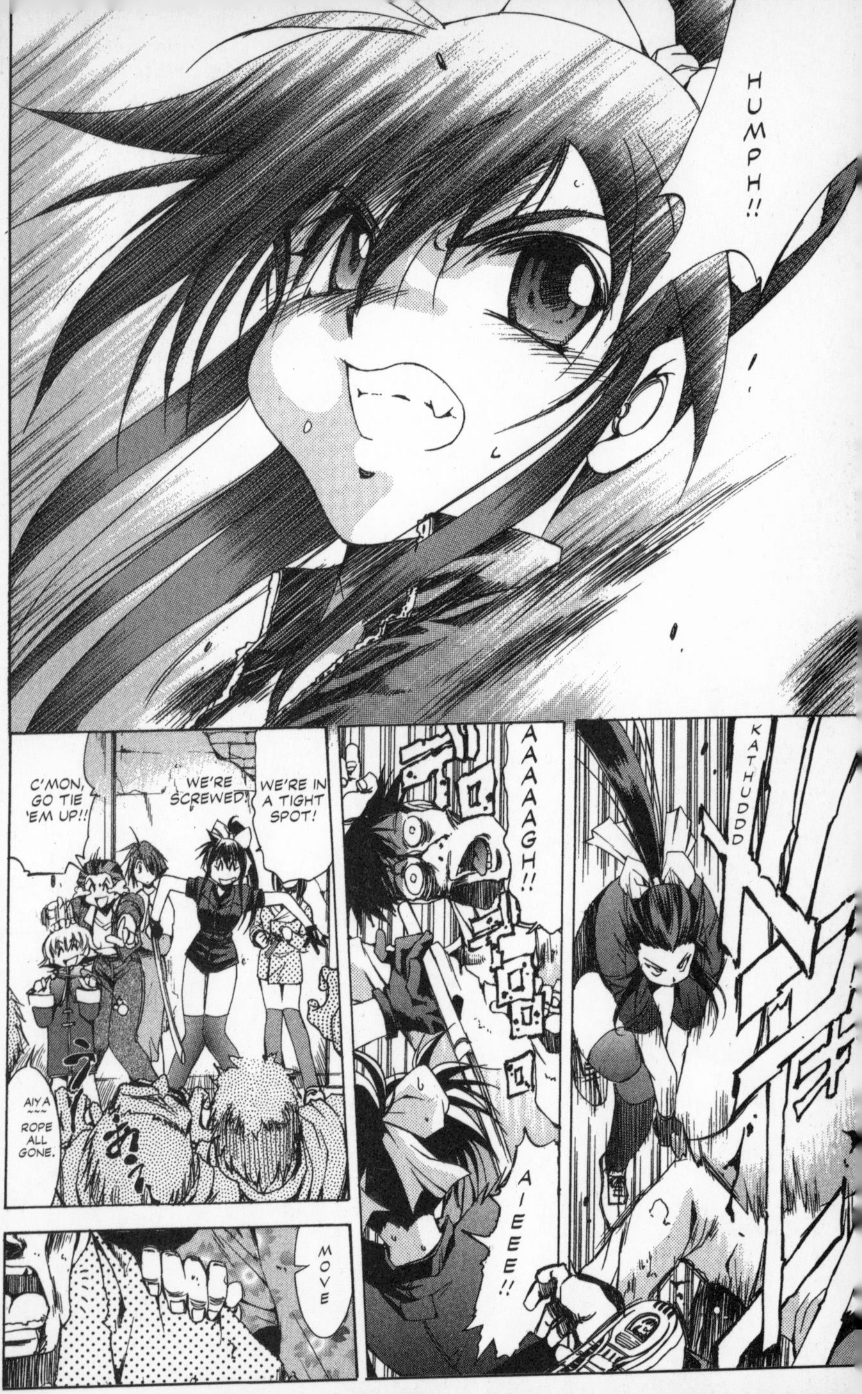
HUMPH!!
KATHUDDD
AAAAAAGH!!
AIEEEE!!
WE'RE IN A TIGHT SPOT!
WE'RE SCREWED!
C'MON, GO TIE 'EM UP!!
AIYA ~~~ ROPE ALL GONE.
MOVE

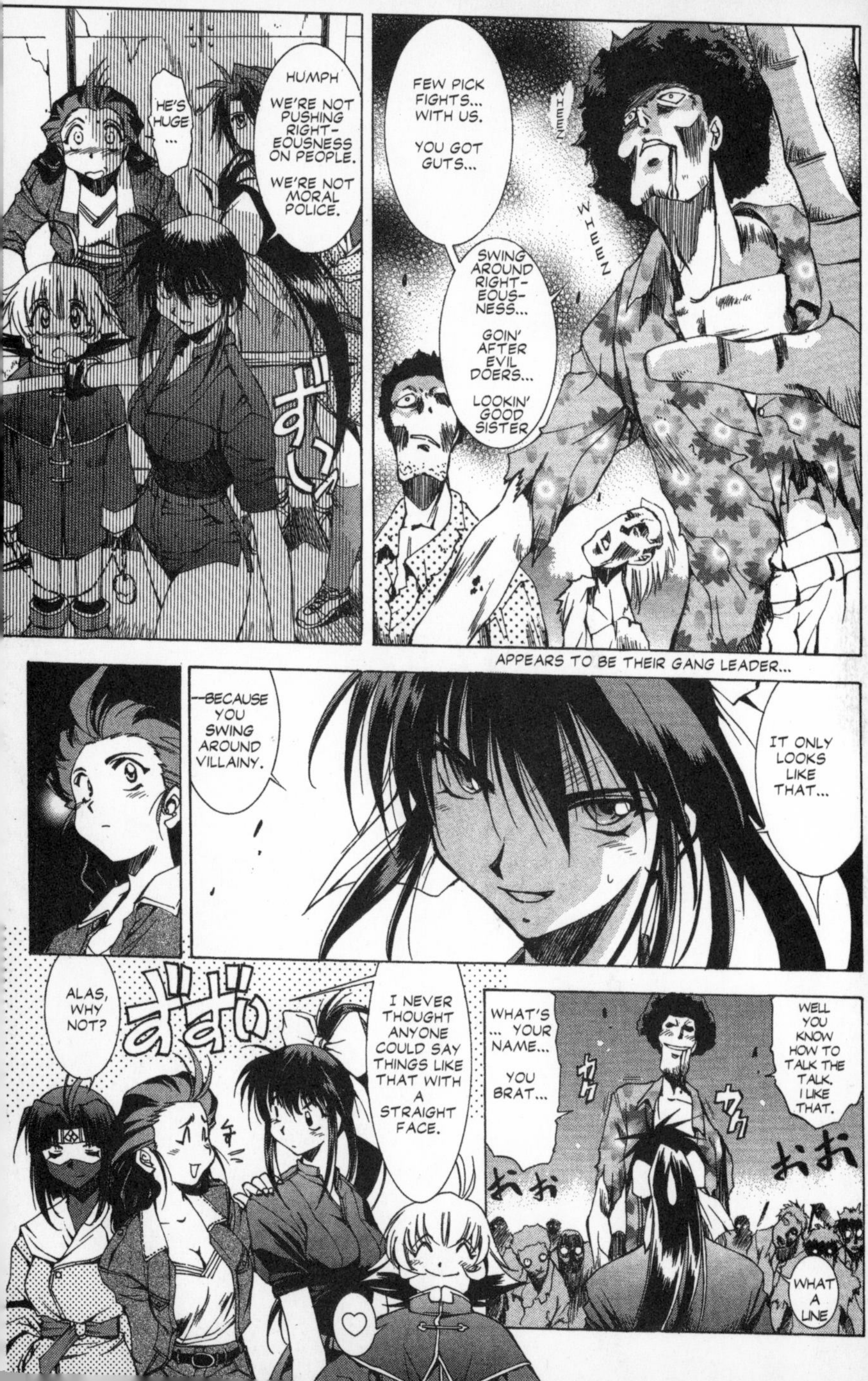
WHEEZ
WHEEZ
FEW PICK FIGHTS... WITH US. YOU GOT GUTS...
SWING AROUND RIGHT-EOUSNESS... GOIN' AFTER EVIL DOERS... LOOKIN' GOOD SISTER
APPEARS TO BE THEIR GANG LEADER...
HUMPH WE'RE NOT PUSHING RIGHT-EOUSNESS ON PEOPLE. WE'RE NOT MORAL POLICE.
HE'S HUGE ...
IT ONLY LOOKS LIKE THAT...
--BECAUSE YOU SWING AROUND VILLAINY.
WELL YOU KNOW HOW TO TALK THE TALK. I LIKE THAT.
WHAT'S ... YOUR NAME... YOU BRAT...
おお
おお
WHAT A LINE
I NEVER THOUGHT ANYONE COULD SAY THINGS LIKE THAT WITH A STRAIGHT FACE.
ALAS, WHY NOT?
ずずい

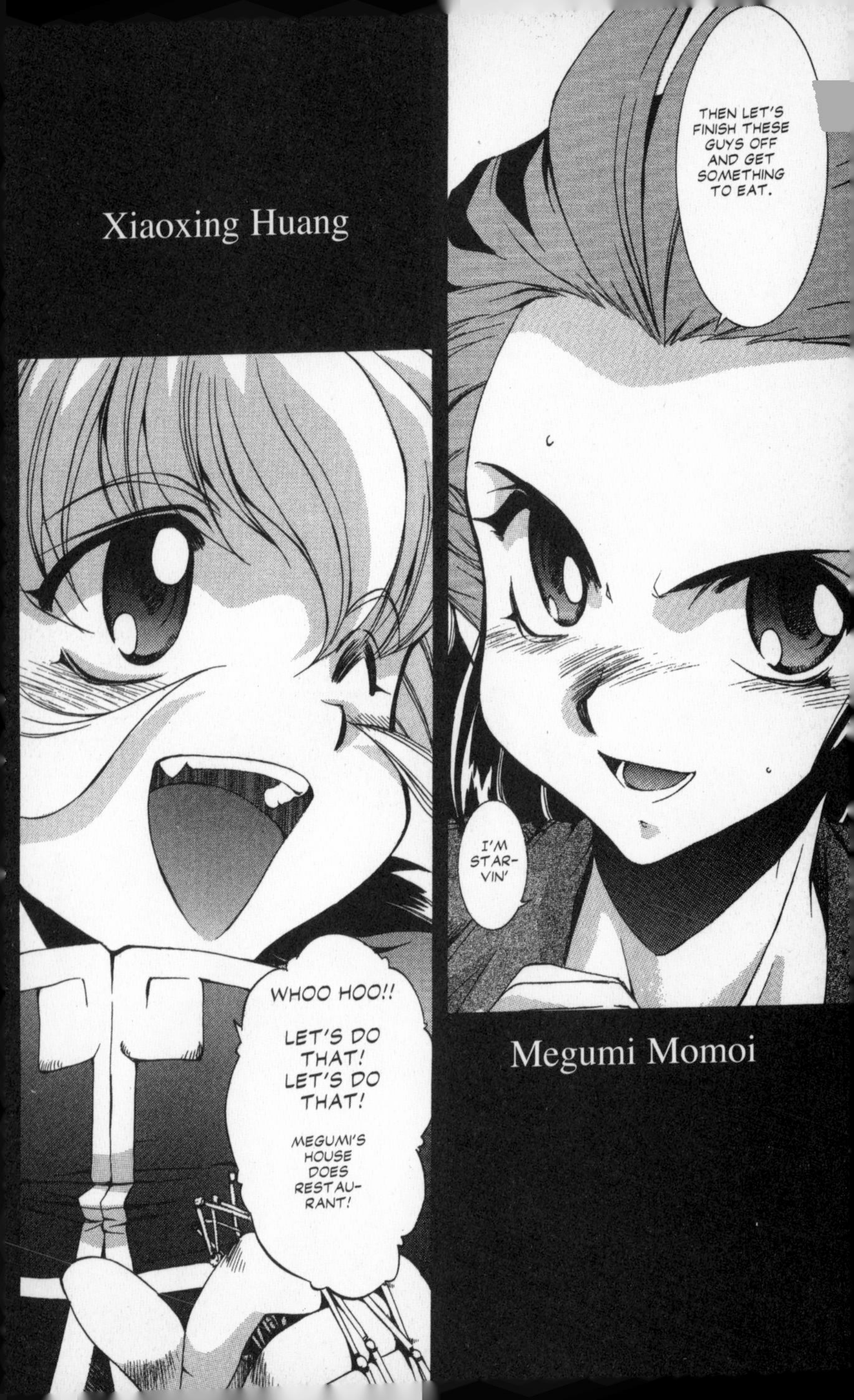
THEN LET'S FINISH THESE GUYS OFF AND GET SOMETHING TO EAT.
I'M STAR-VIN'
Megumi Momoi
Xiaoxing Huang
WHOO HOO!! LET'S DO THAT! LET'S DO THAT!
MEGUMI'S HOUSE DOES RESTAU-RANT!

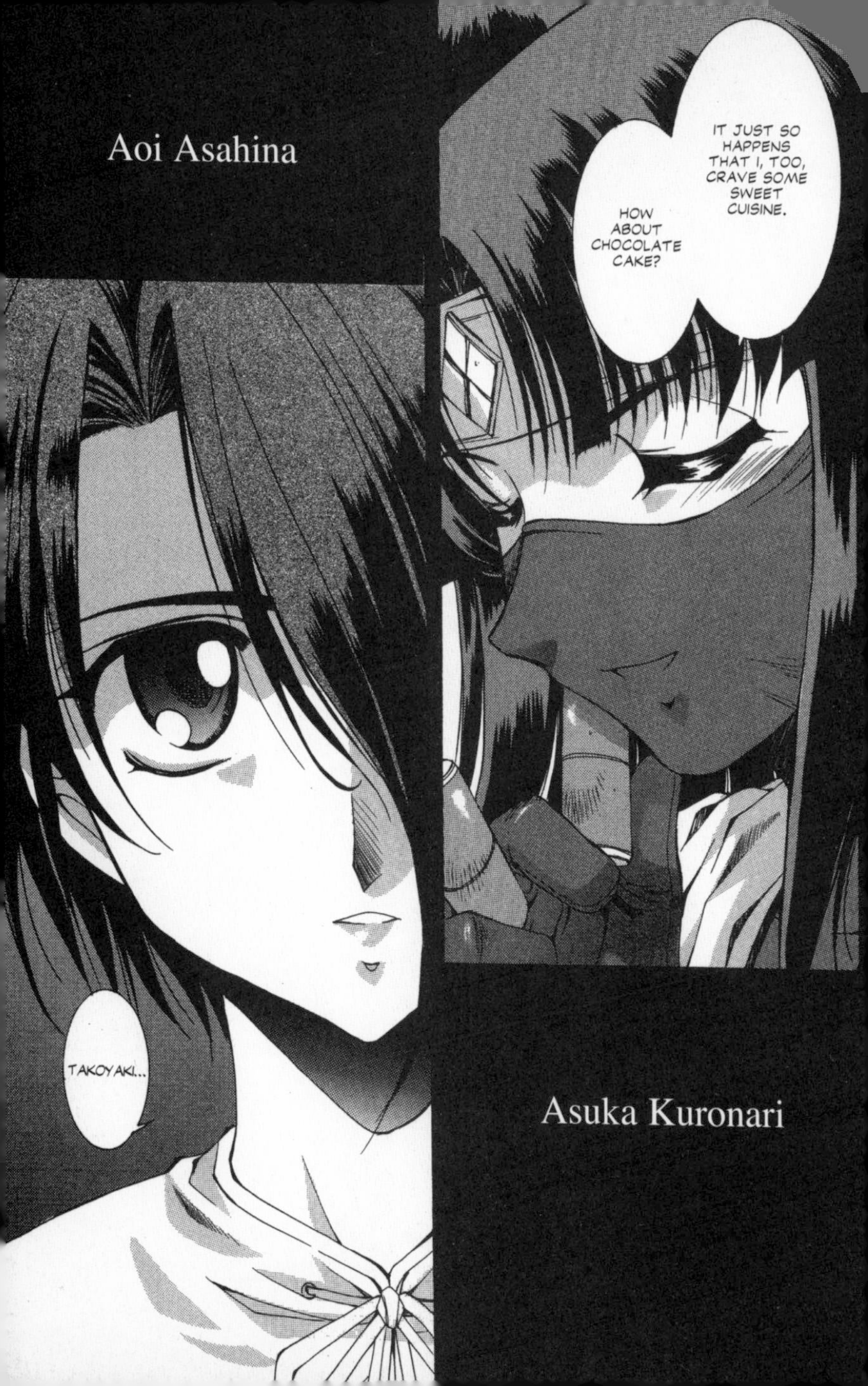
IT JUST SO HAPPENS THAT I, TOO, CRAVE SOME SWEET CUISINE.
HOW ABOUT CHOCOLATE CAKE?
Asuka Kuronari
Aoi Asahina
TAKOYAKI...

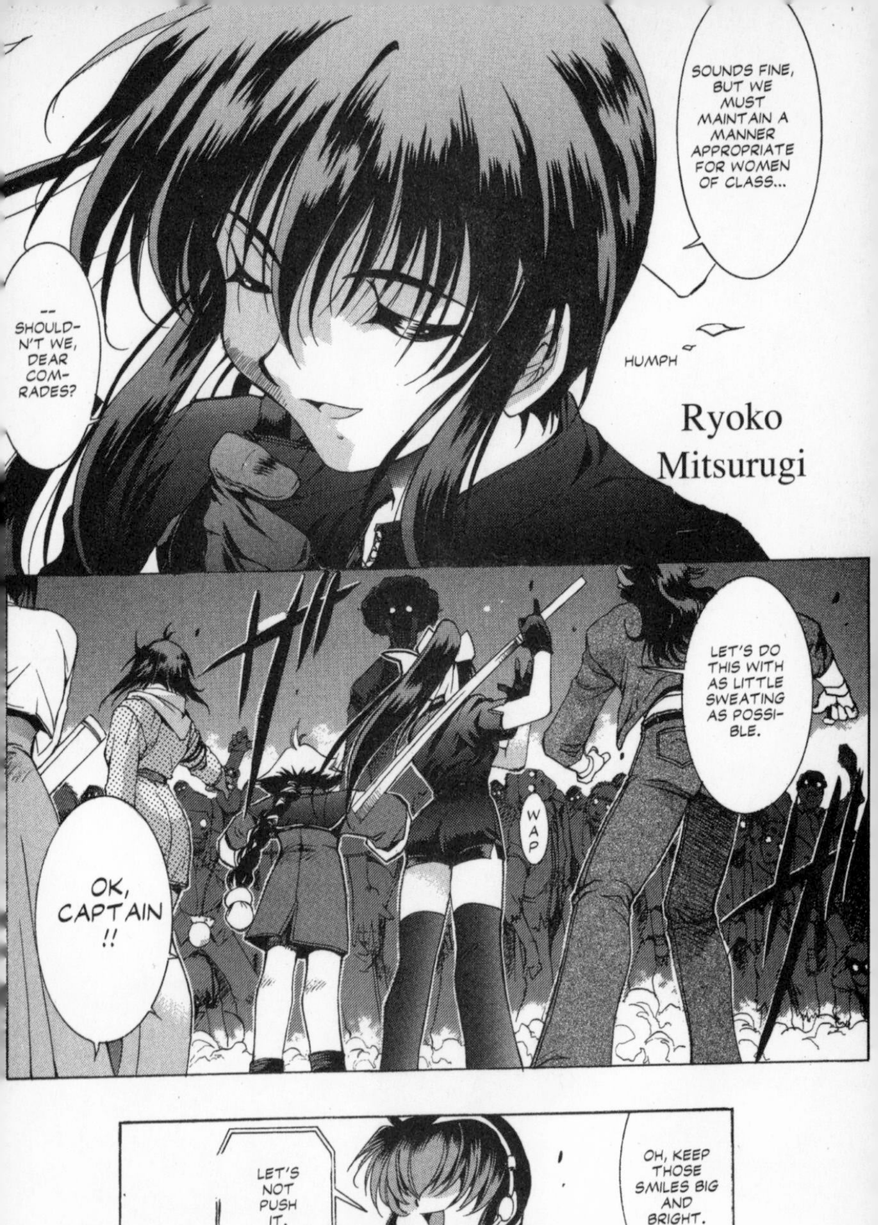
SOUNDS FINE, BUT WE MUST MAINTAIN A MANNER APPROPRIATE FOR WOMEN OF CLASS...
HUMPH
--SHOULDN'T WE, DEAR COMRADES?
Ryoko Mitsurugi
LET'S DO THIS WITH AS LITTLE SWEATING AS POSSIBLE.
WAP
OK, CAPTAIN !!
OH, KEEP THOSE SMILES BIG AND BRIGHT.
LET'S NOT PUSH IT.

Midori Misato

Extra Episode: A Peaceful Moment After the Battle

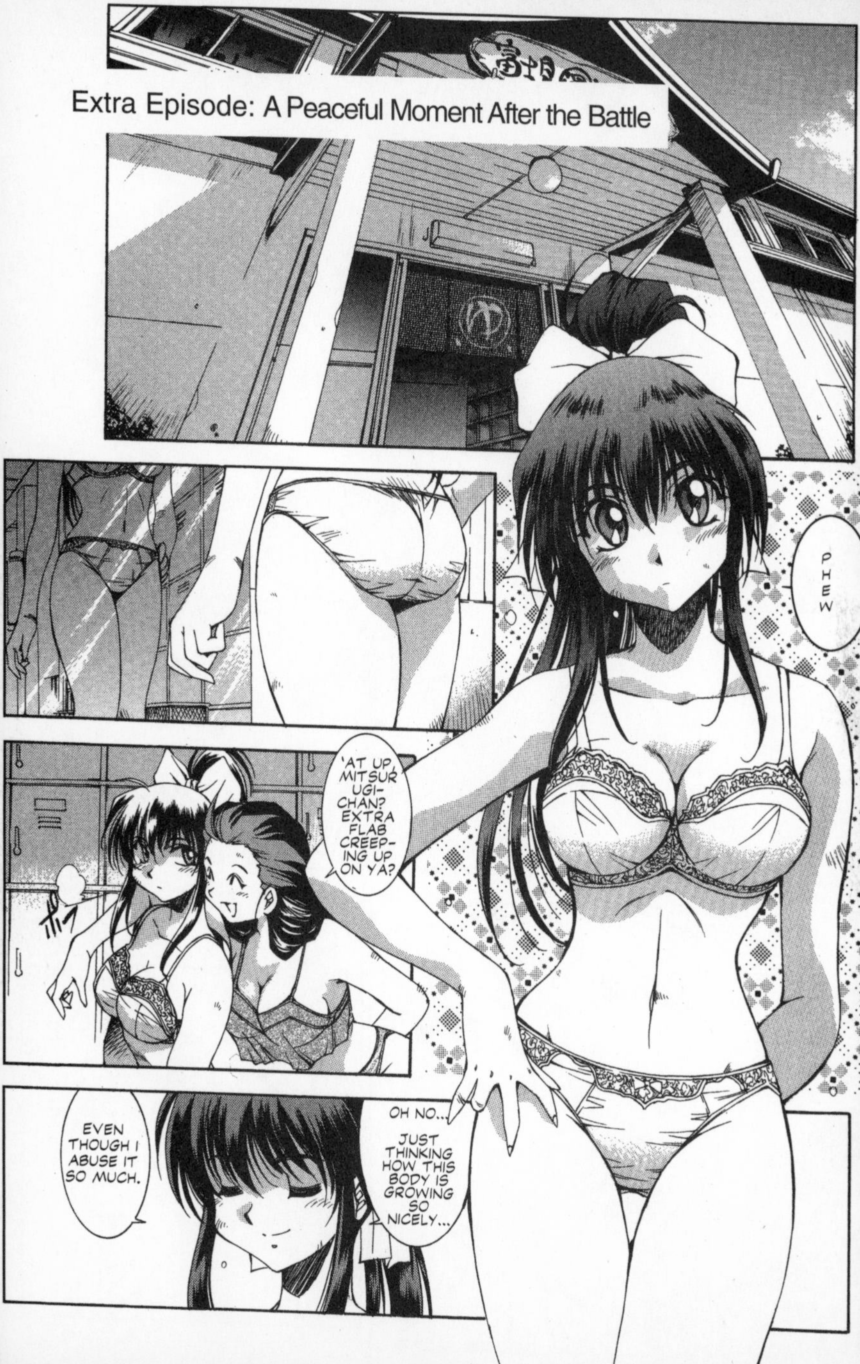
PHEW
'AT UP, MITSURUGI-CHAN? EXTRA FLAB CREEPING UP ON YA?
OH NO... JUST THINKING HOW THIS BODY IS GROWING SO NICELY...
EVEN THOUGH I ABUSE IT SO MUCH.

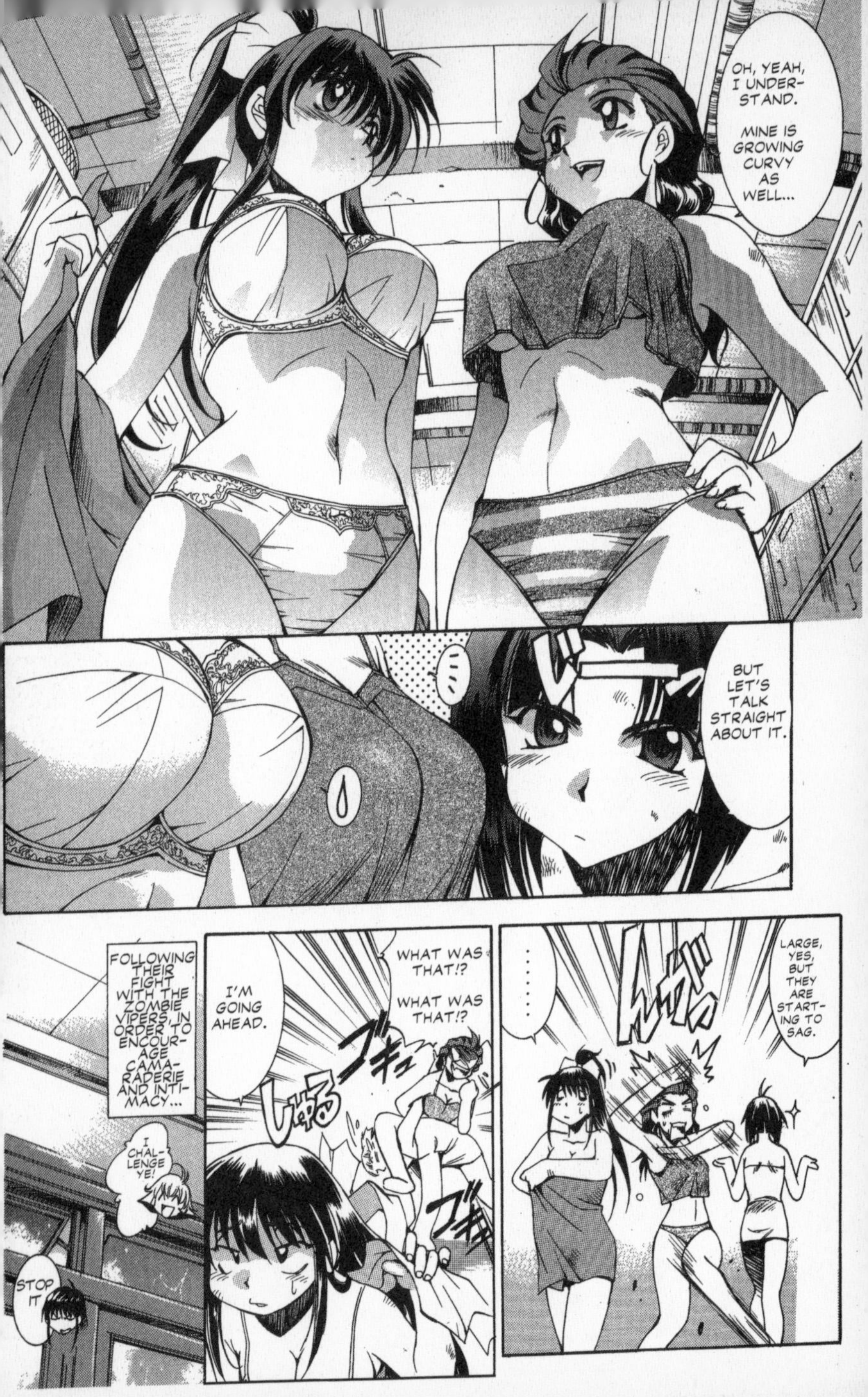

OH, YEAH, I UNDERSTAND.
MINE IS GROWING CURVY AS WELL...
BUT LET'S TALK STRAIGHT ABOUT IT.
LARGE, YES, BUT THEY ARE STARTING TO SAG.
....
WHAT WAS THAT!? WHAT WAS THAT!?
I'M GOING AHEAD.
FOLLOWING THEIR FIGHT WITH THE ZOMBIE VIPERS, IN ORDER TO ENCOURAGE CAMARADERIE AND INTIMACY...
I CHALLENGE YE!
STOP IT

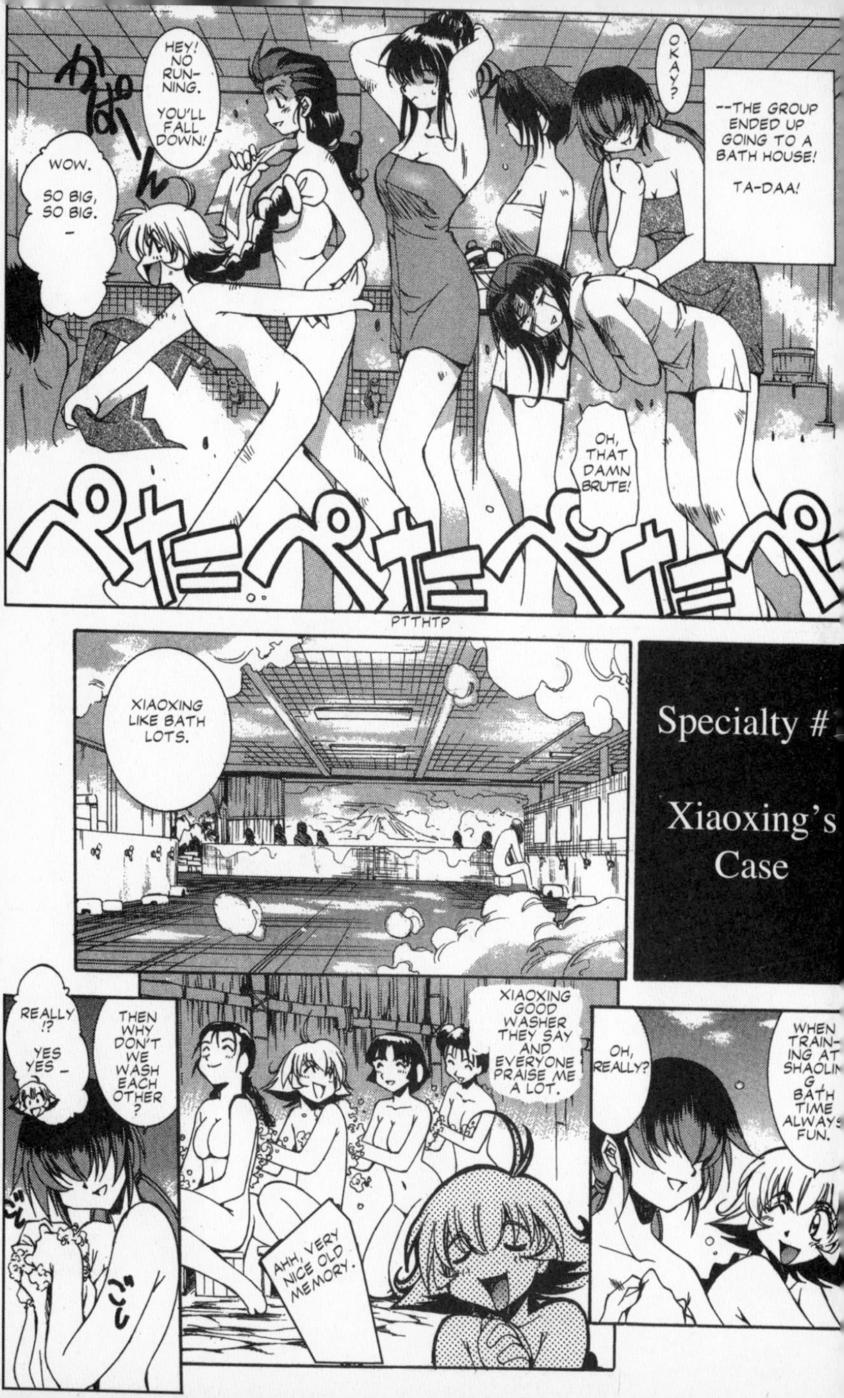
--THE GROUP ENDED UP GOING TO A BATH HOUSE! TA-DAA!
OKAY?
HEY! NO RUN-NING. YOU'LL FALL DOWN!
かぽーん
WOW. SO BIG, SO BIG. –
OH, THAT DAMN BRUTE!
ぺたぺたぺたぺたぺた
PTTHTP
Specialty #
Xiaoxing's Case
XIAOXING LIKE BATH LOTS.
WHEN TRAIN-ING AT SHAOLING, BATH TIME ALWAYS FUN.
OH, REALLY?
XIAOXING GOOD WASHER THEY SAY AND EVERYONE PRAISE ME A LOT.
AHH, VERY NICE OLD MEMORY.
THEN WHY DON'T WE WASH EACH OTHER?
REALLY!? YES YES –
ごし ごし

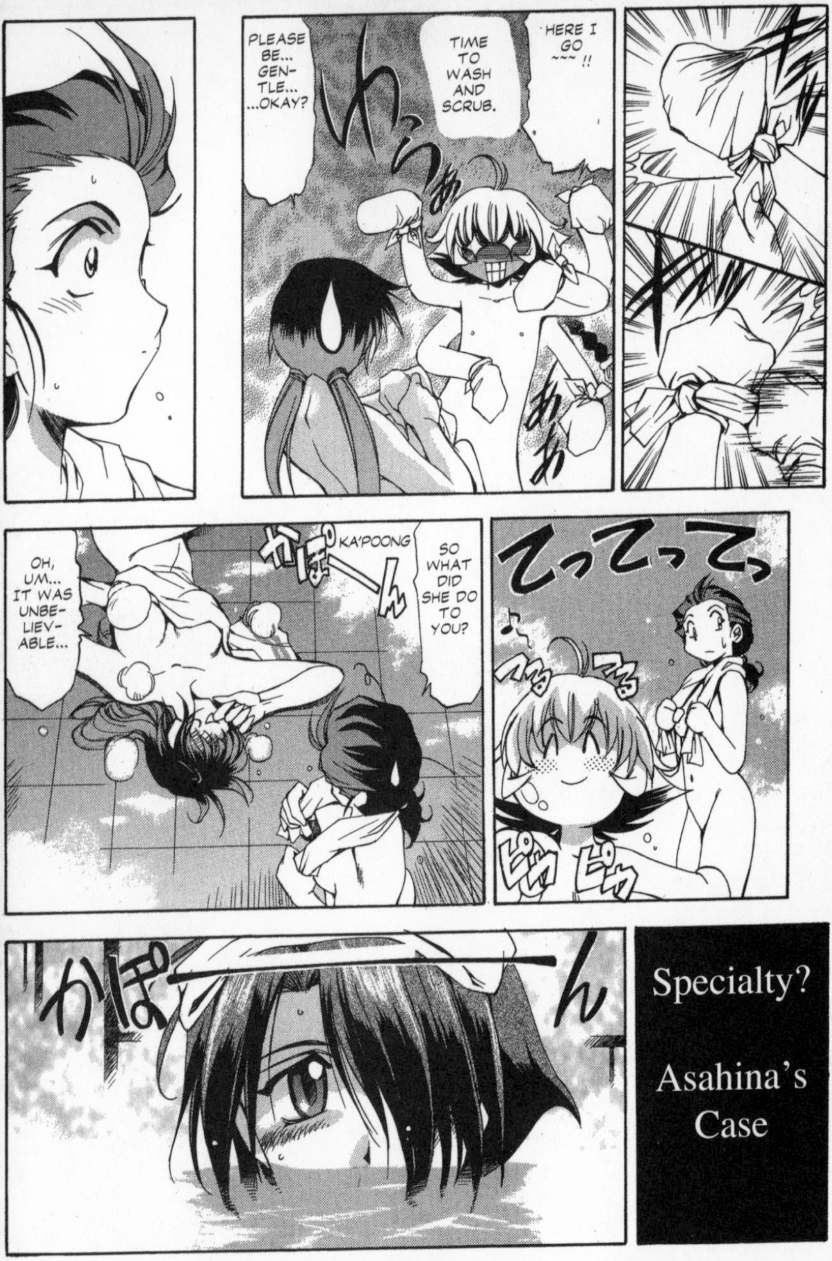
HERE I GO ~~~ !!
TIME TO WASH AND SCRUB.
PLEASE BE... GEN-TLE... ...OKAY?
てっ てっ てっ
SO WHAT DID SHE DO TO YOU?
KA'POONG
OH, UM... IT WAS UNBE-LIEV-ABLE...
Specialty?
Asahina's Case
かぽーん

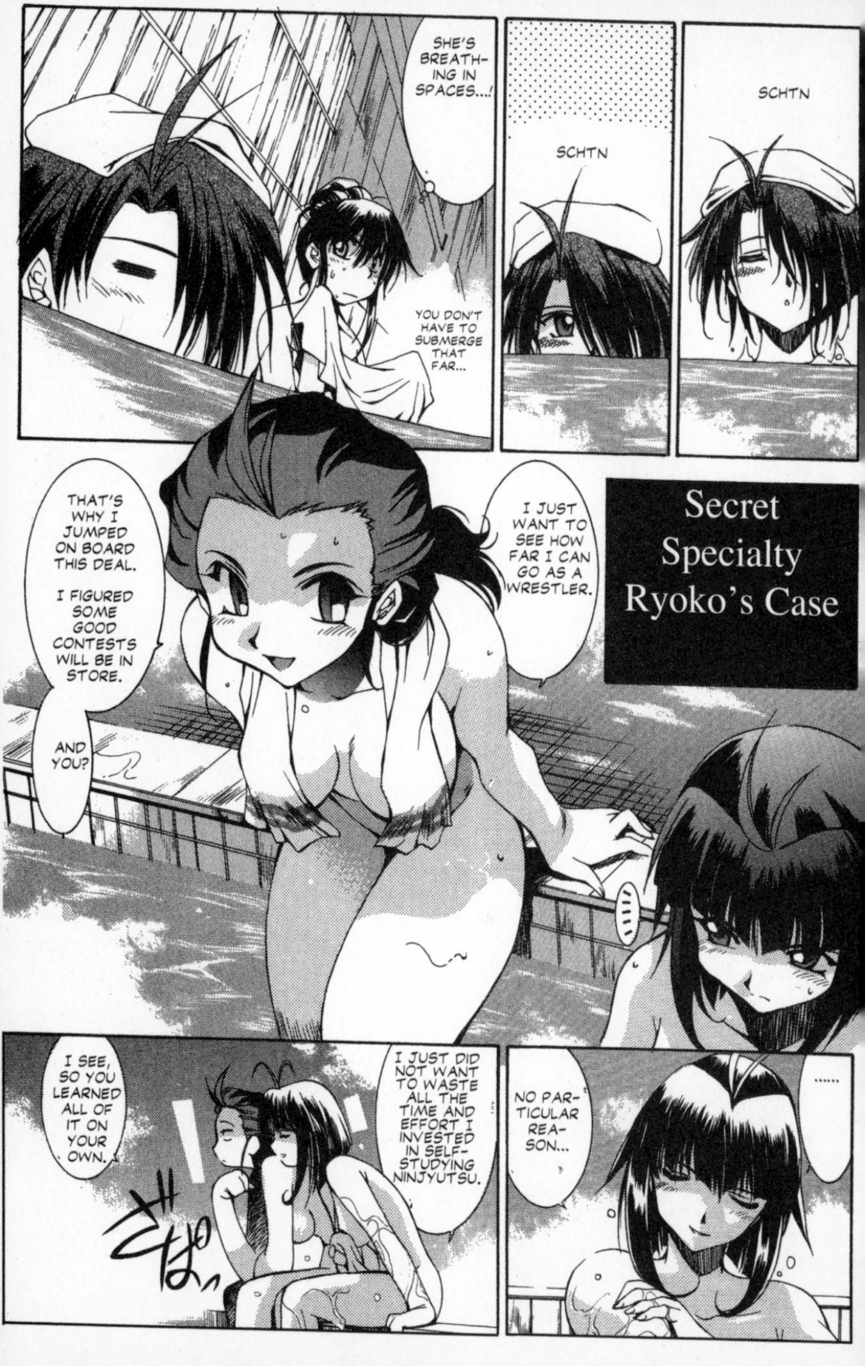
SCHTN
SCHTN
SHE'S BREATHING IN SPACES...!
YOU DON'T HAVE TO SUBMERGE THAT FAR...
Secret Specialty Ryoko's Case
I JUST WANT TO SEE HOW FAR I CAN GO AS A WRESTLER.
THAT'S WHY I JUMPED ON BOARD THIS DEAL.
I FIGURED SOME GOOD CONTESTS WILL BE IN STORE.
AND YOU?
......
NO PARTICULAR REASON...
I JUST DID NOT WANT TO WASTE ALL THE TIME AND EFFORT I INVESTED IN SELF-STUDYING NINJYUTSU.
I SEE, SO YOU LEARNED ALL OF IT ON YOUR OWN.
ざぱっ

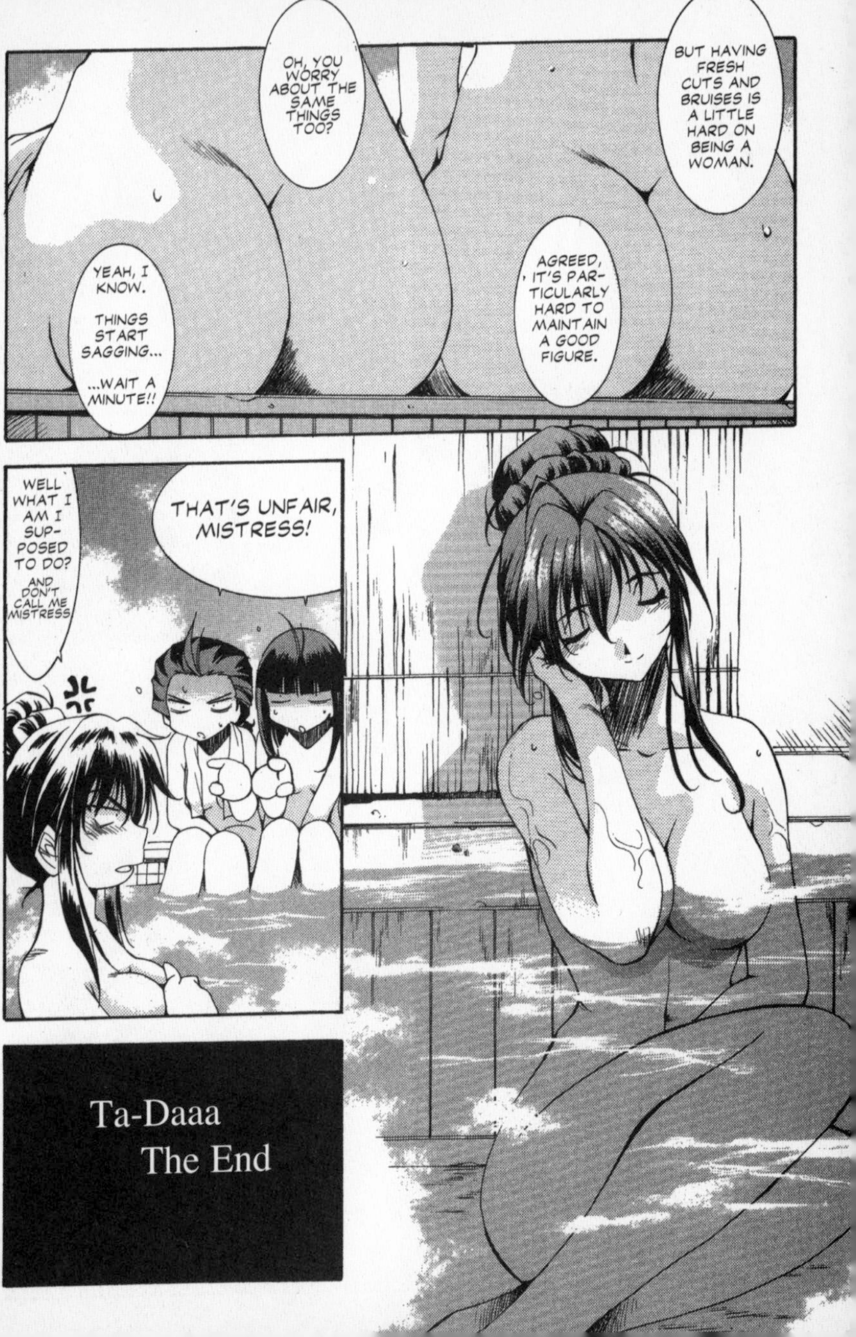
BUT HAVING FRESH CUTS AND BRUISES IS A LITTLE HARD ON BEING A WOMAN.
OH, YOU WORRY ABOUT THE SAME THINGS TOO?
AGREED, IT'S PARTICULARLY HARD TO MAINTAIN A GOOD FIGURE.
YEAH, I KNOW.
THINGS START SAGGING...
...WAIT A MINUTE!!
THAT'S UNFAIR, MISTRESS!
WELL WHAT AM I SUPPOSED TO DO?
AND DON'T CALL ME MISTRESS.
Ta-Daaa The End

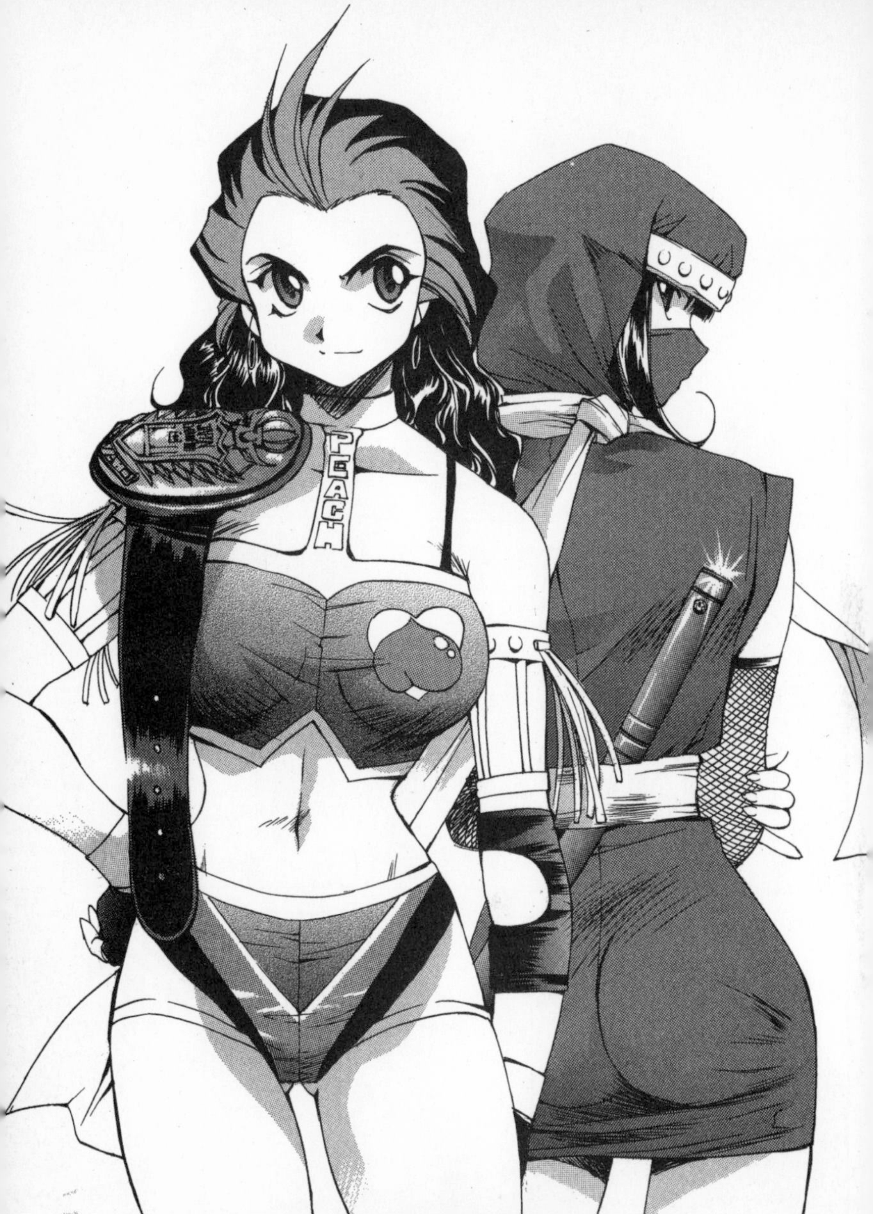
PEACH

Episode 25 A Fighting Débutante's Morning,
A Friendly Debauchee's Afternoon.

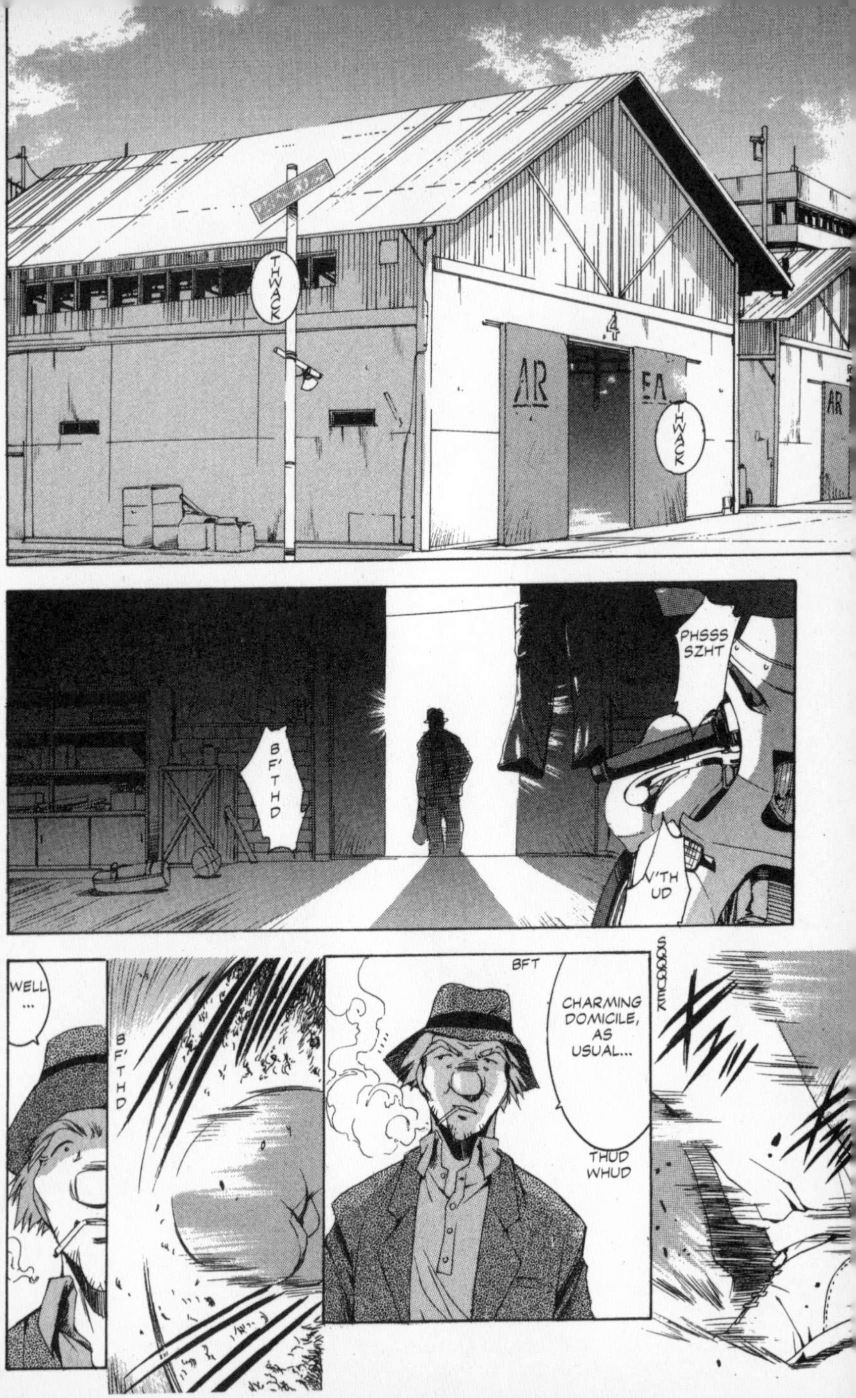
THWACK
THWACK
PHSSS SZHT
V'THUD
BF'THD
SQQQUEK
BFT
CHARMING DOMICILE, AS USUAL...
THUD WHUD
BF'THD
WELL ...

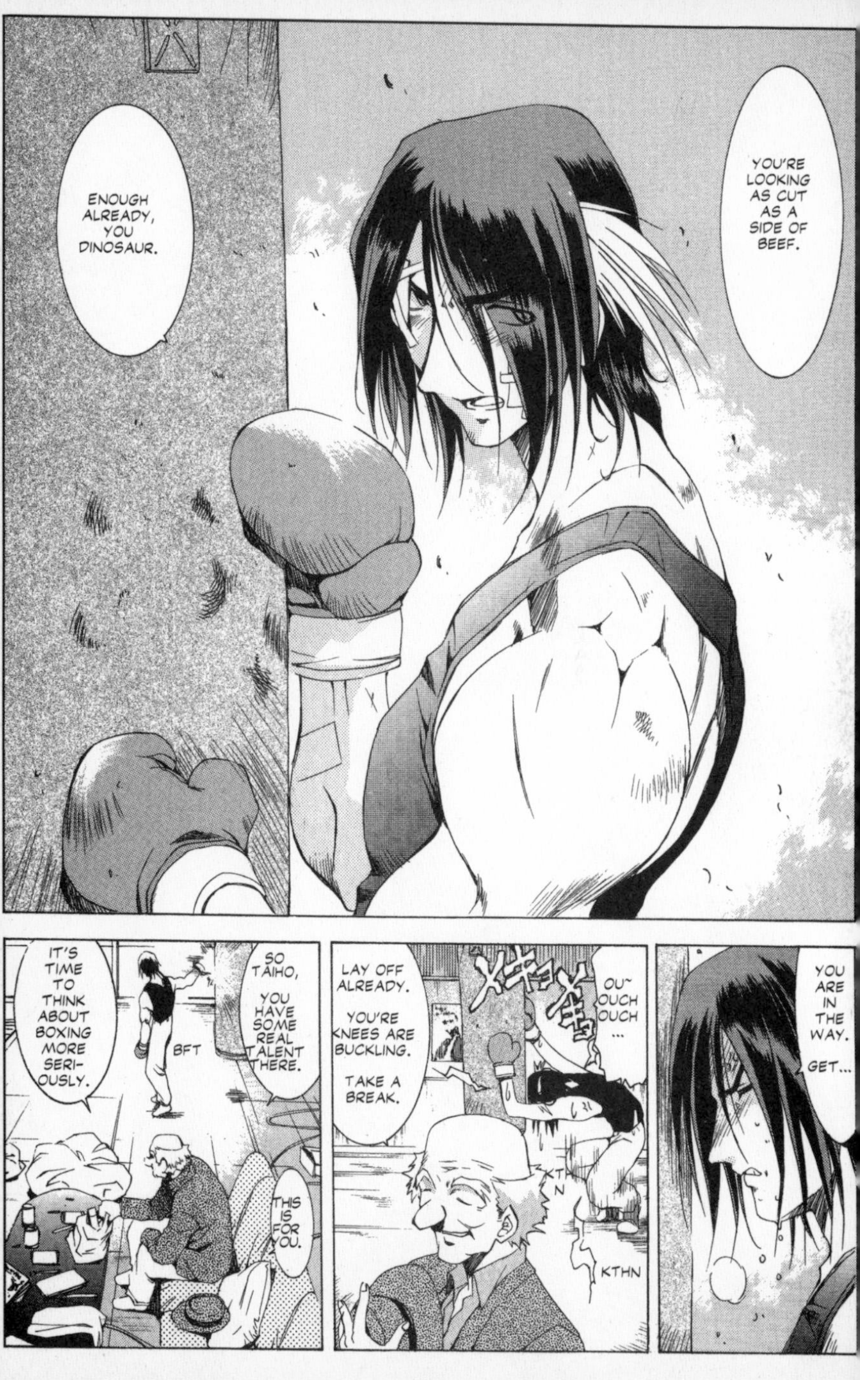
YOU'RE LOOKING AS CUT AS A SIDE OF BEEF.
ENOUGH ALREADY, YOU DINOSAUR.
YOU ARE IN THE WAY.
GET...
OU~ OUCH OUCH ...
LAY OFF ALREADY.
YOU'RE KNEES ARE BUCKLING.
TAKE A BREAK.
KTHN
KTHN
SO TAIHO, YOU HAVE SOME REAL TALENT THERE.
IT'S TIME TO THINK ABOUT BOXING MORE SERI-OUSLY.
BFT
THIS IS FOR YOU.

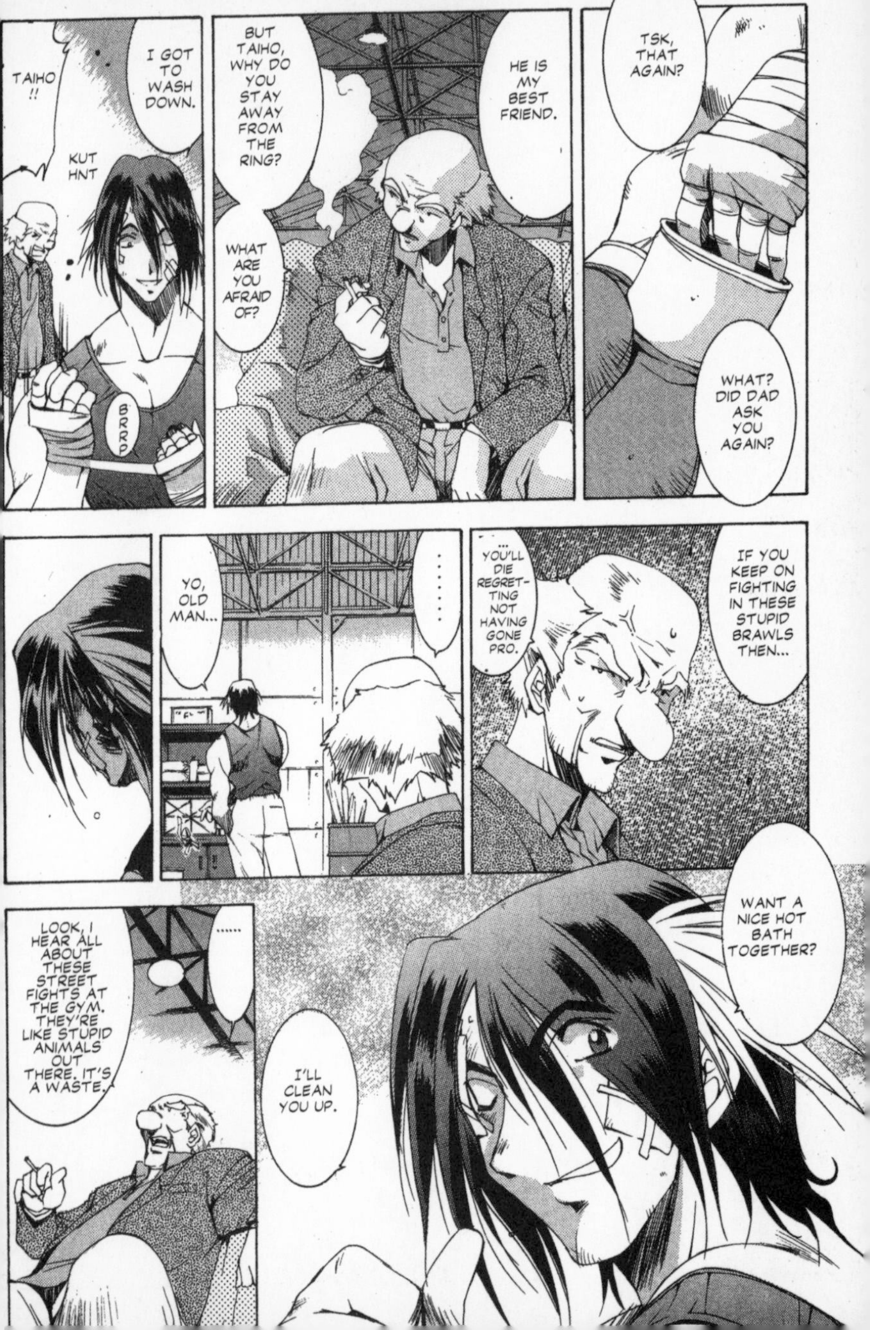
TSK, THAT AGAIN?
WHAT? DID DAD ASK YOU AGAIN?
HE IS MY BEST FRIEND.
BUT TAIHO, WHY DO YOU STAY AWAY FROM THE RING?
WHAT ARE YOU AFRAID OF?
I GOT TO WASH DOWN.
TAIHO !!
KUT HNT
BRRP
IF YOU KEEP ON FIGHTING IN THESE STUPID BRAWLS THEN...
... YOU'LL DIE REGRETTING NOT HAVING GONE PRO.
......
YO, OLD MAN...
WANT A NICE HOT BATH TOGETHER?
I'LL CLEAN YOU UP.
......
LOOK, I HEAR ALL ABOUT THESE STREET FIGHTS AT THE GYM. THEY'RE LIKE STUPID ANIMALS OUT THERE. IT'S A WASTE.

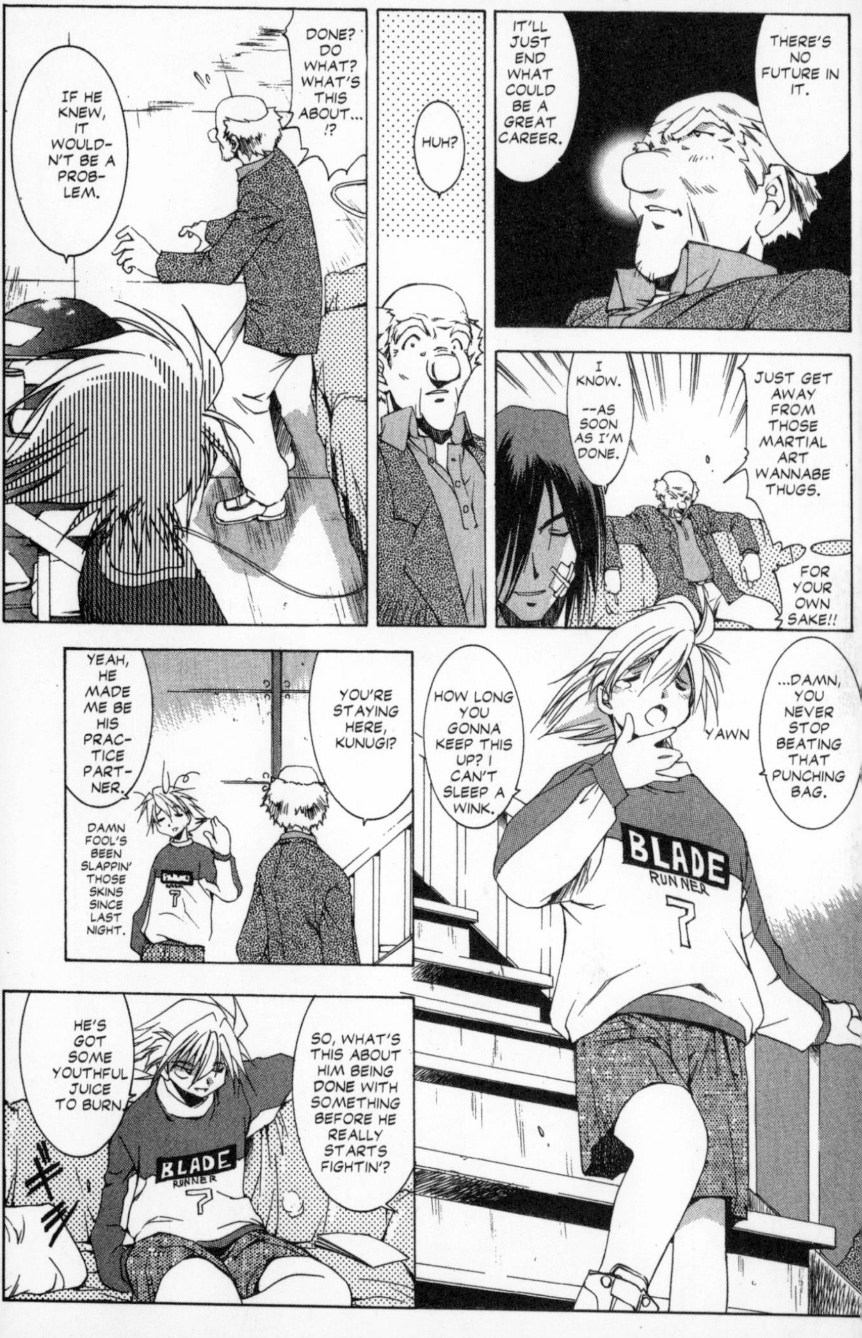
THERE'S NO FUTURE IN IT.
IT'LL JUST END WHAT COULD BE A GREAT CAREER.
JUST GET AWAY FROM THOSE MARTIAL ART WANNABE THUGS.
FOR YOUR OWN SAKE!!
I KNOW.
--AS SOON AS I'M DONE.
HUH?
DONE? DO WHAT? WHAT'S THIS ABOUT...!?
IF HE KNEW, IT WOULDN'T BE A PROBLEM.
...DAMN, YOU NEVER STOP BEATING THAT PUNCHING BAG.
YAWN
HOW LONG YOU GONNA KEEP THIS UP? I CAN'T SLEEP A WINK.
BLADE RUNNER 7
YOU'RE STAYING HERE, KUNUGI?
YEAH, HE MADE ME BE HIS PRACTICE PARTNER.
DAMN FOOL'S BEEN SLAPPIN' THOSE SKINS SINCE LAST NIGHT.
SO, WHAT'S THIS ABOUT HIM BEING DONE WITH SOMETHING BEFORE HE REALLY STARTS FIGHTIN'?
HE'S GOT SOME YOUTHFUL JUICE TO BURN.
BLADE RUNNER 7

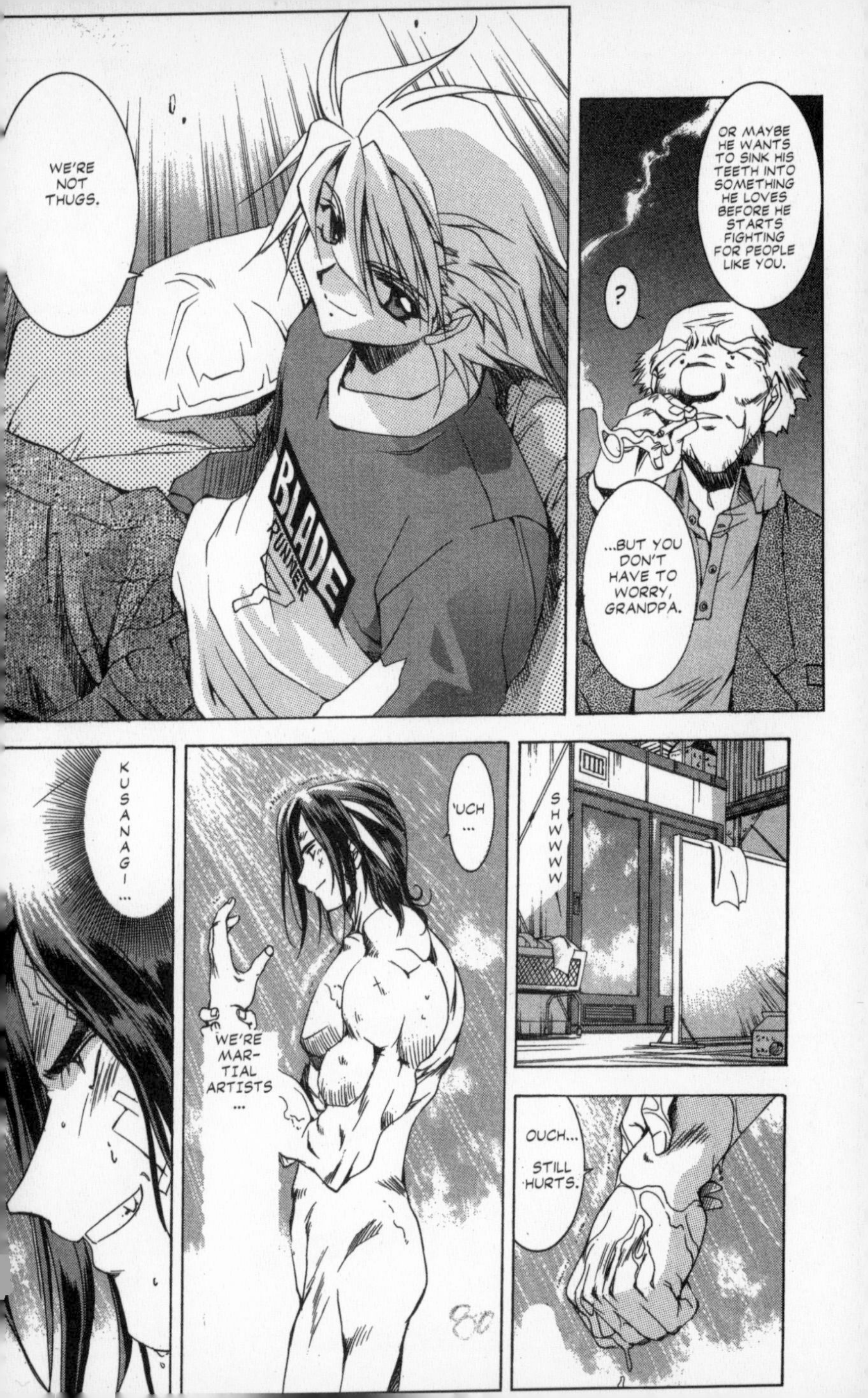
OR MAYBE HE WANTS TO SINK HIS TEETH INTO SOMETHING HE LOVES BEFORE HE STARTS FIGHTING FOR PEOPLE LIKE YOU.
?
...BUT YOU DON'T HAVE TO WORRY, GRANDPA.
WE'RE NOT THUGS.
SHWWWW
OUCH... STILL HURTS.
'UCH ...
WE'RE MAR-TIAL ARTISTS ...
KUSANAGI ...

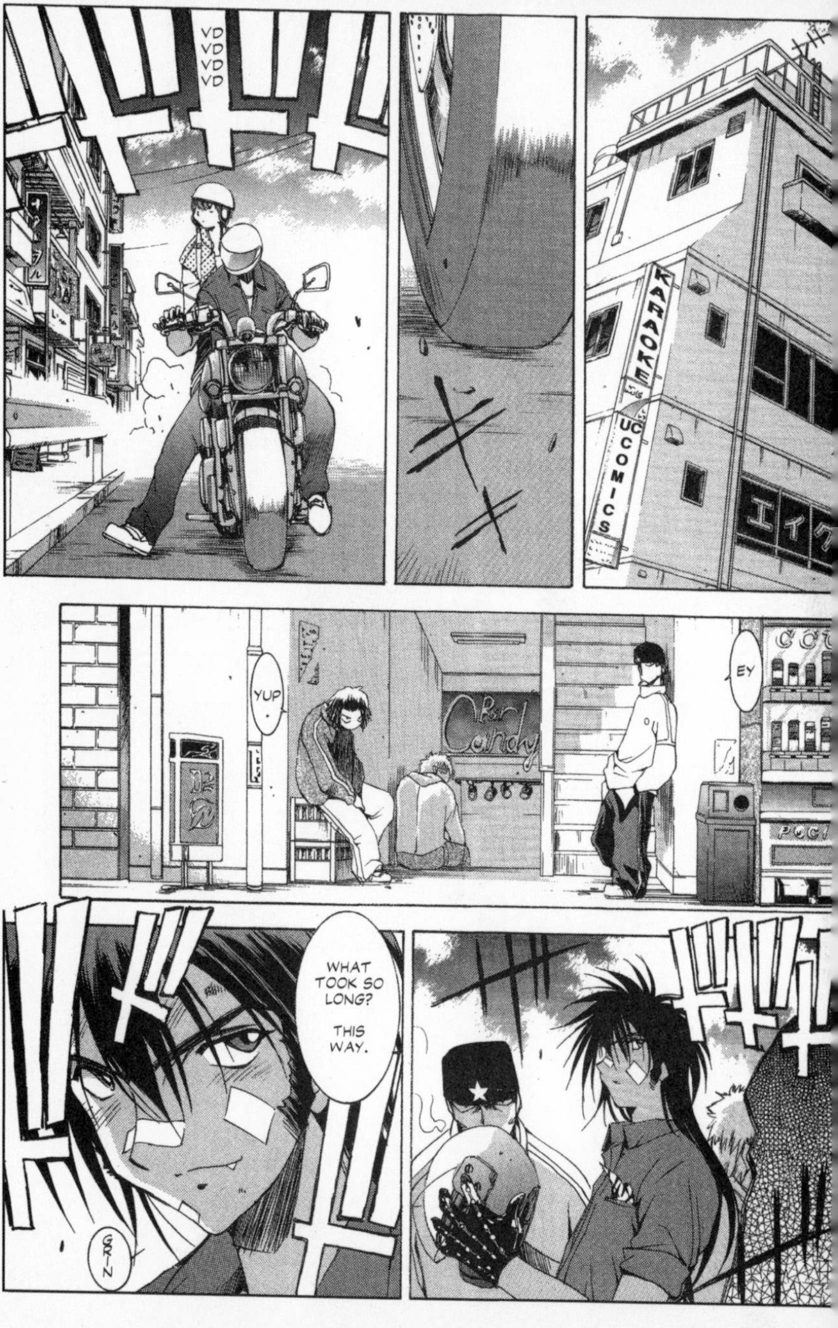
KARAOKE
UC COMICS
VD VD VD VD
EY
Bar Candy
YUP
WHAT TOOK SO LONG?
THIS WAY.
GRIN

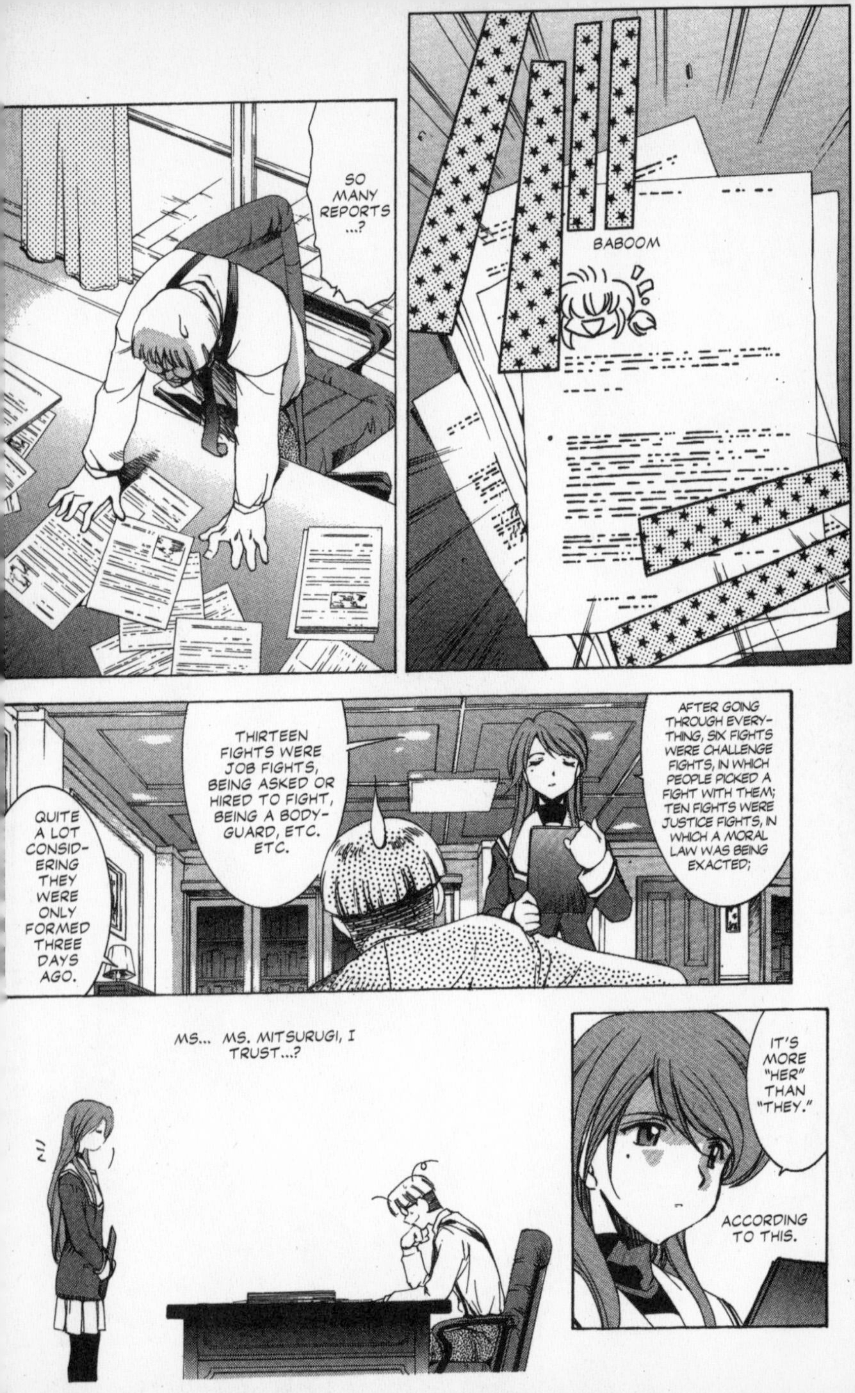
BABOOM
SO MANY REPORTS ...?
AFTER GOING THROUGH EVERYTHING, SIX FIGHTS WERE CHALLENGE FIGHTS, IN WHICH PEOPLE PICKED A FIGHT WITH THEM; TEN FIGHTS WERE JUSTICE FIGHTS, IN WHICH A MORAL LAW WAS BEING EXACTED;
THIRTEEN FIGHTS WERE JOB FIGHTS, BEING ASKED OR HIRED TO FIGHT, BEING A BODYGUARD, ETC. ETC.
QUITE A LOT CONSIDERING THEY WERE ONLY FORMED THREE DAYS AGO.
IT'S MORE "HER" THAN "THEY."
ACCORDING TO THIS.
MS... MS. MITSURUGI, I TRUST...?

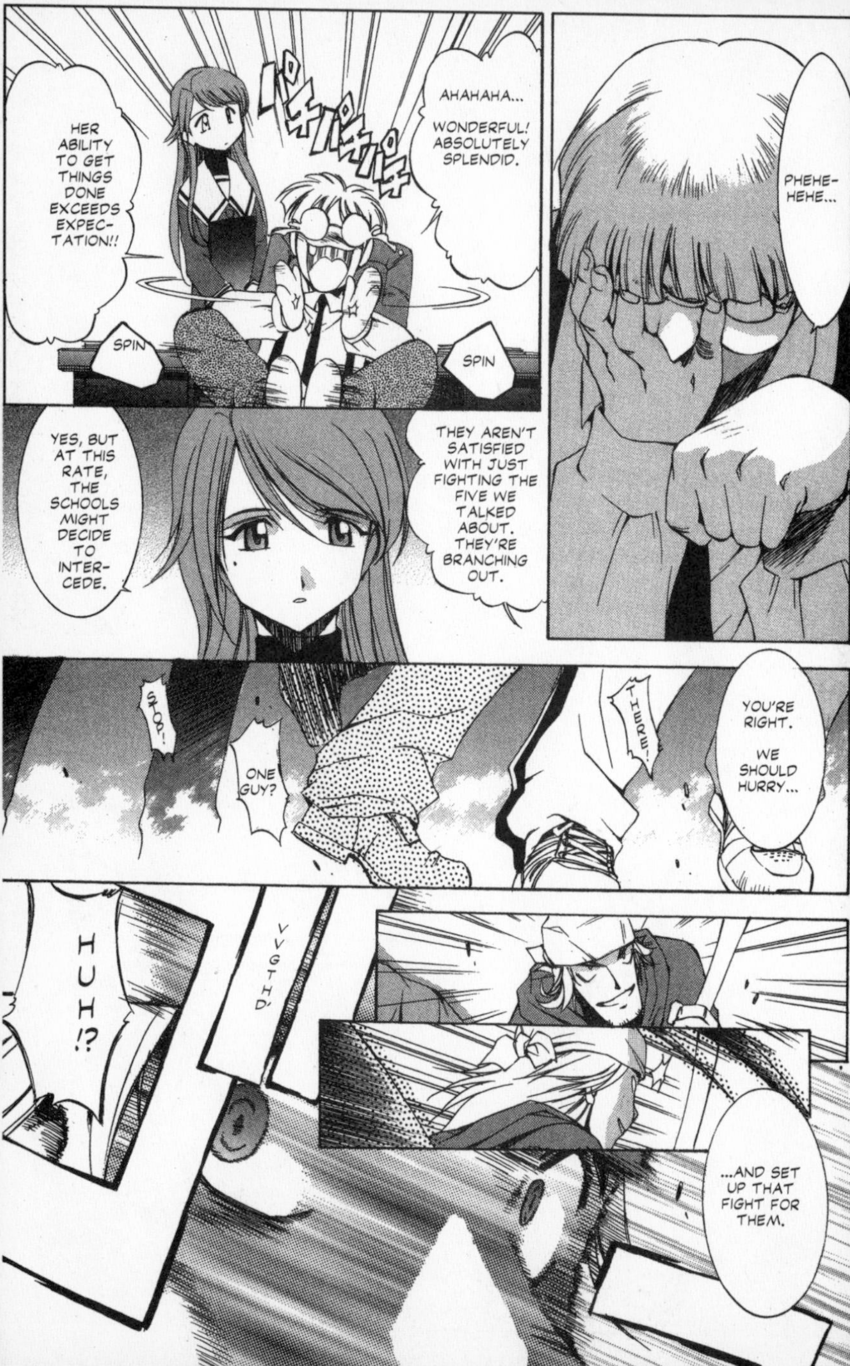
PHEHE-HEHE...
AHAHAHA...
WONDERFUL! ABSOLUTELY SPLENDID.
HER ABILITY TO GET THINGS DONE EXCEEDS EXPECTATION!!
SPIN
SPIN
THEY AREN'T SATISFIED WITH JUST FIGHTING THE FIVE WE TALKED ABOUT. THEY'RE BRANCHING OUT.
YES, BUT AT THIS RATE, THE SCHOOLS MIGHT DECIDE TO INTERCEDE.
YOU'RE RIGHT.
WE SHOULD HURRY...
THERE!
ONE GUY?
STOP!
...AND SET UP THAT FIGHT FOR THEM.
VVGTHD!
HUH!?

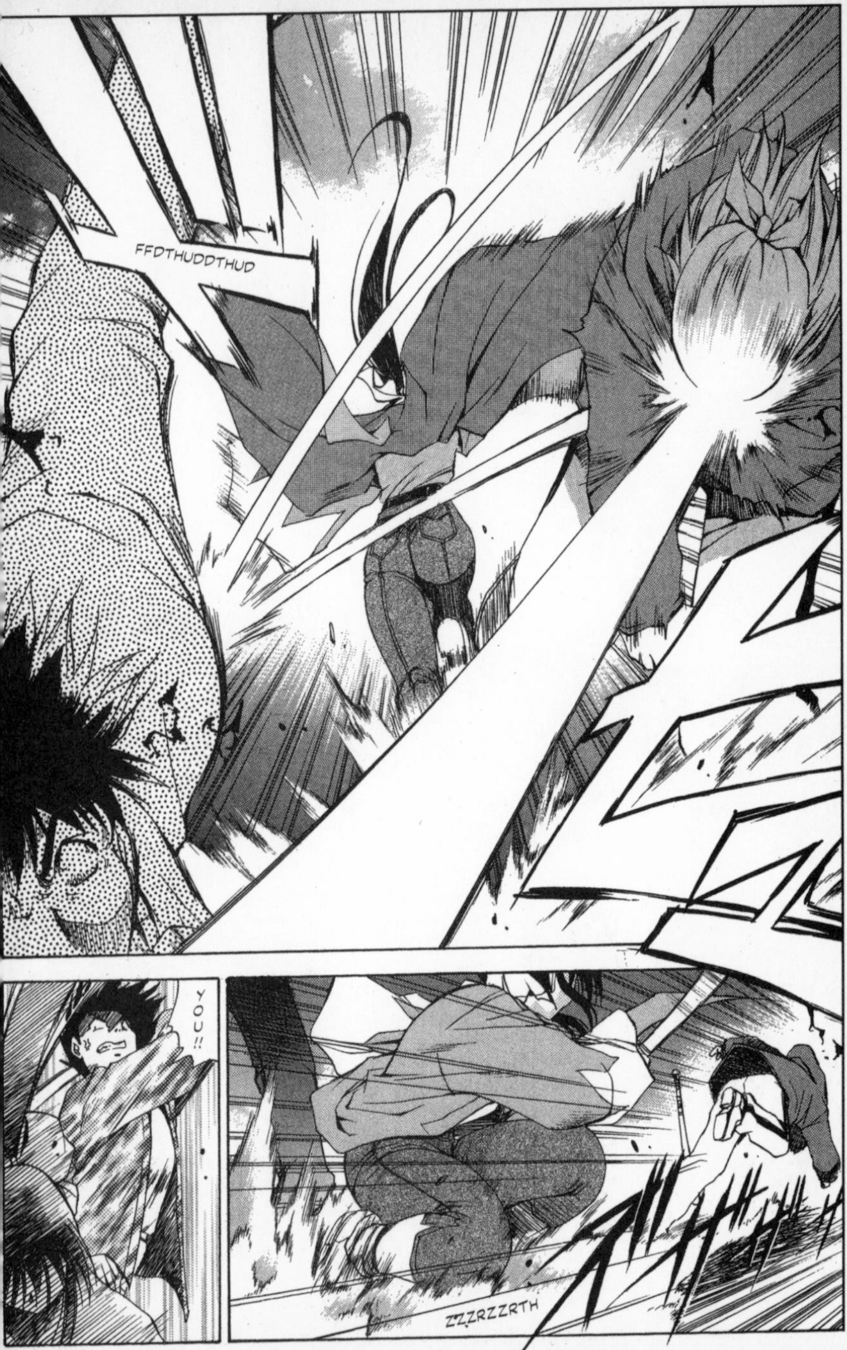
FFDTHUDDTHUD
ZZZRZZRTH
YOU!!

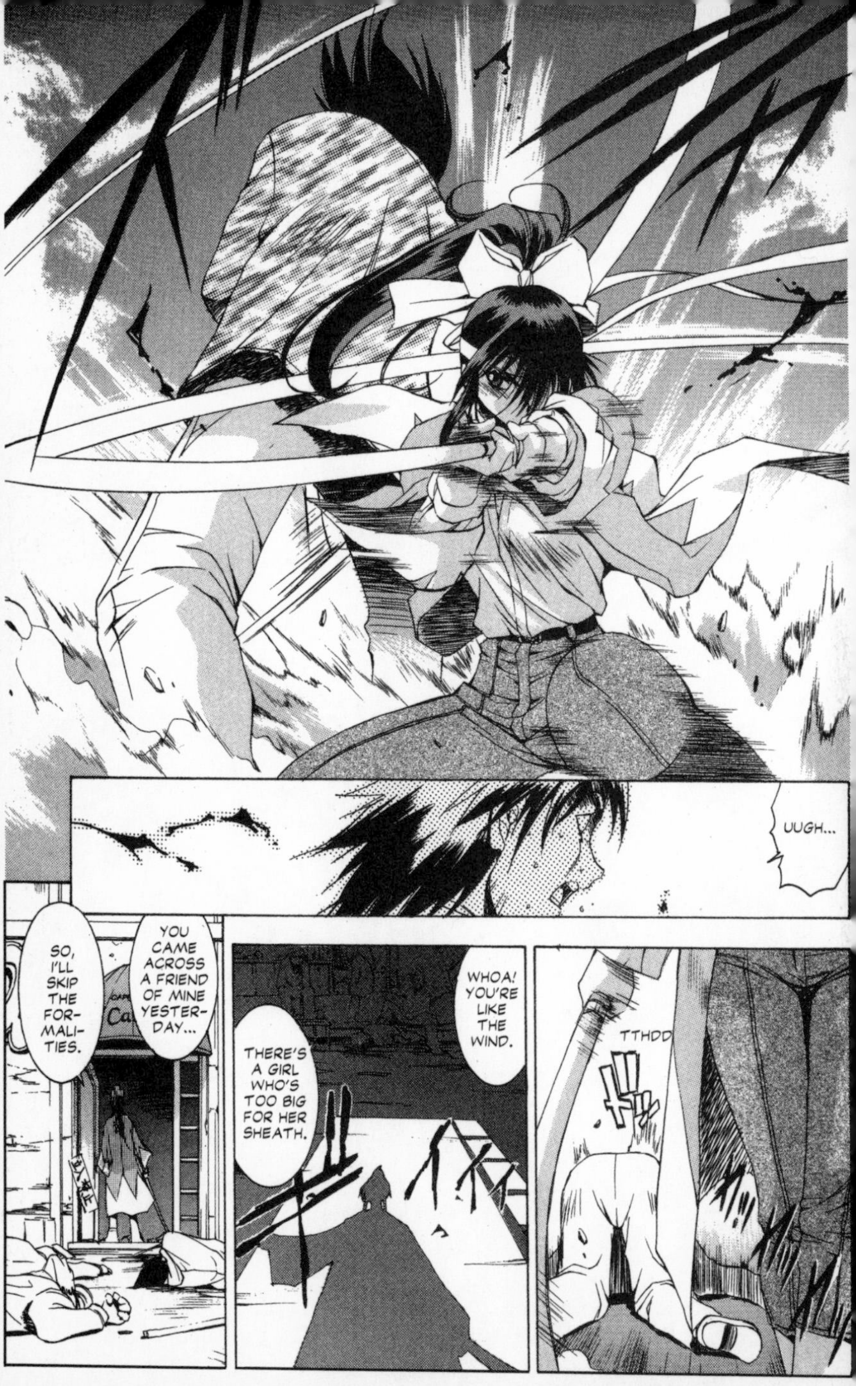
UUGH...
TTHDD
WHOA! YOU'RE LIKE THE WIND.
THERE'S A GIRL WHO'S TOO BIG FOR HER SHEATH.
YOU CAME ACROSS A FRIEND OF MINE YESTERDAY...
SO, I'LL SKIP THE FORMALITIES.

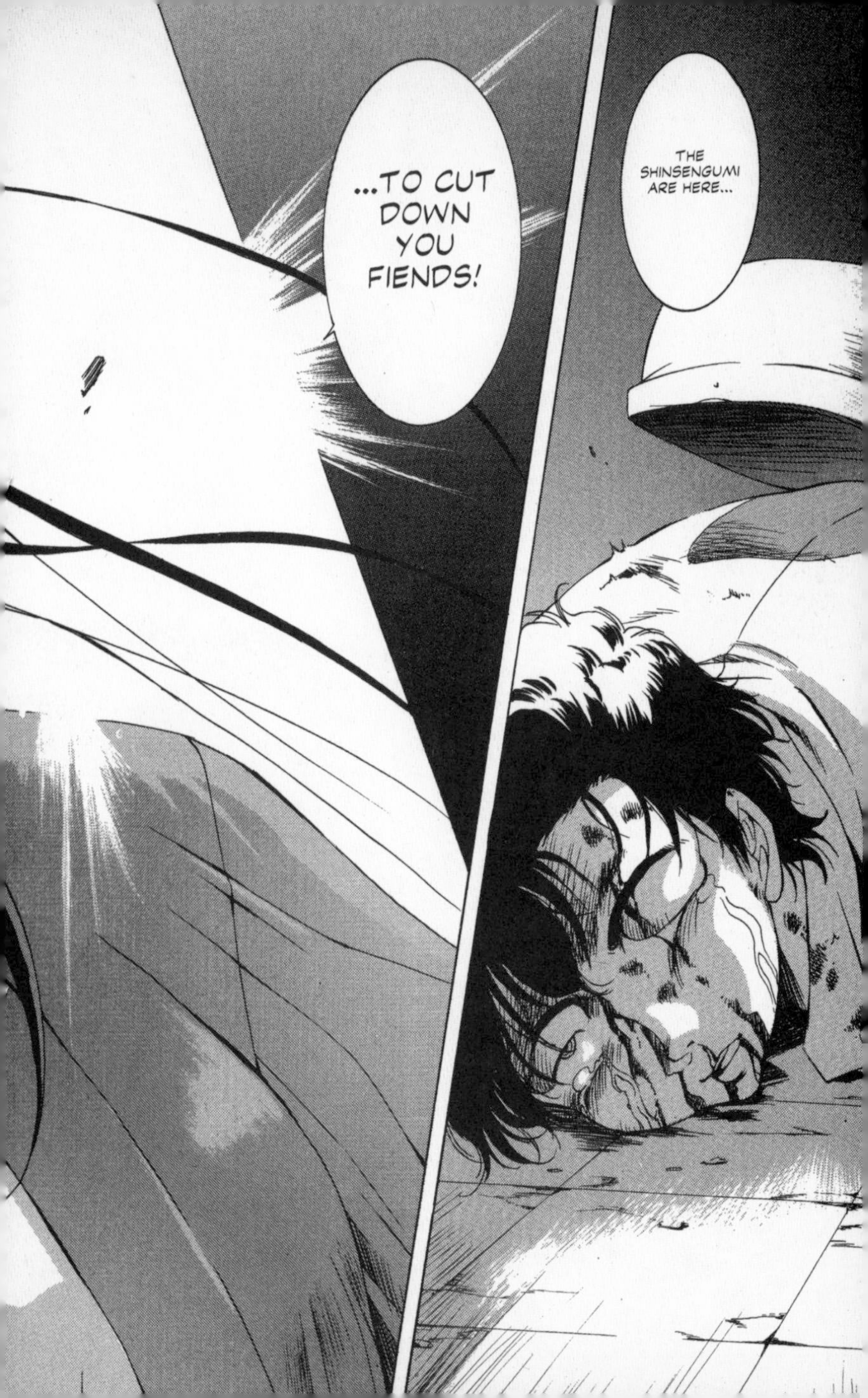
THE SHINSENGUMI ARE HERE...
...TO CUT DOWN YOU FIENDS!

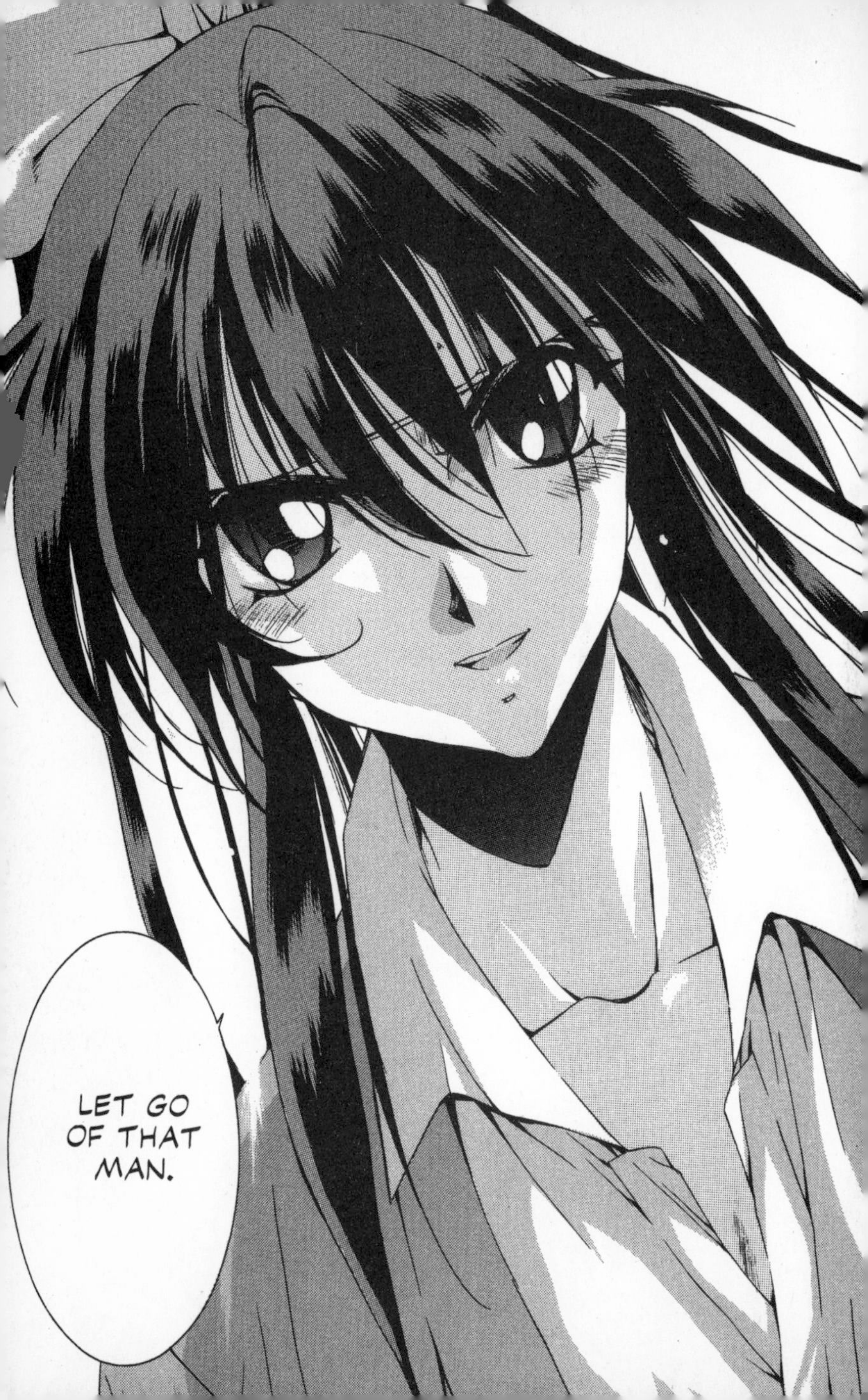
LET GO OF THAT MAN.

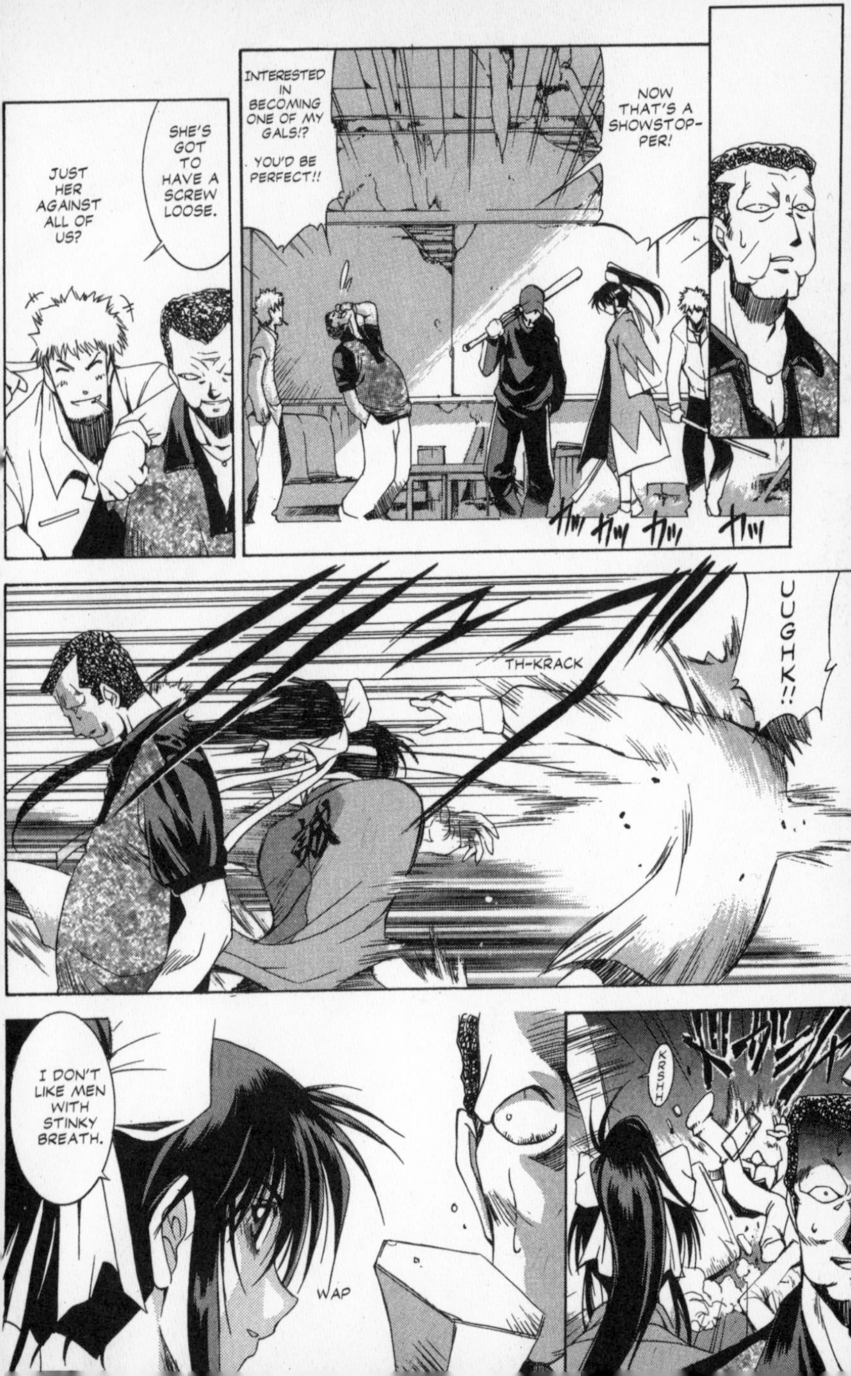
NOW THAT'S A SHOWSTOPPER!
INTERESTED IN BECOMING ONE OF MY GALS!?
YOU'D BE PERFECT!!
SHE'S GOT TO HAVE A SCREW LOOSE.
JUST HER AGAINST ALL OF US?
UUGHK!!
TH-KRACK
KRSHH
I DON'T LIKE MEN WITH STINKY BREATH.
WAP

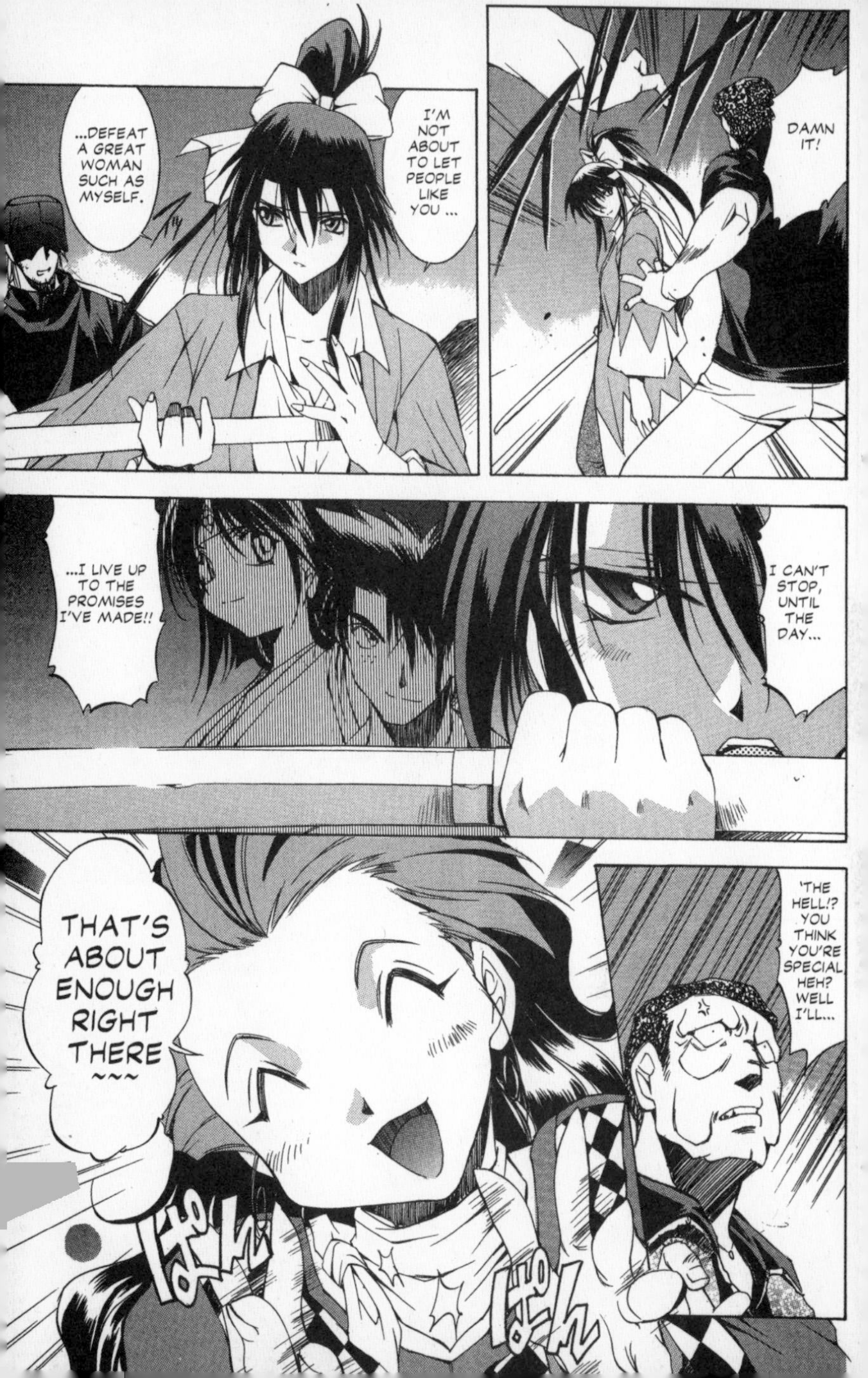
DAMN IT!
I'M NOT ABOUT TO LET PEOPLE LIKE YOU ...
...DEFEAT A GREAT WOMAN SUCH AS MYSELF.
I CAN'T STOP, UNTIL THE DAY...
...I LIVE UP TO THE PROMISES I'VE MADE!!
'THE HELL!? YOU THINK YOU'RE SPECIAL HEH? WELL I'LL...
THAT'S ABOUT ENOUGH RIGHT THERE ~~~

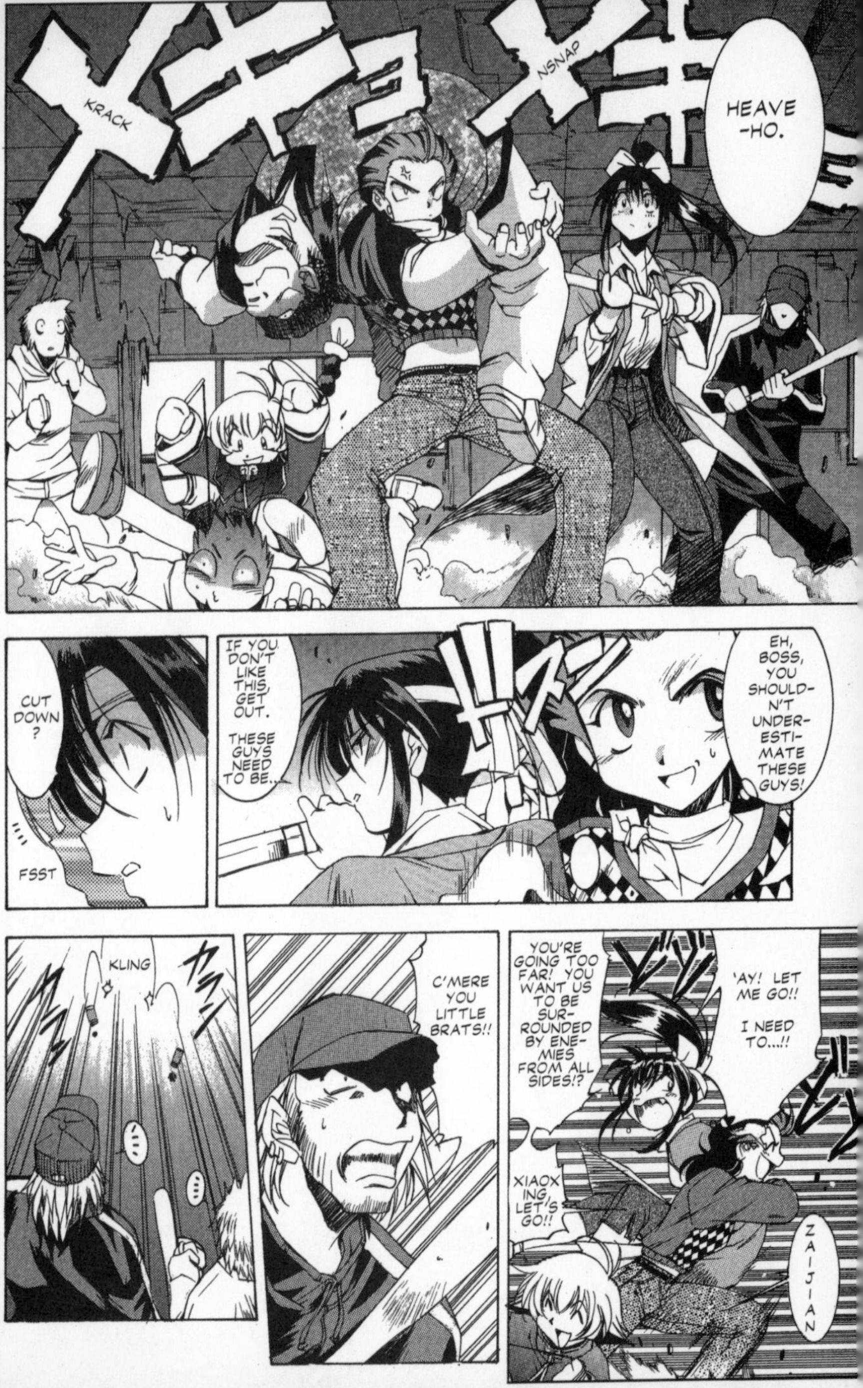
HEAVE-HO.
NSNAP
KRACK
EH, BOSS, YOU SHOULDN'T UNDERESTIMATE THESE GUYS!
IF YOU DON'T LIKE THIS, GET OUT.
THESE GUYS NEED TO BE...
CUT DOWN?
...
FSST
'AY! LET ME GO!!
I NEED TO...!!
YOU'RE GOING TOO FAR! YOU WANT US TO BE SURROUNDED BY ENEMIES FROM ALL SIDES!?
XIAOXING, LET'S GO!!
ZAIJIAN
C'MERE YOU LITTLE BRATS!!
KLING
!...
...

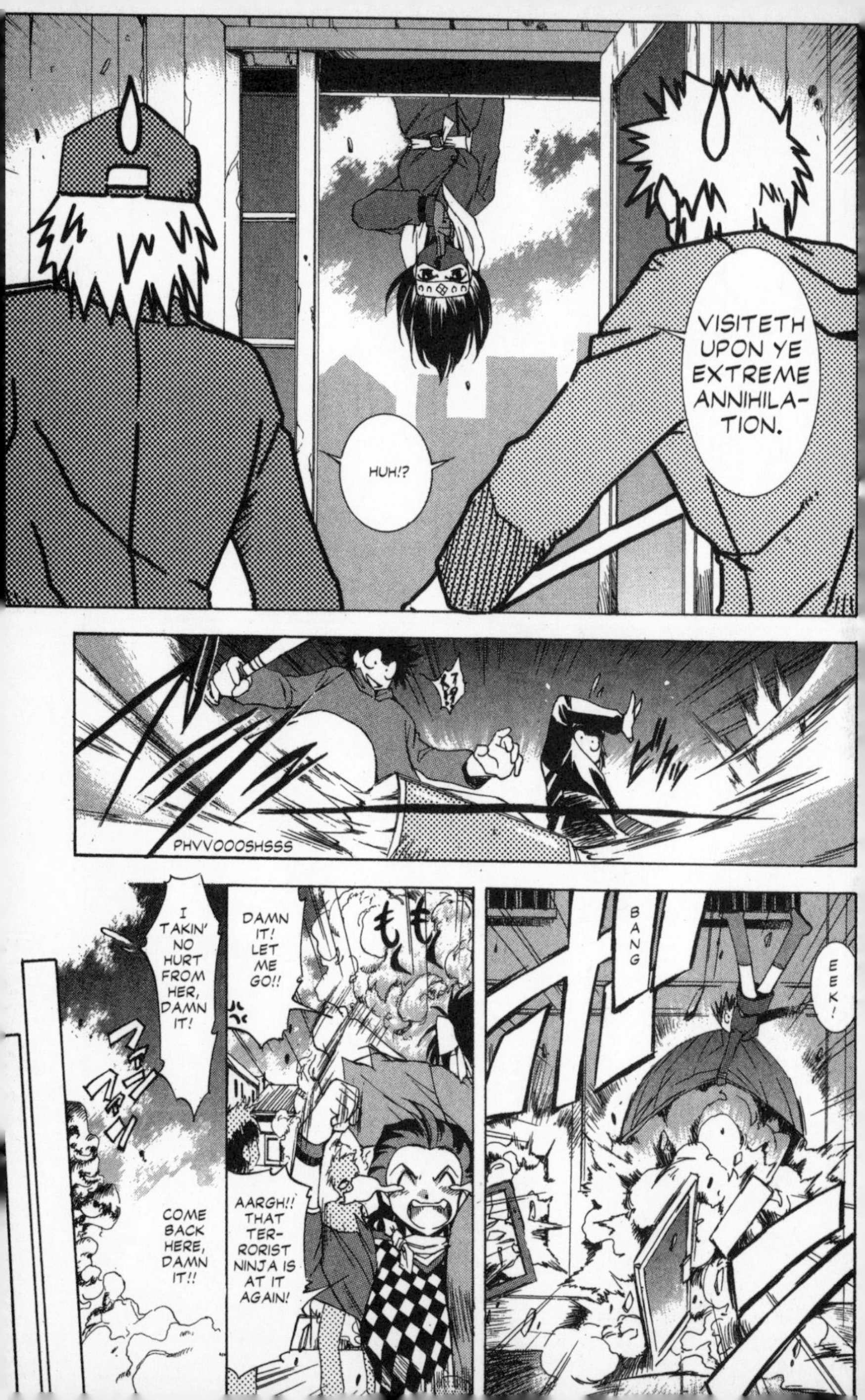
VISITETH UPON YE EXTREME ANNIHILATION.
HUH!?
PHVVOOOSHSSS
EEK!
BANG
DAMN IT! LET ME GO!!
AARGH!! THAT TERRORIST NINJA IS AT IT AGAIN!
I TAKIN' NO HURT FROM HER, DAMN IT!
COME BACK HERE, DAMN IT!!

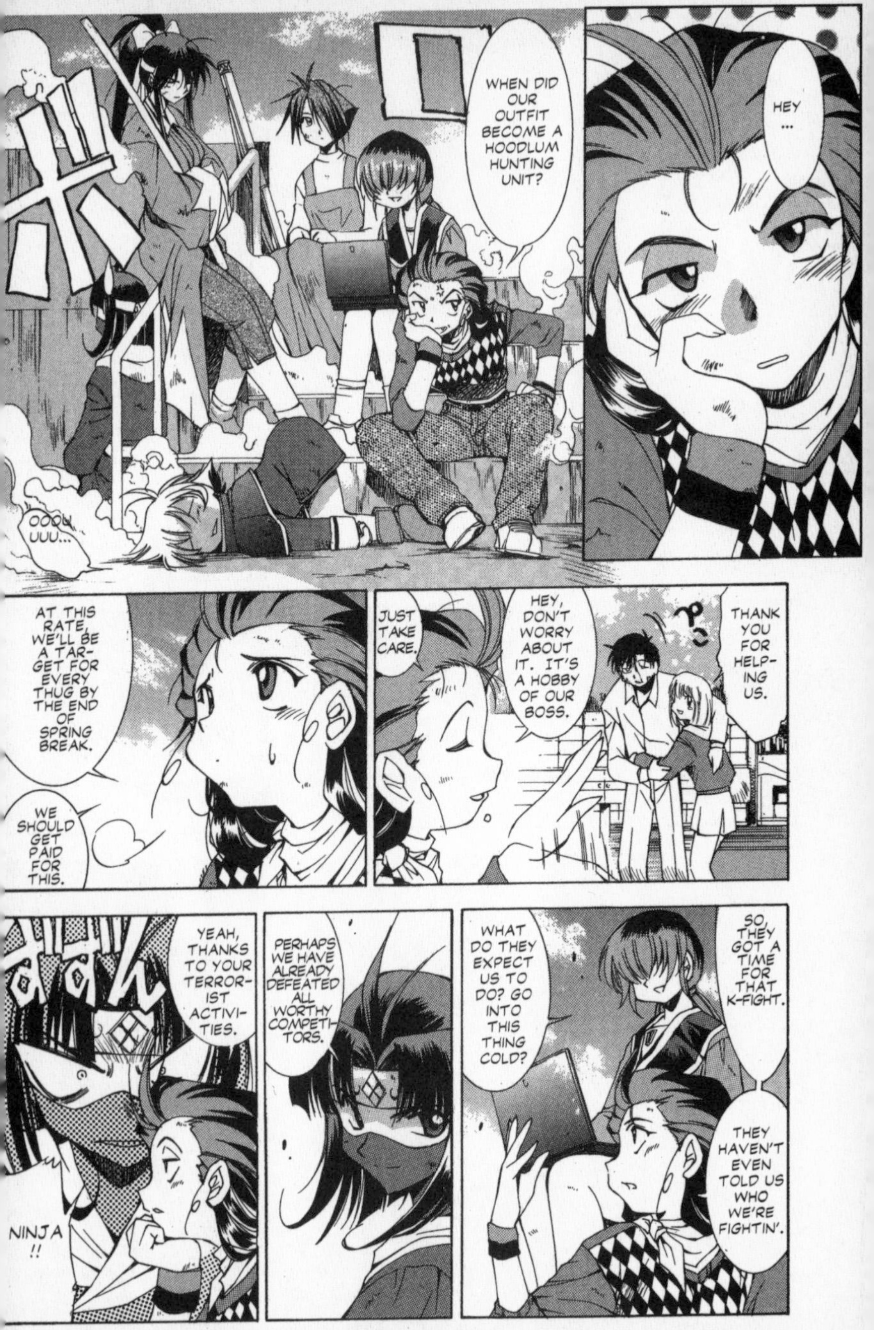
HEY ...
WHEN DID OUR OUTFIT BECOME A HOODLUM HUNTING UNIT?
OOOU UUU...
THANK YOU FOR HELPING US.
HEY, DON'T WORRY ABOUT IT. IT'S A HOBBY OF OUR BOSS.
JUST TAKE CARE.
AT THIS RATE, WE'LL BE A TARGET FOR EVERY THUG BY THE END OF SPRING BREAK.
WE SHOULD GET PAID FOR THIS.
SO, THEY GOT A TIME FOR THAT K-FIGHT.
THEY HAVEN'T EVEN TOLD US WHO WE'RE FIGHTIN'.
WHAT DO THEY EXPECT US TO DO? GO INTO THIS THING COLD?
PERHAPS WE HAVE ALREADY DEFEATED ALL WORTHY COMPETITORS.
YEAH, THANKS TO YOUR TERRORIST ACTIVITIES.
NINJA !!

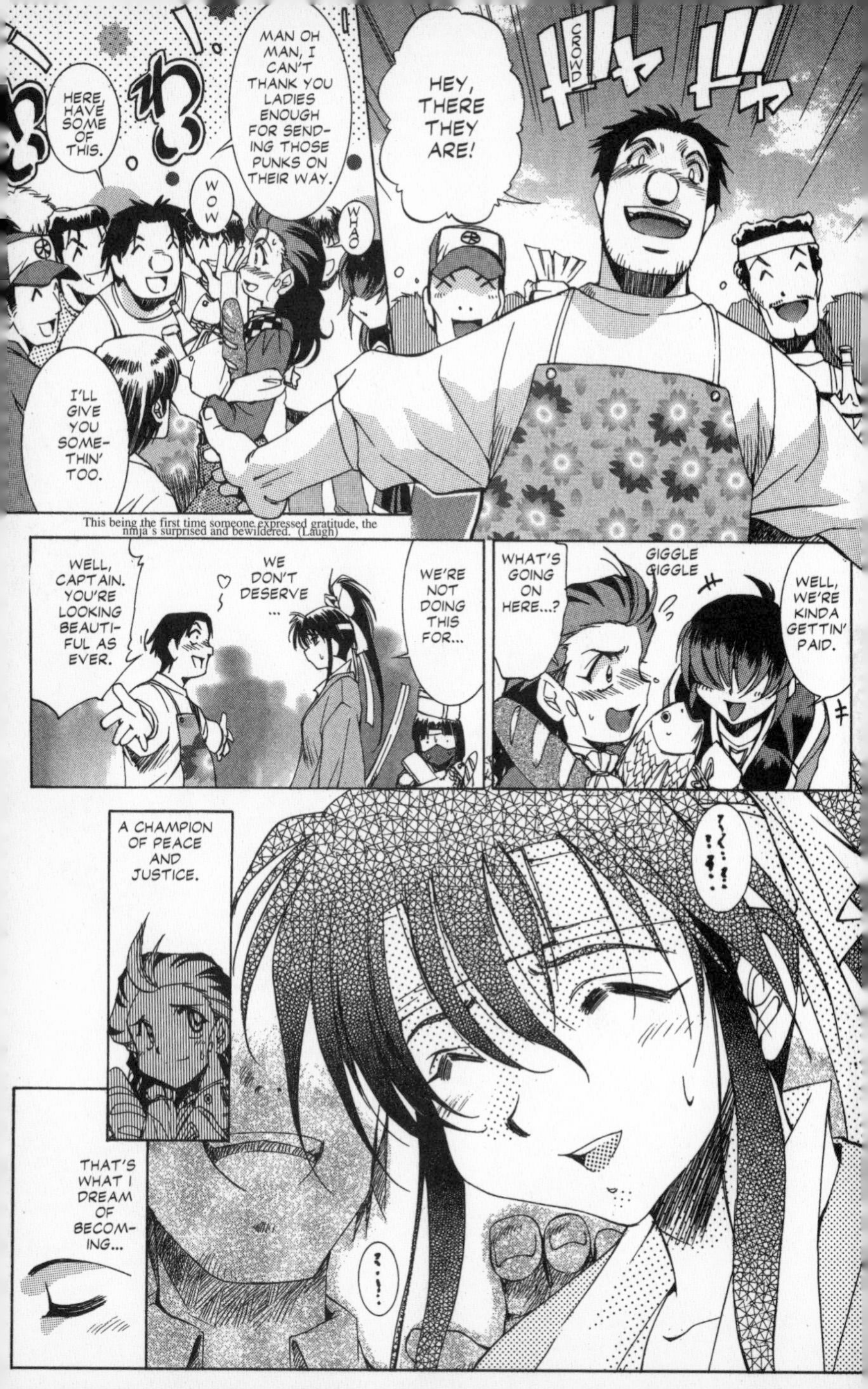
CROWD
HEY, THERE THEY ARE!
MAN OH MAN, I CAN'T THANK YOU LADIES ENOUGH FOR SENDING THOSE PUNKS ON THEIR WAY.
HERE, HAVE SOME OF THIS.
WOW
WHOA
I'LL GIVE YOU SOMETHIN' TOO.
This being the first time someone expressed gratitude, the ninja's surprised and bewildered. (Laugh)
WELL, WE'RE KINDA GETTIN' PAID.
GIGGLE GIGGLE
WHAT'S GOING ON HERE...?
WE'RE NOT DOING THIS FOR...
WE DON'T DESERVE...
WELL, CAPTAIN. YOU'RE LOOKING BEAUTIFUL AS EVER.
A CHAMPION OF PEACE AND JUSTICE.
THAT'S WHAT I DREAM OF BECOMING...

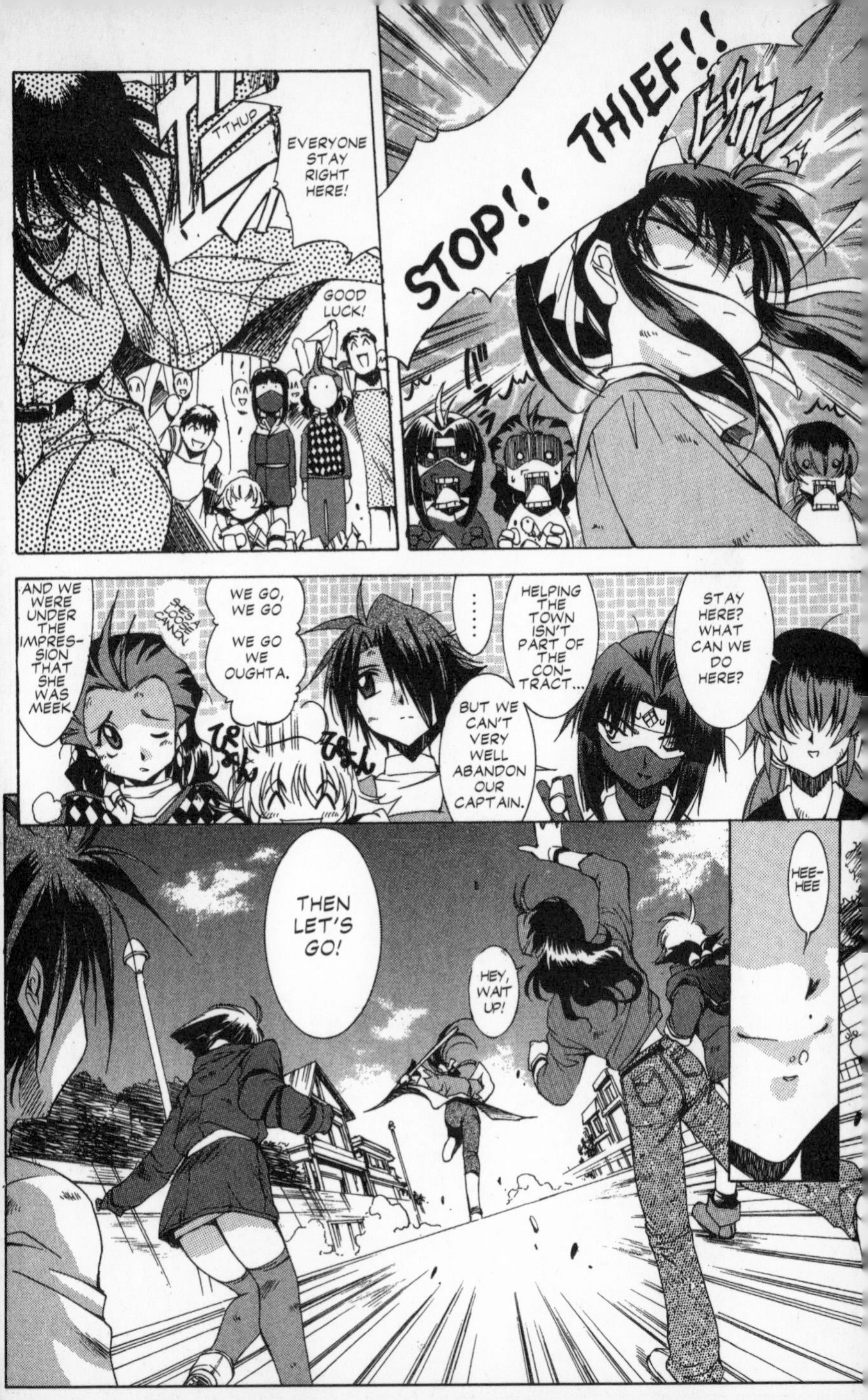
STOP!! THIEF!!
TTHUP
EVERYONE STAY RIGHT HERE!
GOOD LUCK!
STAY HERE? WHAT CAN WE DO HERE?
HELPING THE TOWN ISN'T PART OF THE CON-TRACT...
BUT WE CAN'T VERY WELL ABANDON OUR CAPTAIN.
......
WE GO, WE GO
WE GO WE OUGHTA.
SHE'S A LOOSE CANNON
AND WE WERE UNDER THE IMPRES-SION THAT SHE WAS MEEK.
HEE-HEE
THEN LET'S GO!
HEY, WAIT UP!

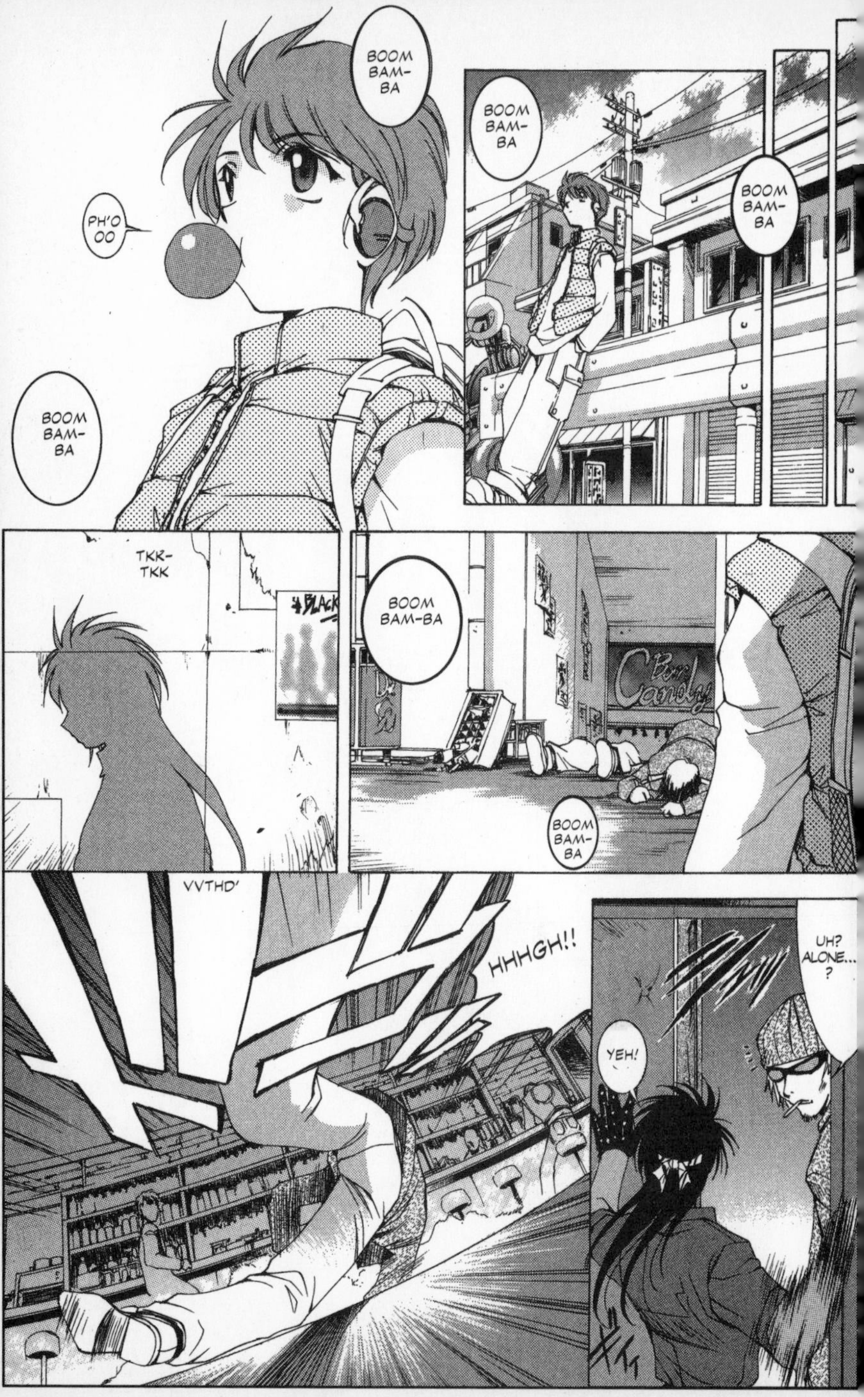

BOOM BAM-BA
BOOM BAM-BA
BOOM BAM-BA
PH'O OO
BOOM BAM-BA
BOOM BAM-BA
BOOM BAM-BA
TKR-TKK
UH? ALONE... ?
YEH!
HHHGH!!
VVTHD'

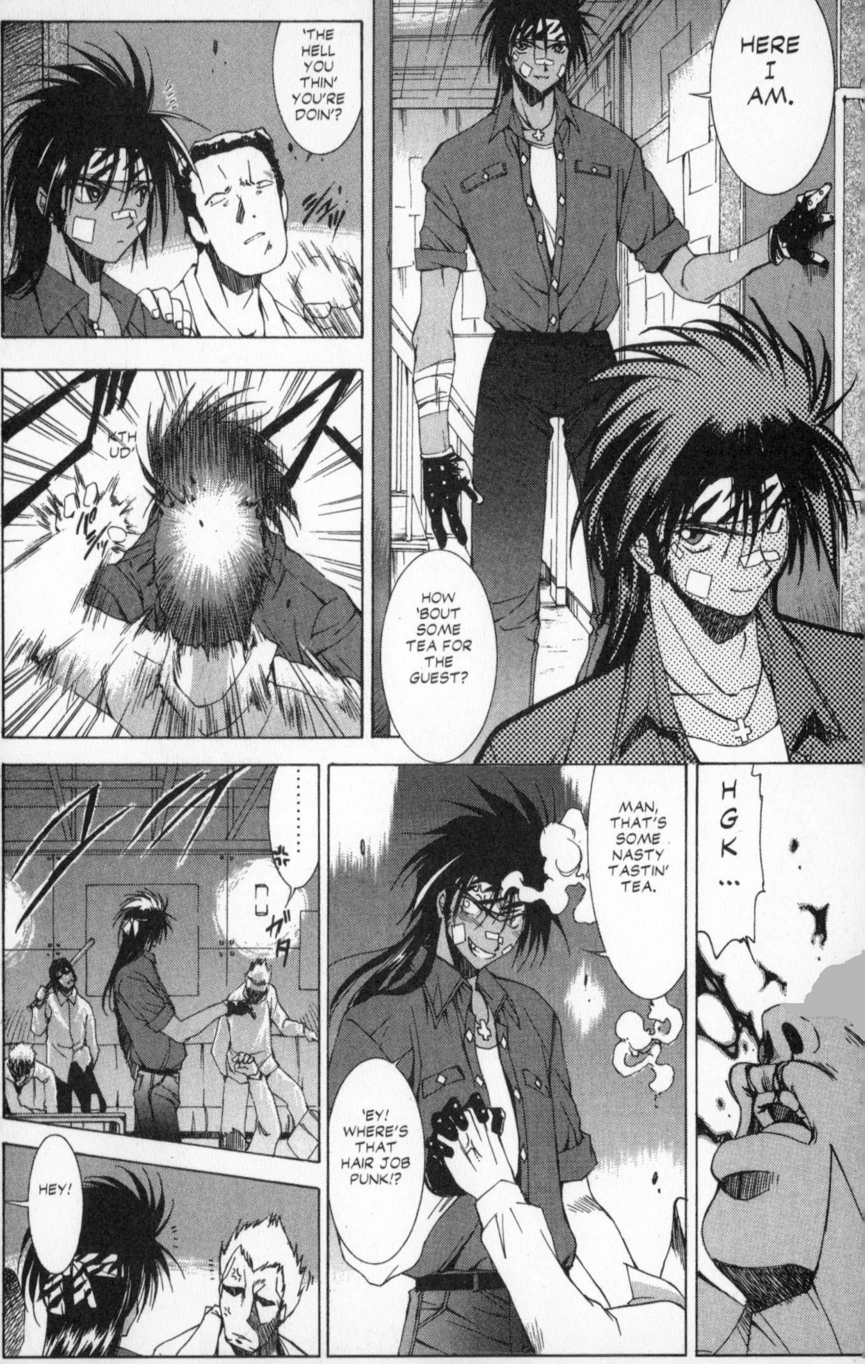

HERE I AM.
HOW 'BOUT SOME TEA FOR THE GUEST?
'THE HELL YOU THIN' YOU'RE DOIN'?
KTH UD'
HGK ...
MAN, THAT'S SOME NASTY TASTIN' TEA.
'EY! WHERE'S THAT HAIR JOB PUNK!?
......
HEY!

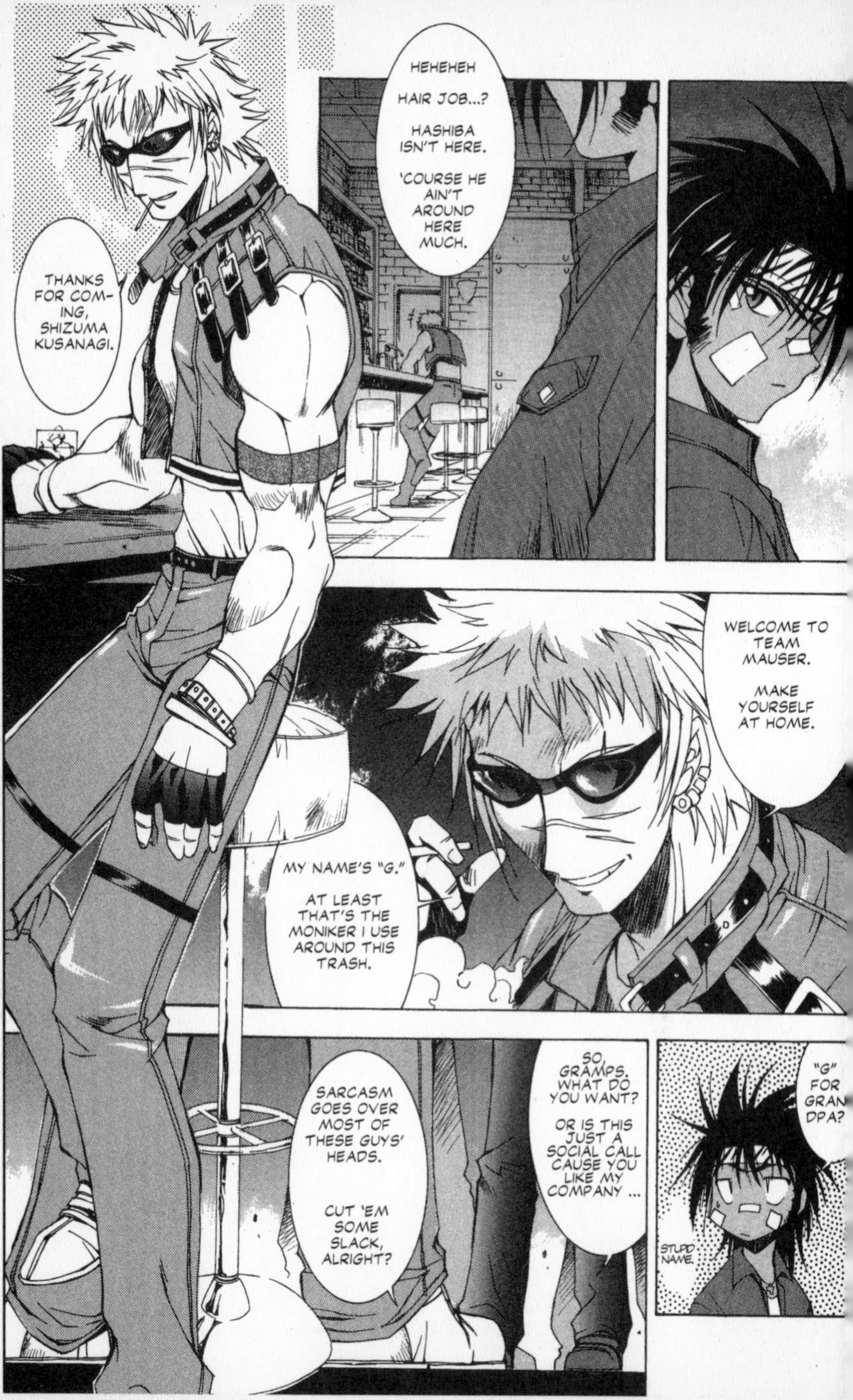
HEHEHEH
HAIR JOB...?
HASHIBA ISN'T HERE.
'COURSE HE AIN'T AROUND HERE MUCH.
THANKS FOR COMING, SHIZUMA KUSANAGI.
WELCOME TO TEAM MAUSER.
MAKE YOURSELF AT HOME.
MY NAME'S "G."
AT LEAST THAT'S THE MONIKER I USE AROUND THIS TRASH.
"G" FOR GRANDPA?
STUPID NAME.
SO, GRAMPS, WHAT DO YOU WANT?
OR IS THIS JUST A SOCIAL CALL CAUSE YOU LIKE MY COMPANY ...
SARCASM GOES OVER MOST OF THESE GUYS' HEADS.
CUT 'EM SOME SLACK, ALRIGHT?

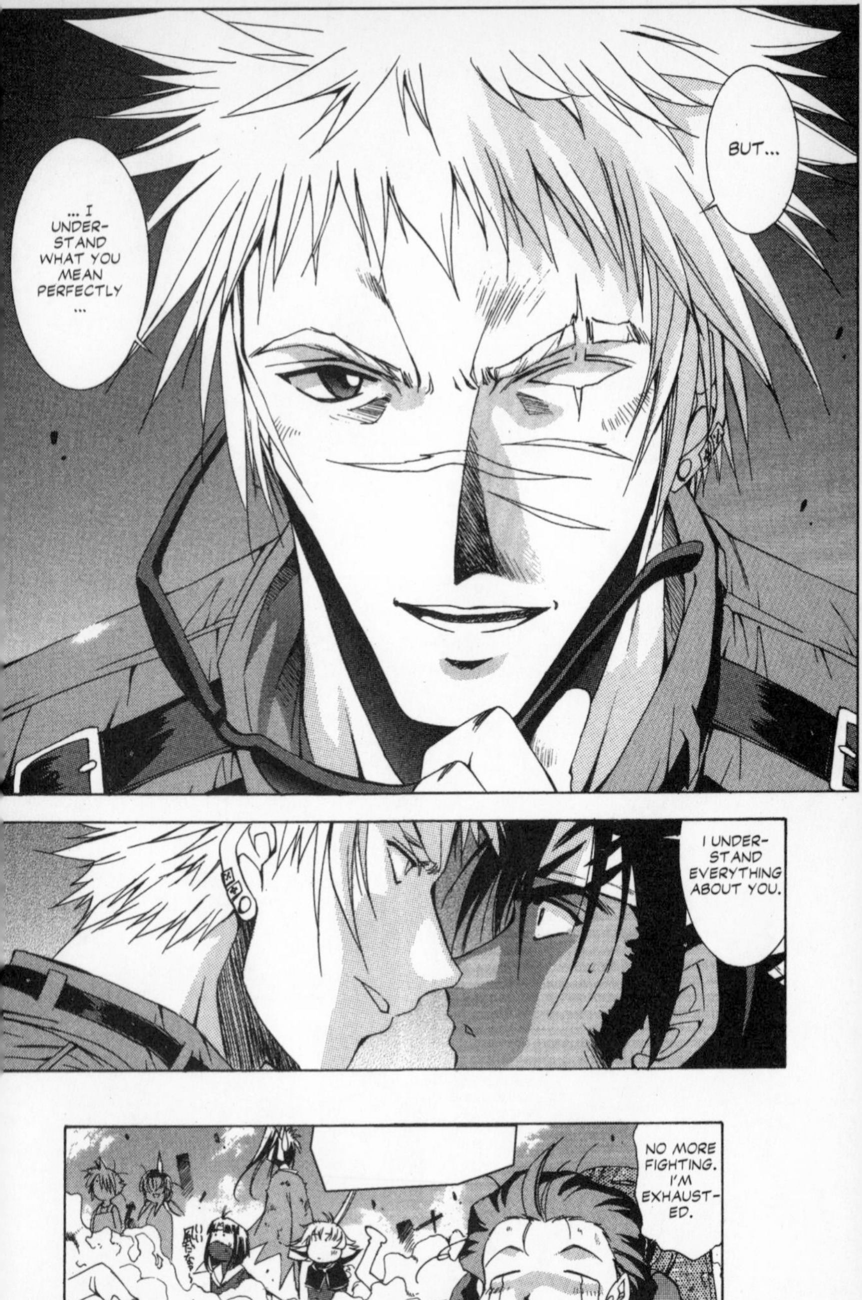
BUT...
... I UNDER-STAND WHAT YOU MEAN PERFECTLY ...
I UNDER-STAND EVERYTHING ABOUT YOU.
NO MORE FIGHTING. I'M EXHAUST-ED.

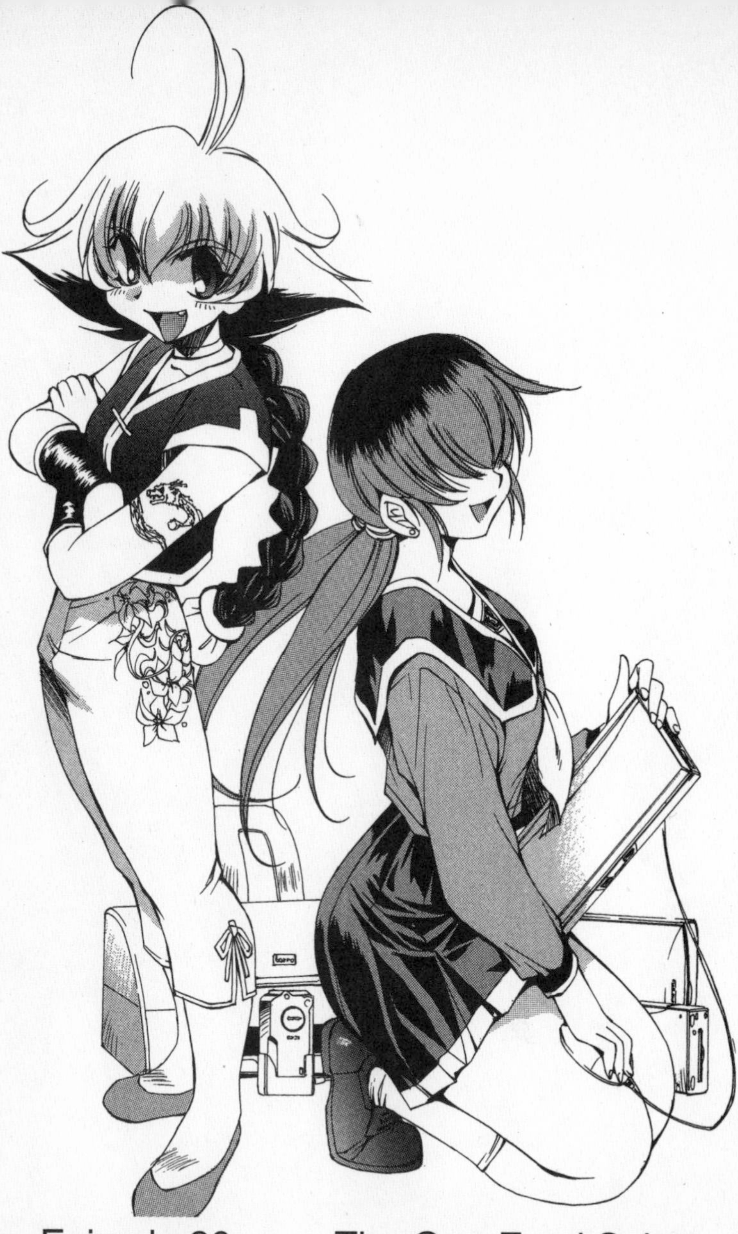

Episode 26 The One-Eyed Saints

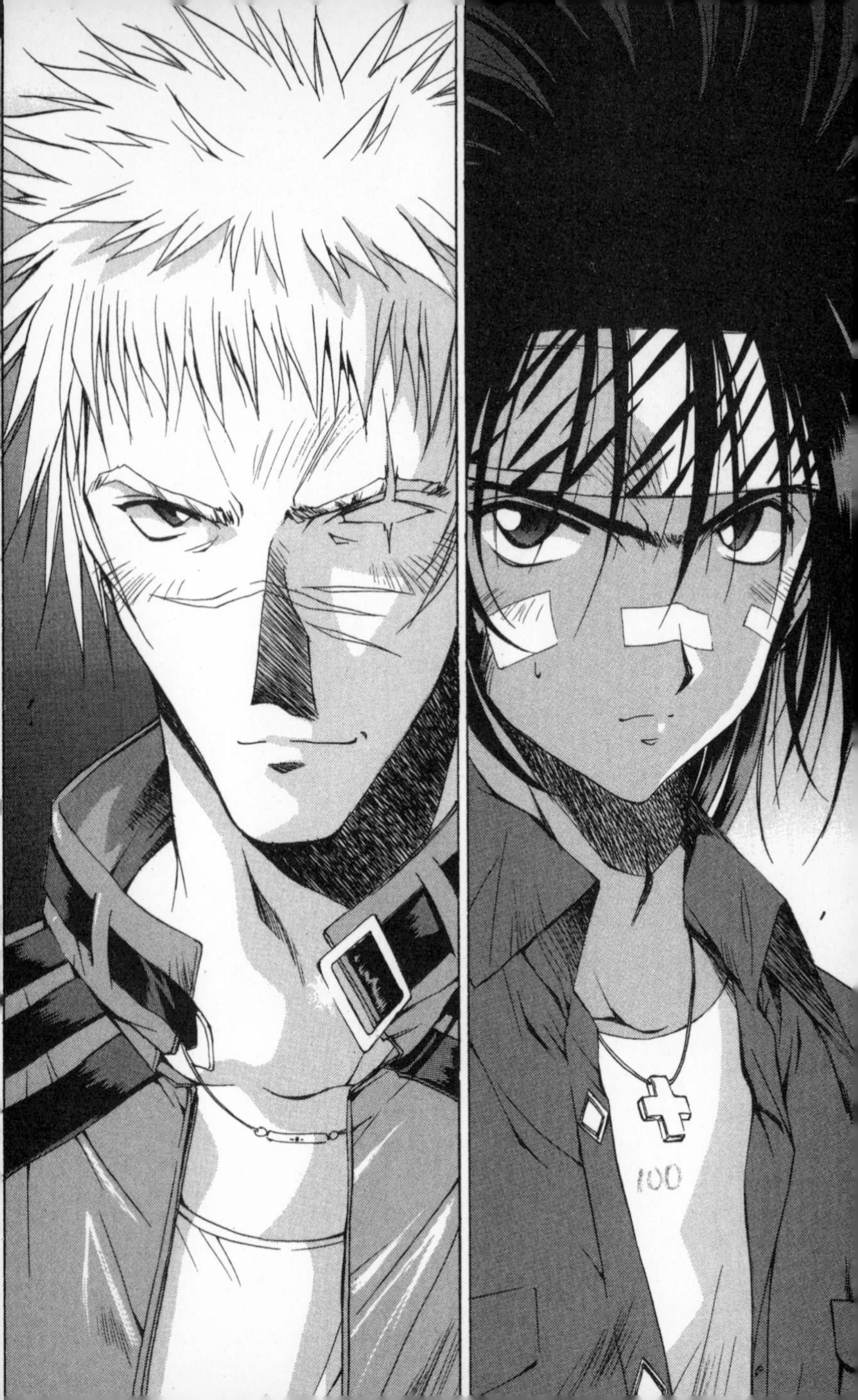
100

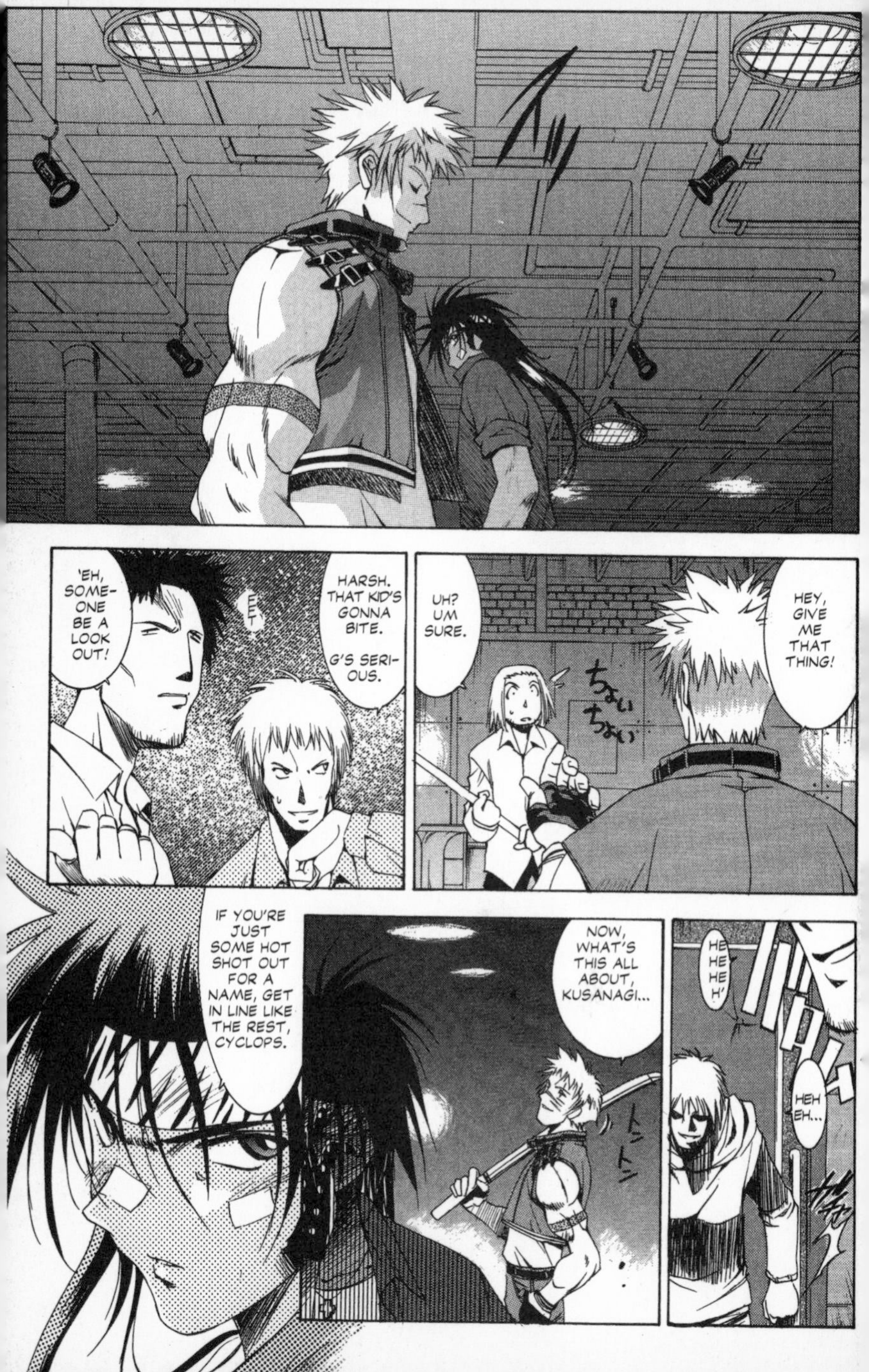
HEY, GIVE ME THAT THING!
UH? UM SURE.
ちょい ちょい
HARSH. THAT KID'S GONNA BITE.
G'S SERIOUS.
'EH, SOMEONE BE A LOOK OUT!
HE HE HE H'
HEH EH...
NOW, WHAT'S THIS ALL ABOUT, KUSANAGI...
IF YOU'RE JUST SOME HOT SHOT OUT FOR A NAME, GET IN LINE LIKE THE REST, CYCLOPS.

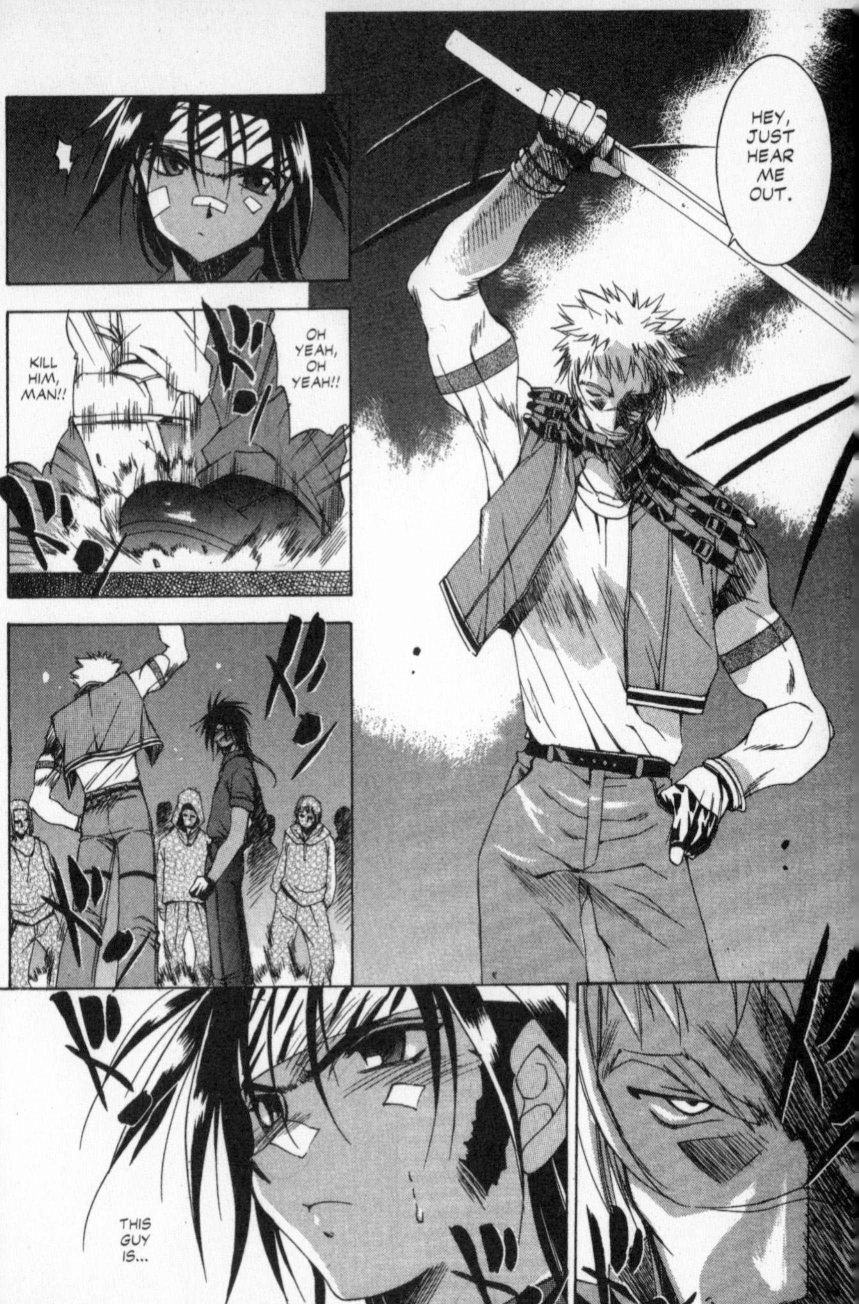
HEY, JUST HEAR ME OUT.
OH YEAH, OH YEAH!!
KILL HIM, MAN!!
THIS GUY IS...

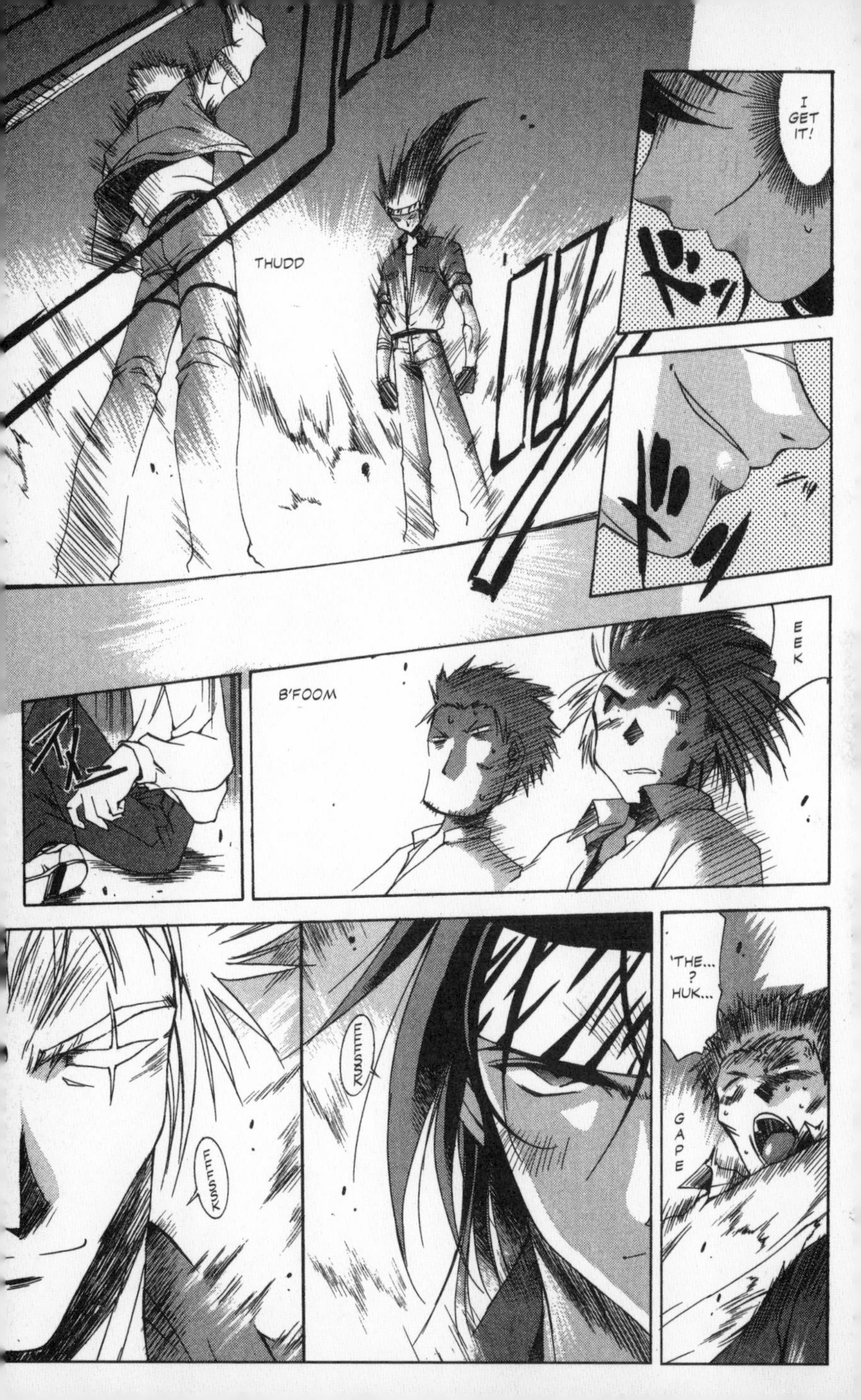
I GET IT!
THUDD
EEK
B'FOOM
'THE...?
HUK...
GAPE
KUSSHHH
KUSSHHH

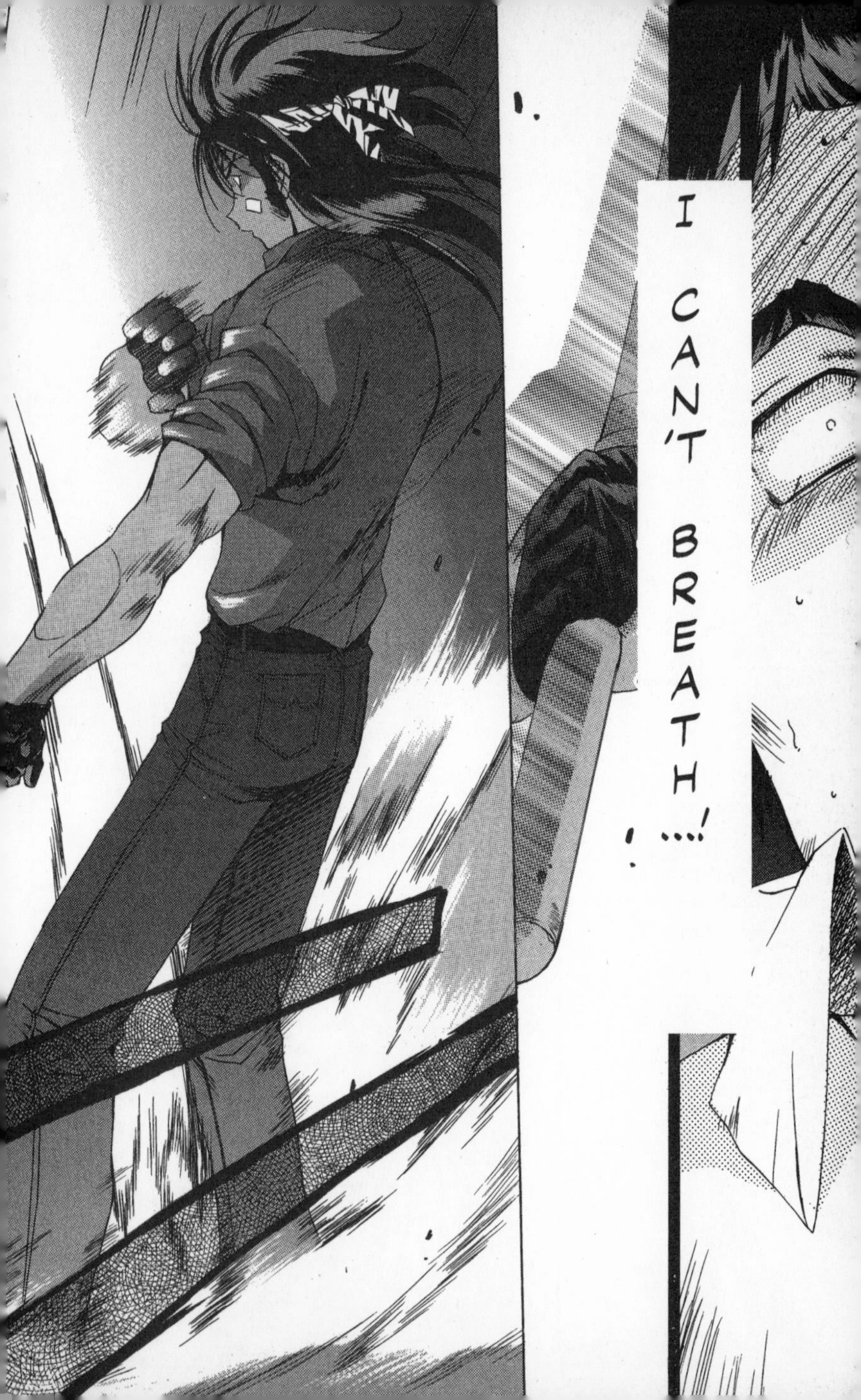
I CAN'T BREATH....!

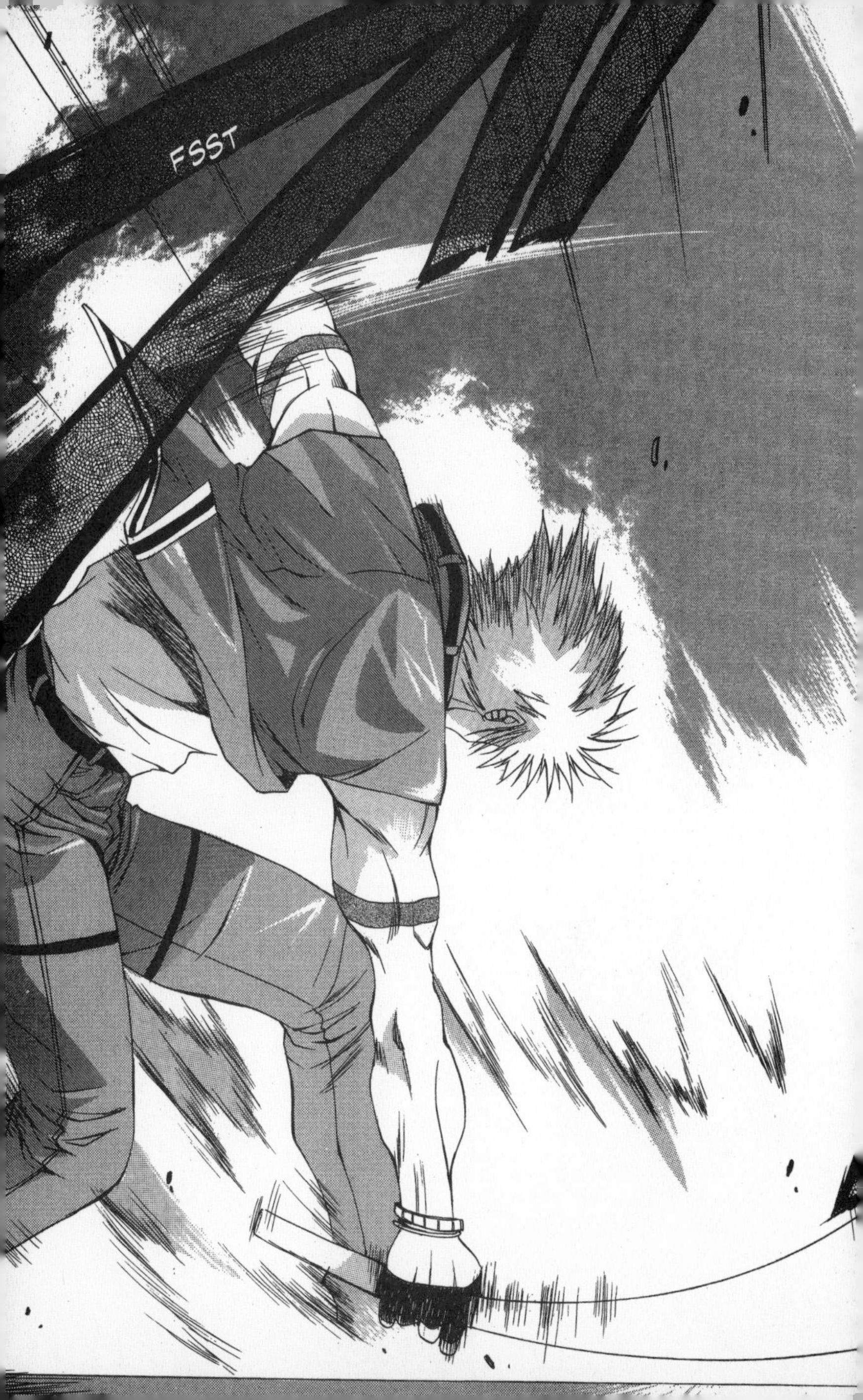
FSST

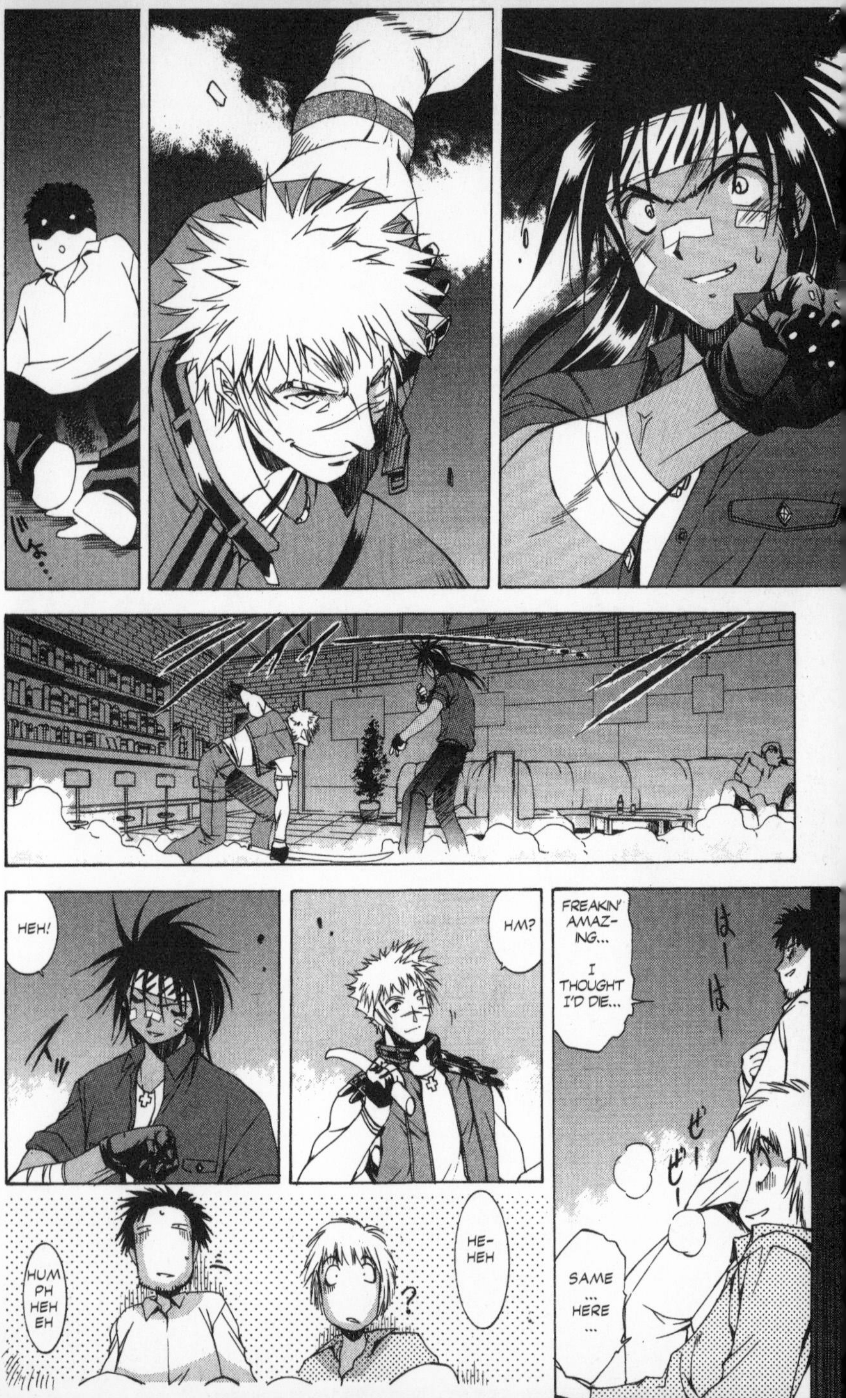
FREAKIN' AMAZ-ING... I THOUGHT I'D DIE...
はーはー
ぜーぜー
SAME ... HERE ...
HM?
HEH!
HE-HEH
HUMPH HEH EH

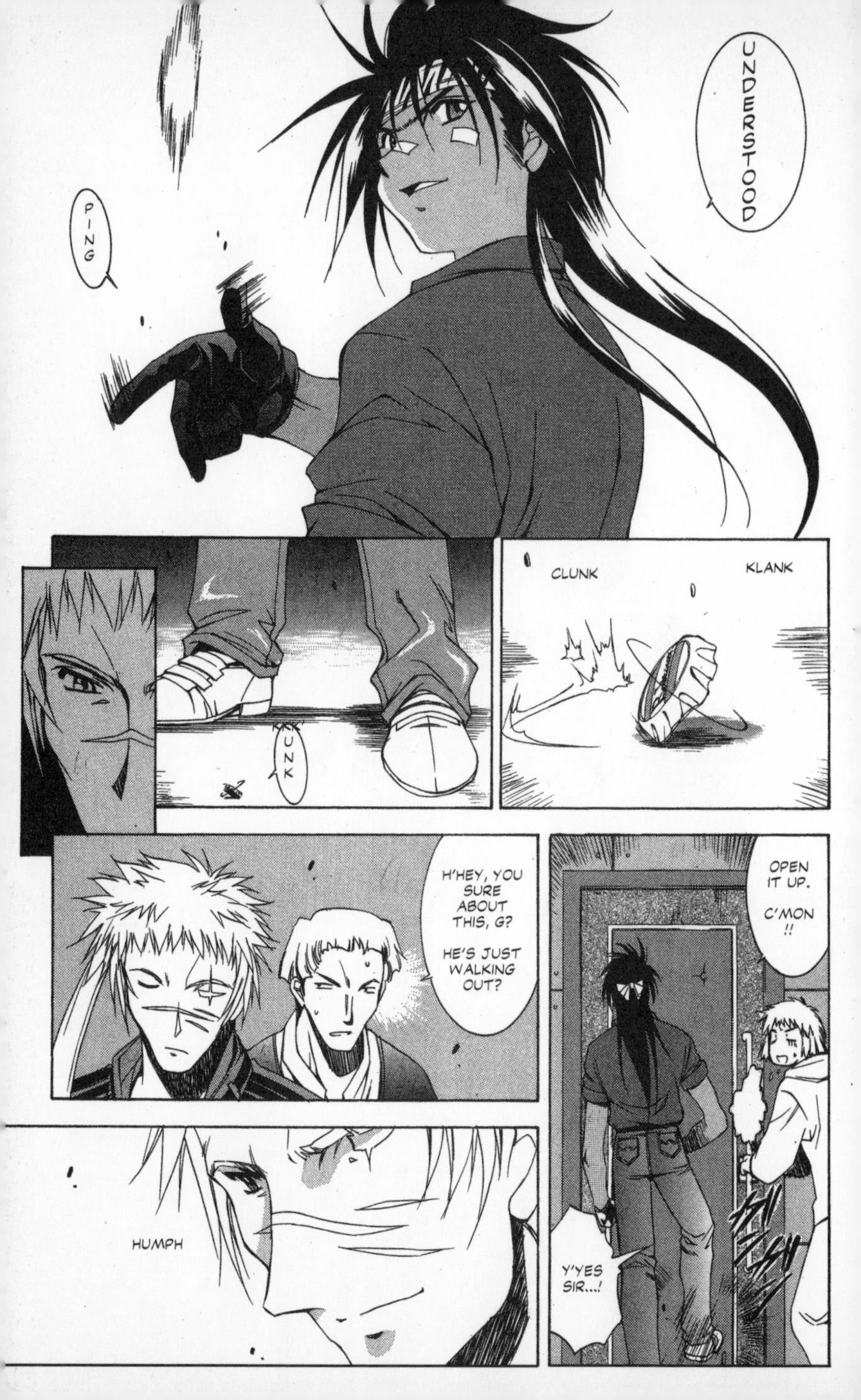
UNDERSTOOD
PING
KLANK
CLUNK
KUNK
OPEN IT UP.
C'MON!!
Y'YES SIR...!
H'HEY, YOU SURE ABOUT THIS, G?
HE'S JUST WALKING OUT?
HUMPH

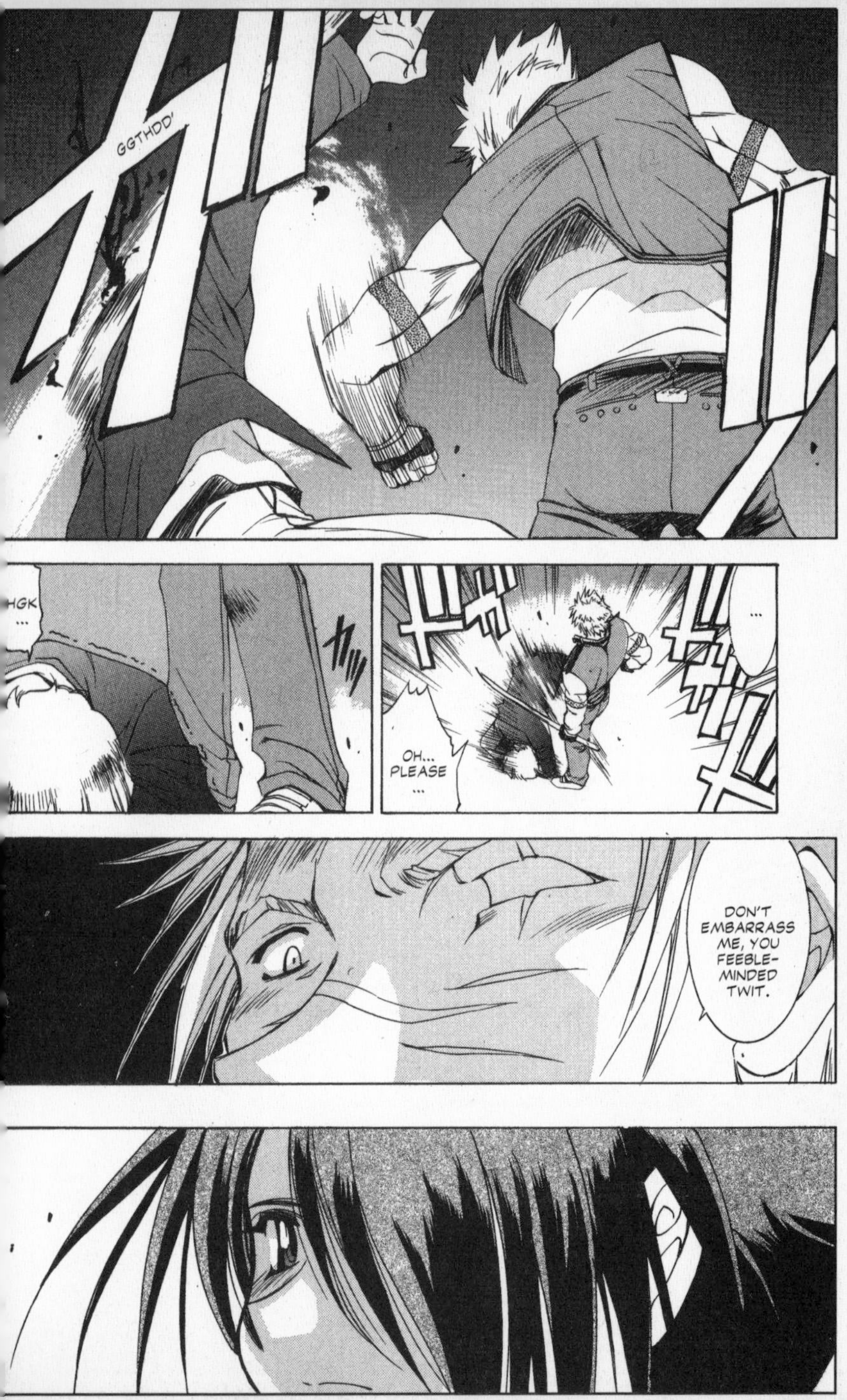
GGTHDD'
...
OH... PLEASE ...
HGK ...
DON'T EMBARRASS ME, YOU FEEBLE-MINDED TWIT.

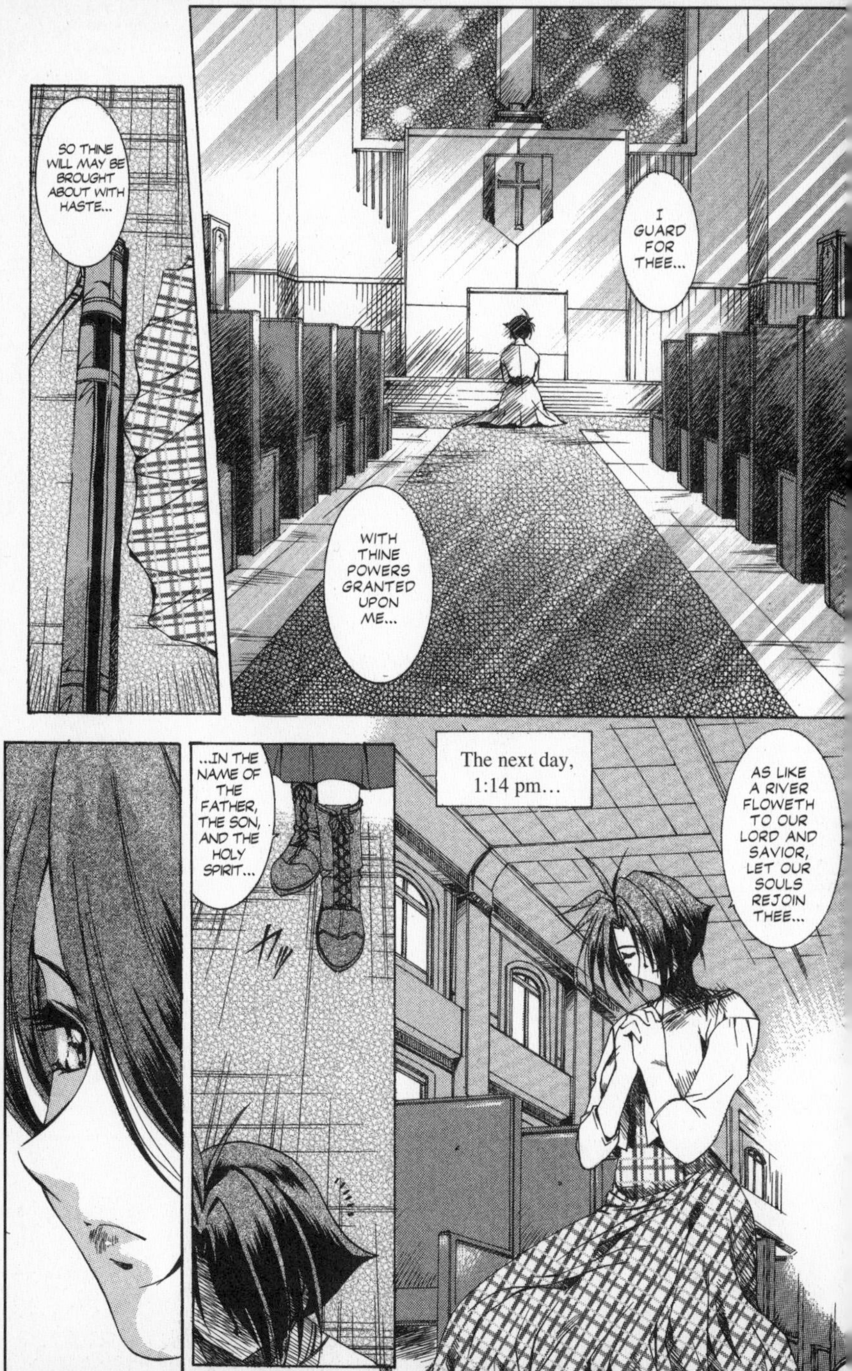
I GUARD FOR THEE...
WITH THINE POWERS GRANTED UPON ME...
SO THINE WILL MAY BE BROUGHT ABOUT WITH HASTE...
The next day, 1:14 pm…
AS LIKE A RIVER FLOWETH TO OUR LORD AND SAVIOR, LET OUR SOULS REJOIN THEE...
...IN THE NAME OF THE FATHER, THE SON, AND THE HOLY SPIRIT...

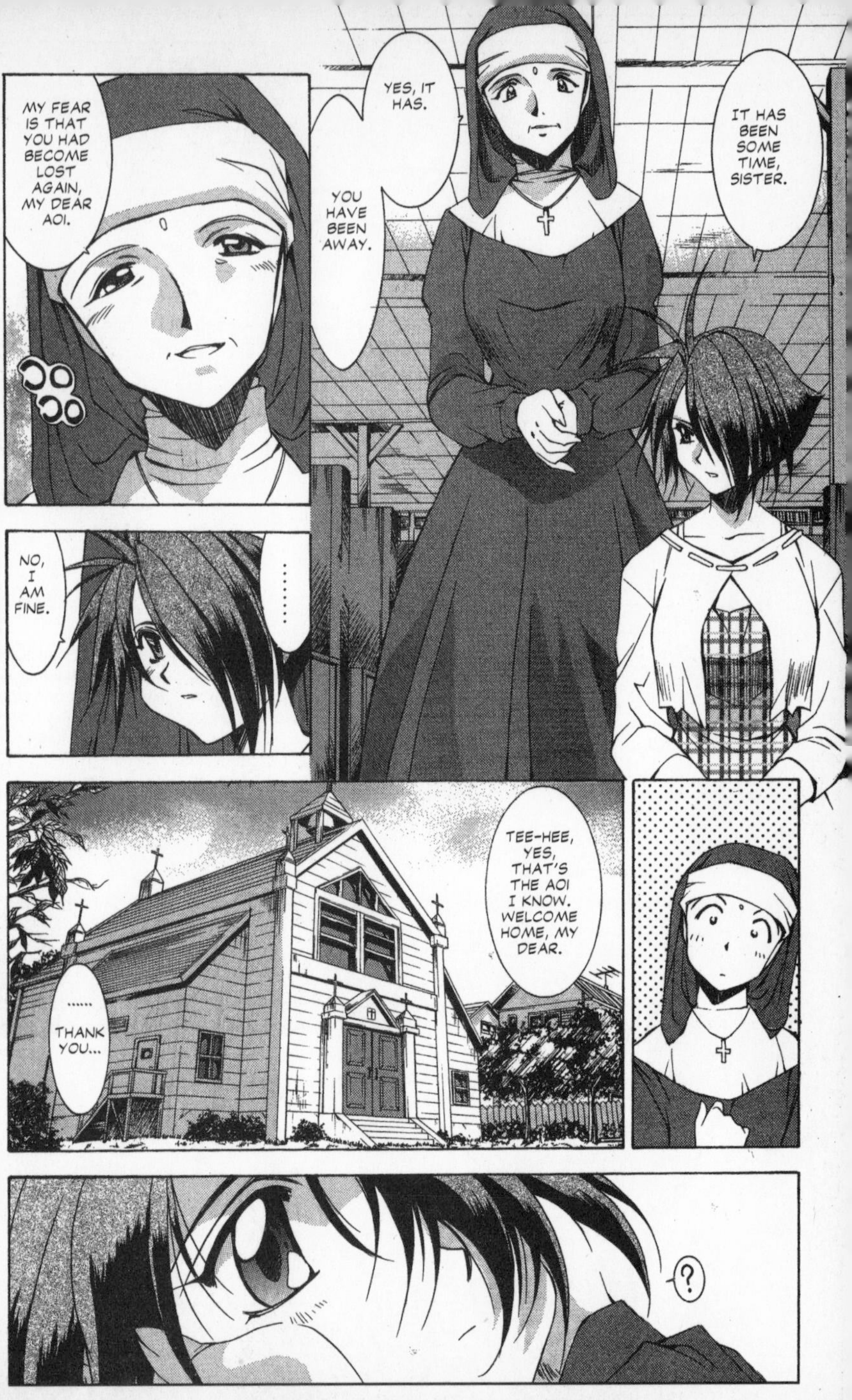
IT HAS BEEN SOME TIME, SISTER.
YES, IT HAS.
YOU HAVE BEEN AWAY.
MY FEAR IS THAT YOU HAD BECOME LOST AGAIN, MY DEAR AOI.
....
NO, I AM FINE.
TEE-HEE, YES, THAT'S THE AOI I KNOW. WELCOME HOME, MY DEAR.
...... THANK YOU...
?

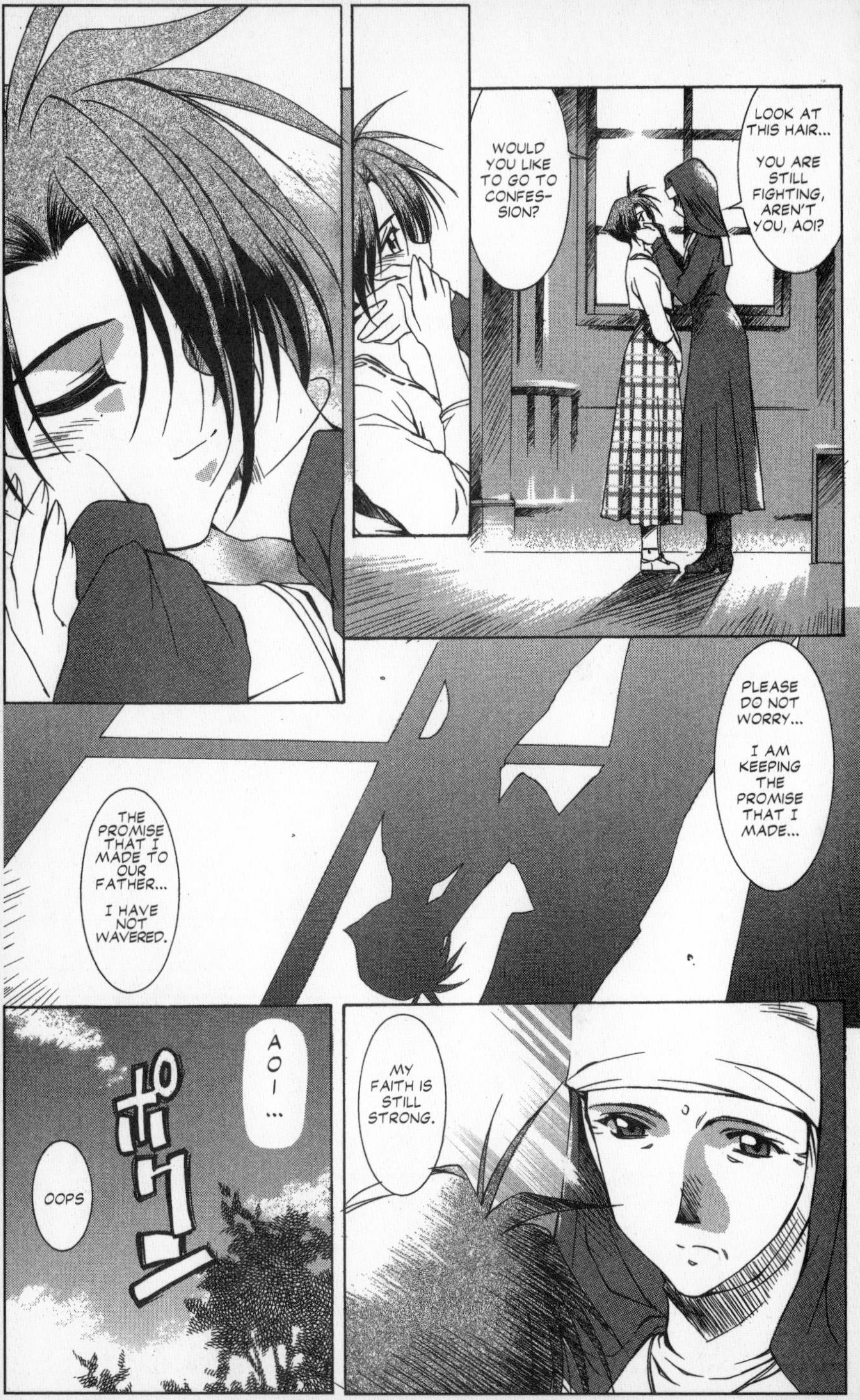
LOOK AT THIS HAIR... YOU ARE STILL FIGHTING, AREN'T YOU, AOI?
WOULD YOU LIKE TO GO TO CONFES-SION?
PLEASE DO NOT WORRY... I AM KEEPING THE PROMISE THAT I MADE...
THE PROMISE THAT I MADE TO OUR FATHER... I HAVE NOT WAVERED.
MY FAITH IS STILL STRONG.
AOI...
OOPS

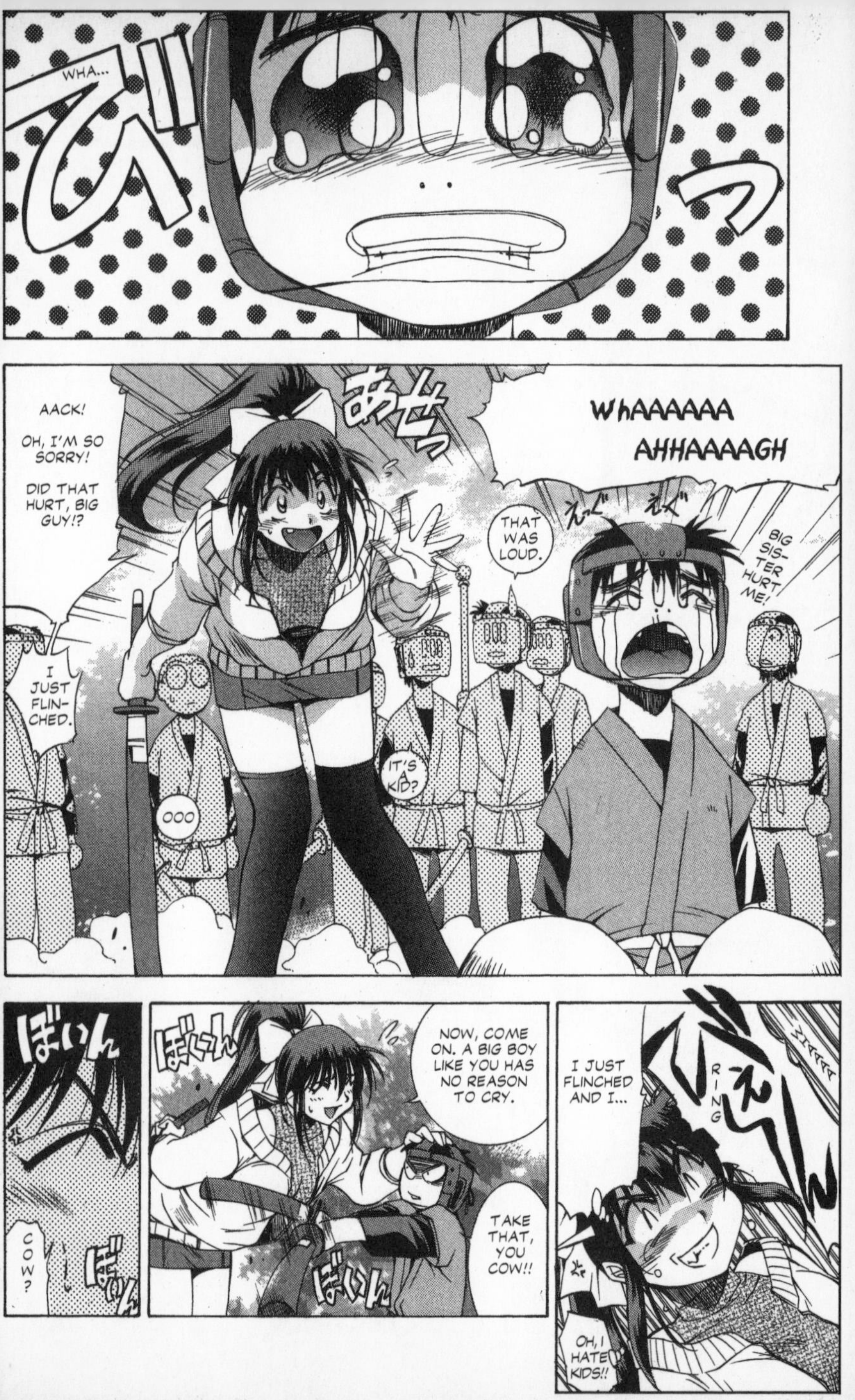
WHA...
BIG SISTER HURT ME!
えぐ えぐ
WhAAAAAA AHHAAAAAGH
THAT WAS LOUD.
あせっ
AACK! OH, I'M SO SORRY! DID THAT HURT, BIG GUY!?
IT'S A KID?
I JUST FLINCHED.
OOO
I JUST FLINCHED AND I...
RING
OH, I HATE KIDS!!
NOW, COME ON. A BIG BOY LIKE YOU HAS NO REASON TO CRY.
TAKE THAT, YOU COW!!
ぼいん
ぼいん
COW?

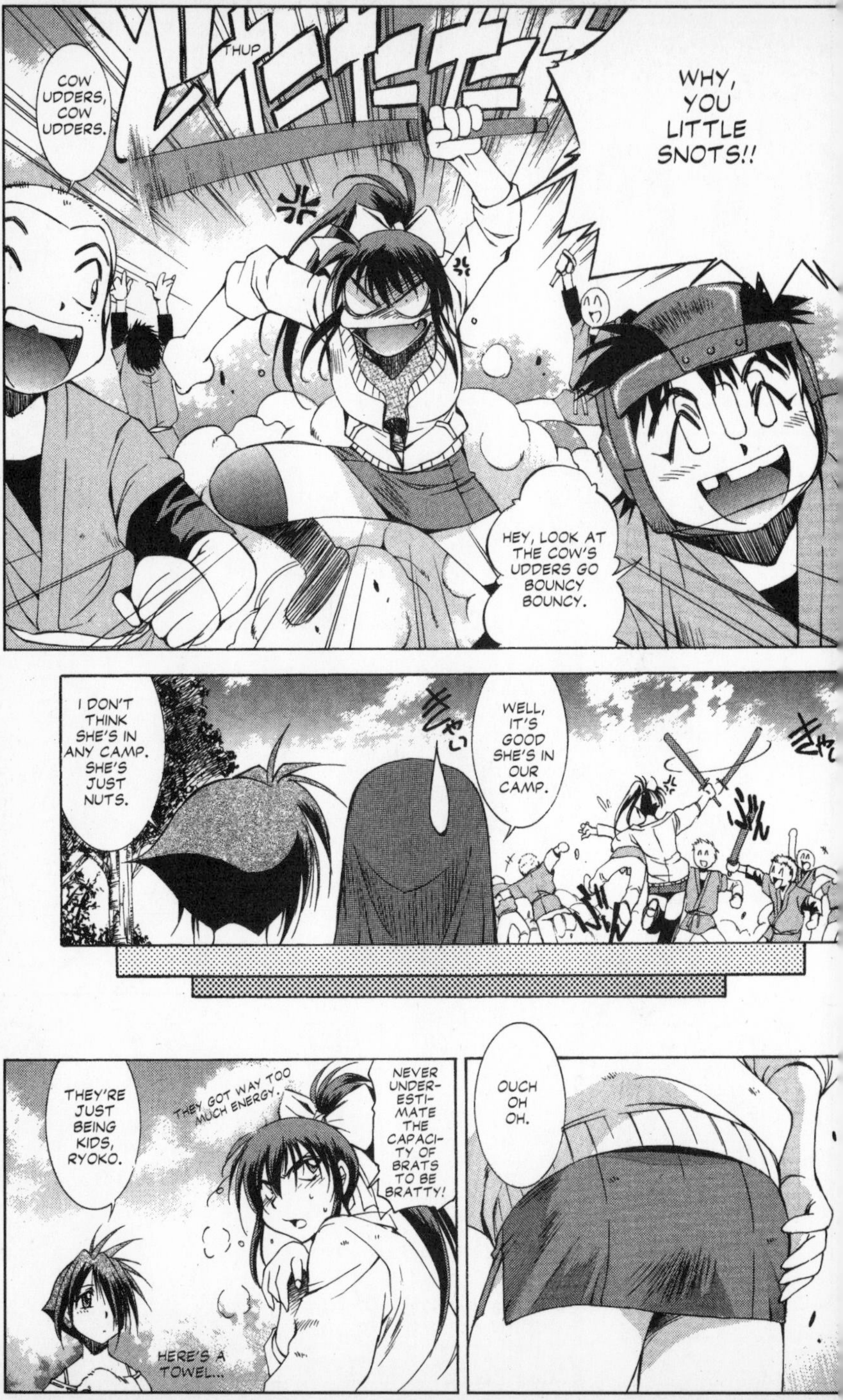
WHY, YOU LITTLE SNOTS!!
HEY, LOOK AT THE COW'S UDDERS GO BOUNCY BOUNCY.
THUP
COW UDDERS, COW UDDERS.
WELL, IT'S GOOD SHE'S IN OUR CAMP.
I DON'T THINK SHE'S IN ANY CAMP. SHE'S JUST NUTS.
OUCH OH OH.
NEVER UNDER-ESTI-MATE THE CAPACI-TY OF BRATS TO BE BRATTY!
THEY GOT WAY TOO MUCH ENERGY.
THEY'RE JUST BEING KIDS, RYOKO.
HERE'S A TOWEL...

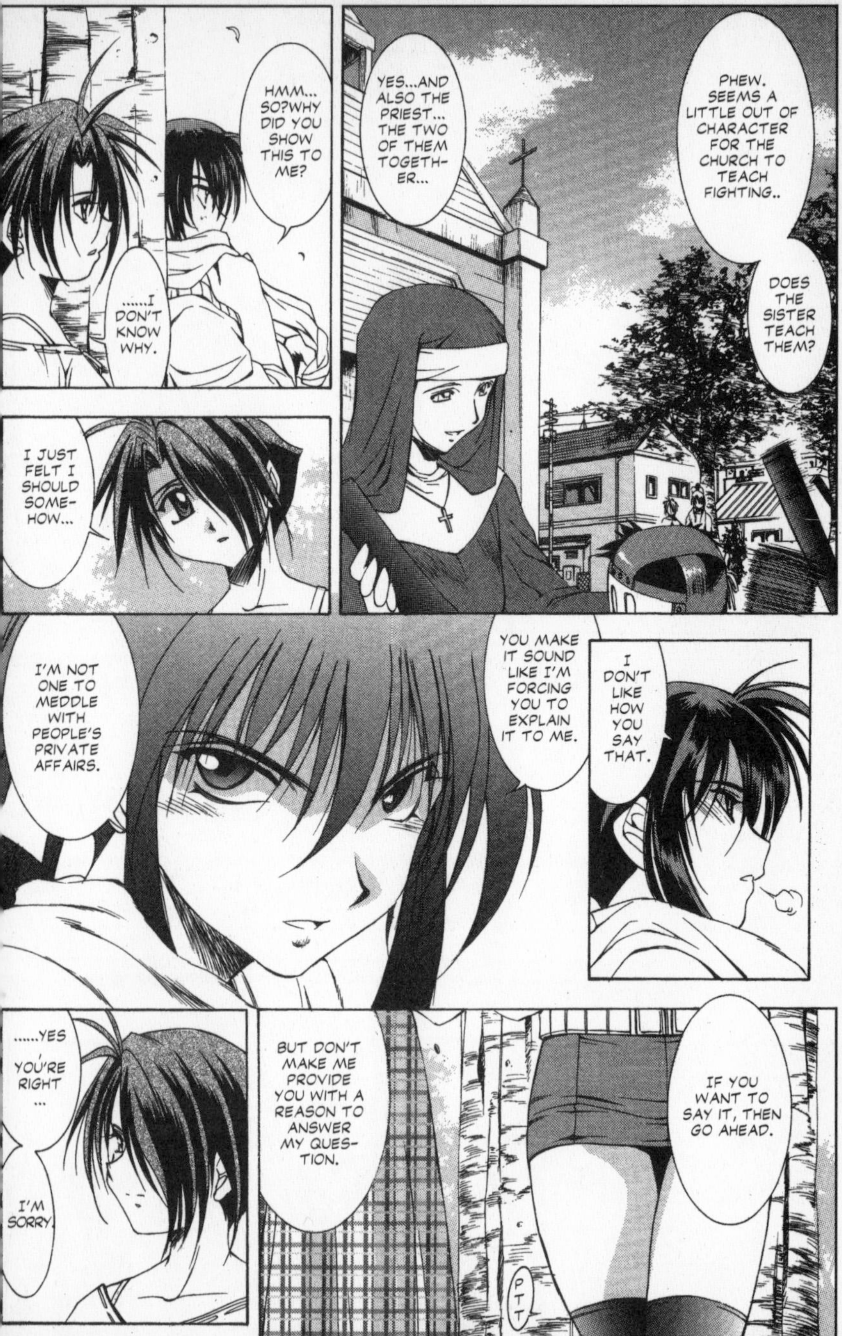
PHEW. SEEMS A LITTLE OUT OF CHARACTER FOR THE CHURCH TO TEACH FIGHTING..
DOES THE SISTER TEACH THEM?
YES...AND ALSO THE PRIEST... THE TWO OF THEM TOGETH-ER...
HMM... SO?WHY DID YOU SHOW THIS TO ME?
......I DON'T KNOW WHY.
I JUST FELT I SHOULD SOME-HOW...
I DON'T LIKE HOW YOU SAY THAT.
YOU MAKE IT SOUND LIKE I'M FORCING YOU TO EXPLAIN IT TO ME.
I'M NOT ONE TO MEDDLE WITH PEOPLE'S PRIVATE AFFAIRS.
IF YOU WANT TO SAY IT, THEN GO AHEAD.
PTT
BUT DON'T MAKE ME PROVIDE YOU WITH A REASON TO ANSWER MY QUES-TION.
......YES, YOU'RE RIGHT ...
I'M SORRY.

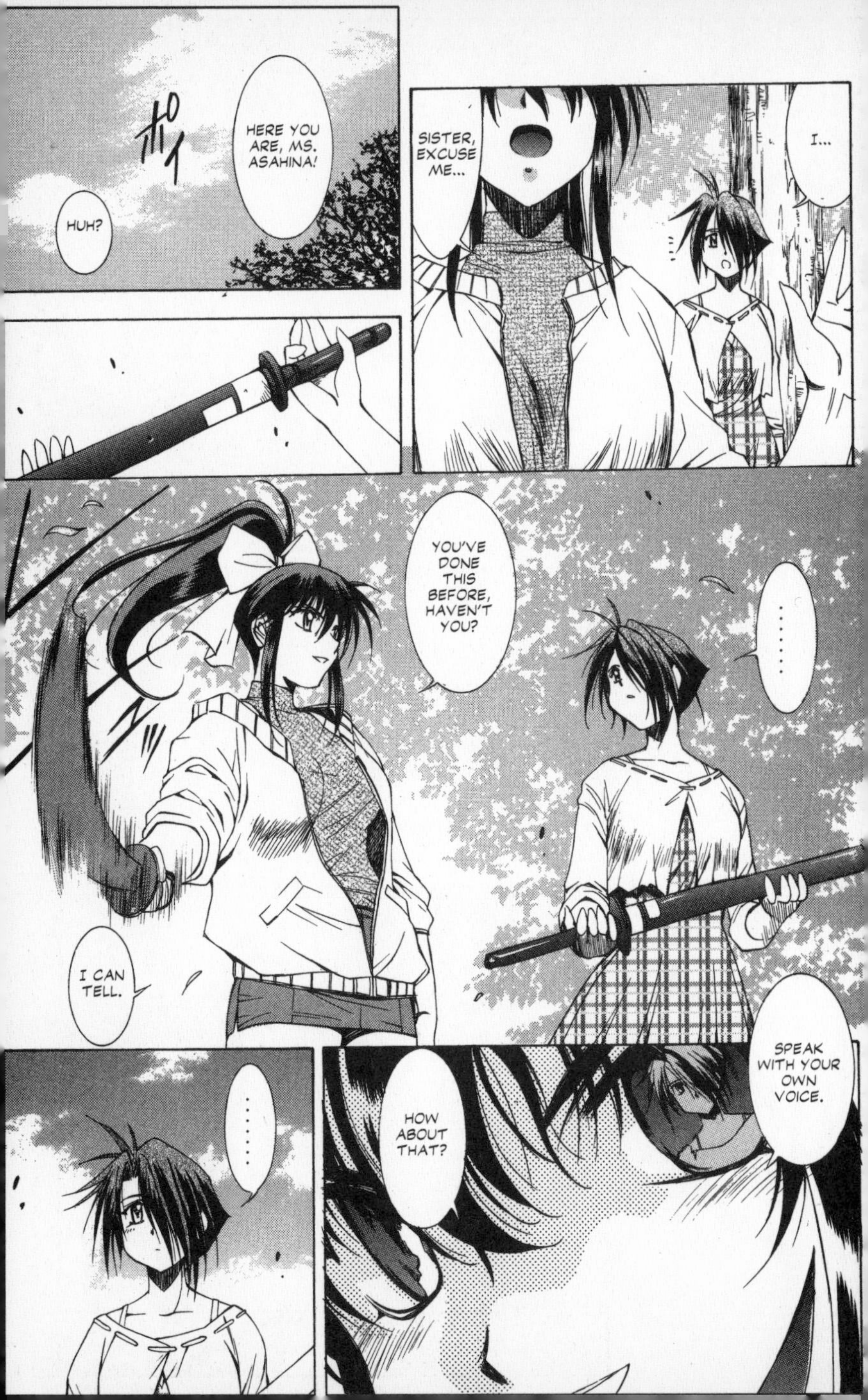
I...
SISTER, EXCUSE ME...
ポイ
HERE YOU ARE, MS. ASAHINA!
HUH?
....
YOU'VE DONE THIS BEFORE, HAVEN'T YOU?
I CAN TELL.
SPEAK WITH YOUR OWN VOICE.
HOW ABOUT THAT?
......

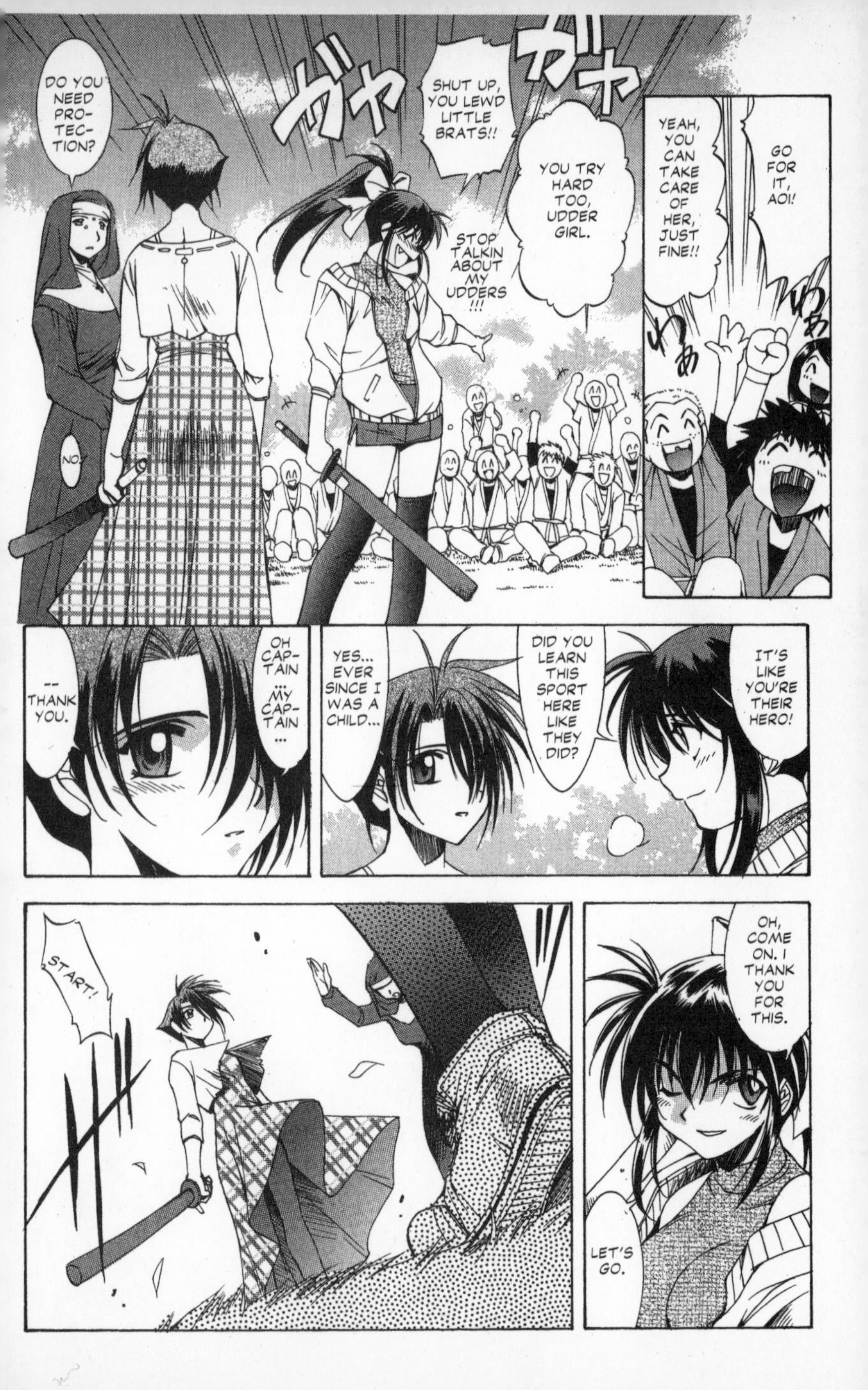
GO FOR IT, AOI!
YEAH, YOU CAN TAKE CARE OF HER, JUST FINE!!
わあ
わあ
がや
がや
YOU TRY HARD TOO, UDDER GIRL.
SHUT UP, YOU LEWD LITTLE BRATS!!
STOP TALKIN ABOUT MY UDDERS!!!
DO YOU NEED PRO-TEC-TION?
NO.
IT'S LIKE YOU'RE THEIR HERO!
DID YOU LEARN THIS SPORT HERE LIKE THEY DID?
YES... EVER SINCE I WAS A CHILD...
OH CAP-TAIN ... MY CAP-TAIN ...
-- THANK YOU.
OH, COME ON. I THANK YOU FOR THIS.
LET'S GO.
START!

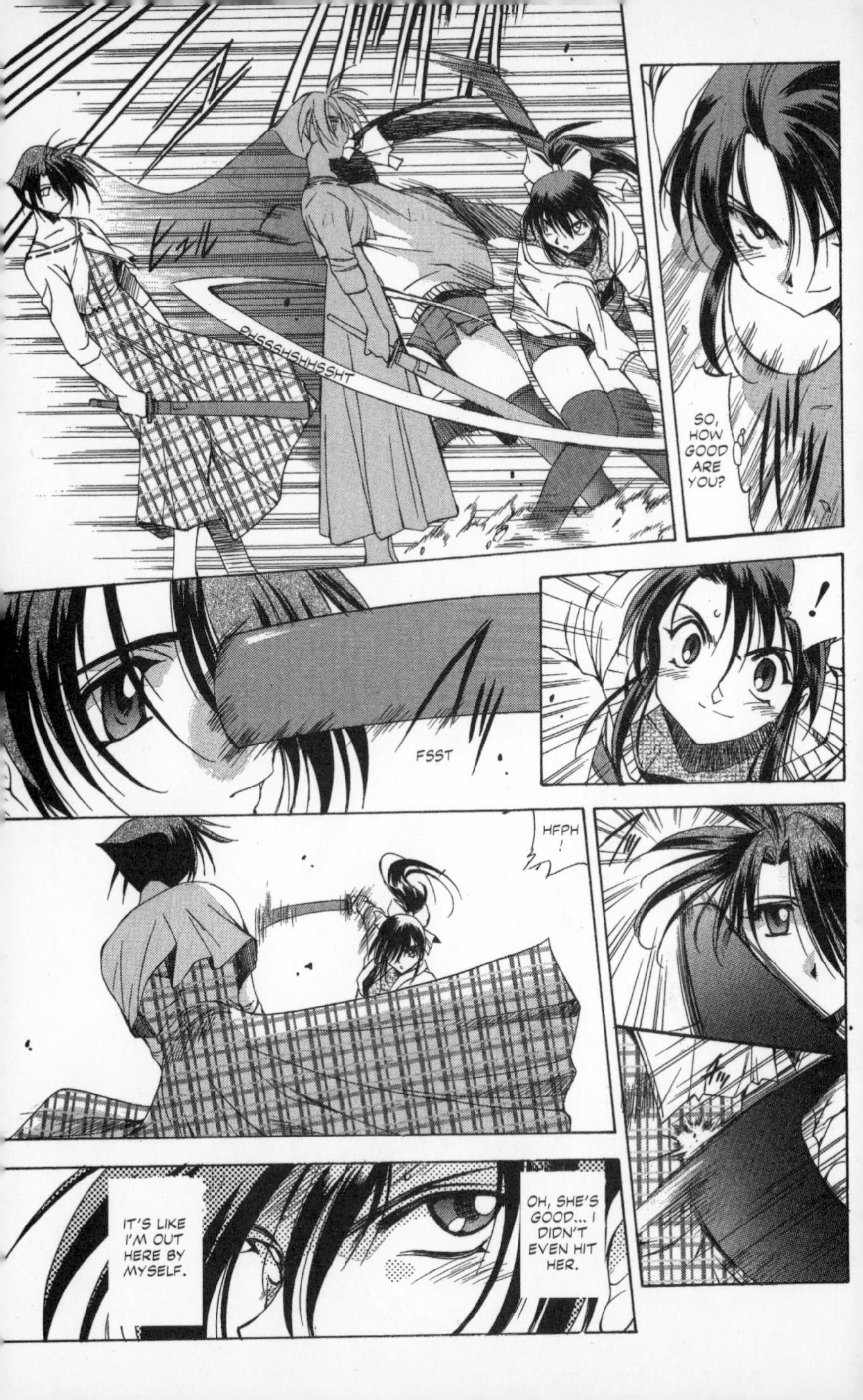
SO, HOW GOOD ARE YOU?
ヒュル
PHSSSHSHHSSHT
!
FSST
HFPH!
OH, SHE'S GOOD... I DIDN'T EVEN HIT HER.
IT'S LIKE I'M OUT HERE BY MYSELF.

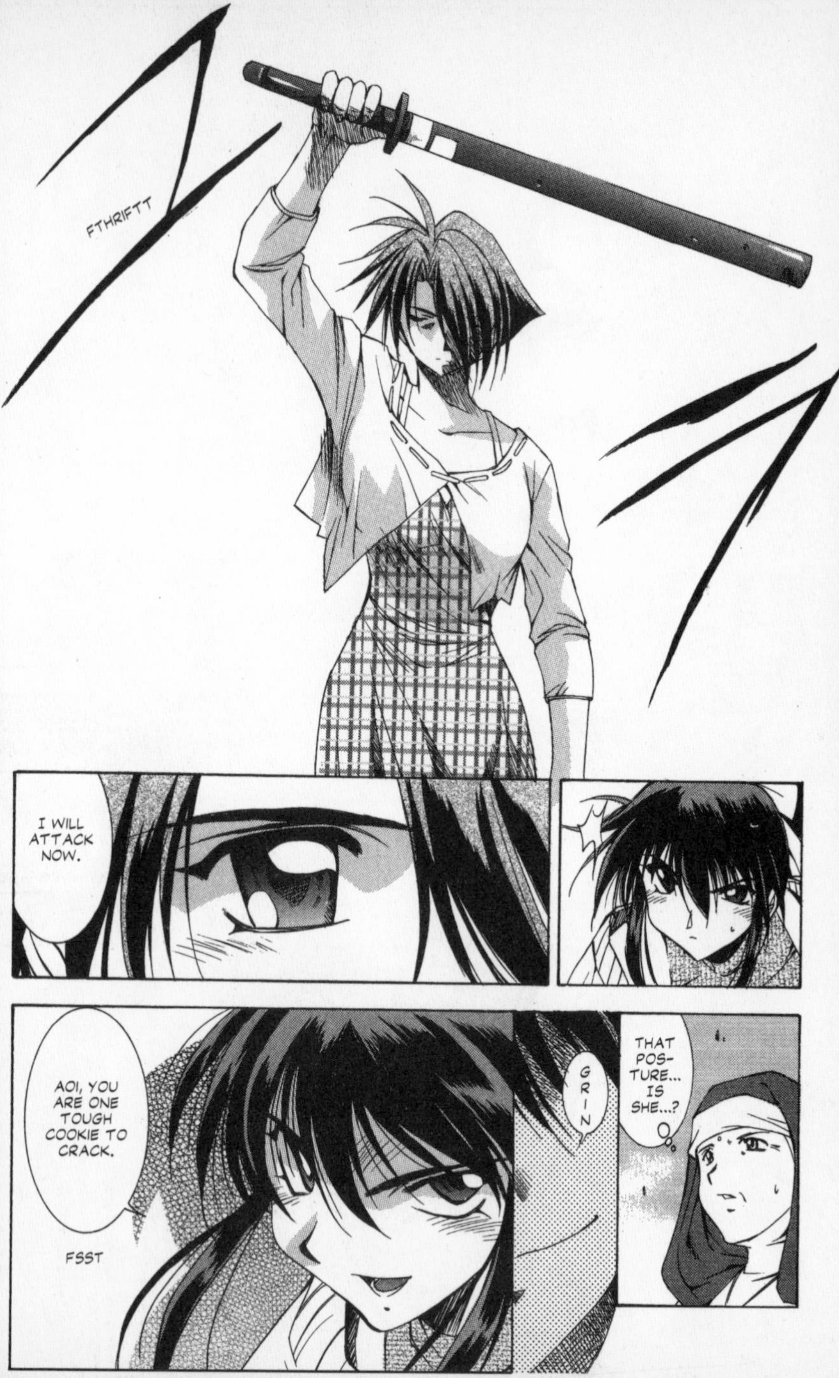
FTHRIFTT
I WILL ATTACK NOW.
THAT POS-TURE... IS SHE...?
GRIN
AOI, YOU ARE ONE TOUGH COOKIE TO CRACK.
FSST

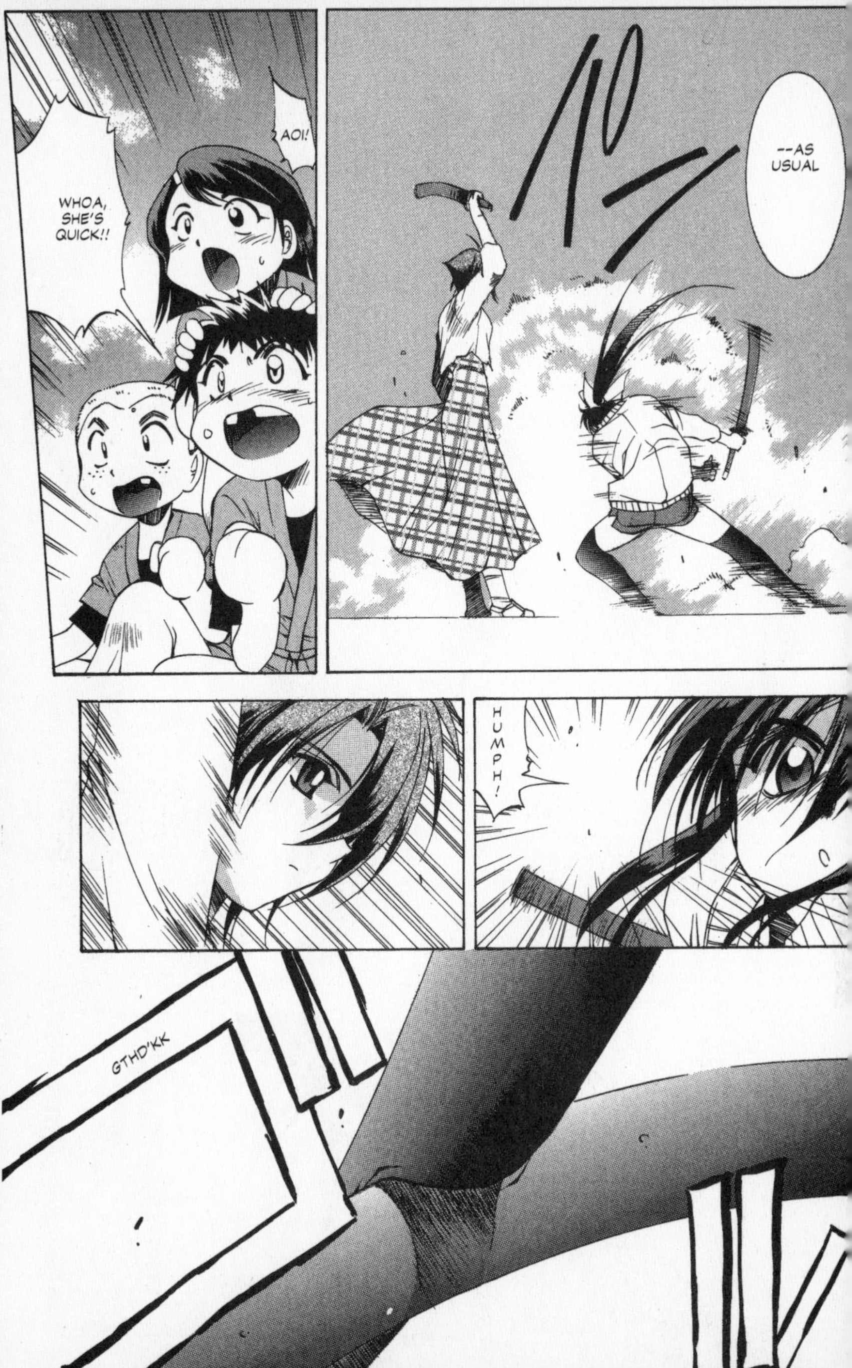
--AS USUAL
AOI!
WHOA, SHE'S QUICK!!
HUMPH!
GTHD'KK

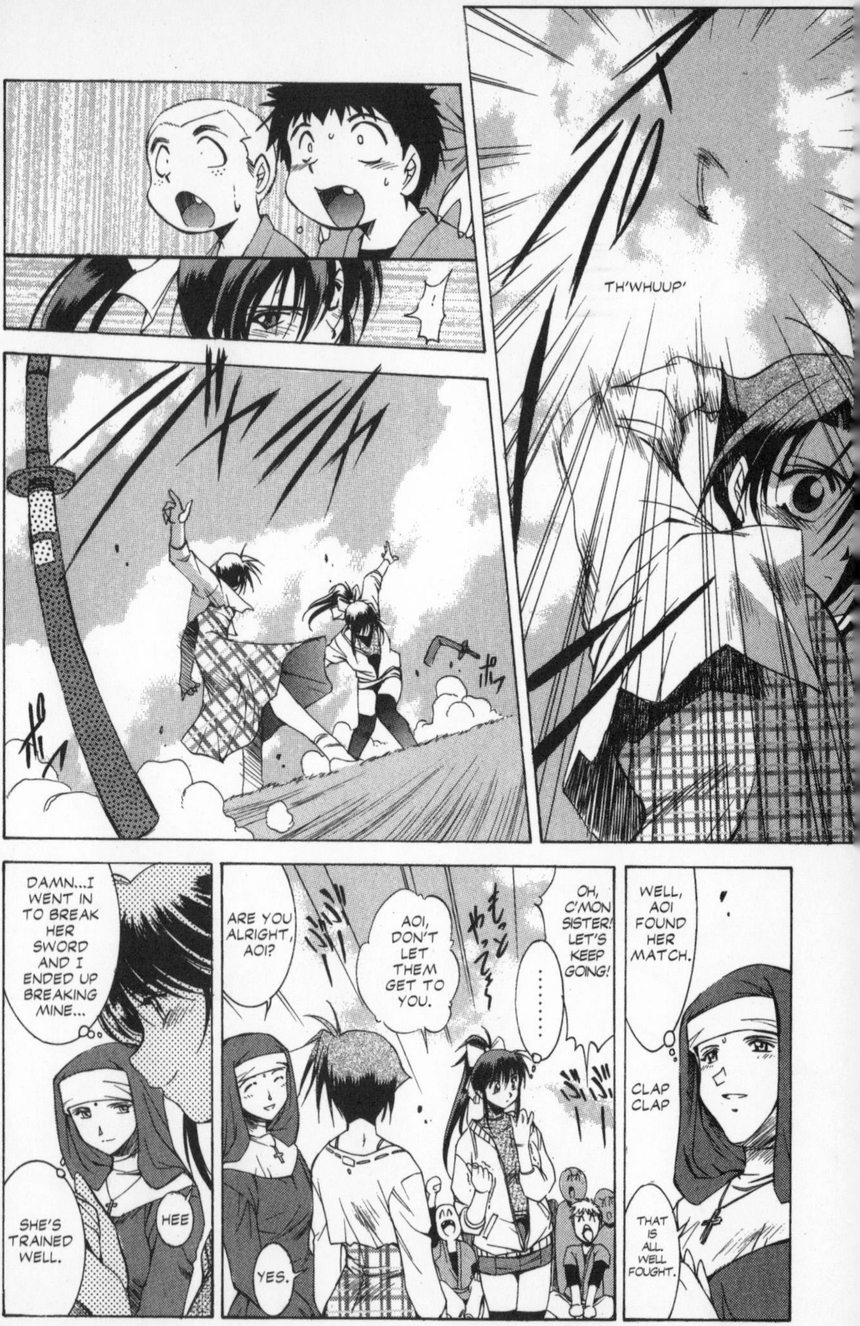
TH'WHUUP'
!
WELL, AOI FOUND HER MATCH.
CLAP CLAP
THAT IS ALL. WELL FOUGHT.
OH, C'MON SISTER! LET'S KEEP GOING!
......
AOI, DON'T LET THEM GET TO YOU.
ARE YOU ALRIGHT, AOI?
YES.
DAMN...I WENT IN TO BREAK HER SWORD AND I ENDED UP BREAKING MINE...
HEE
SHE'S TRAINED WELL.

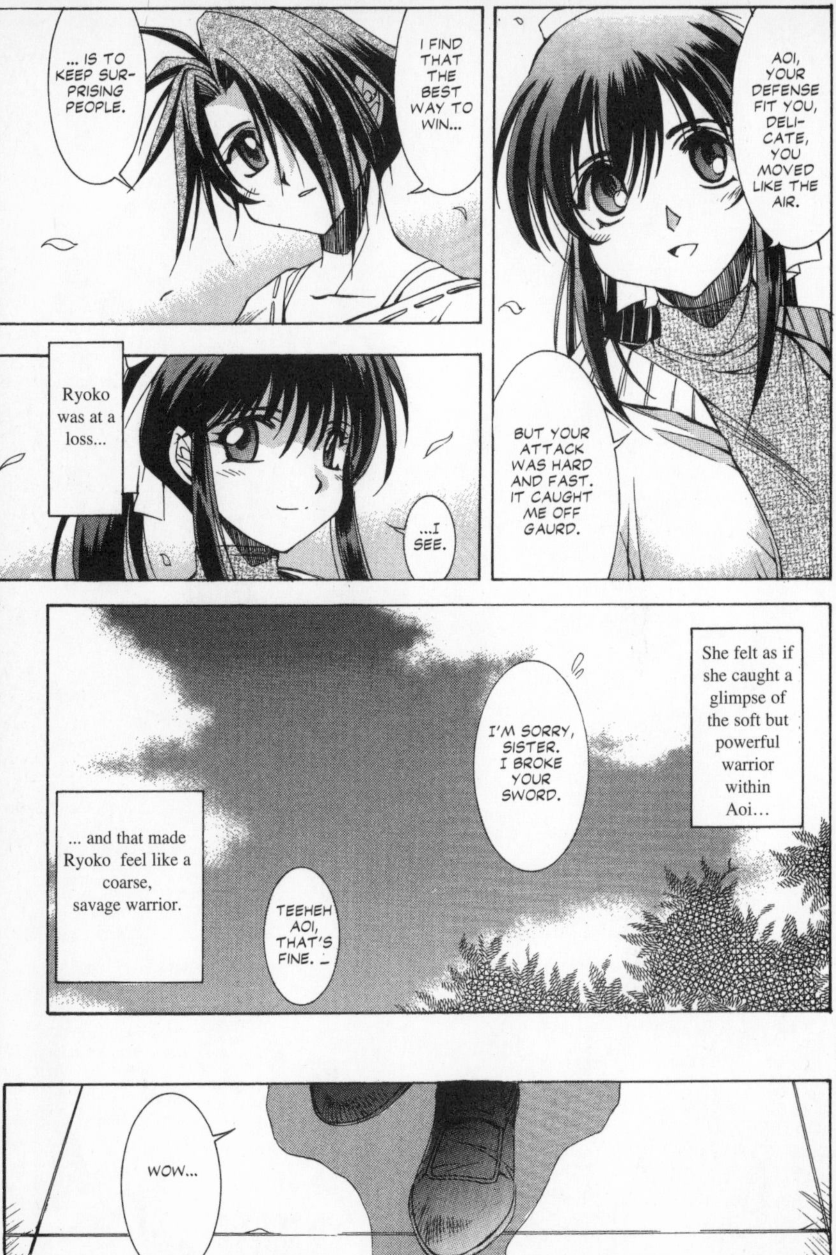
AOI, YOUR DEFENSE FIT YOU, DELICATE, YOU MOVED LIKE THE AIR.
BUT YOUR ATTACK WAS HARD AND FAST. IT CAUGHT ME OFF GAURD.
I FIND THAT THE BEST WAY TO WIN...
... IS TO KEEP SURPRISING PEOPLE.
Ryoko was at a loss...
...I SEE.
She felt as if she caught a glimpse of the soft but powerful warrior within Aoi…
I'M SORRY, SISTER. I BROKE YOUR SWORD.
TEEHEH AOI, THAT'S FINE.
... and that made Ryoko feel like a coarse, savage warrior.
WOW...

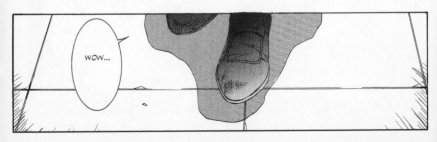

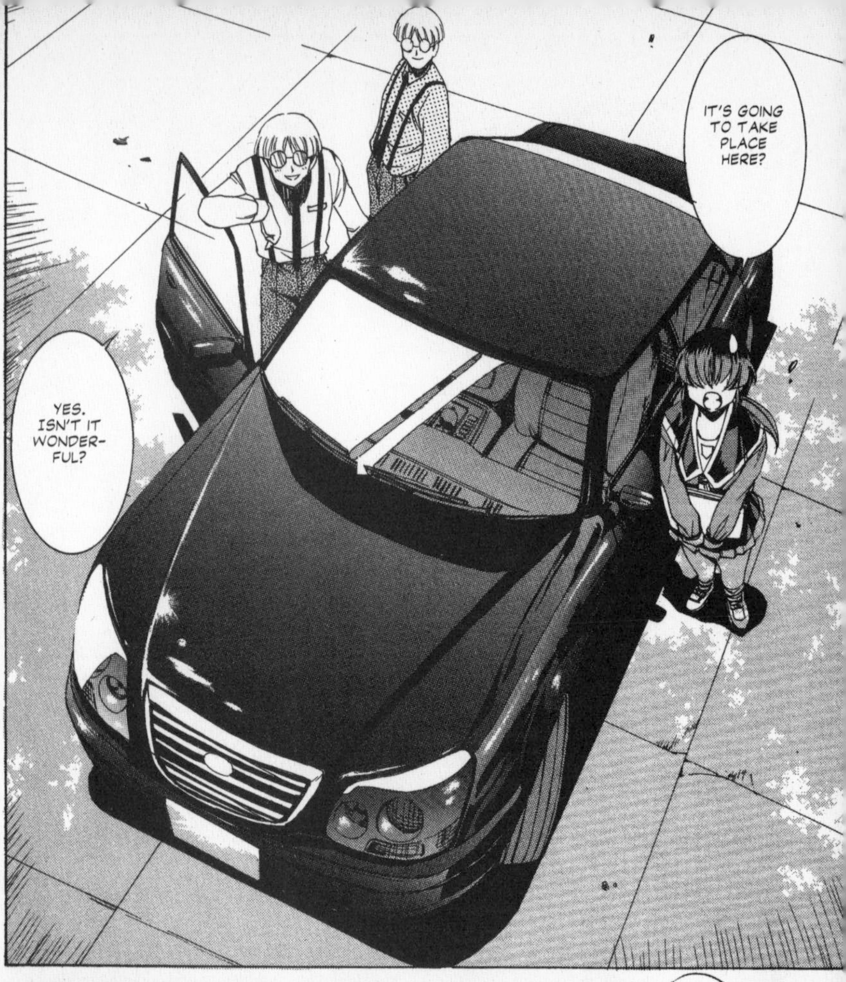
IT'S GOING TO TAKE PLACE HERE?
YES. ISN'T IT WONDER-FUL?

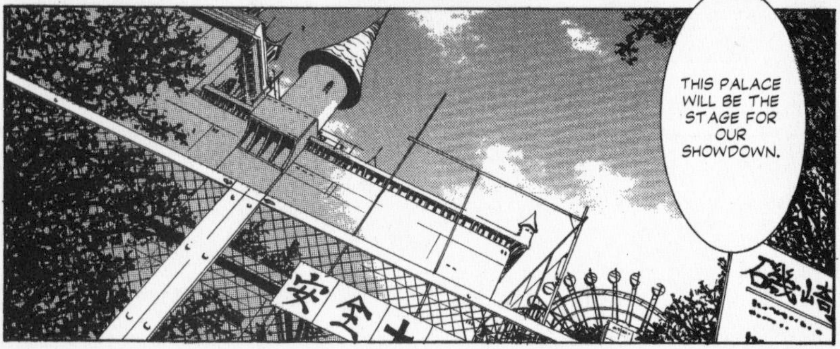
THIS PALACE WILL BE THE STAGE FOR OUR SHOWDOWN.
磯崎
安全

Episode 27 Sword to Sword, Ninja to Ninja

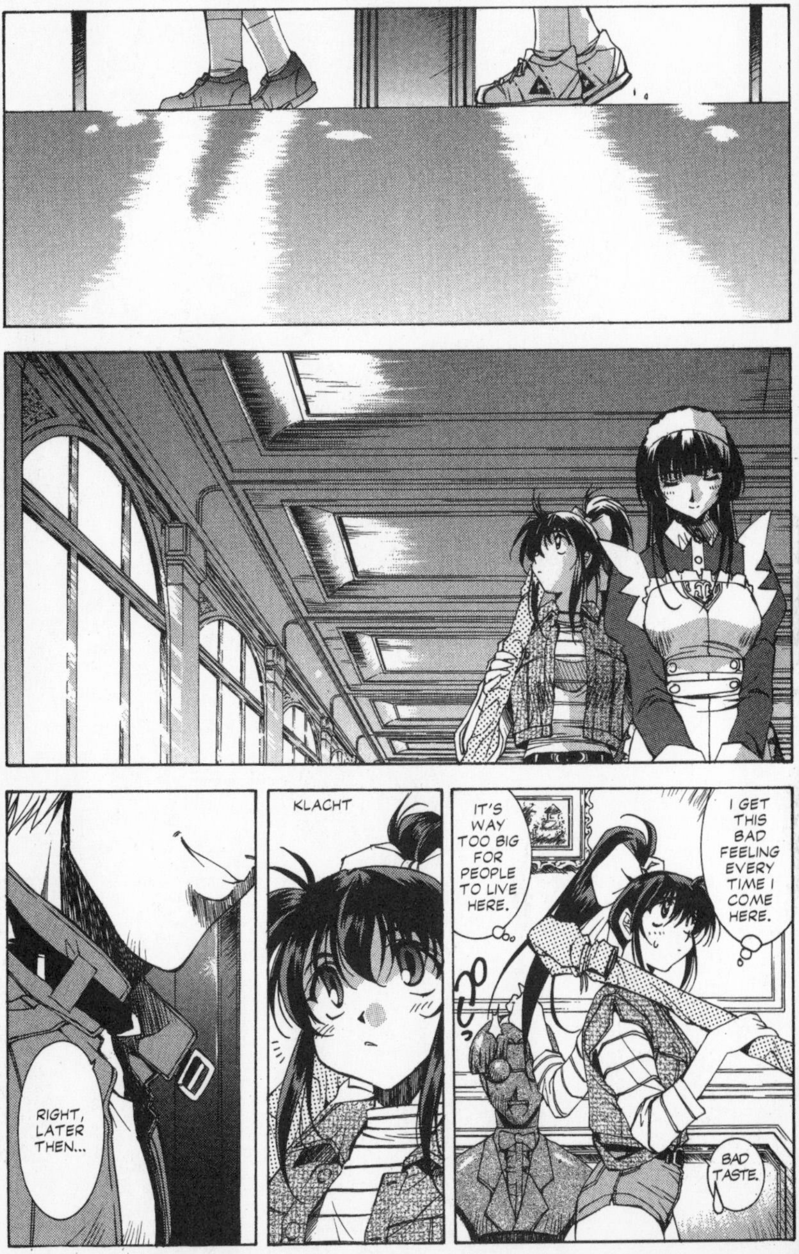
I GET THIS BAD FEELING EVERY TIME I COME HERE.
IT'S WAY TOO BIG FOR PEOPLE TO LIVE HERE.
BAD TASTE.
KLACHT
RIGHT, LATER THEN...

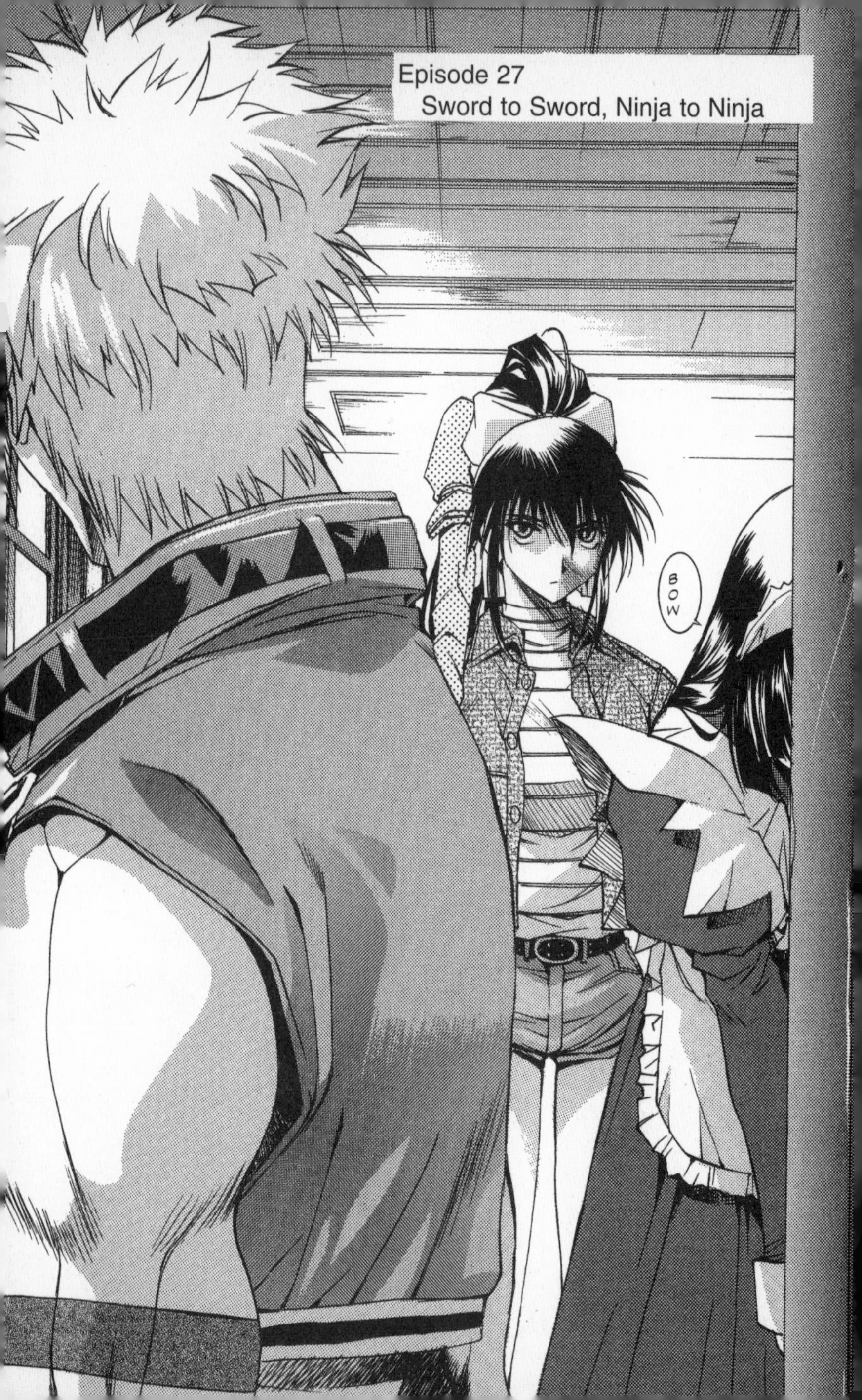
Episode 27
Sword to Sword, Ninja to Ninja
BOW

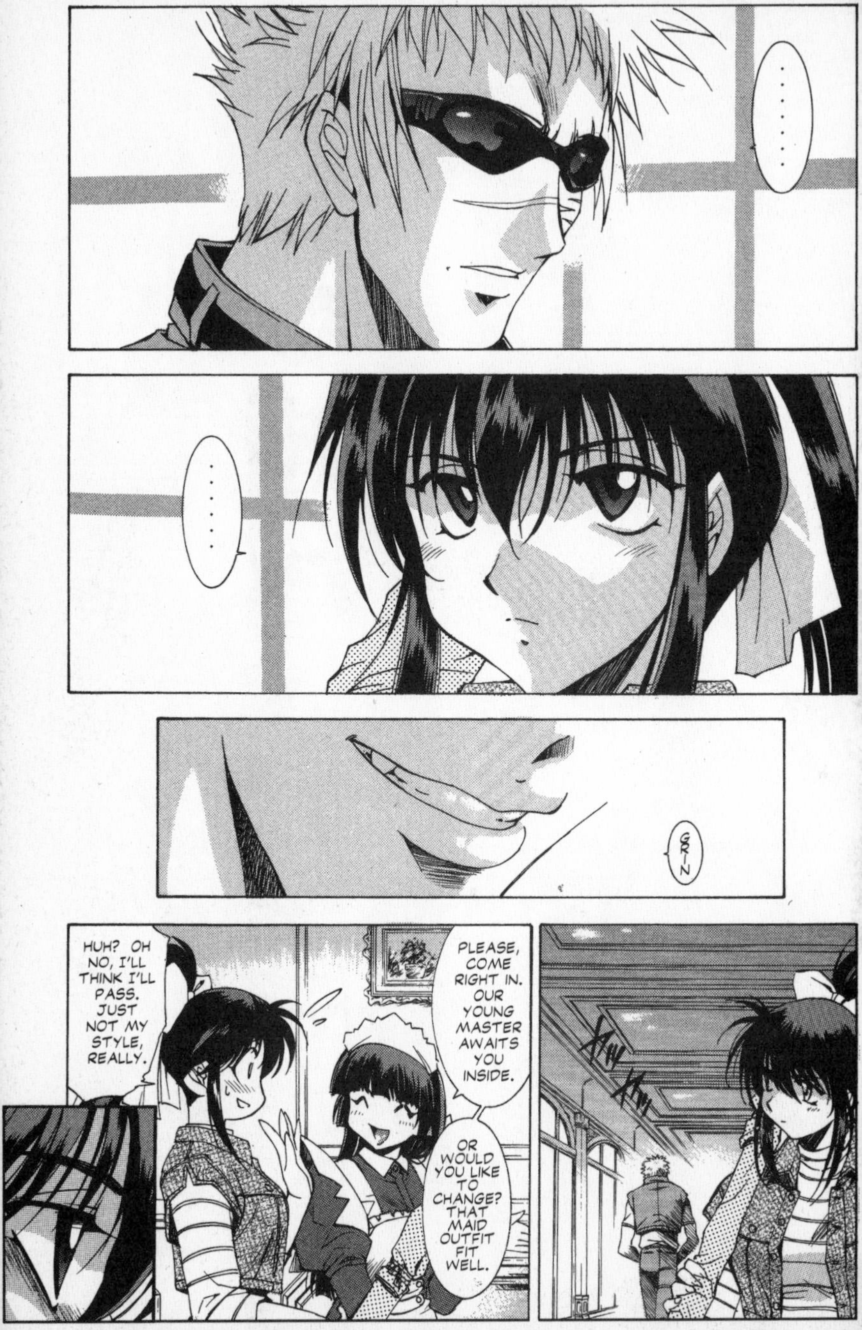

......
......
GRIN
PLEASE, COME RIGHT IN. OUR YOUNG MASTER AWAITS YOU INSIDE.
OR WOULD YOU LIKE TO CHANGE? THAT MAID OUTFIT FIT WELL.
HUH? OH NO, I'LL THINK I'LL PASS. JUST NOT MY STYLE, REALLY.

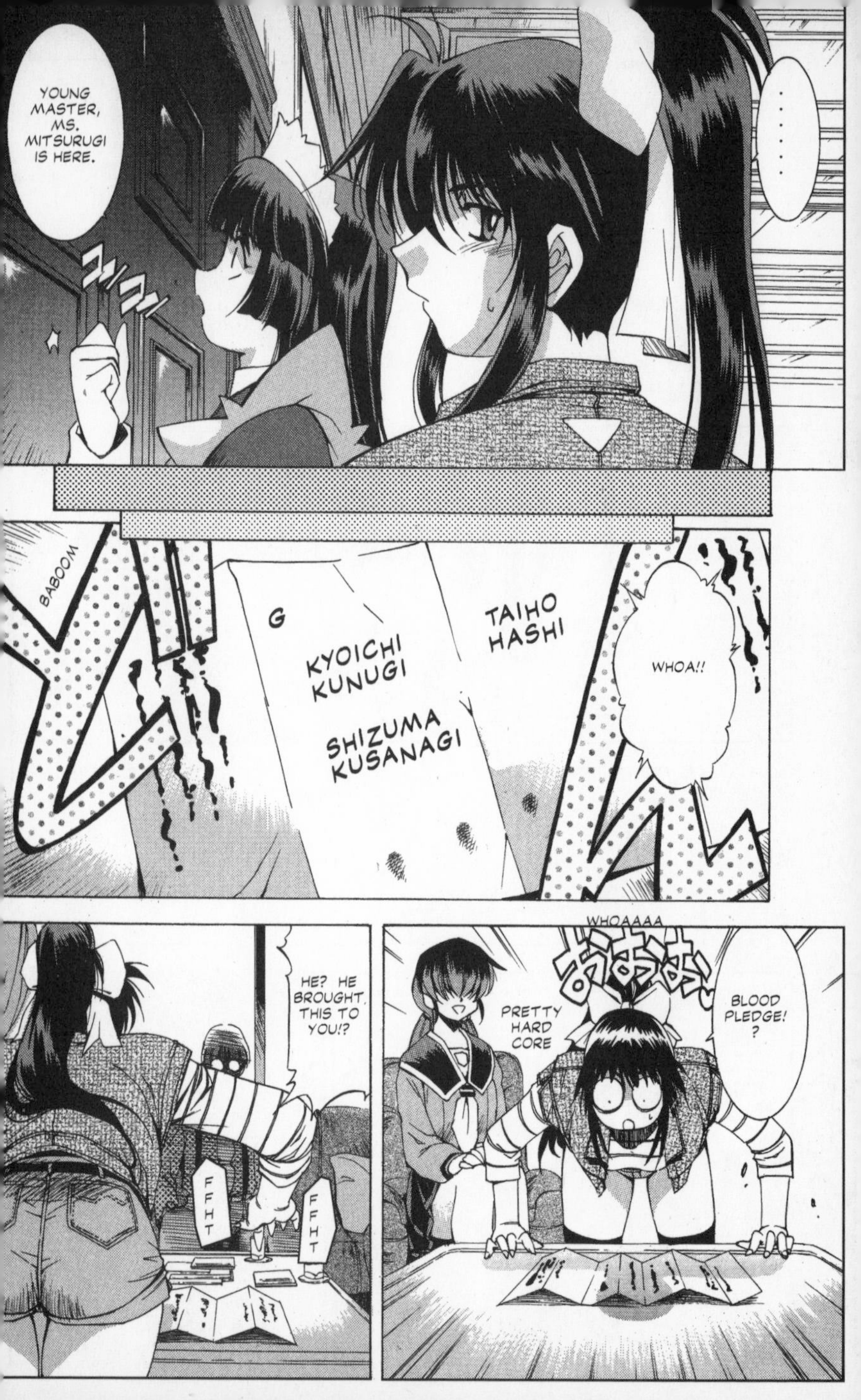
. . . . . .
YOUNG MASTER, MS. MITSURUGI IS HERE.
WHOA!!
TAIHO HASHI
KYOICHI KUNUGI
SHIZUMA KUSANAGI
G
BABOOM
BLOOD PLEDGE!?
WHOAAAA
PRETTY HARD CORE
HE? HE BROUGHT THIS TO YOU!?
FFHT
FFHT

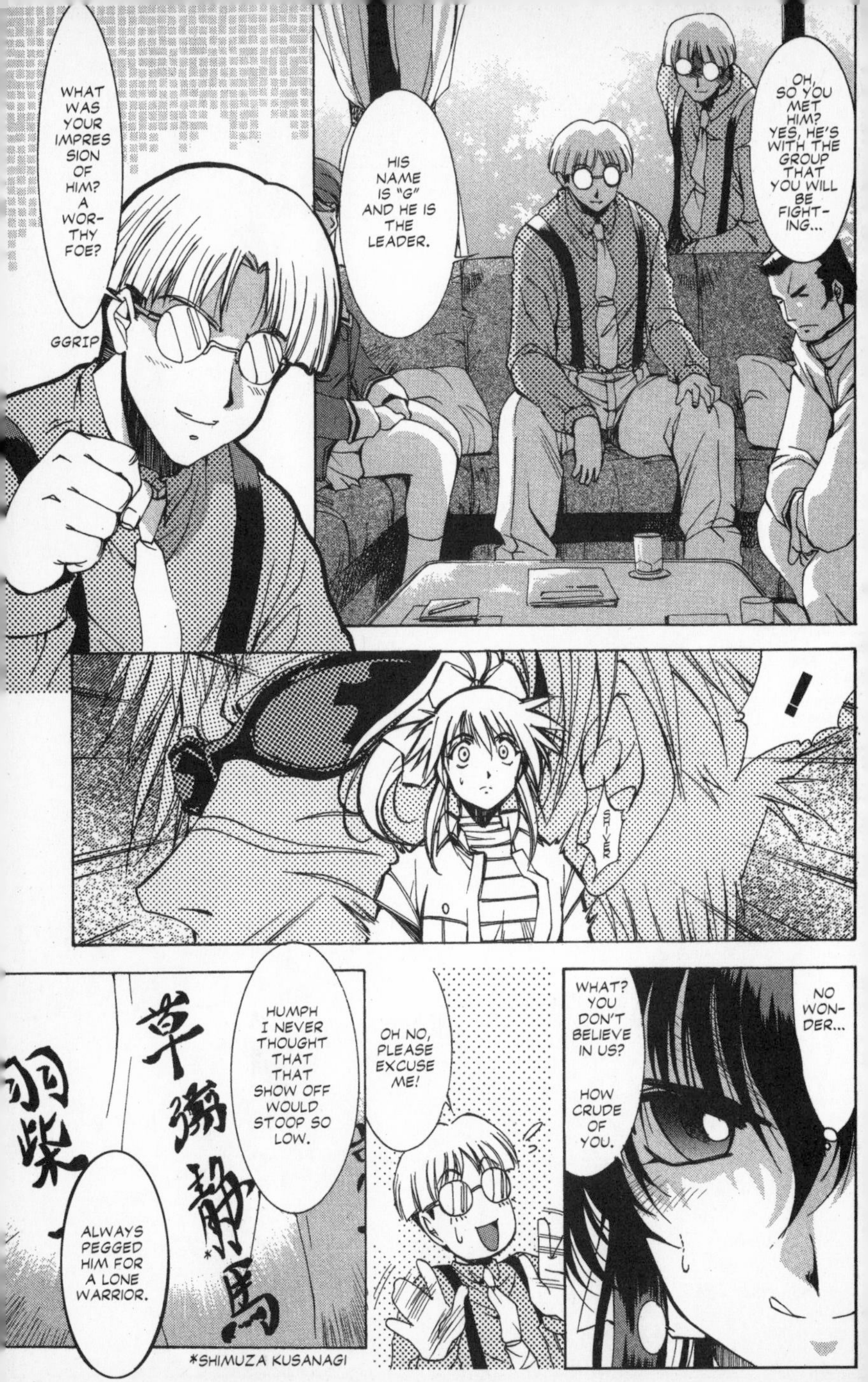
OH, SO YOU MET HIM? YES, HE'S WITH THE GROUP THAT YOU WILL BE FIGHT-ING...
HIS NAME IS "G" AND HE IS THE LEADER.
WHAT WAS YOUR IMPRES SION OF HIM? A WOR-THY FOE?
GGRIP
!
SHIVER
NO WON-DER...
WHAT? YOU DON'T BELIEVE IN US?
HOW CRUDE OF YOU.
OH NO, PLEASE EXCUSE ME!
HUMPH I NEVER THOUGHT THAT THAT SHOW OFF WOULD STOOP SO LOW.
草薙静馬*
羽柴
ALWAYS PEGGED HIM FOR A LONE WARRIOR.
*SHIMUZA KUSANAGI

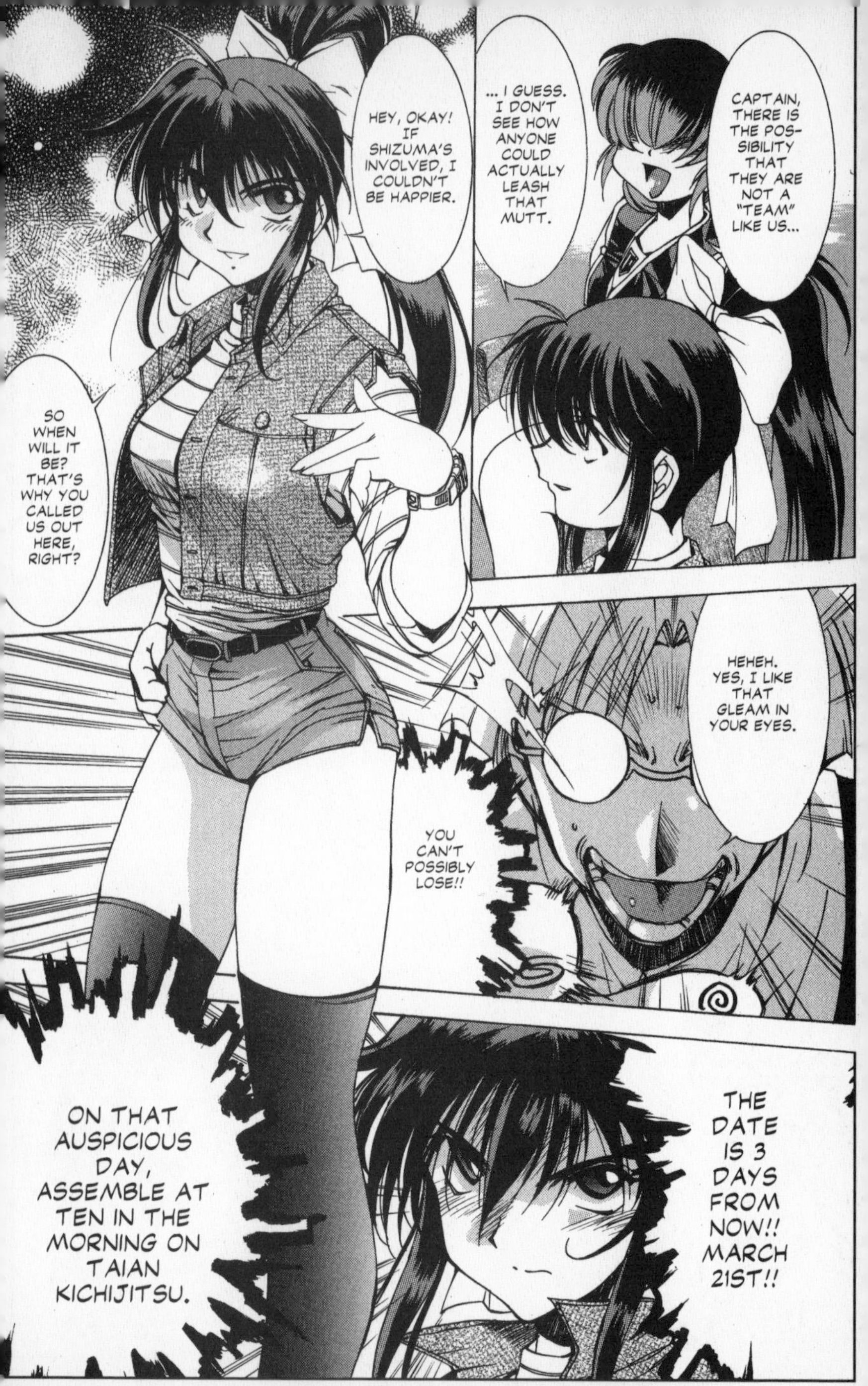
CAPTAIN, THERE IS THE POSSIBILITY THAT THEY ARE NOT A "TEAM" LIKE US...
... I GUESS. I DON'T SEE HOW ANYONE COULD ACTUALLY LEASH THAT MUTT.
HEY, OKAY! IF SHIZUMA'S INVOLVED, I COULDN'T BE HAPPIER.
SO WHEN WILL IT BE? THAT'S WHY YOU CALLED US OUT HERE, RIGHT?
HEHEH. YES, I LIKE THAT GLEAM IN YOUR EYES.
YOU CAN'T POSSIBLY LOSE!!
THE DATE IS 3 DAYS FROM NOW!! MARCH 21ST!!
ON THAT AUSPICIOUS DAY, ASSEMBLE AT TEN IN THE MORNING ON TAIAN KICHIJITSU.

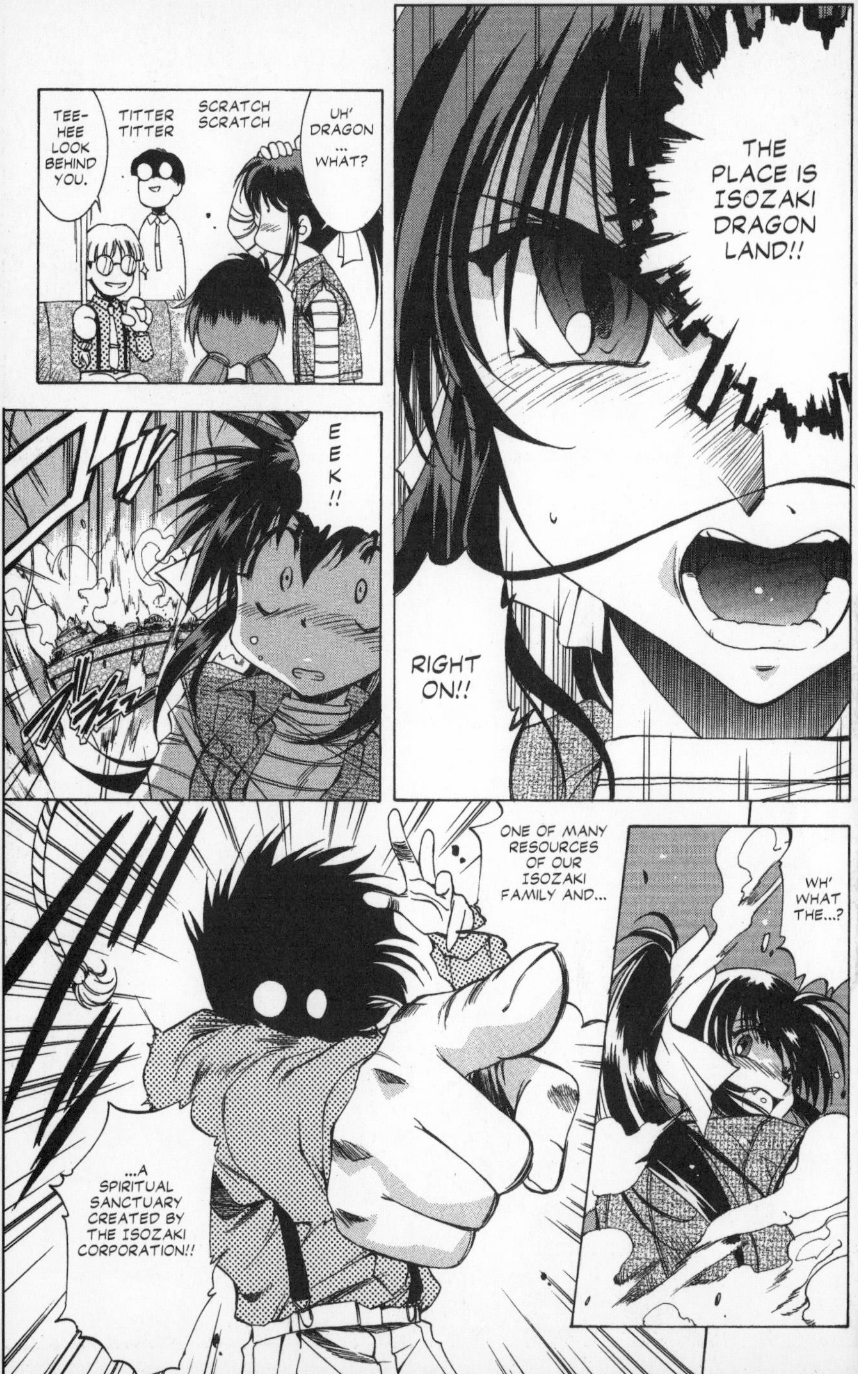
THE PLACE IS ISOZAKI DRAGON LAND!!
RIGHT ON!!
UH' DRAGON ... WHAT?
SCRATCH SCRATCH
TITTER TITTER
TEE-HEE LOOK BEHIND YOU.
EEEK!!
WH' WHAT THE...?
ONE OF MANY RESOURCES OF OUR ISOZAKI FAMILY AND...
...A SPIRITUAL SANCTUARY CREATED BY THE ISOZAKI CORPORATION!!

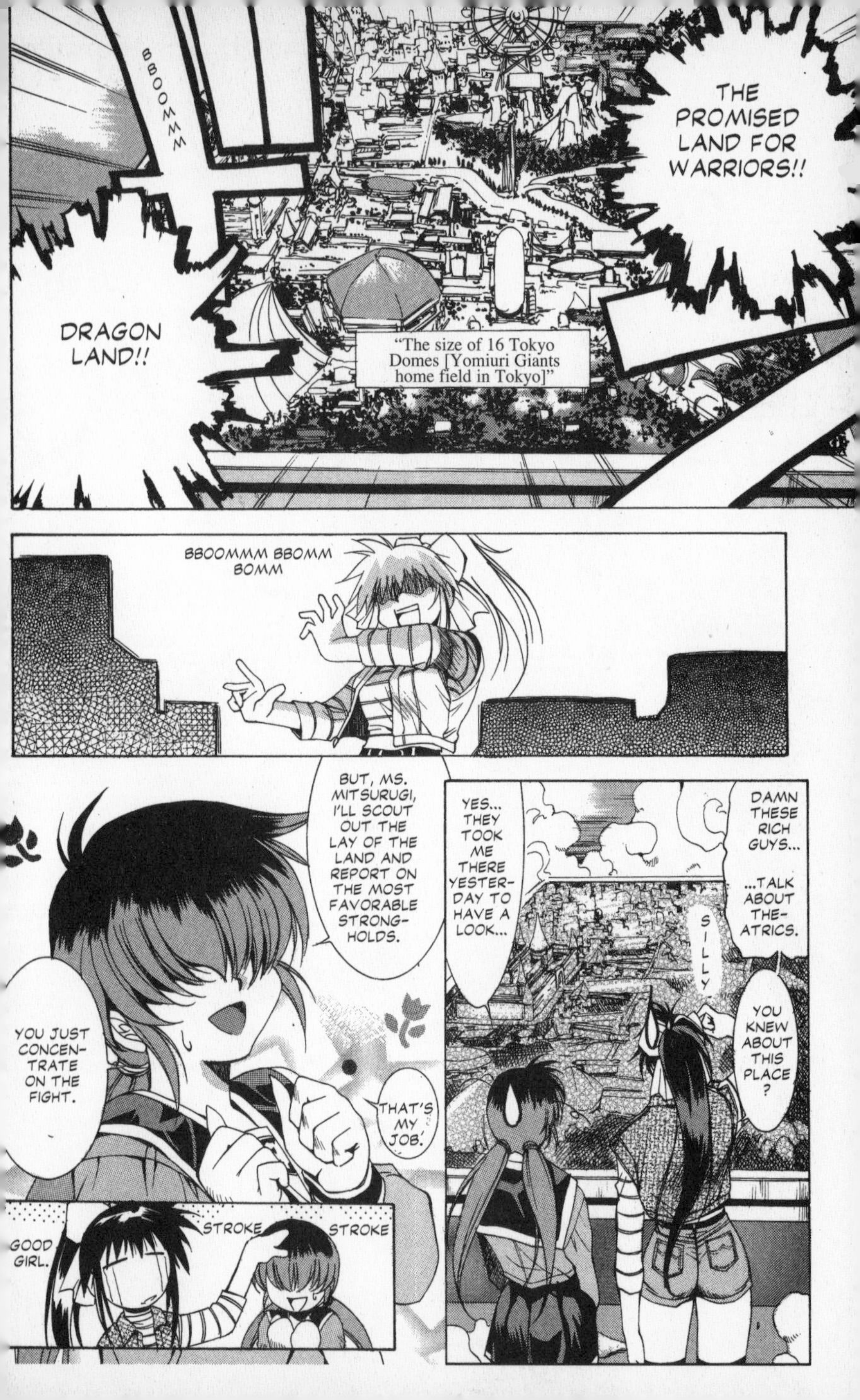
THE PROMISED LAND FOR WARRIORS!!
BBOOMMM
"The size of 16 Tokyo Domes [Yomiuri Giants home field in Tokyo]"
DRAGON LAND!!
BBOOMMM BBOMM BOMM
DAMN THESE RICH GUYS...
...TALK ABOUT THEATRICS.
SILLY
YOU KNEW ABOUT THIS PLACE?
YES... THEY TOOK ME THERE YESTERDAY TO HAVE A LOOK...
BUT, MS. MITSURUGI, I'LL SCOUT OUT THE LAY OF THE LAND AND REPORT ON THE MOST FAVORABLE STRONGHOLDS.
YOU JUST CONCENTRATE ON THE FIGHT.
THAT'S MY JOB.
STROKE
STROKE
GOOD GIRL.

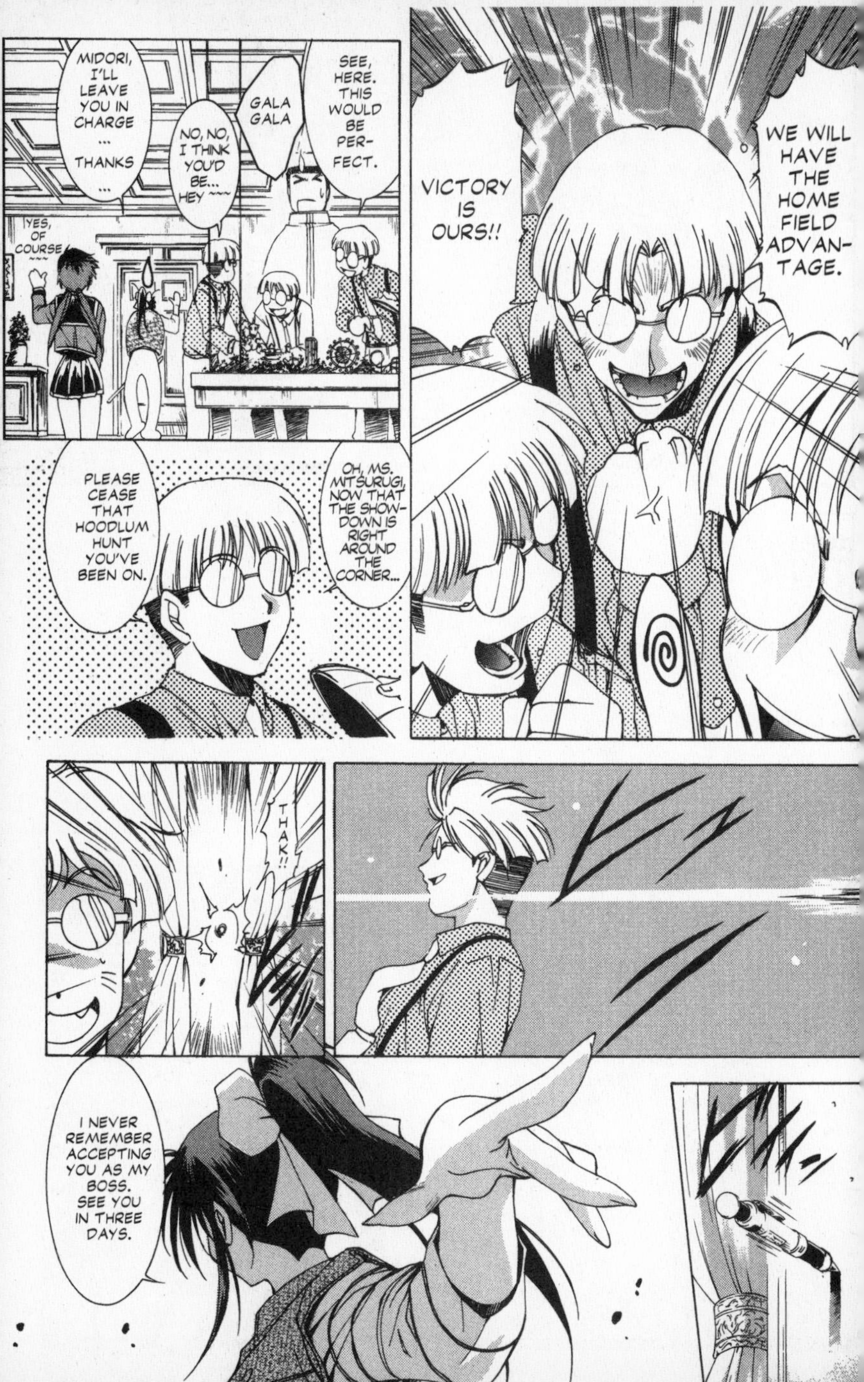
WE WILL HAVE THE HOME FIELD ADVANTAGE.
VICTORY IS OURS!!
SEE, HERE. THIS WOULD BE PERFECT.
GALA GALA
NO, NO, I THINK YOU'D BE... HEY ~~~
MIDORI, I'LL LEAVE YOU IN CHARGE ... THANKS ...
YES, OF COURSE ~~~
OH, MS. MITSURUGI, NOW THAT THE SHOWDOWN IS RIGHT AROUND THE CORNER...
PLEASE CEASE THAT HOODLUM HUNT YOU'VE BEEN ON.
THAK!!
I NEVER REMEMBER ACCEPTING YOU AS MY BOSS. SEE YOU IN THREE DAYS.

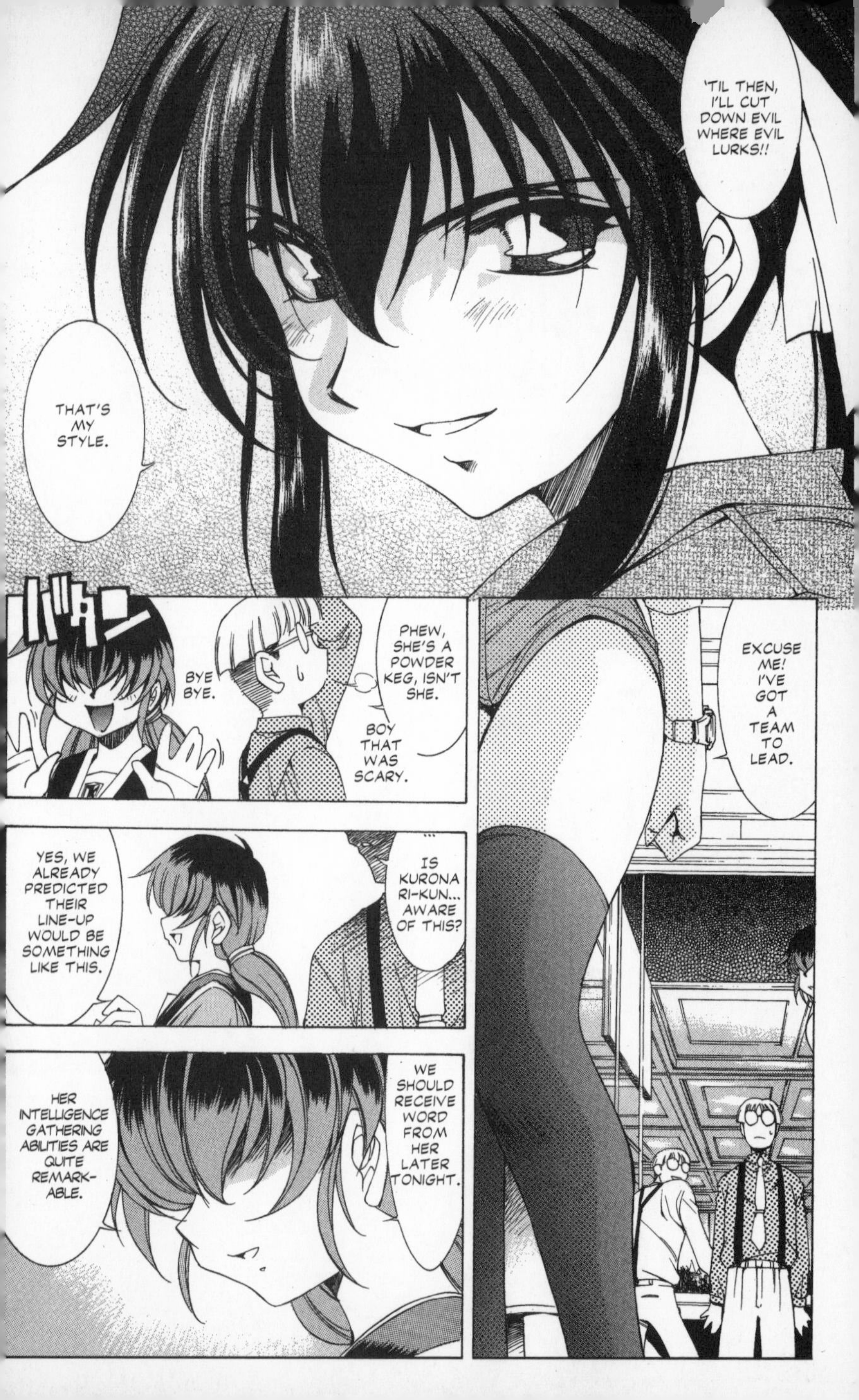
'TIL THEN, I'LL CUT DOWN EVIL WHERE EVIL LURKS!!
THAT'S MY STYLE.
EXCUSE ME! I'VE GOT A TEAM TO LEAD.
バタン
PHEW, SHE'S A POWDER KEG, ISN'T SHE.
BOY THAT WAS SCARY.
BYE BYE.
...
IS KURONARI-KUN... AWARE OF THIS?
YES, WE ALREADY PREDICTED THEIR LINE-UP WOULD BE SOMETHING LIKE THIS.
WE SHOULD RECEIVE WORD FROM HER LATER TONIGHT.
HER INTELLIGENCE GATHERING ABILITIES ARE QUITE REMARK-ABLE.

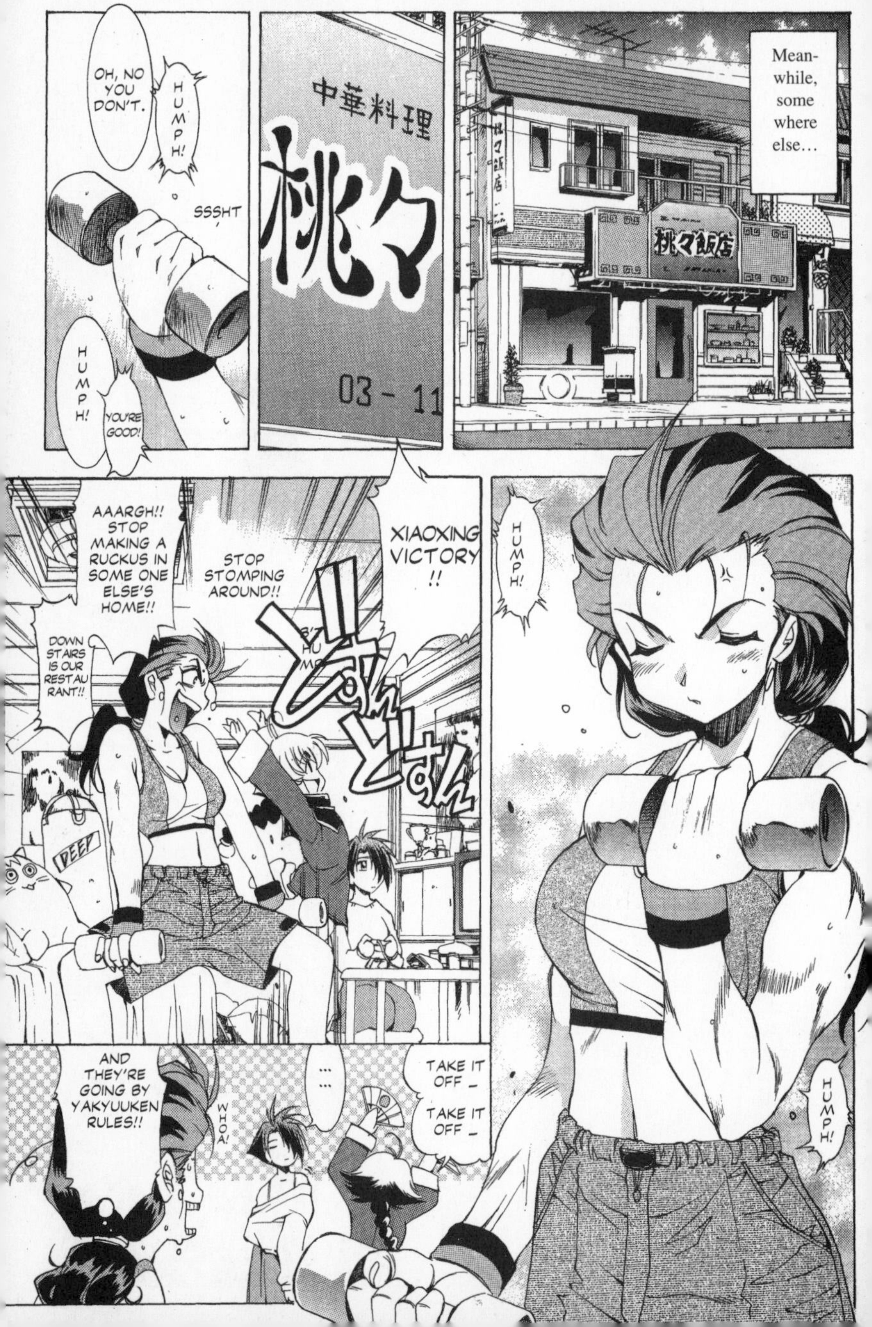
Mean-while, some where else…
桃々飯店
中華料理
桃々
03 - 11
OH, NO YOU DON'T.
HUMPH!
SSSHT
HUMPH!
YOU'RE GOOD!
HUMPH!
XIAOXING VICTORY!!
どすん どすん
STOP STOMPING AROUND!!
AAARGH!! STOP MAKING A RUCKUS IN SOME ONE ELSE'S HOME!!
DOWN STAIRS IS OUR RESTAU RANT!!
DEEP
HUMPH!
TAKE IT OFF _
TAKE IT OFF _
……
WHOA!
AND THEY'RE GOING BY YAKYUUKEN RULES!!

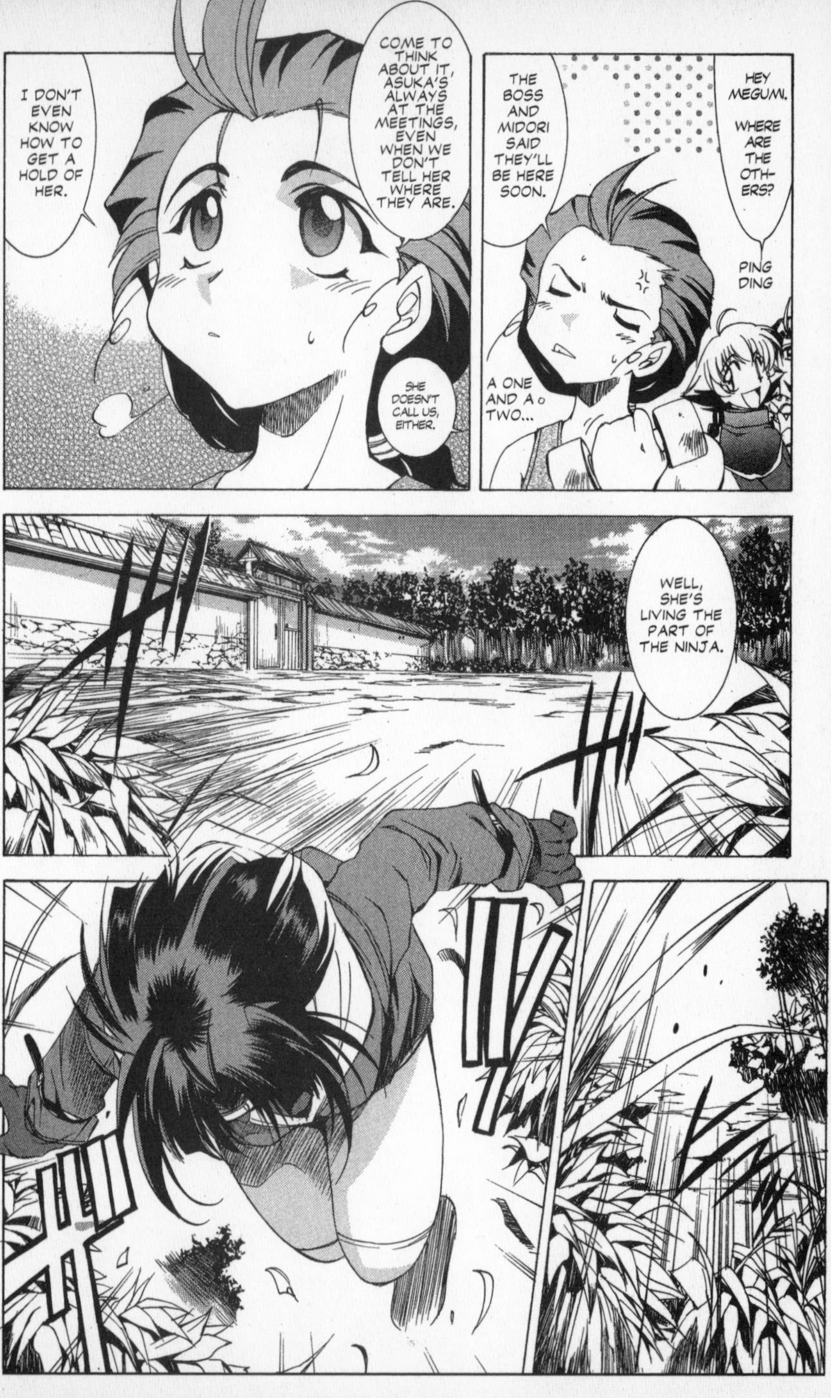
HEY MEGUMI. WHERE ARE THE OTH-ERS?
PING DING
THE BOSS AND MIDORI SAID THEY'LL BE HERE SOON.
A ONE AND A TWO...
COME TO THINK ABOUT IT, ASUKA'S ALWAYS AT THE MEETINGS, EVEN WHEN WE DON'T TELL HER WHERE THEY ARE.
SHE DOESN'T CALL US, EITHER.
I DON'T EVEN KNOW HOW TO GET A HOLD OF HER.
WELL, SHE'S LIVING THE PART OF THE NINJA.

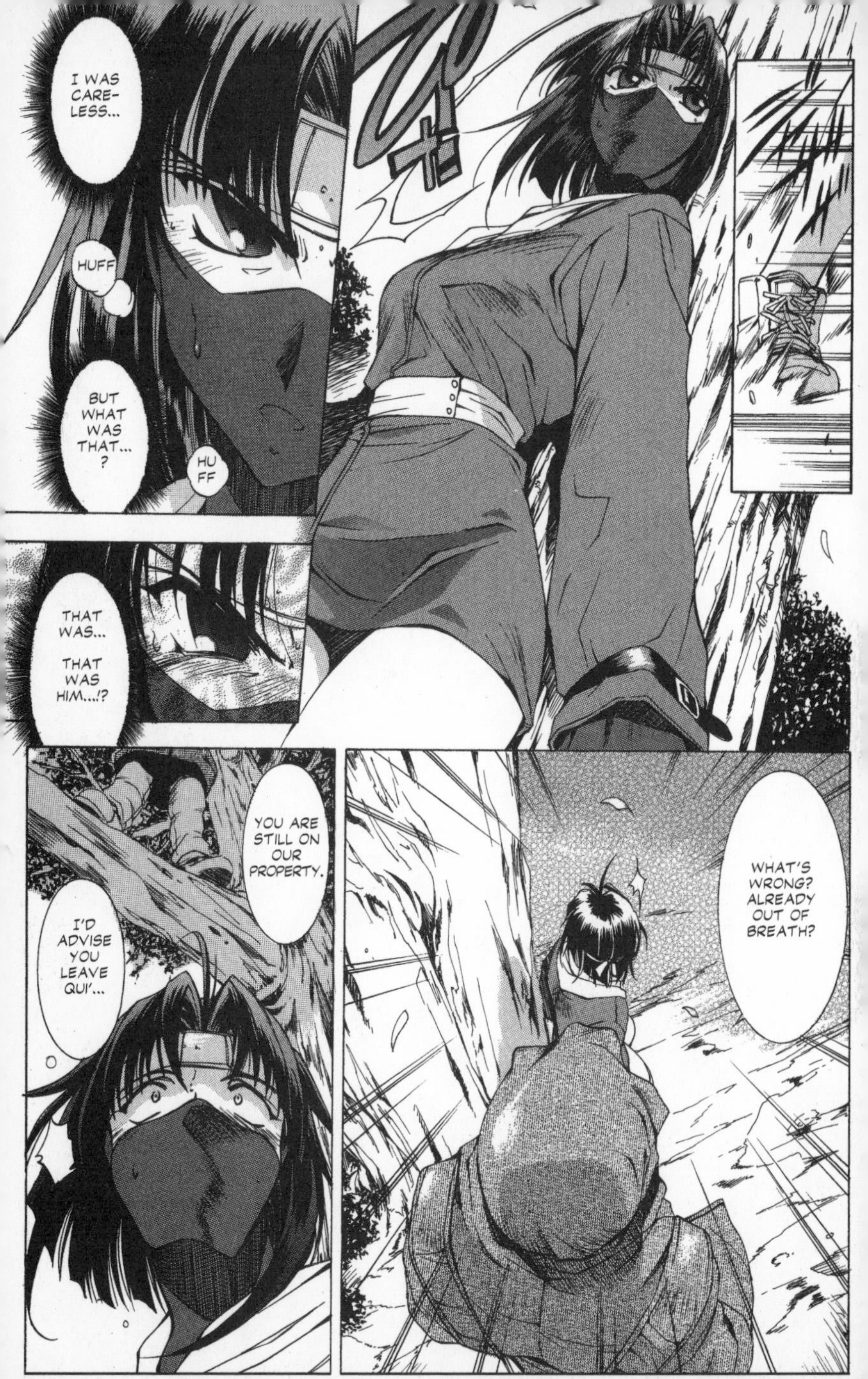
I WAS CARE-LESS...
HUFF
BUT WHAT WAS THAT...?
HU FF
THAT WAS...
THAT WAS HIM...!?
WHAT'S WRONG? ALREADY OUT OF BREATH?
YOU ARE STILL ON OUR PROPERTY.
I'D ADVISE YOU LEAVE QUI'...

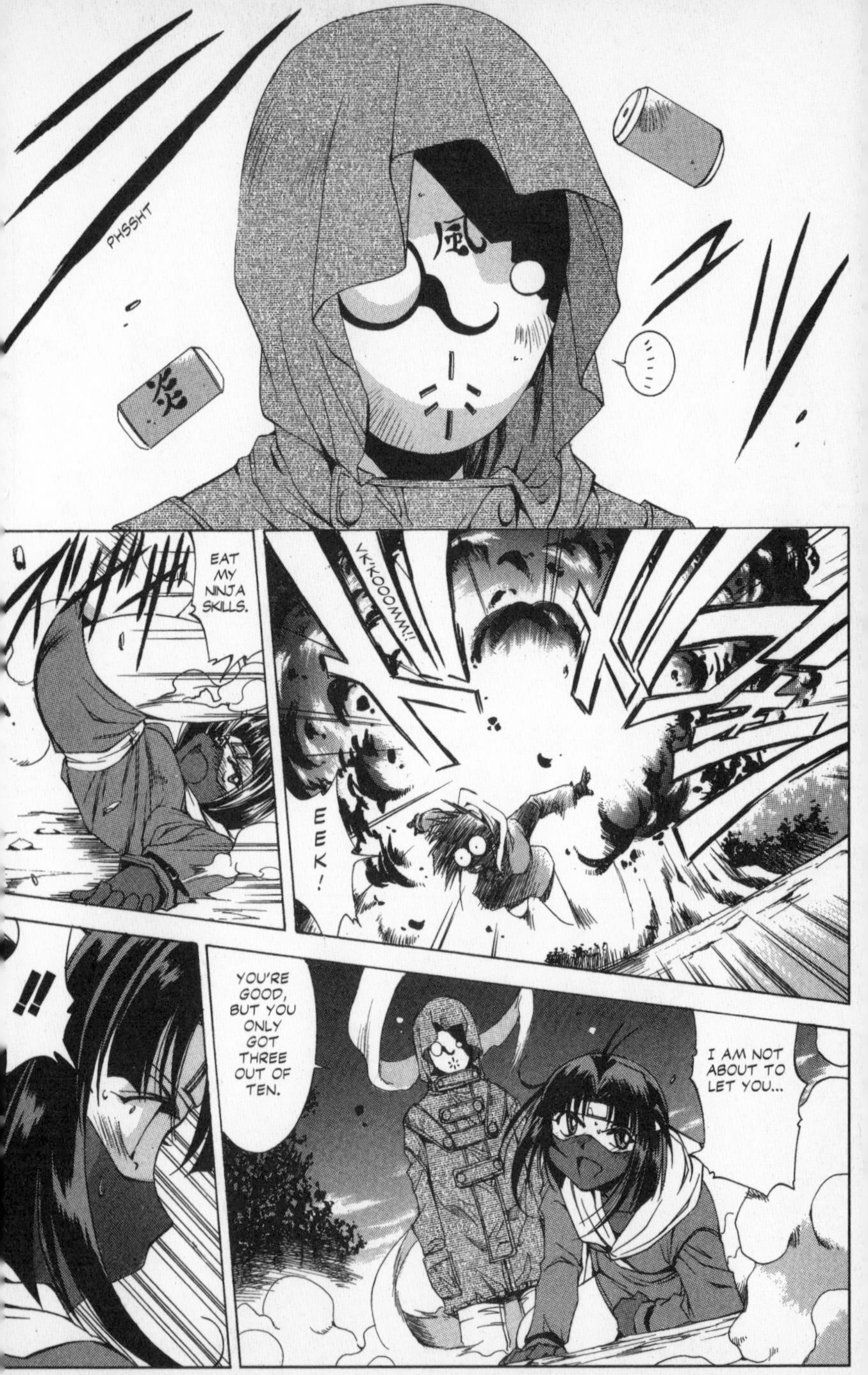
PHSSHT
...
VK'KOOOMM!!
EEK!
EAT MY NINJA SKILLS.
I AM NOT ABOUT TO LET YOU...
YOU'RE GOOD, BUT YOU ONLY GOT THREE OUT OF TEN.
!!

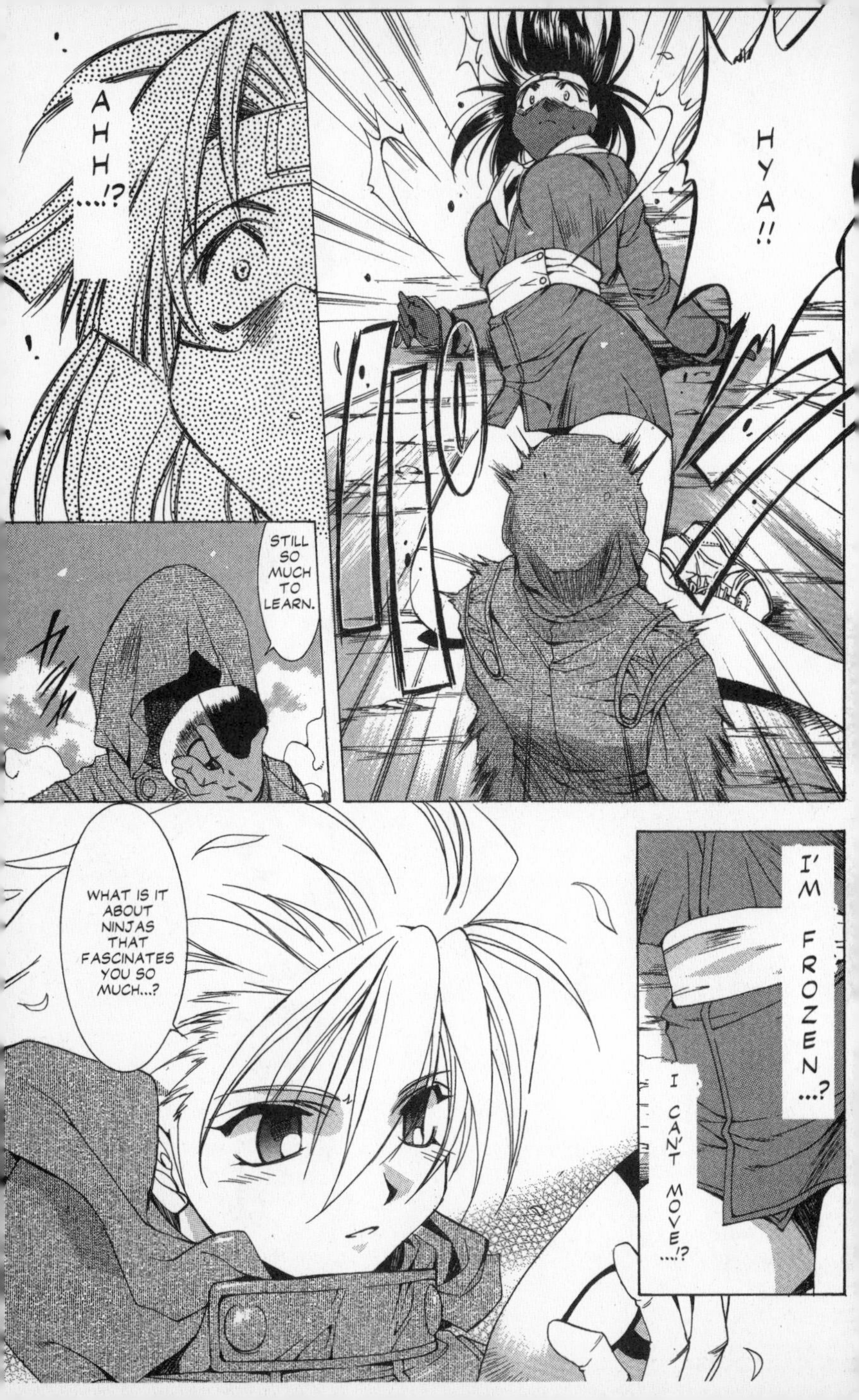

HYA!!
AHH...!?
STILL SO MUCH TO LEARN.
I'M FROZEN...?
I CAN'T MOVE...!?
WHAT IS IT ABOUT NINJAS THAT FASCINATES YOU SO MUCH...?

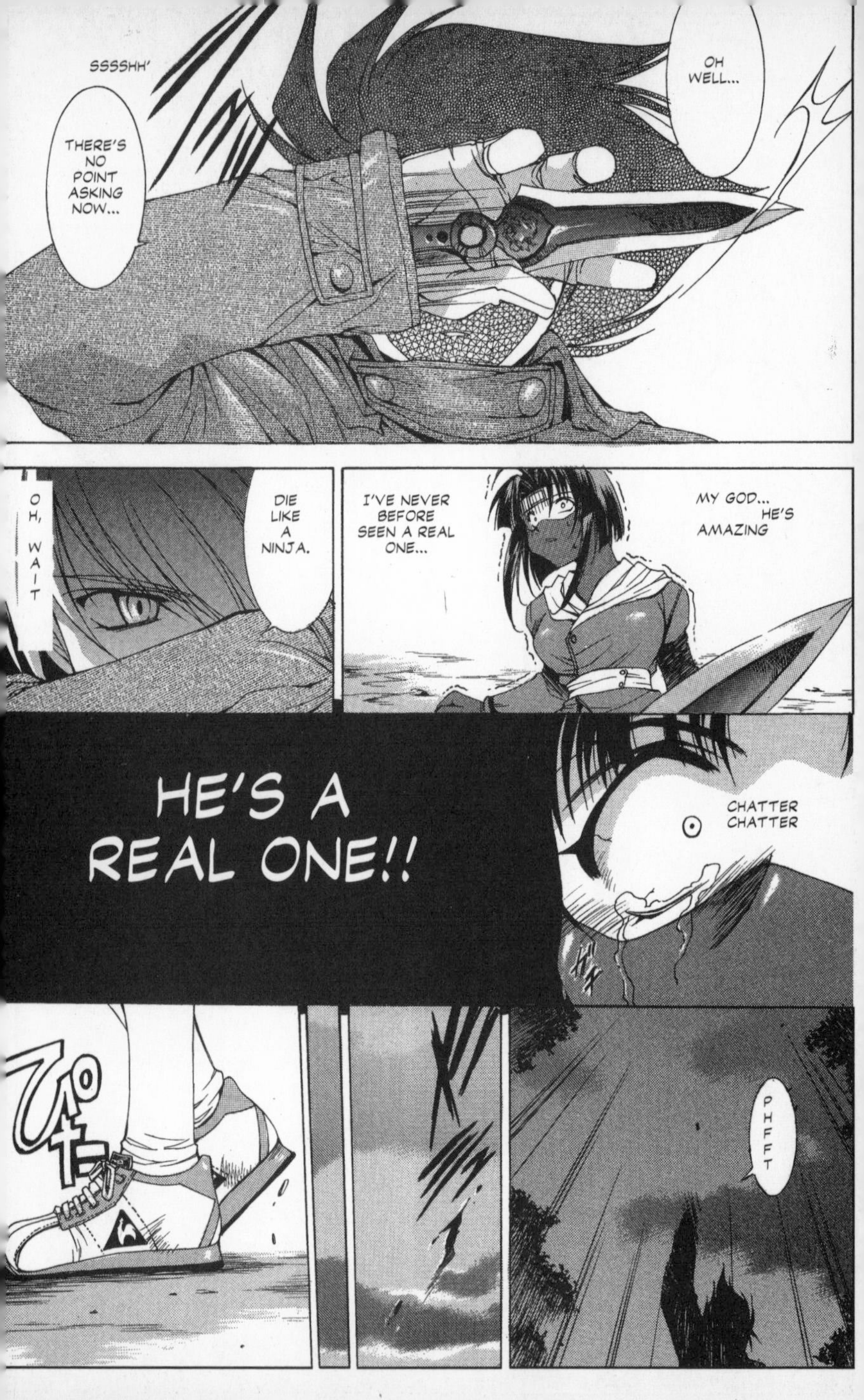
OH WELL...
SSSSHH'
THERE'S NO POINT ASKING NOW...
MY GOD... HE'S AMAZING
I'VE NEVER BEFORE SEEN A REAL ONE...
DIE LIKE A NINJA.
OH, WAIT
CHATTER CHATTER
HE'S A REAL ONE!!
PHFFT

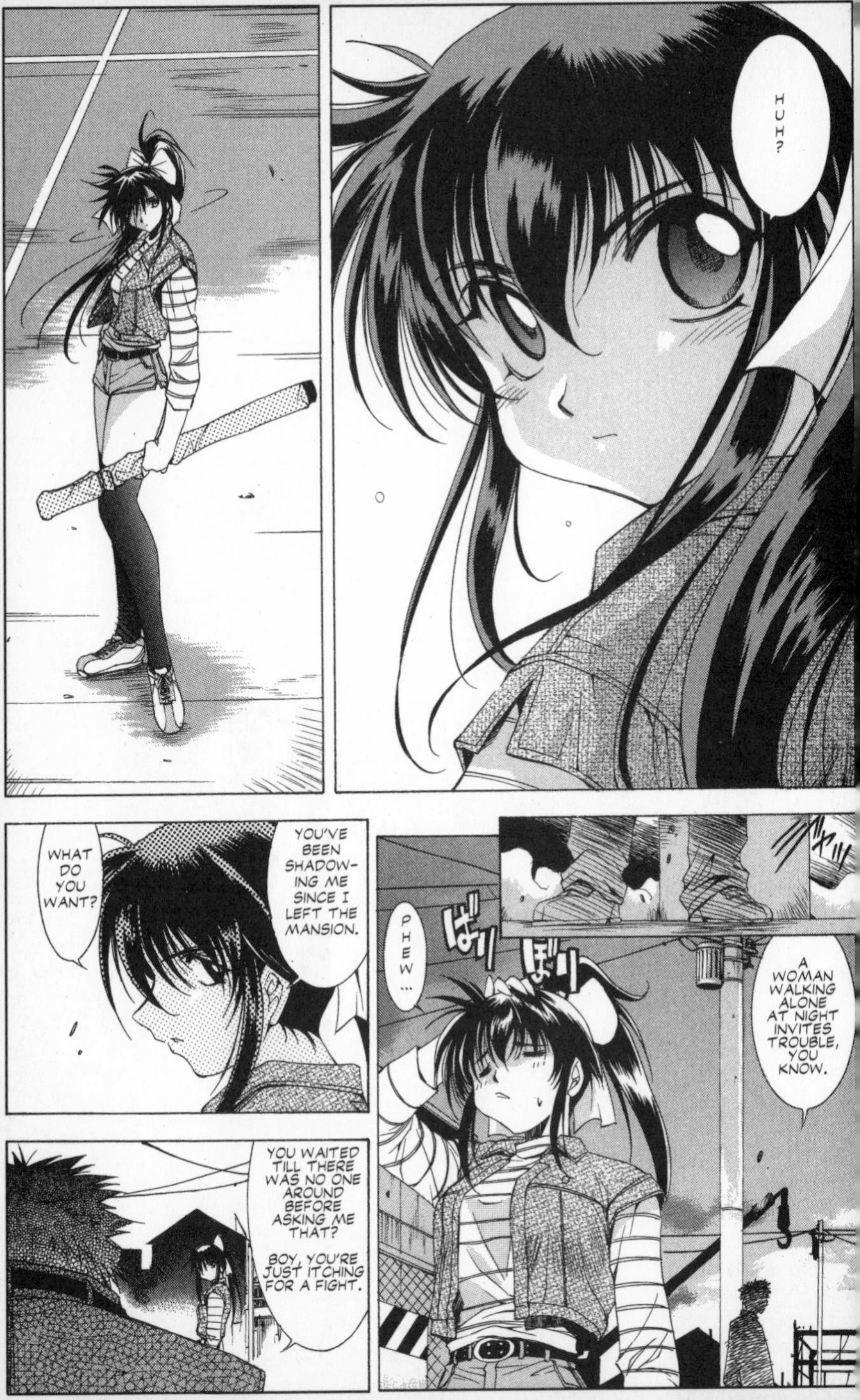
HUH?
A WOMAN WALKING ALONE AT NIGHT INVITES TROUBLE, YOU KNOW.
PHEW...
YOU'VE BEEN SHADOWING ME SINCE I LEFT THE MANSION.
WHAT DO YOU WANT?
YOU WAITED TILL THERE WAS NO ONE AROUND BEFORE ASKING ME THAT?
BOY, YOU'RE JUST ITCHING FOR A FIGHT.

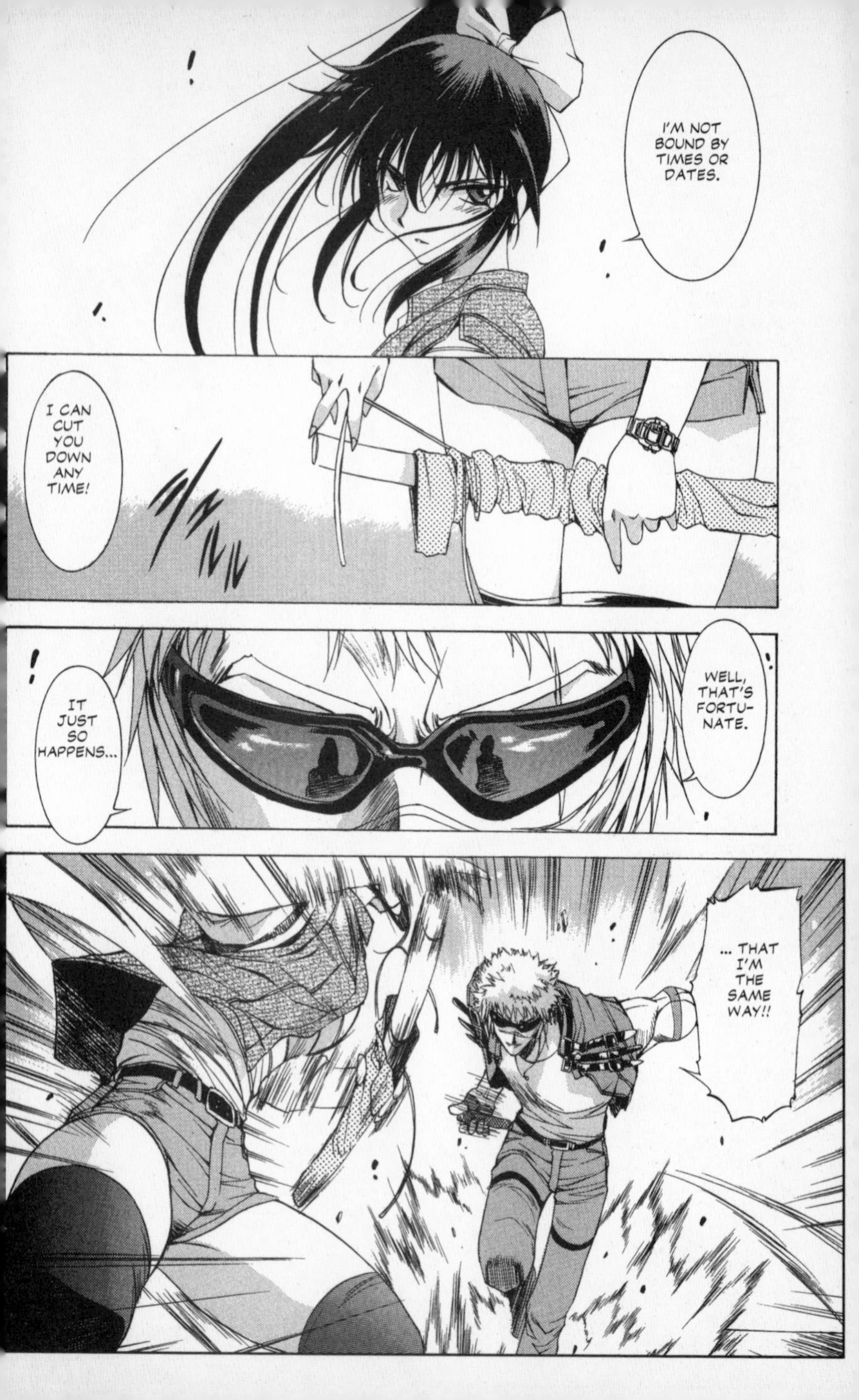
I'M NOT BOUND BY TIMES OR DATES.
I CAN CUT YOU DOWN ANY TIME!
WELL, THAT'S FORTU-NATE.
IT JUST SO HAPPENS...
... THAT I'M THE SAME WAY!!

Episode 28 The Kinds of Days That Are Poison for the Soul

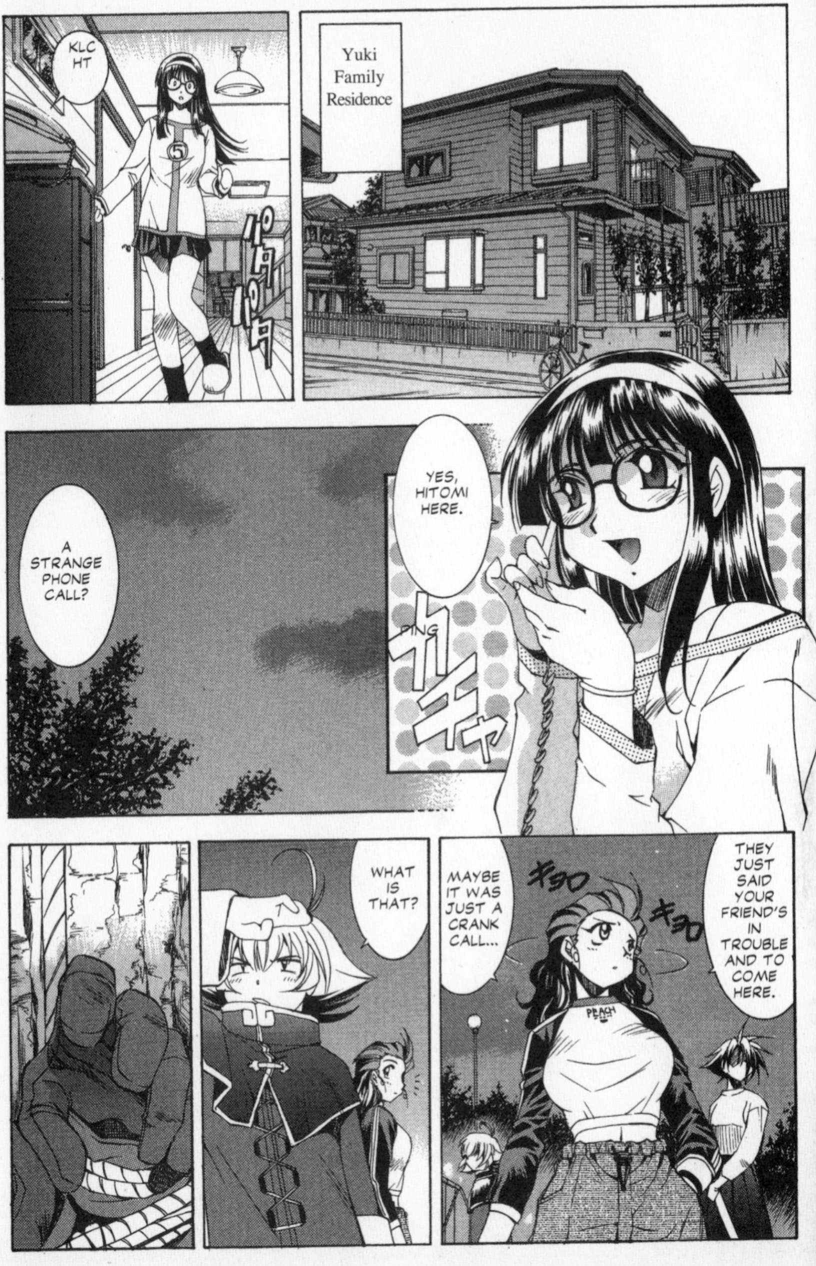
Yuki Family Residence
KLC HT
パタパタ
YES, HITOMI HERE.
PING
カチャ
A STRANGE PHONE CALL?
THEY JUST SAID YOUR FRIEND'S IN TROUBLE AND TO COME HERE.
MAYBE IT WAS JUST A CRANK CALL...
PEACH
WHAT IS THAT?

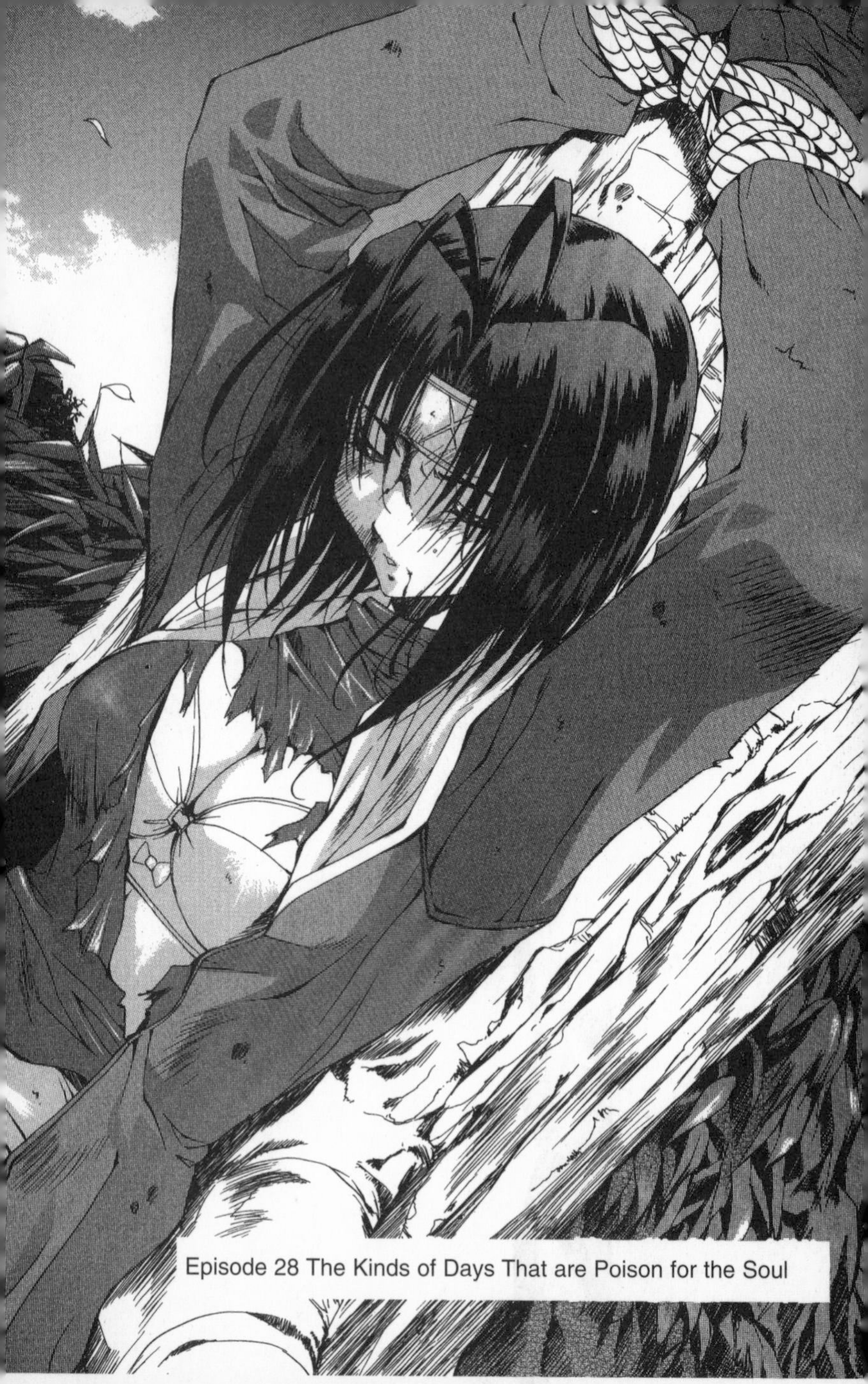

Episode 28 The Kinds of Days That are Poison for the Soul

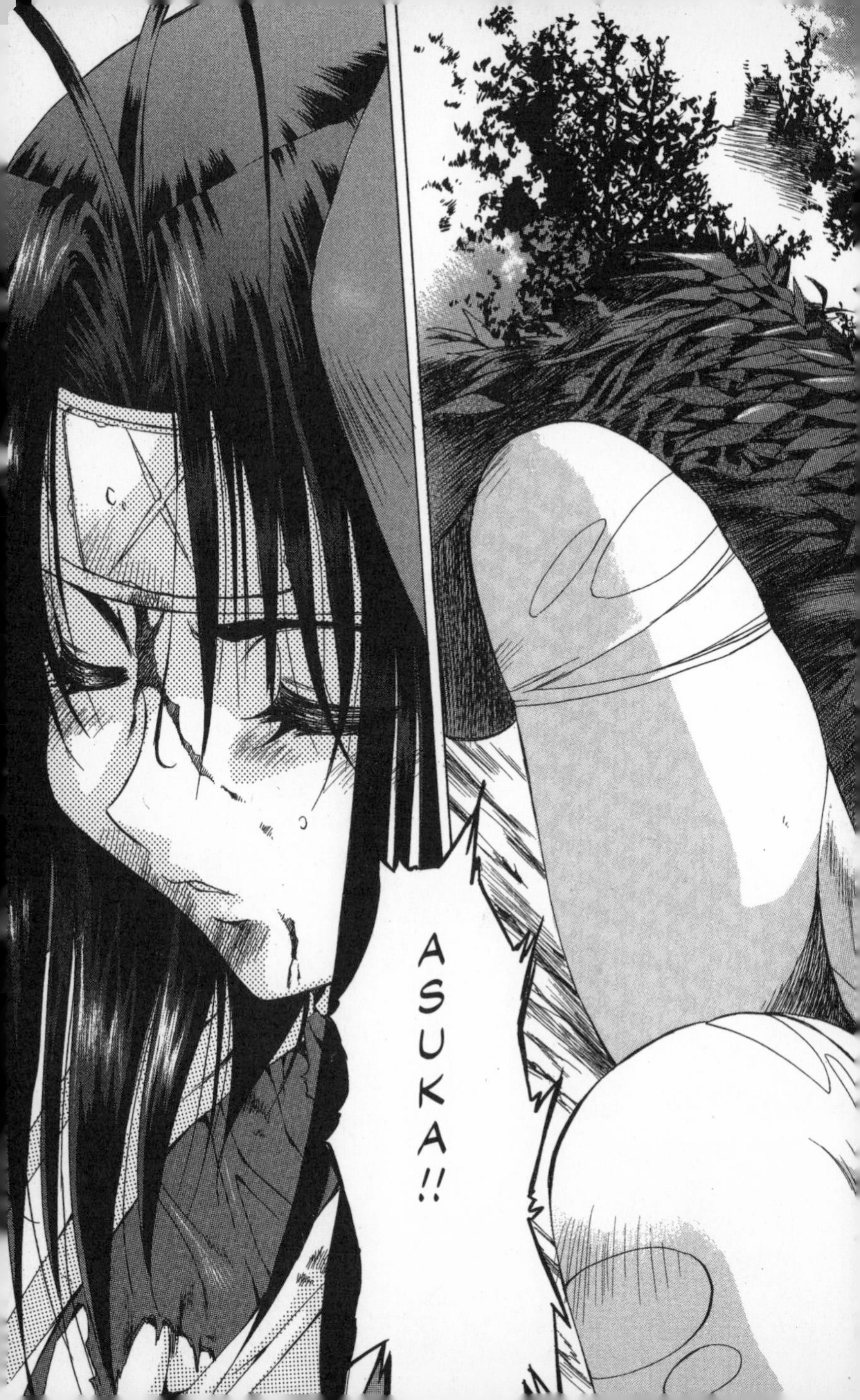
ASUKA!!

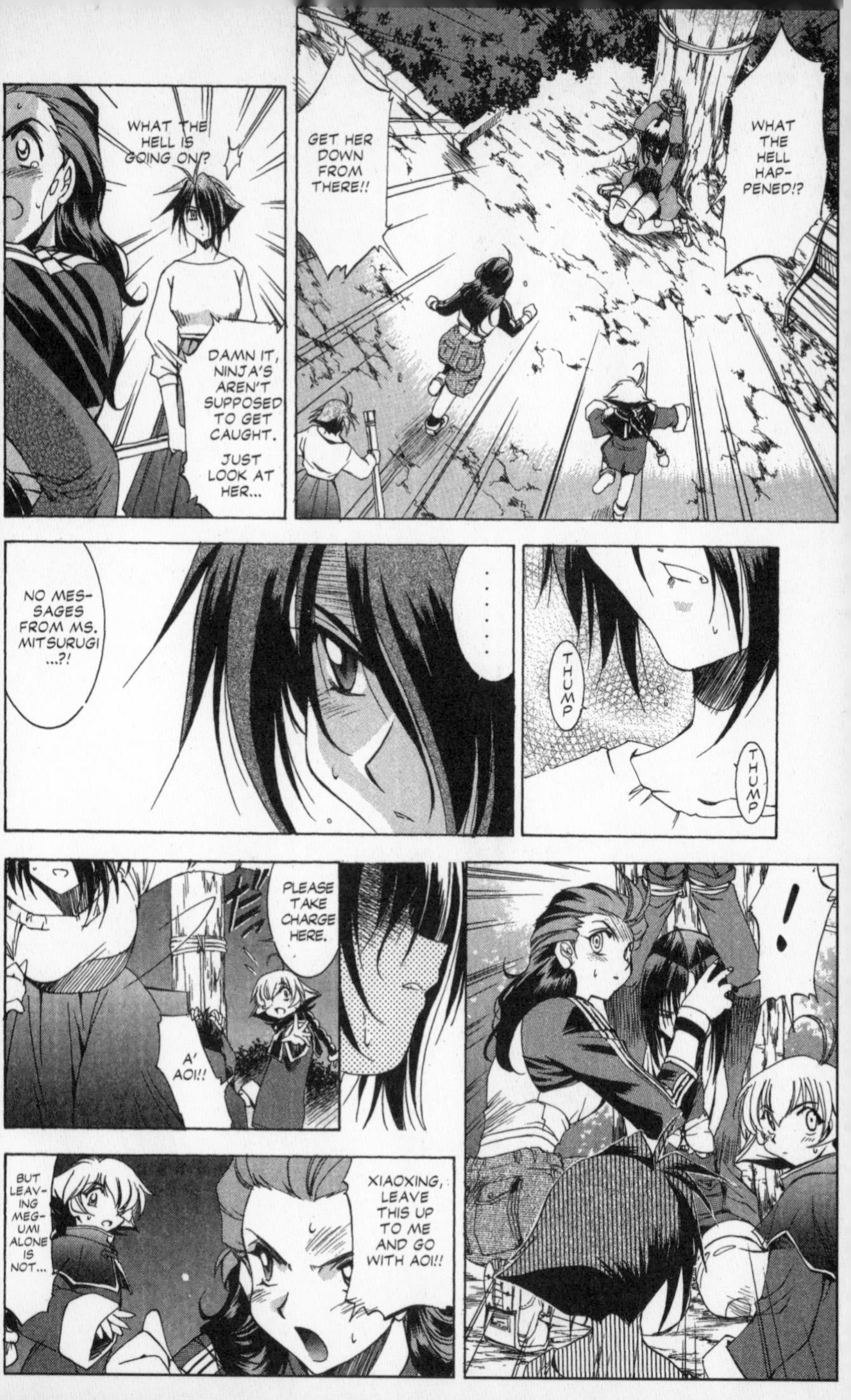
WHAT THE HELL HAP-PENED!?
GET HER DOWN FROM THERE!!
WHAT THE HELL IS GOING ON!?
DAMN IT, NINJA'S AREN'T SUPPOSED TO GET CAUGHT.
JUST LOOK AT HER...
THUMP
THUMP
......
NO MES-SAGES FROM MS. MITSURUGI ...?!
!
PLEASE TAKE CHARGE HERE.
A' AOI!!
XIAOXING, LEAVE THIS UP TO ME AND GO WITH AOI!!
BUT LEAV-ING MEG-UMI ALONE IS NOT...

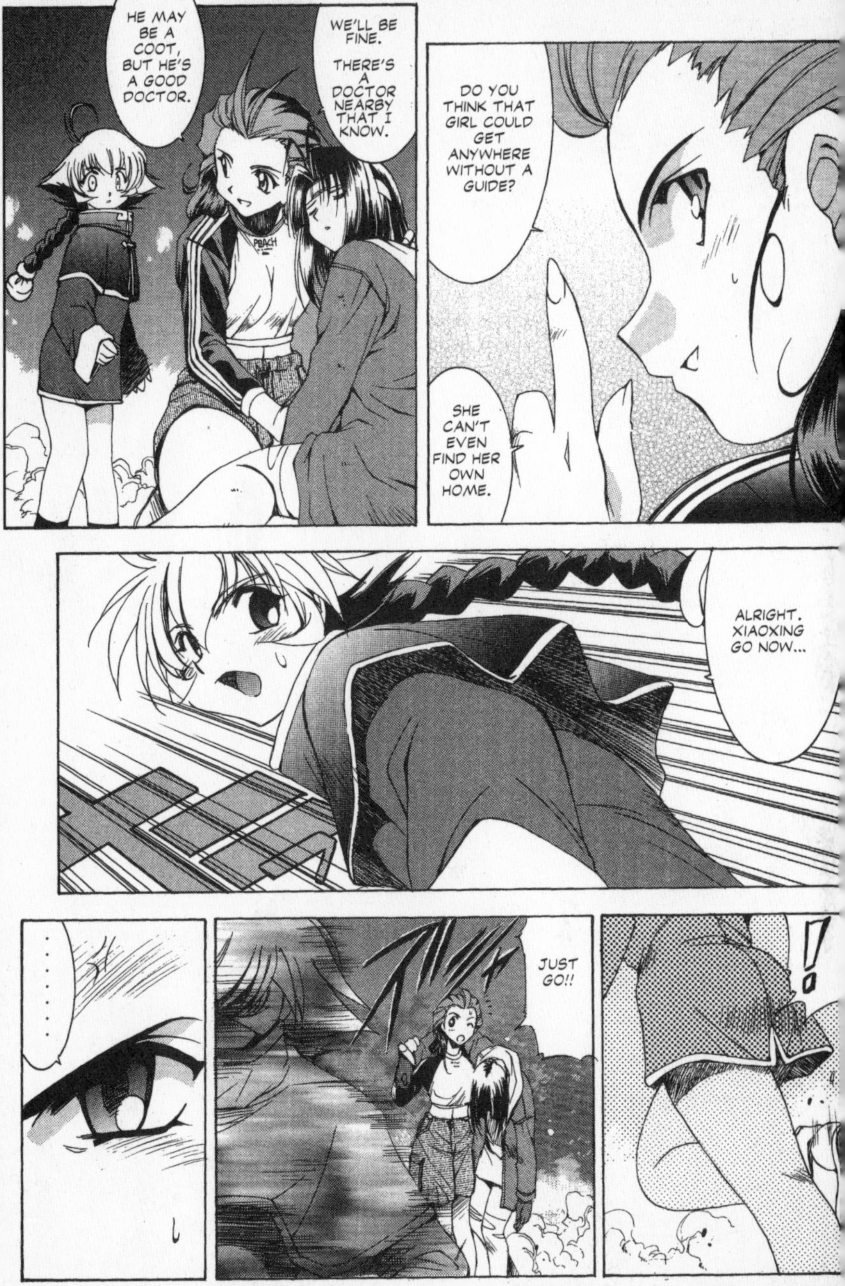
DO YOU THINK THAT GIRL COULD GET ANYWHERE WITHOUT A GUIDE?
SHE CAN'T EVEN FIND HER OWN HOME.
WE'LL BE FINE.
THERE'S A DOCTOR NEARBY THAT I KNOW.
HE MAY BE A COOT, BUT HE'S A GOOD DOCTOR.
ALRIGHT. XIAOXING GO NOW...
!?
JUST GO!!
......

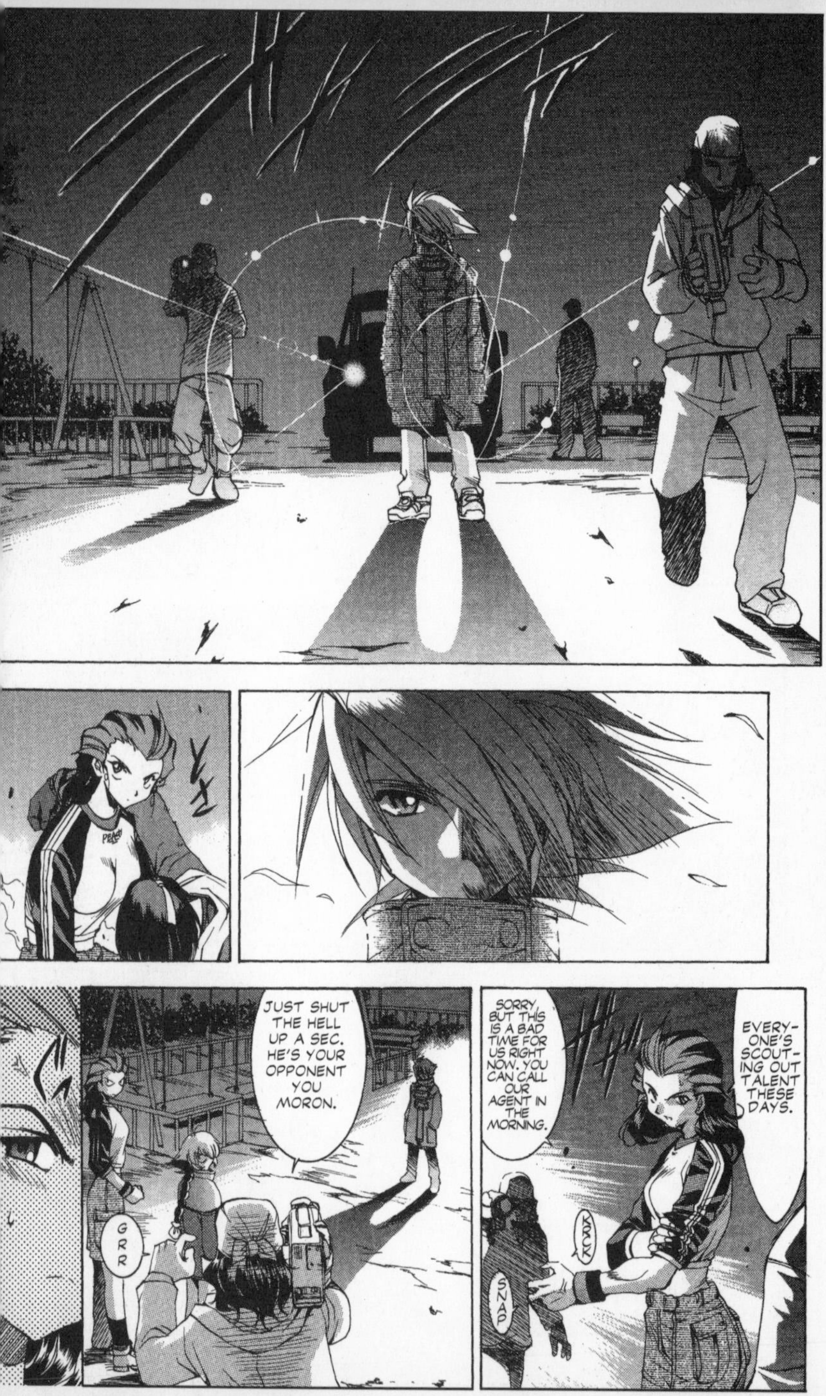
EVERY-ONE'S SCOUTING OUT TALENT THESE DAYS.
SORRY, BUT THIS IS A BAD TIME FOR US RIGHT NOW. YOU CAN CALL OUR AGENT IN THE MORNING.
KRCK
SNAP
JUST SHUT THE HELL UP A SEC. HE'S YOUR OPPONENT YOU MORON.
GRR

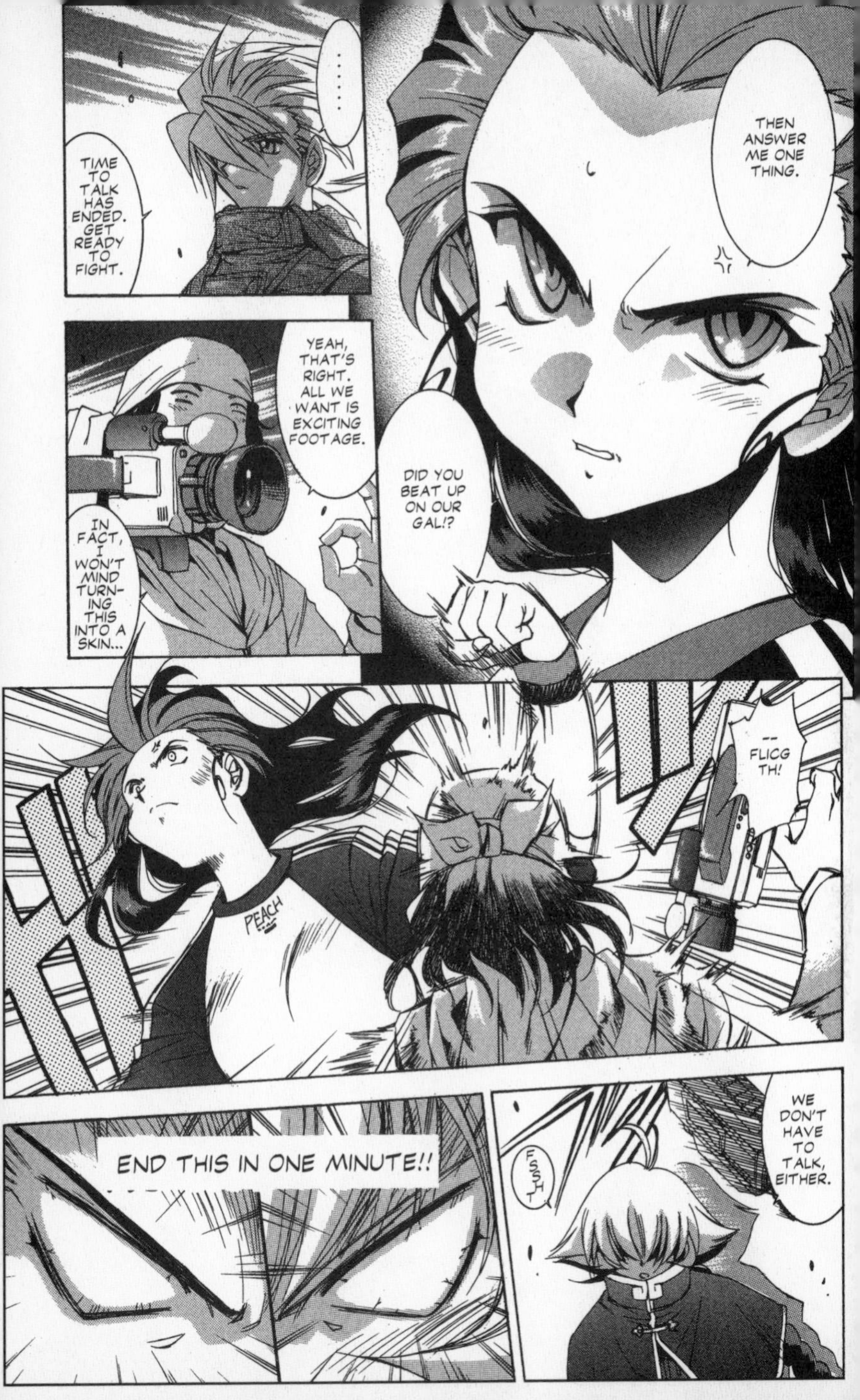
THEN ANSWER ME ONE THING.
DID YOU BEAT UP ON OUR GAL!?
......
TIME TO TALK HAS ENDED. GET READY TO FIGHT.
YEAH, THAT'S RIGHT. ALL WE WANT IS EXCITING FOOTAGE.
IN FACT, I WON'T MIND TURNING THIS INTO A SKIN...
-- FLICG TH!
PEACH
WE DON'T HAVE TO TALK, EITHER.
FSSHT
END THIS IN ONE MINUTE!!

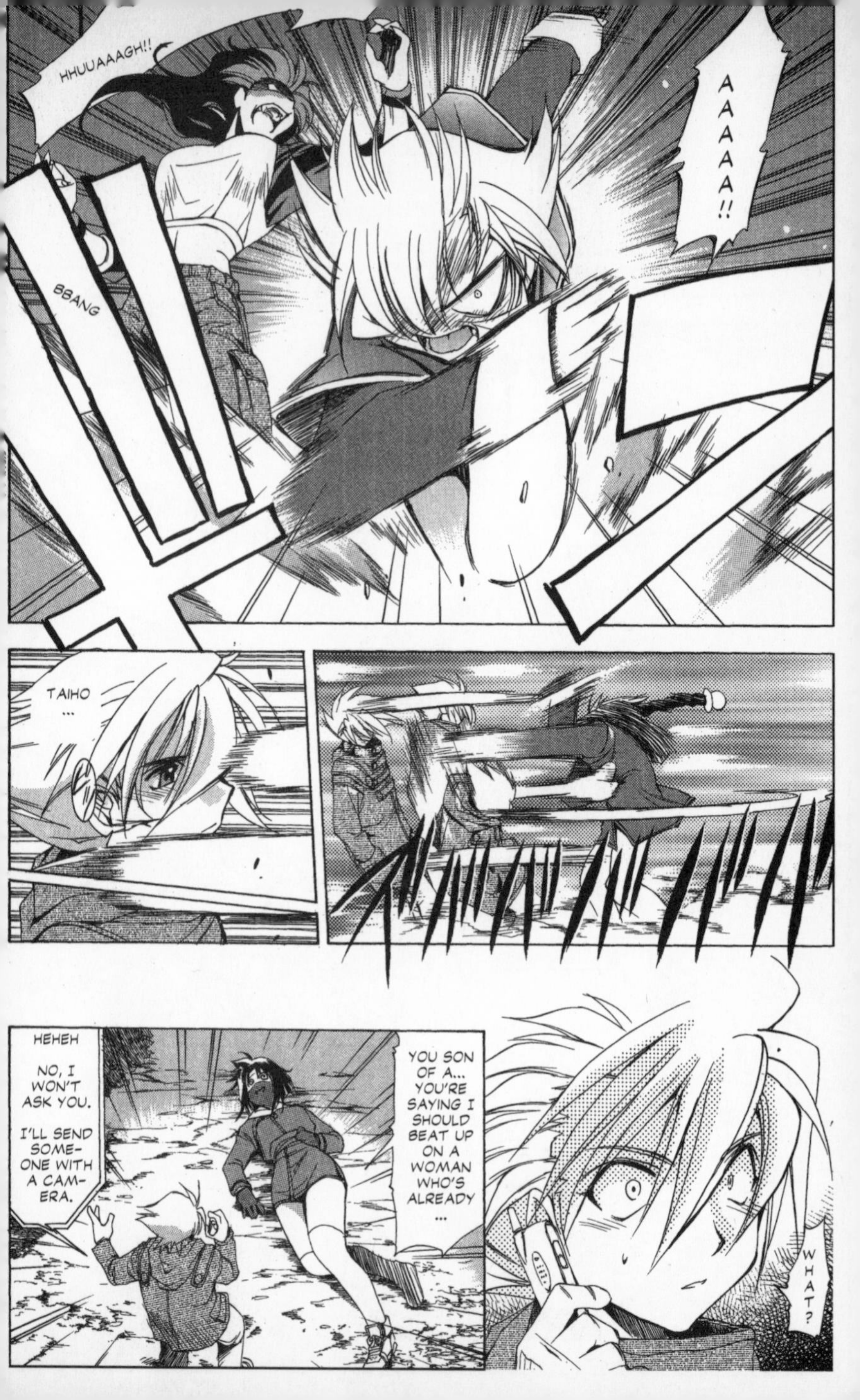
AAAAA!!
HHUUAAAGH!!
BBANG
TAIHO ...
WHAT?
YOU SON OF A... YOU'RE SAYING I SHOULD BEAT UP ON A WOMAN WHO'S ALREADY ...
HEHEH
NO, I WON'T ASK YOU.
I'LL SEND SOME-ONE WITH A CAM-ERA.

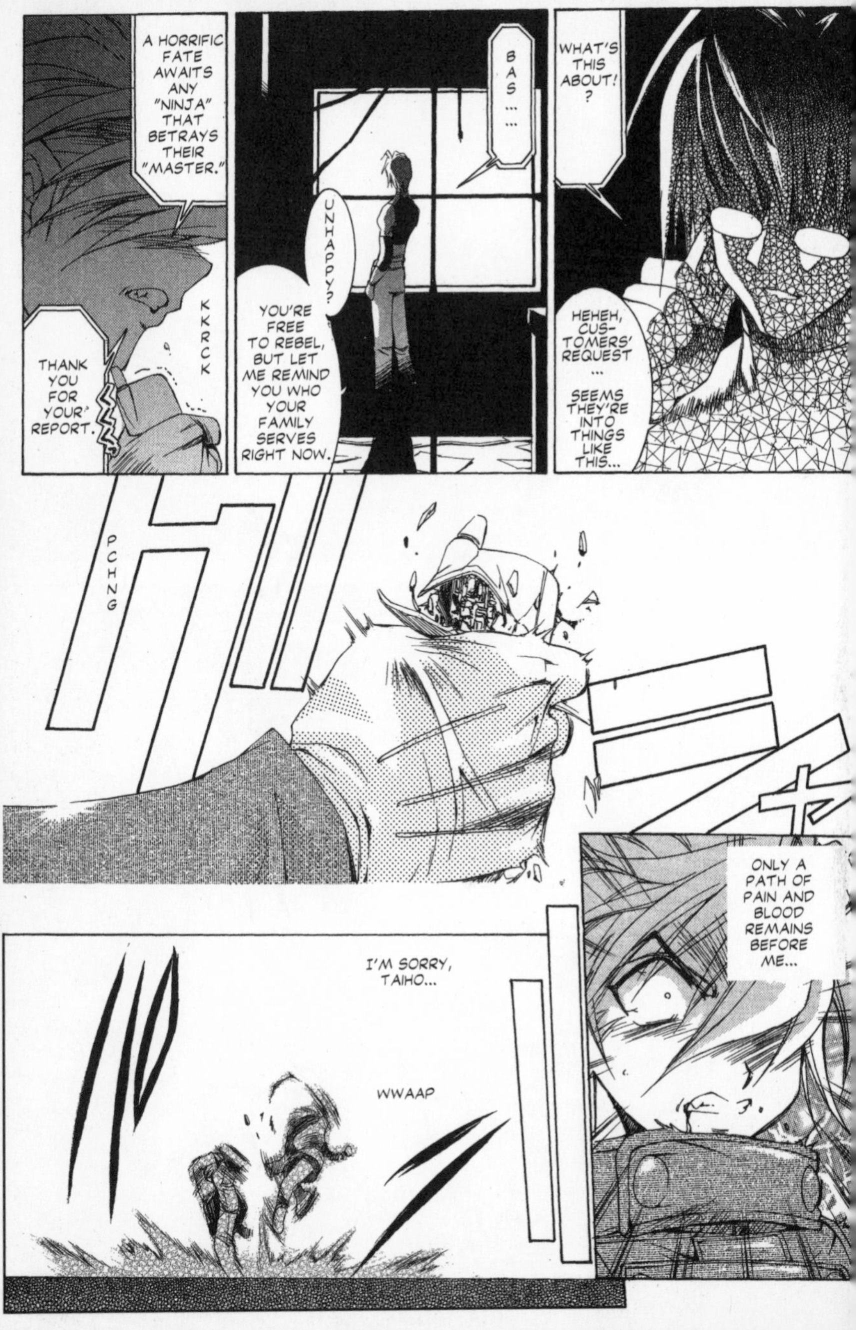
WHAT'S THIS ABOUT!?
HEHEH, CUS-TOMERS' REQUEST... SEEMS THEY'RE INTO THINGS LIKE THIS...
BAS......
UNHAPPY?
YOU'RE FREE TO REBEL, BUT LET ME REMIND YOU WHO YOUR FAMILY SERVES RIGHT NOW.
A HORRIFIC FATE AWAITS ANY "NINJA" THAT BETRAYS THEIR "MASTER."
KKRCK
THANK YOU FOR YOUR REPORT.
PCHNG
ONLY A PATH OF PAIN AND BLOOD REMAINS BEFORE ME...
I'M SORRY, TAIHO...
WWAAP

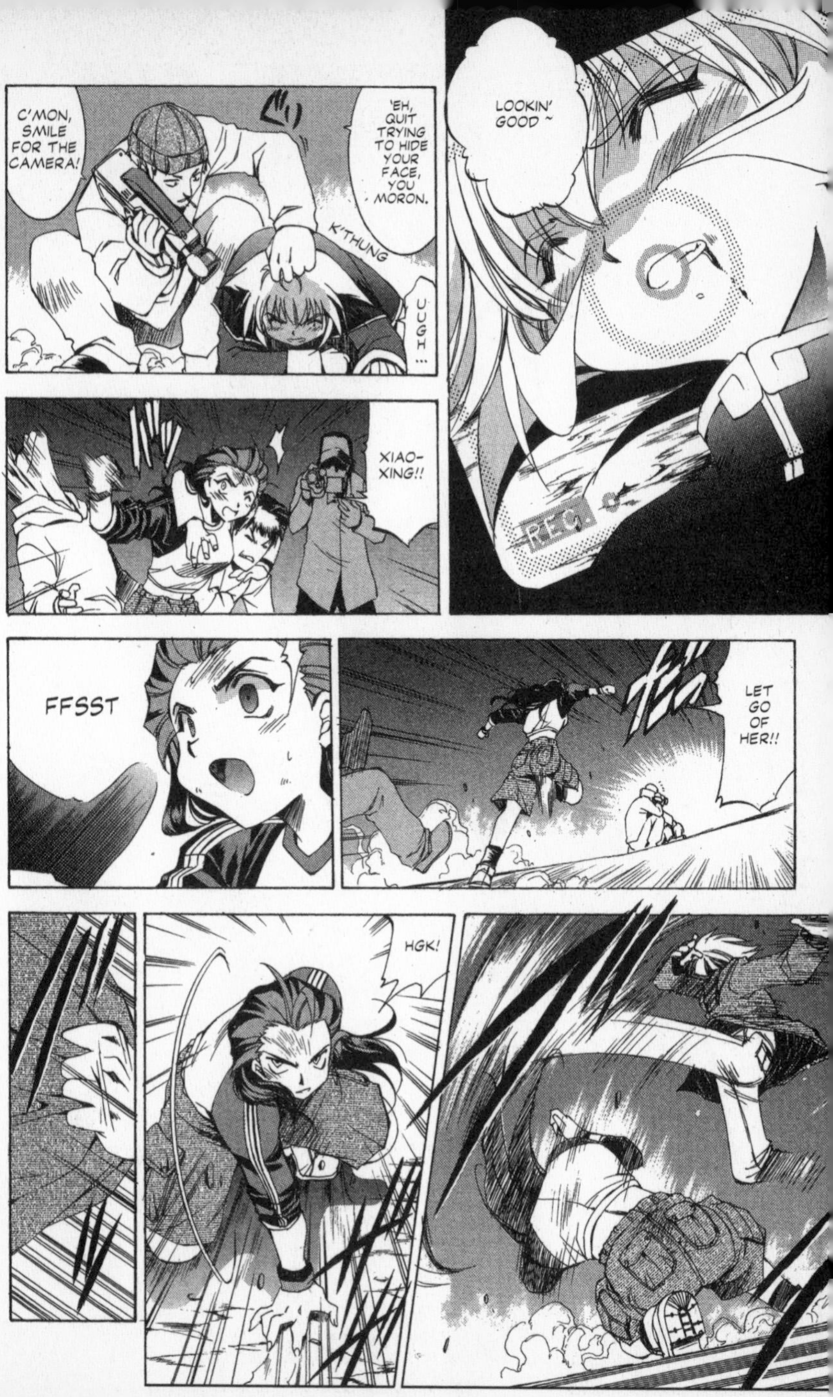
LOOKIN' GOOD ~
REC
'EH, QUIT TRYING TO HIDE YOUR FACE, YOU MORON.
C'MON, SMILE FOR THE CAMERA!
K'THUNG
UUGH...
XIAO-XING!!
LET GO OF HER!!
FFSST
HGK!

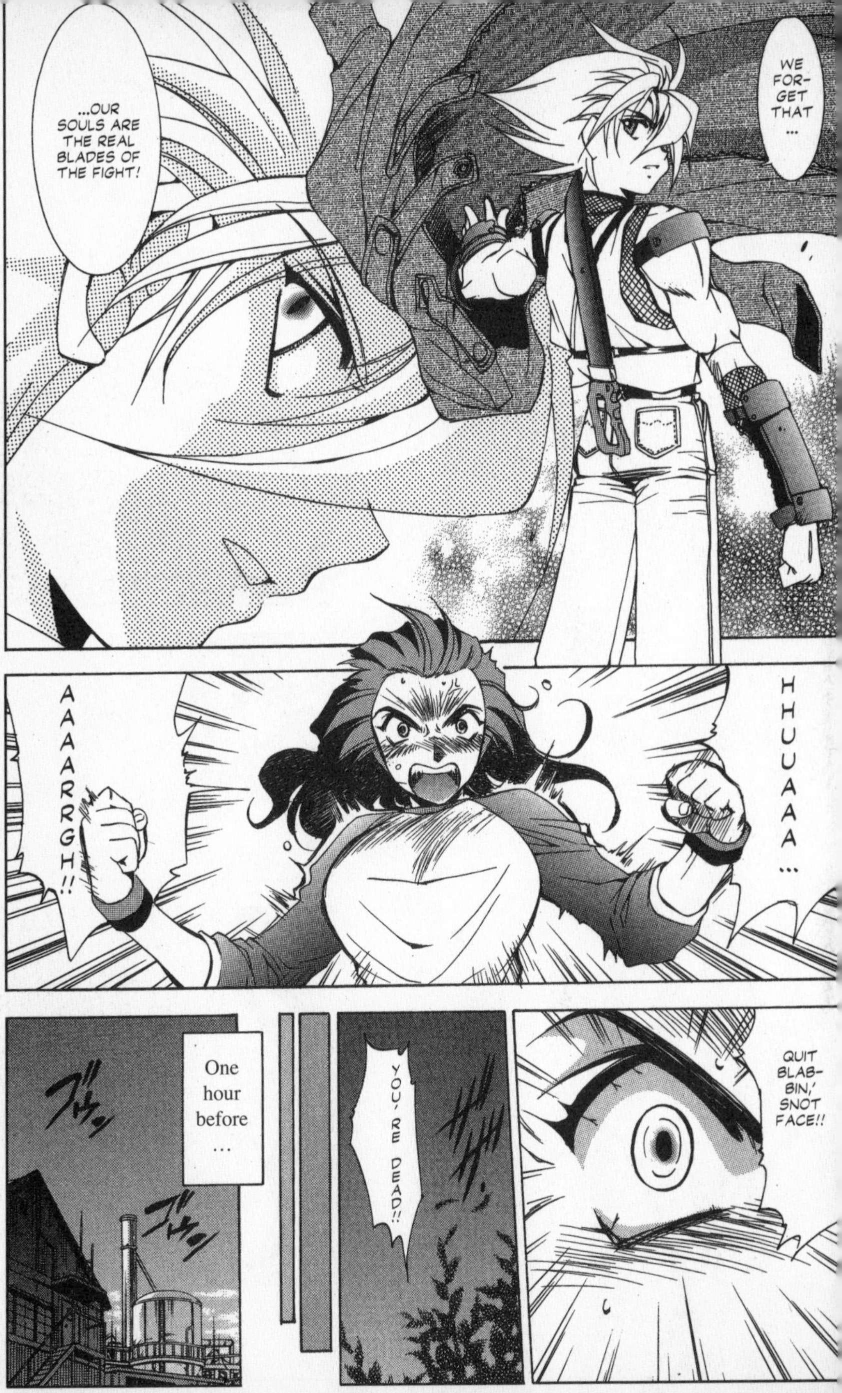
WE FOR-GET THAT ...
...OUR SOULS ARE THE REAL BLADES OF THE FIGHT!
HHUUAAAA ...
AAAAARRGH!!
QUIT BLAB-BIN,' SNOT FACE!!
YOU'RE DEAD!!
One hour before …

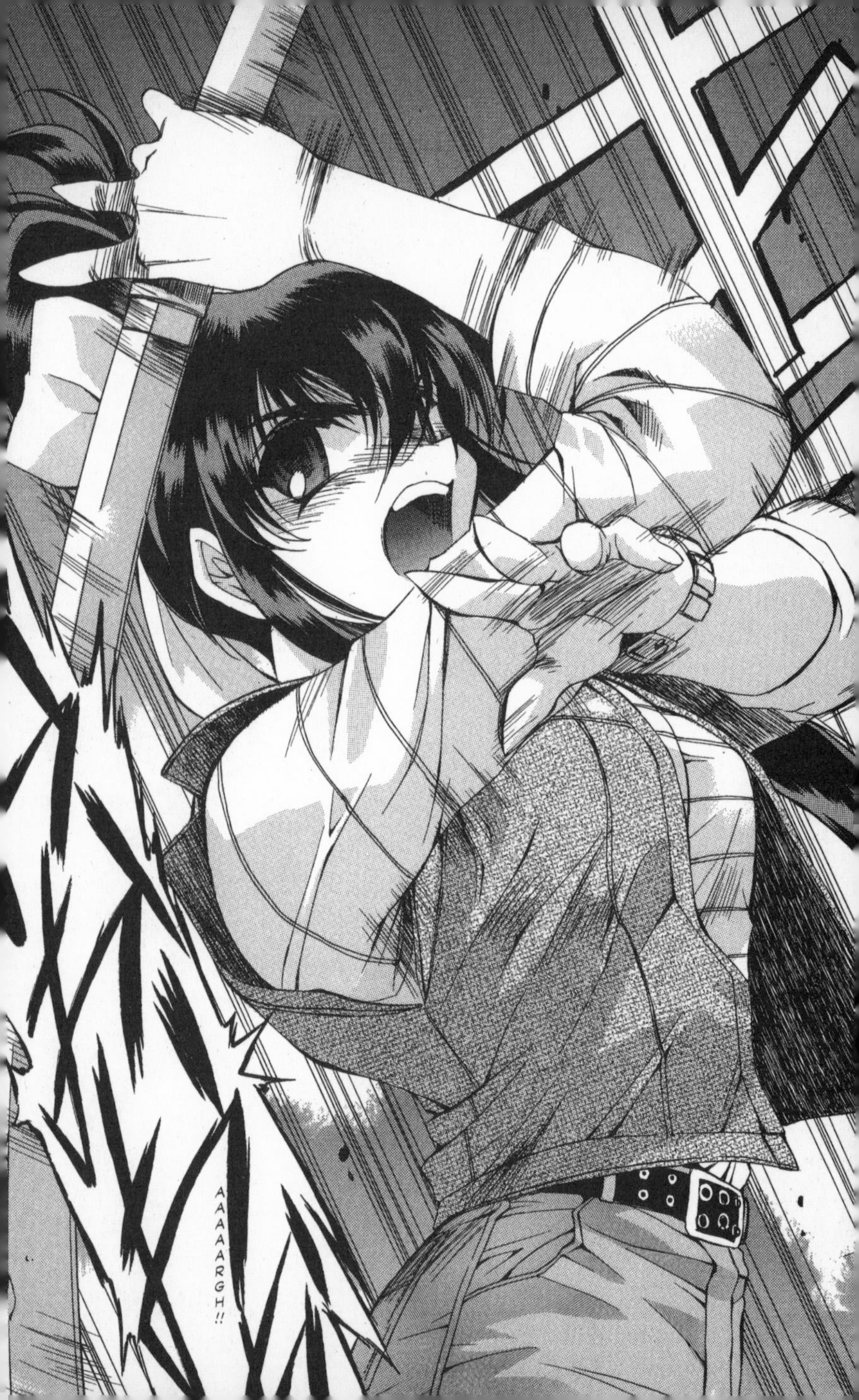
AAAAARGH!!

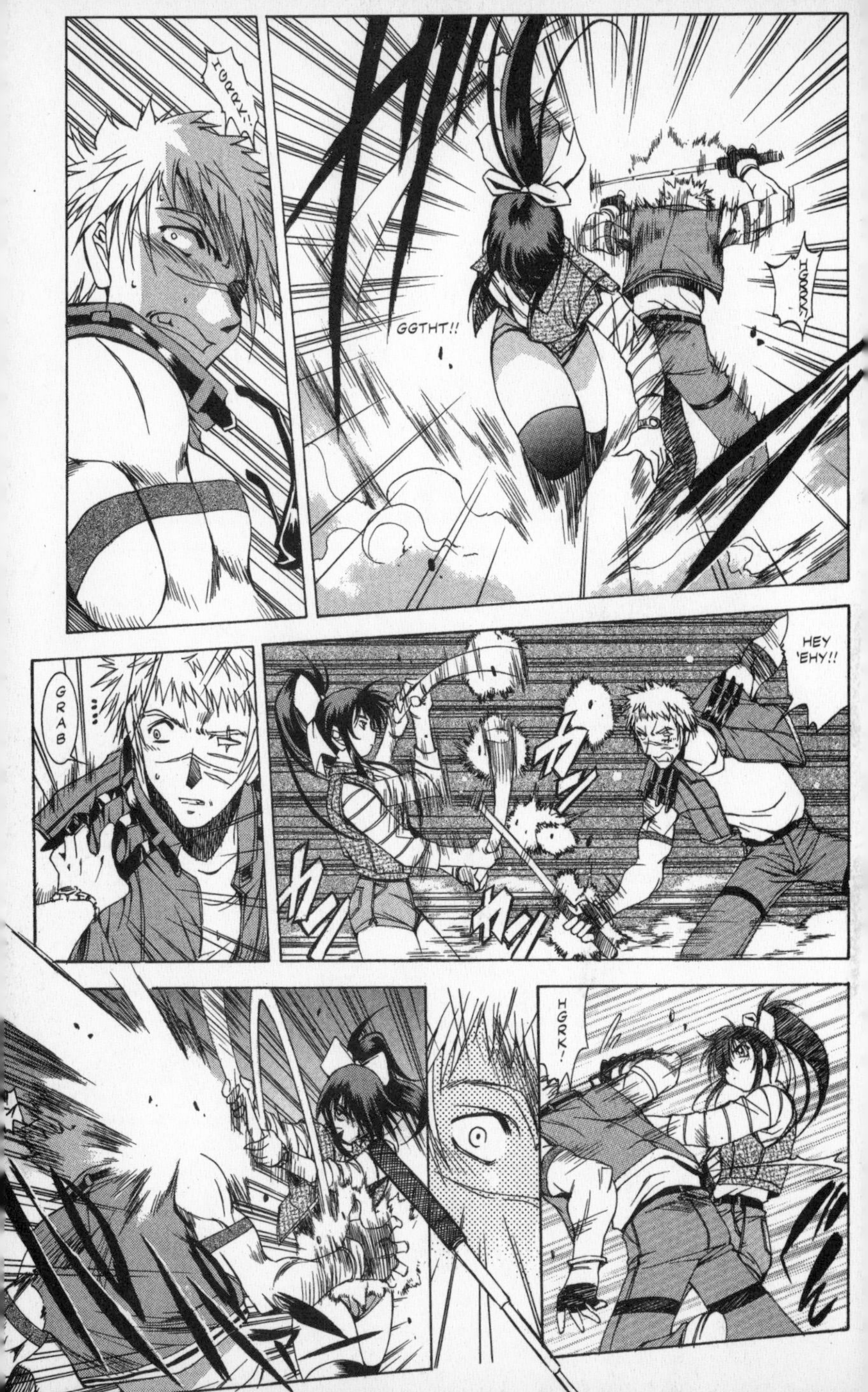
HGRRRK!
GGTHT!!
HGRRRK!!
HEY 'EHY!!
GRAB
HGRK!

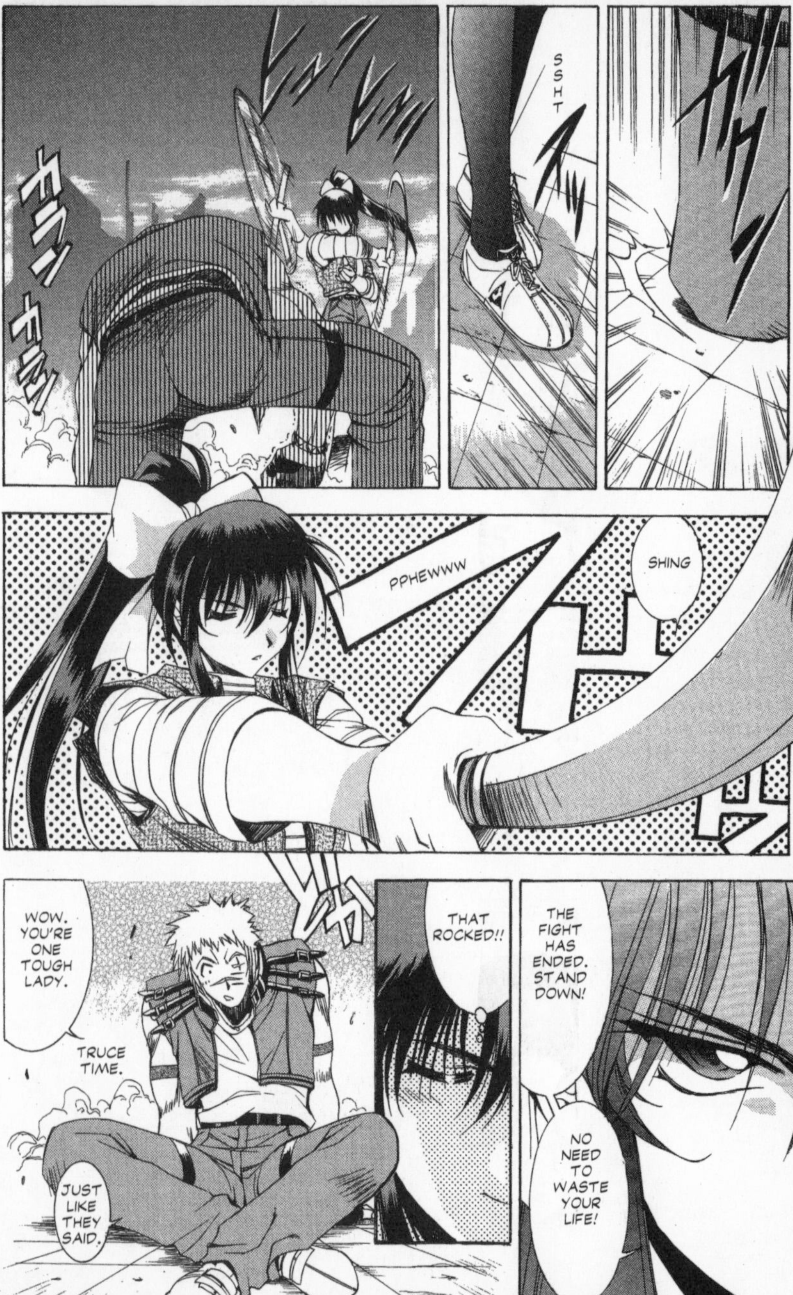
SSHT
SHING
PPHEWWW
THE FIGHT HAS ENDED. STAND DOWN!
NO NEED TO WASTE YOUR LIFE!
THAT ROCKED!!
WOW. YOU'RE ONE TOUGH LADY.
TRUCE TIME.
JUST LIKE THEY SAID.

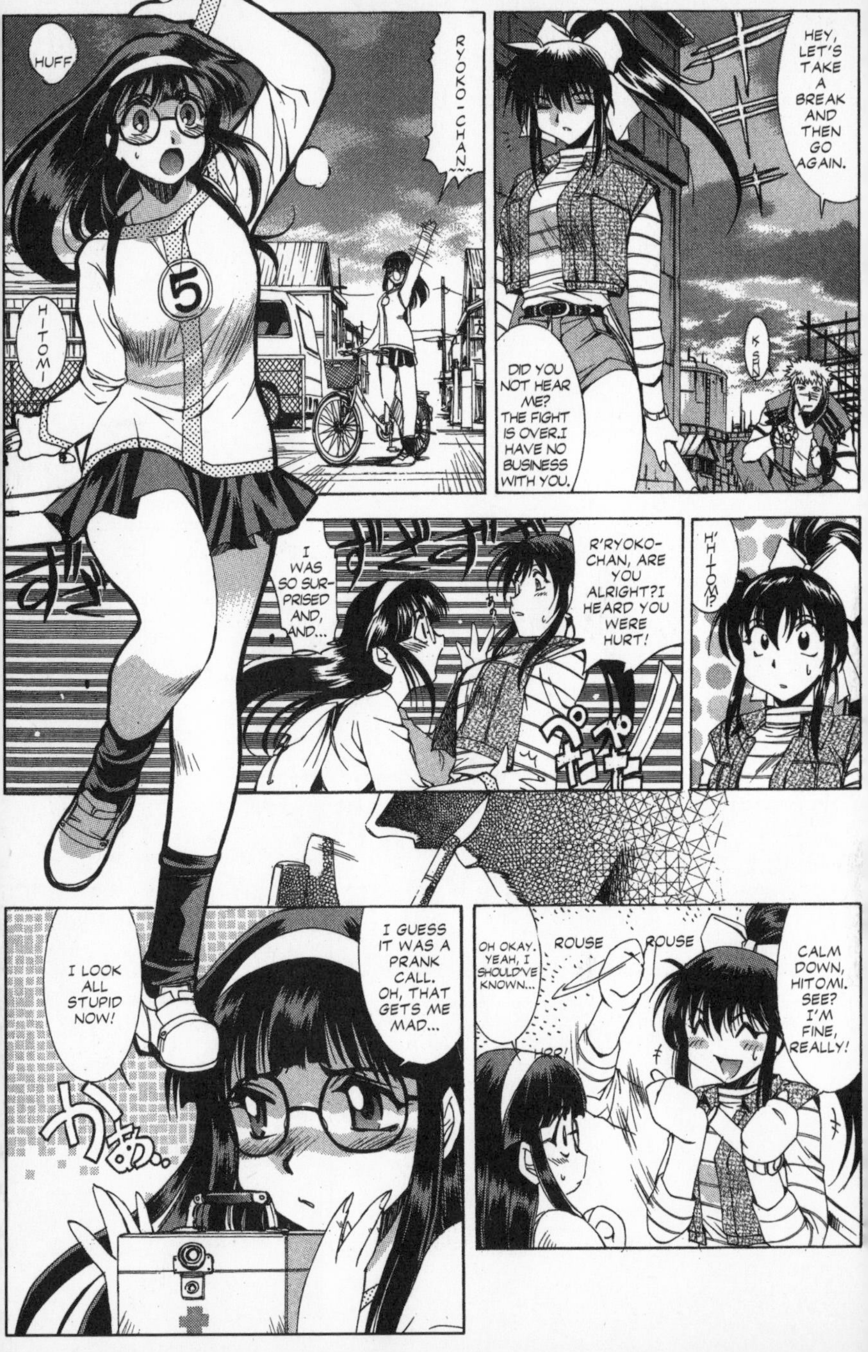
HEY, LET'S TAKE A BREAK AND THEN GO AGAIN.
DID YOU NOT HEAR ME? THE FIGHT IS OVER. I HAVE NO BUSINESS WITH YOU.
RYOKO-CHAN~~~
HUFF
HITOMI
H'ITOMI!?
R'RYOKO-CHAN, ARE YOU ALRIGHT? I HEARD YOU WERE HURT!
I WAS SO SURPRISED AND, AND...
CALM DOWN, HITOMI. SEE? I'M FINE, REALLY!
ROUSE
ROUSE
OH OKAY. YEAH, I SHOULD'VE KNOWN...
I GUESS IT WAS A PRANK CALL. OH, THAT GETS ME MAD...
I LOOK ALL STUPID NOW!

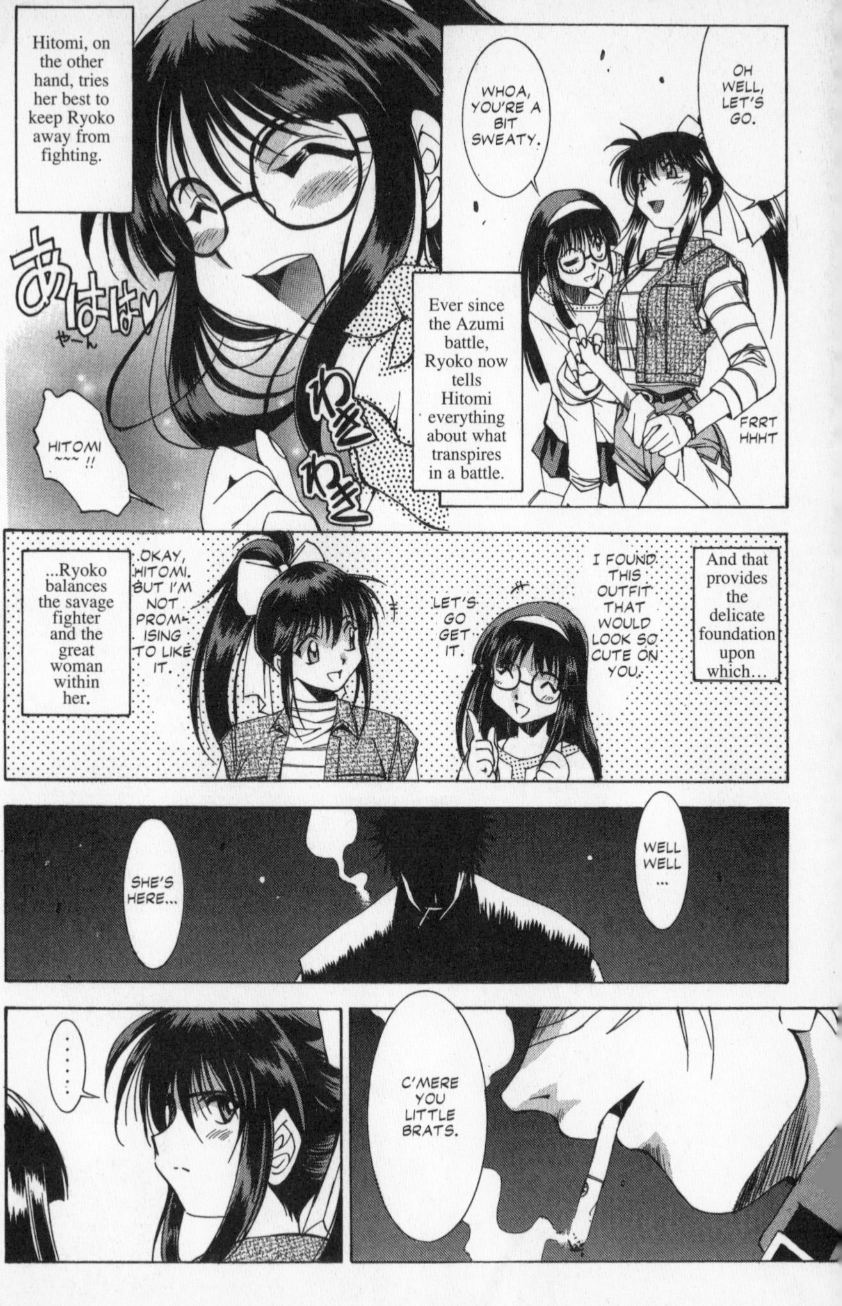
OH WELL, LET'S GO.
WHOA, YOU'RE A BIT SWEATY.
Ever since the Azumi battle, Ryoko now tells Hitomi everything about what transpires in a battle.
FRRT HHHT
Hitomi, on the other hand, tries her best to keep Ryoko away from fighting.
あはは♥
やーん
わきわき
HITOMI ~~~ !!
And that provides the delicate foundation upon which...
I FOUND THIS OUTFIT THAT WOULD LOOK SO CUTE ON YOU.
LET'S GO GET IT.
OKAY, HITOMI. BUT I'M NOT PROMISING TO LIKE IT.
...Ryoko balances the savage fighter and the great woman within her.
WELL WELL ...
SHE'S HERE...
C'MERE YOU LITTLE BRATS.
....

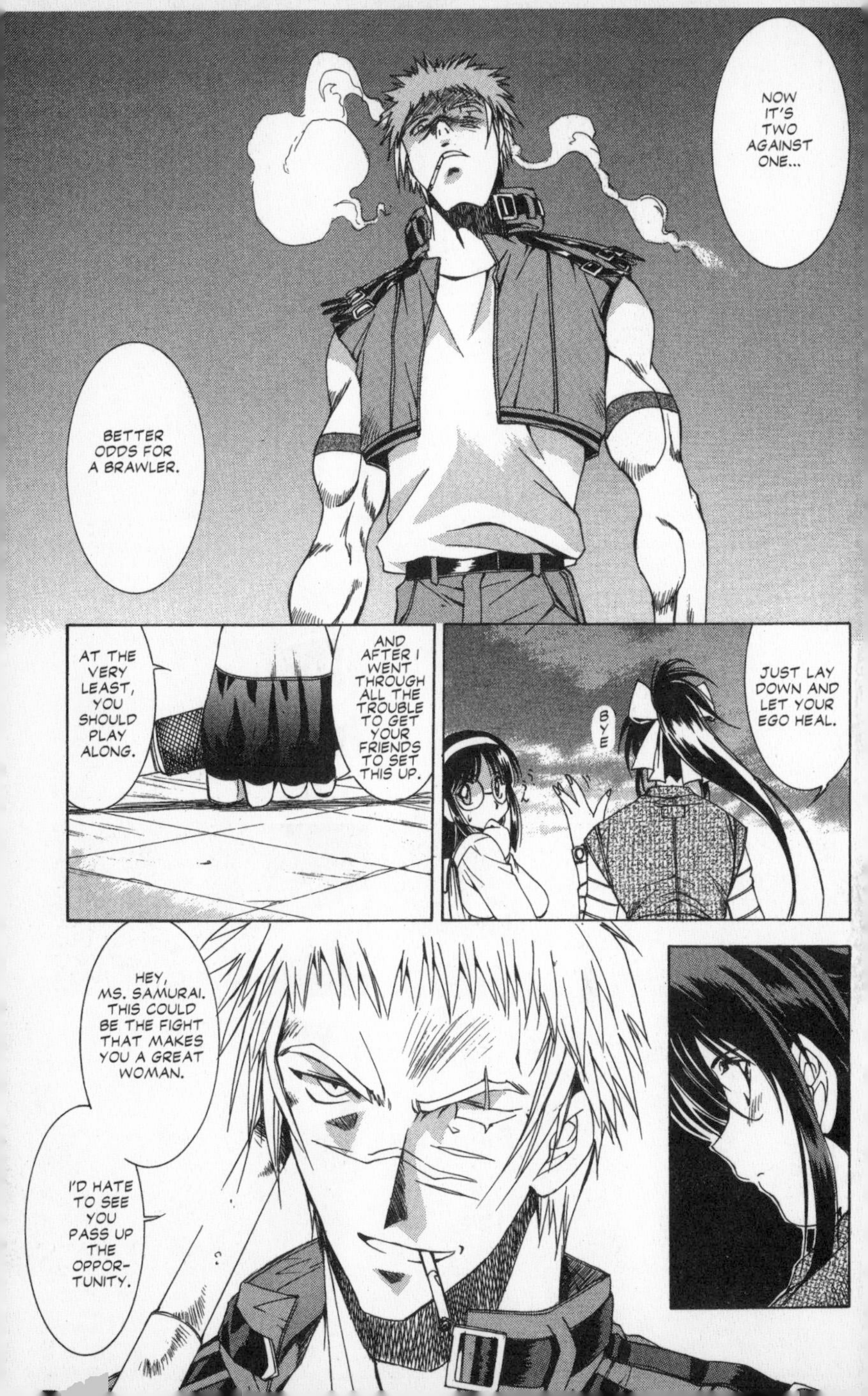
NOW IT'S TWO AGAINST ONE...
BETTER ODDS FOR A BRAWLER.
JUST LAY DOWN AND LET YOUR EGO HEAL.
BYE
AND AFTER I WENT THROUGH ALL THE TROUBLE TO GET YOUR FRIENDS TO SET THIS UP.
AT THE VERY LEAST, YOU SHOULD PLAY ALONG.
HEY, MS. SAMURAI. THIS COULD BE THE FIGHT THAT MAKES YOU A GREAT WOMAN.
I'D HATE TO SEE YOU PASS UP THE OPPOR-TUNITY.

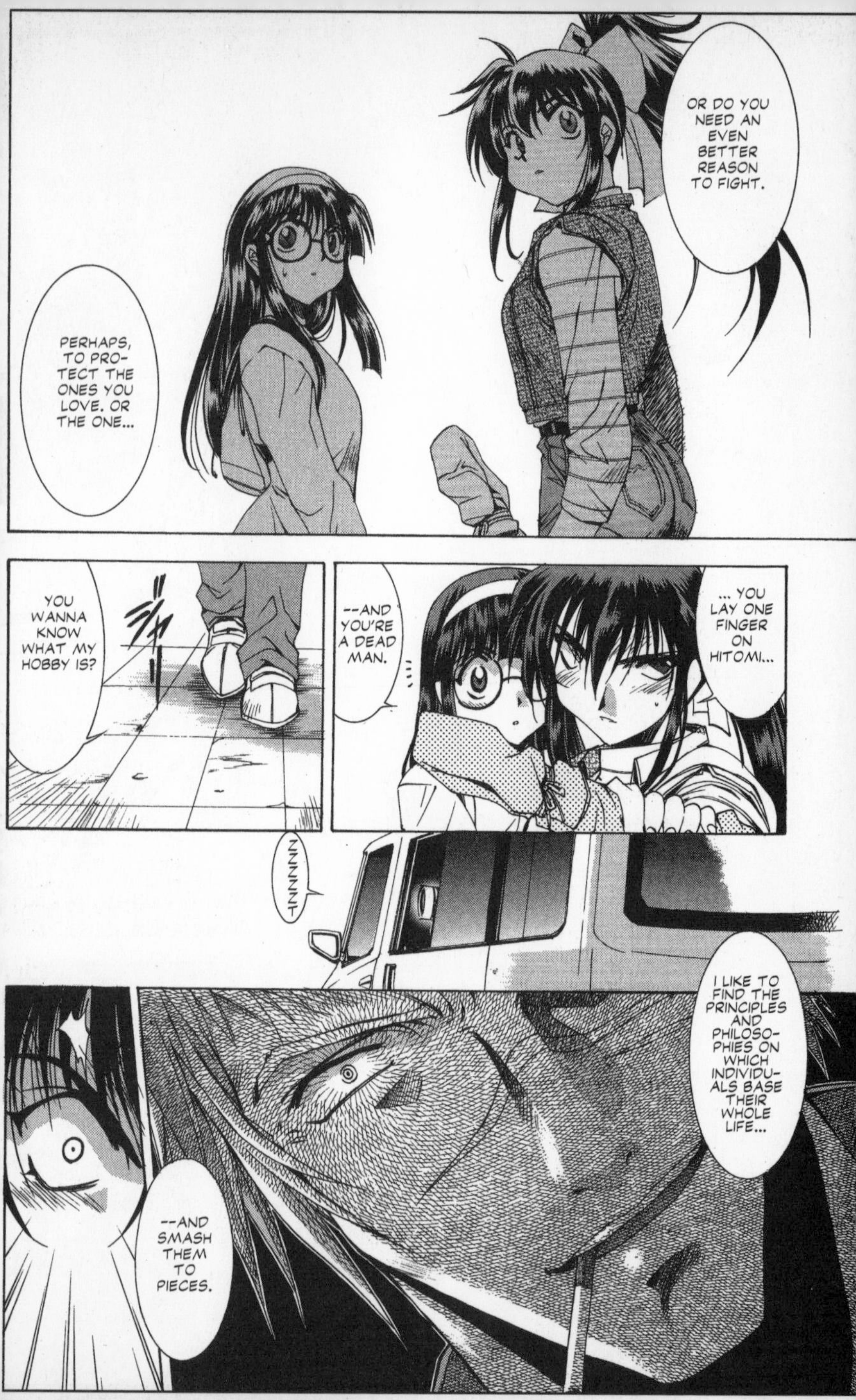
OR DO YOU NEED AN EVEN BETTER REASON TO FIGHT.
PERHAPS, TO PROTECT THE ONES YOU LOVE. OR THE ONE...
... YOU LAY ONE FINGER ON HITOMI...
--AND YOU'RE A DEAD MAN.
YOU WANNA KNOW WHAT MY HOBBY IS?
ZZZZZZ
I LIKE TO FIND THE PRINCIPLES AND PHILOSOPHIES ON WHICH INDIVIDUALS BASE THEIR WHOLE LIFE...
--AND SMASH THEM TO PIECES.

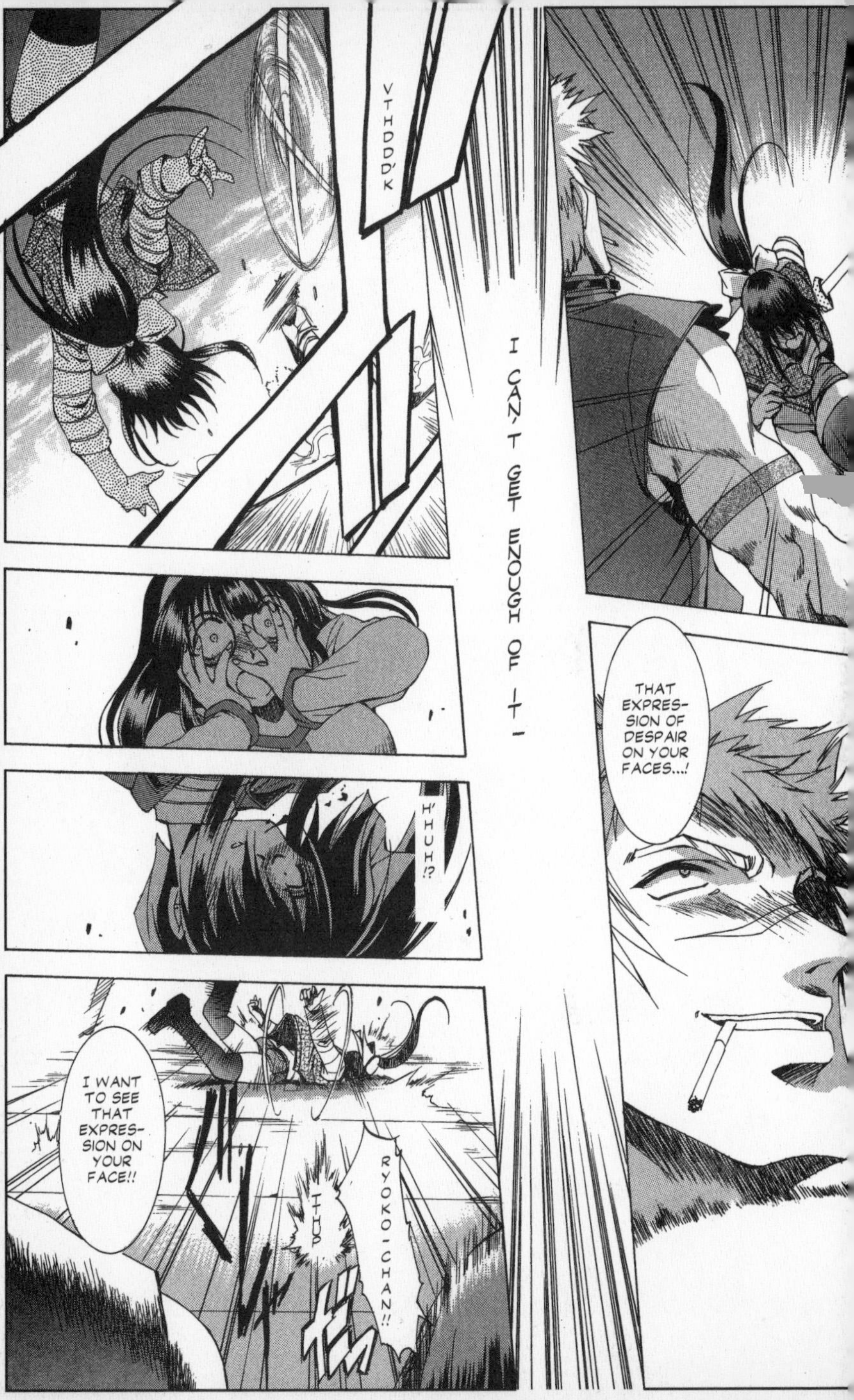
I CAN'T GET ENOUGH OF IT—
THAT EXPRESSION OF DESPAIR ON YOUR FACES...!
VTHDDD'K
H'HUH!?
RYOKO-CHAN!!
THUP
I WANT TO SEE THAT EXPRESSION ON YOUR FACE!!

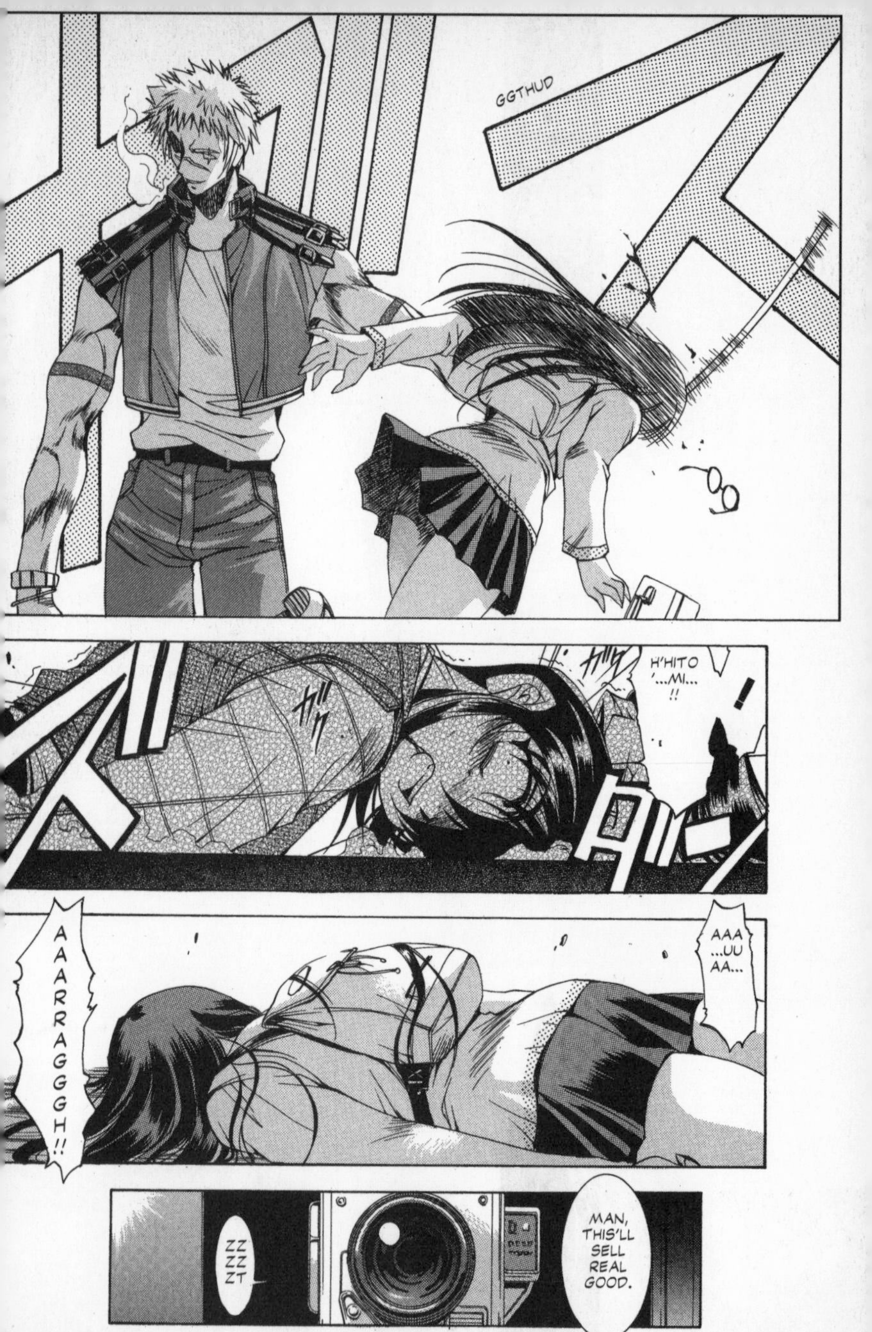
GGTHUD
H'HITO '...MI... !!
AAA ...UU AA...
AAAARRAGGGH!!
MAN, THIS'LL SELL REAL GOOD.
ZZ ZZ ZT

To Be Continued in Volume 5

ALAS, REAL BOUT-ESQUE DAYS.

A WORD FROM REIJI SAIGA AND SORA INOUE

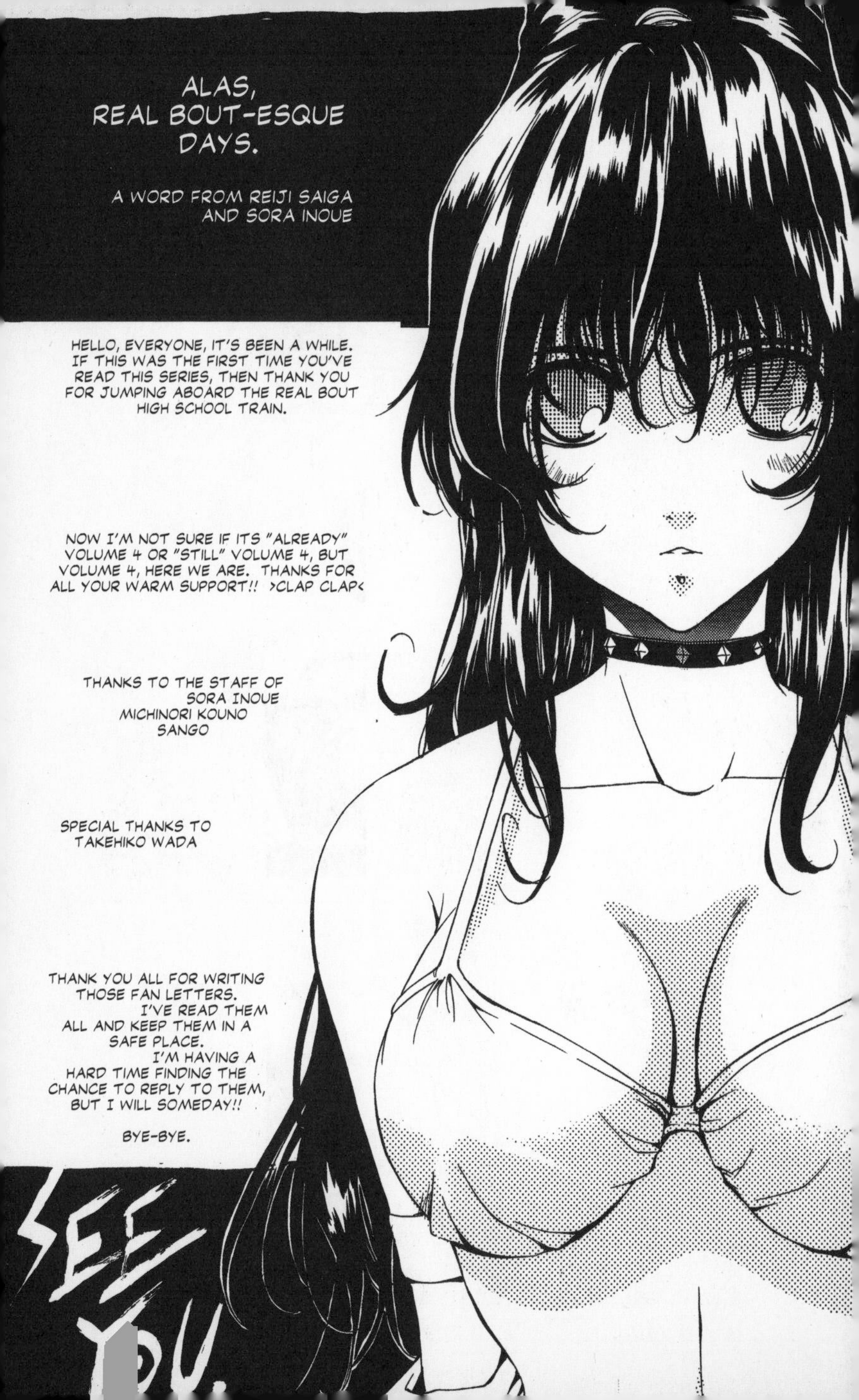

HELLO, EVERYONE, IT'S BEEN A WHILE. IF THIS WAS THE FIRST TIME YOU'VE READ THIS SERIES, THEN THANK YOU FOR JUMPING ABOARD THE REAL BOUT HIGH SCHOOL TRAIN.

NOW I'M NOT SURE IF ITS "ALREADY" VOLUME 4 OR "STILL" VOLUME 4, BUT VOLUME 4, HERE WE ARE. THANKS FOR ALL YOUR WARM SUPPORT!! >CLAP CLAP<

THANKS TO THE STAFF OF
SORA INOUE
MICHINORI KOUNO
SANGO

SPECIAL THANKS TO
TAKEHIKO WADA

THANK YOU ALL FOR WRITING THOSE FAN LETTERS. I'VE READ THEM ALL AND KEEP THEM IN A SAFE PLACE. I'M HAVING A HARD TIME FINDING THE CHANCE TO REPLY TO THEM, BUT I WILL SOMEDAY!!

BYE-BYE.

SEE YOU.

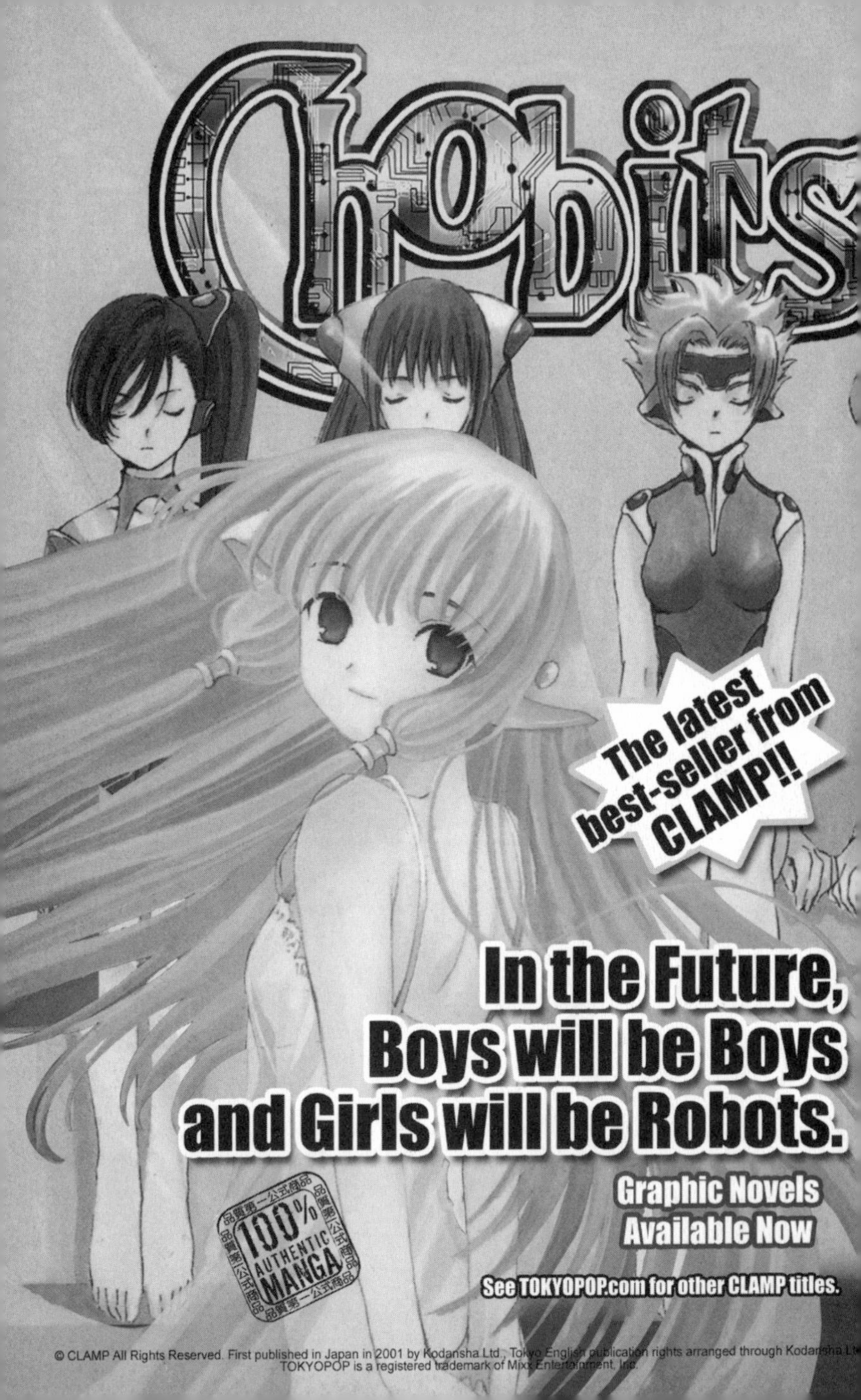
Chobits
The latest best-seller from CLAMP!!
In the Future, Boys will be Boys and Girls will be Robots.
Graphic Novels Available Now
100% AUTHENTIC MANGA
See TOKYOPOP.com for other CLAMP titles.
© CLAMP All Rights Reserved. First published in Japan in 2001 by Kodansha Ltd., Tokyo English publication rights arranged through Kodansha Ltd.
TOKYOPOP is a registered trademark of Mixx Entertainment, Inc.

STOP!

This is the back of the book.
You wouldn't want to spoil a great ending!

This book is printed "manga-style," in the authentic Japanese right-to-left format. Since none of the artwork has been flipped or altered, readers get to experience the story just as the creator intended. You've been asking for it, so TOKYOPOP® delivered: authentic, hot-off-the-press, and far more fun!

DIRECTIONS

If this is your first time reading manga-style, here's a quick guide to help you understand how it works.

It's easy... just start in the top right panel and follow the numbers. Have fun, and look for more 100% authentic manga from TOKYOPOP®!